RESIDENTIAL
TENANCIES

AUSTRALIA
LBC Information Services
Sydney

CANADA AND THE USA
Carswell
Toronto

NEW ZEALAND
Brooker's
Auckland

SINGAPORE AND MALAYSIA
Thomson Information (S.E. Asia)
Singapore

RESIDENTIAL TENANCIES

Second Edition

By

Peter Robson, LL.B., Ph.D., Solicitor
Professor of Social Welfare Law,
University of Strathclyde

and

Simon Halliday, LL.B. (Hons), Dip.L.P.
Research Fellow, Law School,
University of Strathclyde

W. Green / Sweet & Maxwell
Edinburgh
1998

First published 1994
Second edition 1998

Published in 1998 by W. Green & Son Limited
21 Alva Street
Edinburgh EH2 4PS

Typeset by Trinity Typesetting Services
Edinburgh

Printed in Great Britain by Redwood Books Ltd
Kennet Way, Trowbridge, Wiltshire

No natural forests were destroyed to make this product;
only farmed timber was used and replanted

A CIP catalogue record of this book is available from the British Library

ISBN 0 414 01215 1

© 1998
Peter Robson and Simon Halliday

AIGUAS BLANCS RAIS ROIGS

PREFACE TO SECOND EDITION

It has been almost five years since the publication of the first edition of this book. During this time there have been a number of developments in the law of housing in Scotland which warranted a second edition. Housing law continues to be a particularly tricky subject and the continuing jurisprudence from both north and south of the border has not eased this situation. Writing the second edition has allowed us to grapple with these problems and to undertake a certain amount of tinkering with the structure of the book. We hope that the reader finds this edition an accessible and intelligible introduction to this difficult subject. Law, by its nature, remains uncertain and this book merely represents our own attempts to construct a reasonably coherent picture from the number of incoherent sources. We are now part of a team actively engaged in preparing a fuller discussion of the development of the law concerning tenancies which we hope will be published in due course by the Scottish Universities Law Institute.

A number of people have been helpful to us in the preparation of this edition and we would like to acknowledge our thanks to them: Liz Aitken, Katherine Astill, John Blackie, Anne-Marie Cuddihy, Clare Elliott, John Huntley, Ron Pipkin, Mark Praustie, Stephen Savage and Chas from S.H.A.S. The book has also much benefited from discussions over the years with the students of Housing Law and Property Law at Strathclyde University and at the University of Stirling which we taught with our colleague Denise Mina. Despite the unfortunate affair of the credit for the Stirling Housing Law Reader, we trust that by thanking her here she will remember us now that she's rich and famous. A special mention must also be made of Sharon Cowan and Justeen Hyde who helped us navigate the Slaughterhouse Falls and to Jim for his special encouragement of Peter.

Thanks are once again due to the staff at Greens.

Peter Robson
Simon Halliday

October 1998

PREFACE TO FIRST EDITION

This work is designed as an introduction to the topic of residential tenancies. Since W. Green published my annotations to the Housing (Scotland) Act 1998, I have been approached by representatives of tenants and landlords to consider a wide range of problems of those involved in the renting of residential property. The nature and extent of these inquiries suggested a possible need for a concise guide to the law dealing with some of the complexities stemming from having several parallel statutes operating in the area of residential property. This text reflects the concerns and queries which I have been involved with over the years. It is the first stage of a more extensive project on which I am working to cover the law of housing in Scotland. All omissions from the current work will be dealt with in the more extensive treatment of the law. All errors will be excised at that stage. All irrelevant material will be jettisoned. I am sure there will be no shortage of suggestions.

Any author providing a preface since 1971 does so in the shadow of Steven Box's classic which graces both editions of *Deviance, Reality and Society*. Any readers who are not familiar with this introduction will find it a rewarding read. Like, I am sure, most authors I have enjoyed the support and assistance which Box describes. Andrina, Les and Florence Robson did not, however, conform to the Box familial typology for which I am very grateful. I would also like to acknowledge the influence of the A.S.F., Zenon Bankowski, Paul D. Brown, Bob Burgess, Jessica Burns, Chris Clark, Robert J. Cook, Gordon Cowie, Ann Dickson, Noel Dolan, Martyn Evans, Alan Ferguson, John Ferguson, Paul Gadd, Ray Geary, Jim Gray, Ann Marie Hughes, Neil Hutton, Chris Himsworth, David Hoath, John Irwin, Amy Isaac, Alice Ann Jackson, David Johnston, Robert Keenan, David Kieran, Margaret Kieran, Ian Lloyd, Martin Loughlin, Benny Lynch, Neil MacCormick, John R. McBeth, Roody McColl, Francis McGarvey, Sheila McKechnie, Angus McIntosh, Howard Meek, Kenny Miller, Jonathan Mitchell, Tom Mullen, Derek O'Carroll, Martin Partington, Ian Porterfield, D. W. Ramblers, Andrew Robertson, Jim Robertson, Marie Robertson, Philip Rodney, Keith Rowe, Duncan Sim, Paul Watchman, Andrew Wilkin, Ian Willock, Sharon Wood and Eric Young. Those at Green's and Roody Devlin have helped to bring us this work to its current state.

Peter Robson

March 25, 1994

CONTENTS

TABLE OF CASES

xviii   *Residential Tenancies*

TABLE OF STATUTES

TABLE OF STATUTORY INSTRUMENTS

CHAPTER 1

INTRODUCTION

1. Twentieth-century Development of Tenants' and Landlords' Rights

Introduction

There are different kinds of rights which those occupying property may have: 1–01
some of these are absolute property rights in so far as they allow the occupier to
remain in the property indefinitely, *e.g.* ownership; others are restricted in that
they provide for the occupancy by that individual for a limited period of time
only. This period of time may depend on the terms of a contract. Thus it may be
as little as a few days or as extensive as many years. At common law there were
very few limitations on what individuals could agree. Statute has both limited
the formal length of leases of dwelling-houses as well as having provided that
individuals can stay on beyond the term of the agreement. In addition, in some
situations members of the family of the occupier may be entitled to stay on in
the property on the death of the original occupier.

The most common form of occupancy at the start of the twentieth century
was as a tenant of a private landlord. Traditionally such leases of residential
property involved the grant of the use of a house by one party to another for a
period of time in return for money, commodities or even services. The precise
nature of the rights individuals enjoyed as tenants depended on the contracts
they were able to negotiate. At different times the bargaining power of owners
and potential tenants has shifted but in the twentieth century the undersupply of
accommodation, particularly decent accommodation, has been a chronic feature
of housing throughout Europe.[1] Scotland has been no exception. In the United
Kingdom, protection for tenants was first introduced in 1915[2] and has been
continued in subsequent legislation. The extent and nature of this protection
has altered over the years depending on both the political complexion of the
party in office and the wider developments in housing availability and population
changes.

Pre-1965

Traditionally the lease was a contract where the rent as fixed by the parties 1–02
was conclusive and there was no body to whom either party could appeal.
Similarly when the tenancy came to an end the tenant had no right to remain
provided that notice to quit had been served thus preventing tacit relocation
operating. Soon after the outbreak of the First World War landlords throughout
Britain took advantage of their market position and responded to the increase in

---

[1] See L. Neville Brown, "Comparative Rent Control" (1970) 19 I.C.L.Q. 205.
[2] Increase of Rent and Mortgage Interest (War Restrictions) Act 1915.

1

demand for housing in industrial areas by raising rents. The responses of tenants'
groups and the support of the industrial workers together with the threat to arms
and munitions production led the Government to appoint a committee under
Lord Hunter and Professor Scott to examine the problem in, among other places,
Glasgow.[3] Their findings led to government proposals to deal with the problem
of profiteering. Rents were to be set at the level operating on the outbreak of the
war. Landlords who wished to evict tenants at the end of the tenancy henceforth
had to establish that they had a good reason, such as requiring the property for
their own use or that of their family.[4] This was a major shift from the market
principle of housing allocation and pricing. As the Government was at pains to
stress when the Increase of Rents and Mortgage Interest (War Restrictions) Act
1915 was enacted, this was to be a temporary measure to end six months after
hostilities. Various committees and experts advised subsequent interwar
governments that a return to market principles would be impolitic.[5] This theme
was strengthened after the extensive destruction of housing during the Second
World War and control of rents and security of tenure was retained after 1945.[6]
    The rise of market-orientated politics in the Conservative Party in the mid-
1950s resulted in an attempt to abolish rent control and security of tenure in the
Rent Act 1957. This Act abolished control over rents and security of tenure
beyond the term of the tenancy for properties above a certain rateable value.
For lower rated properties the Act provided that these would cease to be covered
by legislative controls on rents and security when the landlord obtained vacant
possession. This controversial legislation was abused by landlords who sought
to persuade their tenants to leave by a variety of methods. These included
payments of money, threats of harm and terror tactics. Housing policy was one
of the features which the Labour Party was able to fasten on to at the start of the
1960s and they promised to repeal the 1957 Act. Their plans as to how to deal
with private rented housing were not clear. There was a brief flirtation with
municipalisation of rental housing but in the end a compromise was reached
between policies which favoured landlords with power in the market place and
removing rental housing from the arena of profit.

The return to regulation in 1965

1–03   On achieving office in October 1964 the Labour Party set up an investigation
into the abuse of the private rented sector. Richard Crossman with the assistance
of a variety of experts and academics produced a fresh policy to the alternatives
hitherto tried. The Rent Act 1965 provided a new means of dealing with the
question of rents for private rented housing. In place of the policy of "freezing"
rents the 1965 legislation provided for fixing rents in accordance with specified
criteria and a mechanism for reviewing them.
    The new legislation applied to all properties previously under the "controlled"
regime. However, there were transitional arrangements provided in cases where
the accommodation had certain facilities such as a w.c. and bathroom and reached
a reasonable standard of repair. Not all rented properties met these criteria and
despite the availability of grants to allow facilities to be installed this upgrading
was not done in all cases. In Scotland, the remaining controlled properties which

---

[3] Departmental Committee Report, Cmnd 8111 (1914–16) (Chairman, Lord Hunter).
[4] Increase of Rent and Mortgage Interest (War Restrictions) Act 1915.
[5] M. Barnett, *The Politics of Legislation* (1969).
[6] Ridley Committee (1945).

did not meet these criteria were dealt with initially under the Housing (Financial Provisions) (Scotland) Act 1972[7] and finally by the Tenants' Rights Etc. (Scotland) Act 1980. The remaining 200,000[8] properties left in the controlled category were declared to be "regulated tenancies" as from December 1, 1980.[9]

The legislation originally introduced in 1965 was common to all of Great Britain. However, since 1968 the law has generally been split into Acts covering housing in England and Wales and statutes applying solely to Scotland. The Scottish legislation was consolidated originally in 1971 and most recently in 1984. As we shall see, however, the legislation of 1988 provides a different approach and covers private sector tenancies entered into from the beginning of 1989.

Extension of Rent Act protection to furnished tenancies

When the Rent Acts were introduced in 1915 they did not cover furnished   1–04 lets. The regulation of rents through the fair rent system was applied only to unfurnished tenancies. Tenants in furnished accommodation had limited protection in terms of rent levels and postponement of eviction. A measure of protection for such tenants was first introduced in Scotland in the Rent of Furnished Houses Control (Scotland) Act 1943. This lesser degree of protection meant that landlords seeking to evade the provisions of the Rent Acts could do so by providing minimal furniture and thereby bringing their properties under the furnished code contained in Part VI of the Rent Act 1965 (subsequently Part VII of the Rent (Scotland) Act 1971). Crossman claimed that furnished tenancies were left out of the 1965 Rent Act for "purely administrative reasons" because the officials said they could not get the Bill drafted in time. He later described this as a fatal flaw.[10]

Part VII of the 1971 Act provided, so far as security was concerned, that if an individual received a notice to quit from the landlord then the tenant could apply to the Rent Tribunal, which could suspend the notice to quit for a maximum period of six months. This period was meant to provide a breathing space for a tenant to obtain fresh accommodation.[11] Furnished tenants were in a much weaker position than their unfurnished counterparts since they were only entitled to a postponement of a notice to quit rather than enjoying proper security of tenure. The landlord did not require to establish any ground for possession provided that a notice to quit had been duly served.

A committee was appointed in 1969 to review the operation of the Rent Acts   1–05 and also the relationship between the furnished and unfurnished codes. Although the 1971 Francis Report came out against amalgamation of the codes, it was the strongly worded Minority Report which was acted upon by the next Labour Government.[12] The Rent Act 1974 provided that leases of furnished property should be treated the same way as leases of unfurnished property as to both rent fixing and security of tenure.

---

[7] Pt V; the timetable for automatic conversion was slowed down by S.I. 1973 No. 782 and S.I. 1974 No. 2004 and then suspended by s. 10 of the Housing Rents and Subsidies (Scotland) Act 1975.

[8] *Hansard*, H.C. Vol. 976, col. 1557 (January 15, 1980).

[9] Tenants' Rights Etc. (Scotland) Act 1980, s. 46(1).

[10] Richard Crossman, *The Diaries of a Cabinet Minister* (1975), Vol. 1, p. 89n.

[11] Report of the Committee on the Rent Acts, Cmnd 4609 (1971), p. 151.

[12] *ibid.* (Chairman, H. E. Francis, Q.C.); Minority Report by Miss L. Evans, pp. 228–237.

The old Rent Tribunals retained jurisdiction in a number of areas, the main one being where a resident landlord was involved, but these formed only a small proportion of the cases coming before the Rent Registration Service. The jurisdiction of the Rent Tribunals was transferred to the Rent Assessment Committees by the Tenants' Rights Etc. (Scotland) Act 1980 as from December 1980. The Housing (Scotland) Act 1988 abolished subsequent protection for such occupiers.[13-14] The latter are left with their contractual rights only.

The return to the market

1–06   The subsequent apparent disappearance of many properties from the letting market led to concern in some quarters that the amalgamation of the two codes, giving full protection to furnished tenants, had dried up the supply of furnished property. However, at the same time there was an extension of renting by landlords using arrangements which avoided the protection of the Rent Acts.[15] As research indicated, this trend seemed to proceed from a misunderstanding of the nature of the protection given to resident landlords and owner-occupiers wishing to rent out their property.[16]

The Conservative Government's Tenants' Rights Etc. (Scotland) Act 1980 and its English equivalent, the Housing Act 1980 attempted to stimulate the traditional private rented sector. It was thought many potential landlords were deterred from letting out empty property or spare rooms by the fact that tenants would have extensive security of tenure. The 1980 legislation introduced a new form of tenure with no security beyond the agreed term. In Scotland this tenancy was called a "short" tenancy ("shorthold" in England and Wales). In order to qualify as a "short" tenancy a tenancy had to contain certain features. It only applied to tenancies which were for a minimum of one year and not more than five years' duration. In addition a fair rent had to be registered and the tenant had to be notified that his tenancy was a security free short tenancy. The first six months of the new tenure produced a very small number of such agreements. In England, it was decided to remove the obligation to have a fair rent fixed automatically in 1981. This had little impact as tenants could still apply themselves for fair rent registration.

1–07   The original term "assured tenancy" was introduced in 1980 in England and Wales in the Housing Act 1980. It never applied in this form in Scotland. In such tenancies although there was no control over rent levels, the tenant received a degree of security of tenure equivalent to that for business tenancies in the English Landlord and Tenant Act 1954. Potential landlords of these old style assured tenancies had to be approved by the Secretary of State for the Environment and the tenancies applied originally only in buildings built after the Act's introduction. The provision was later extended to conversions. The assured tenancy regime under the Housing Act 1980 was not a success and attracted little investment.

[13-14] Housing (Scotland) Act 1988, s. 44(1).
[15] See paras 2.52–2.62.
[16] P. Robson and R. Nicoll, "Modern Residential Landlords' Holdings, Their Lettings Policies and Perceptions of Legislation" (Social Science Research Council) (1985).

The introduction of the "assured tenancy" in Scotland

The current system of rent protection was enacted by the Housing (Scotland) 1–08
Act 1988. This involves a more sophisticated approach than was attempted in
1957. While allowing those tenants who had protected tenancies to retain them,
the 1988 Act regime operates for new tenancies from 1989. Such tenancies are
described in Scotland as "assured tenancies". These enjoy no protection as far as
rent levels are concerned and there is a reduction in the security of tenure rights of
tenants. There is also a parallel system of tenancies called "short assured tenancies".
These offer no security of tenure and only the possibility of having rents adjusted
where rents significantly in excess of the market rent are being charged.[17] In essence
protection for tenants from market forces has been abolished.

Public sector landlords: the introduction of "secure tenancies"

Until 1919 what local authority housing existed came from local initiatives 1–09
aimed at clearing away city centre slums in cities and towns such as Edinburgh,
Glasgow and Greenock.[18] Before the consideration of housing needs became
obligatory, however, very little was built on the sites of the demolished slums.[19]
Indeed, the obligation to ensure that there were sufficient alternative houses for
those displaced inhibited these demolition activities. Only slightly more than
3,000 local authority buildings existed by 1919—mainly in Glasgow. This
compared with over 20,000 provided by the coal-owners.[20]

In 1917 a Royal Commission on the housing conditions of the industrial and
agricultural workforce found that investment in building housing for the working
classes below the level of the prosperous artisan had all but dried up. This
structural failure of the traditional means of supply of rented housing—rather
than the success of any political movement to secure local authority housing—
provided the impetus for imposing an obligation to consider local housing needs.

The major increase in public sector housing provision, however, did not occur
until the years following the Second World War. Nevertheless, it was not until
relatively recently that public sector tenants enjoyed rights of security of tenure
equivalent to those in the private sector. Previously, they had to rely on the fact
that local authorities were accountable to their tenants through the ballot box
and that this would provide adequate protection. This faith was sometimes
misplaced.[21] In 1980, however, security of tenure was introduced as part of the
Tenants' Rights Etc. (Scotland) Act 1980.

2. Leases and other Contracts for the Occupation of Dwelling-houses

It has also been significant that most of the protections have been granted to 1–10
those who are "tenants". Since the introduction of protection for tenants a
proportion of those renting out property have sought to avoid this legislation by
a variety of means.[22] Distinguishing between tenancies and other rights to occupy
dwelling-houses is, accordingly, important.

---

[17] See paras 2.47 and 2.48.
[18] E. Gauldie, *Cruel Habitations* (1978).
[19] P. Robson, Housing and the Judiciary (1979).
[20] *ibid.*
[21] *Cannock D.C. v. Kelly* [1978] 1 W.L.R. 1; *Edinburgh D.C. v. Parnell*, 1980 S.L.T. (Sh. Ct.) 11.
[22] See para. 2.52 *et seq.*

Leases and licences: English law

1–11   In English law over the past three centuries, starting with *Thomas v. Sorrell,*[23]
a lesser right has developed to deal with situations where there was no clear
intention to create the relationship of landlord and tenant. Such occupancy can
be distinguished from a lease and is known as a "licence". As far as residential
property is concerned it stemmed from the need to deal with agreements where
occupiers allowed friends or relatives to occupy property for a limited period.
These were not accorded the full recognition as leases but were accorded a
second-class status as licences.[24]

One of the crucial distinctions between the landlord-tenant relationship and
that of licensor-licensee was whether exclusive possession had been granted.
Between 1978 and 1985 in England there was extensive litigation in the courts
as landlords sought to avoid the impact of the Rent Acts by claiming that those
occupying their property were not really tenants but had only the lesser rights
of licensees. This was done through requiring their tenants to sign agreements
which indicated that they did not have exclusive possession. These agreements
did not normally reflect the reality of the situation. The House of Lords attempted
to put an end to these sham avoidance techniques in one decision[25] where the
occupier actually enjoyed exclusive possession.

1–12   Where there is exclusive possession, but it is shared by more than one person
at a time, normally the inference would be joint tenancy. Landlords sought to
claim that where there was sharing there was no exclusive possession. Each
occupier was given his own individual agreement which stated that there was
no exclusive possession. These straightforward attempts by landlords to deprive
occupiers of the rights as tenants were rejected by the House of Lords in
Antoniades v. Villiers.[26] The occupiers had one bedroom with a double bed and
a small sitting room where there was a convertible settee. The provisions which
purported to allow the landlord to introduce either an indefinite number of third
parties or himself were rejected as "an attempt to disguise the true character of
the agreement which it was hoped would deceive the court and prevent the
appellants enjoying the protection of the Rent Acts."[27] However, at the same
time the House of Lords was prepared to accept limited licence rights being
granted to people whose agreements to share were rather more elaborate.

The agreements in *A.G. Securities v. Vaughan*[28] involved occupiers who were
also not provided with exclusive possession in their individual agreements. There
were differences though between them and the tenants in *Antoniades*. In
A.G. Securities the occupiers did not come to the property at the same time;
they paid different rents; they had no control over the filling of vacancies; they
were not liable for the costs of other defaulting occupiers nor when there were
vacancies. This was accepted by the House of Lords as a "sensible and realistic
[arrangement] to provide accommodation for shifting population of individuals
who were genuinely prepared to share the flat with others introduced from time
to time who would, at least initially, be strangers to them."[29]

---

[23] (1673) Vaugh. 330.
[24] P. Robson and P. Watchman, "The Hidden Wealth of Licences" [1980] Conv. 27.
[25] *Street v. Mountford* [1985] A.C. 809.
[26] [1988] 3 W.L.R. 1205.
[27] *ibid. per* Lord Bridge of Harwich at 1208.
[28] [1988] 3 All E.R. 1205.
[29] *ibid. per* Lord Bridge of Harwich at 1207.

Leases and licences: Scots law

The lease-licence question is less clear in Scots law. Part of the problem of 1–13 how to deal with such arrangements in Scotland may well stem from the difference in the law as to the requirement for rent. Rent is one of the required elements of a lease in Scots law, while its absence is not fatal to the creation of a tenancy in English law.[30] The friend or family arrangement without rent does not fall within the Scots law of lease. The parties' rights and duties are determined solely by the contract they have entered. In the event that the relationship is actually commercial then the occupier would be treated as a tenant notwithstanding the existence of a family relationship.[31]

The developments in this area of exceptions to leases might have been of limited impact but for the Rent Acts which gave tenants a measure of protection from exploitation. Landlords have attempted various devices to avoid the Rent Acts. One of the simplest has been to rename their tenants "licensees" and call their leases "licences". This makes the distinction between the two kinds of rights of crucial importance. It also means that the question of whether this part of English law has ever become part of Scots law a matter of considerable interest. Sir John Rankine, when he provided his definition of a lease in Scots law, made it clear that he was aware that it was wide enough to cover what those south of the border would have called licences.[32] This means that the substantial body of English case law is of limited help in determining the distinctions between leases and lesser forms of occupancy. Such determinations must be made exclusively accordingly to Scots law, a point emphasised recently by the Inner House.[33]

It is fair to say that since the law of leases was last revised developments in the provision of supported accommodation have occurred which would seem to make a genuine agreement conferring lesser rights than tenancies appropriate. The literature contains some debate about the legal status of occupiers of supported accommodation.[34] However, the current law seems rather inadequate to cope with a diversifying housing sector. Calls have been made for a review of landlord and tenant law to take account of developments in housing provision.[35] The problem for reform is how to prevent the landlord's power, inherent to legal relationships which are lesser than that of lease, from being exploited.

In contrast to the position in England and Wales, there has been relatively 1–14 little exploration in Scotland of the distinctions between leases and lesser forms of relationship. In various cases on valuation and rating, in deciding whether a contract of lease existed, the court has placed emphasis on the temporary or limited use of property for advertising sites[36] and rights of shooting[37] or

---

[30] *Ashburn Anstalt v. Arnold* [1988] 2 W.L.R. 706.
[31] *Nunn v. Dalrymple* (1989) 21 H.L.R. 569.
[32] J. Rankine, *A Treatise on the Law of Leases in Scotland* (3rd ed., 1916), p. 1.
[33] *Brador Properties Ltd v British Telecommunications plc*, 1992 S.L.T. 490.
[34] M. Dailly, "Homeless Hostels, assured tenancies and unlawful eviction", 1995 SCOLAG 131; "Ejection Brevi Manu and Hostel Dwellings" (1995) JLSS 435; "Lease or license in Scots Law", 1996 SCOLAG 126; S. Halliday, "Unlawful Eviction and Hostel Accommodation", 1997 SCOLAG 46.
[35] A. Mina Coull, "Housing Agreements in Supported Accommodation in Scotland" (Shelter, 1997).
[36] *L.N.E.R. v. Assessor for Glasgow*, 1937 S.C. 309.
[37] *Inland Revenue v. Anderson*, 1922 S.C. 284; *L.M.S. Ry v. Assessor of Public Undertakings*, 1937 S.C. 773.

garaging.[38] This case law revolves around what the status of an agreement is for the purposes of valuation and rating. An important factor in determining if these non-residential contracts were leases was the question of exclusivity of the possession. If possession was exclusive, then the agreement could be a lease. If, however, possession was only partial, then it could not be a lease. However, this case law is only of very limited assistance to the task of distinguishing between leases and licences.[39] In these cases a different question was essentially at issue, namely, whether for rating purposes the properties concerned should be regarded as an *unum quid*. Further, in relation to residential property, the concept of limited or partial possession is problematic. There is in standard residential occupancy no genuine position short of exclusive possession. It has only been by shams and fictions that landlords have been able both to allow others to occupy the properties and charge a fee for this while denying that what is involved is a landlord-tenant relationship.

1–15   The Inner House has considered the lease-licence question in two recent cases. *Scottish Residential Estates Development Co. Ltd v. Henderson*[40] concerned an agreement to occupy a cottage for an unspecified period of time in exchange for certain estate duties which were accepted by the parties as amounting to a rent. The court resolved that, in order to decide whether a lease existed, it had to construe the intention of the parties. This intention was to be "found from the words used in the relevant documents together, if necessary, with the inference to be drawn from the actings of parties thereafter".[41] Here, the written agreement of the parties specifically indicated that no relationship of landlord and tenant was to be entered into, but rather that the occupier could have use of the property until the proprietor required possession of it. Accordingly, it was held, no lease existed.

In *Brador Properties Ltd v. British Telecommunications plc,*[42] the issue was whether the tenant of a long lease had created a sub-lease in breach of the terms of the lease. The long lease provided that the tenant was prohibited from sub-letting or assigning any part of the subjects without the consent of the landlord. The tenant sought and was refused permission to sub-let the subjects but subsequently entered into a number of agreements with third parties. In one agreement, the tenant undertook to provide the third party with the use of office accommodation. The agreement expressly stipulated that it did not constitute a lease and that the tenant would retain possession of the subjects. The Inner House held that it was entitled to examine the agreement carefully in order to determine whether it had been deliberately framed to circumvent the express provisions of the lease and to make it appear that the agreement was not a sub-let. It was further entitled to consider this question against the background that the tenant had already sought and been refused permission to sub-let. The Lord Justice-Clerk came to the conclusion that:

> "[W]hen regard is had to the circumstances in which these agreements were entered into, and to the terms of them, it is difficult to avoid the conclusion that the agreements were devised by the [tenant] in an attempt

---

[38] *Broomhill Motor Co. v. Assessor for Glasgow*, 1927 S. C. 447; *Chaplin v. Assessor for Perth*, 1947 S.C. 373.
[39] *Brador Properties Ltd v. British Telecommunications plc*, 1992 S.L.T. 490.
[40] 1991 S.L.T. 490.
[41] *ibid.* at 492.
[42] 1992 S.L.T. 490.

to circumvent the provisions of ... the lease and that [the condition stating that the agreement does not constitute a lease] was inserted in an attempt to disguise the real nature of the transaction."[43]

The foundation, then, from which the lease-licence question is to be resolved 1–16 in Scots law is the intention of the parties in forming the relationship in question. This, of course, begs the question of *how* the intention of the parties is to be determined. This intention is to be divined in the first instance from the words of their agreement unless, as in *Brador Properties*, the factual context in which the agreement is framed is such that the court will regard it as sham disguising the *true* intention of the parties. Alternatively, the actings of the parties subsequent to and giving effect to the written agreement may be examined, but only if such is made necessary by some ambiguity in the wording of the agreement.[44] In both *Scottish Residential Estates* and *Brador Properties* this was not required.

Of course, once the matter of the intentions of the parties has been determined, it must be asked whether the agreement is capable of amounting to a lease in Scots law. For an agreement to create a lease to be realised, it must satisfy the requirements for the creation of the lease, a matter which will be explored later in this chapter.

Service occupancy

In the case of employees whose work entitles them to the occupancy of a 1–17 house belonging to the employer, the contract may well not be one of tenancy. Normally the limited nature of the occupier's rights will be laid down in a contract document, whether it be in a missive of let or contract of service. In order to avoid doubt it will commonly be inserted in such a document that on the cessation of the employment the right of occupancy shall also cease.[45]

This limited right, ceasing on the termination of the employment, may be implied if there are no express provisions. Each case will be judged on its particular circumstances. A service occupancy (*i.e.* the limited right of occupancy) will be inferred only if the occupation of the house is necessary for the performance of the employee's duties. It is not enough that one is only eligible for the house if one is employed in certain jobs. Thus, for example, a railway employee living in a railway-owned house, where there was nothing expressly stated about his occupancy in relation to the performance of his railway duties, would, on ceasing to work for the railway, be able to live in the particular house. In such circumstances the occupancy would in fact be a lease rather than a service occupancy.

The test as to the distinction between a lease and a service occupancy is 1–18 whether the occupation itself is that of an employee. A baker occupied one of the three houses in Dingwall which his employer found for him and to whom he paid a small rent. He was told this "went with the job", but not that the occupation would cease with his termination of employment. This was held to be a lease as where he lived in no way related to his efficiency as a baker.[46] Where, however, a sum was deducted from a teacher's salary equal to the annual value of the

---

[43] 1992 S.L.T. 490 at 497.
[44] *Scottish Residential Estates Development Co. Ltd v. Henderson*, above; *Brador Properties Ltd v. British Telecommunications plc*, above.
[45] *Norris v. Checksfield* [1991] 1 W.L.R. 1241.
[46] *MacGregor v. Dunnett*, 1949 S.C. 510.

Education Authority's house occupied by him, it was held that the contract was one of service not of lease.[47]

Rights more extensive than lease

1–19   Various contracts relating to land produce similar effects such as the grantee obtaining a right to occupy while the granter retains the property rights or provide rights which can be retained for the life of the grantee and passed on death. Basically a feu confers rights in perpetuity while a lease, though it may confer rights, is generally limited to a specified duration. Would-be purchasers may withdraw or resile from a bargain if, unknown to them, the subjects are leasehold as opposed to feudal as they were understood to be.

In the case of a lease, although under Rent Act legislation certain tenants may have almost complete security of tenure during their own lifetime and for the lives of other members of the family,[48] nevertheless the property never becomes that of the tenant. The landlord remains the owner and if the conditions of the lease are broken the tenant may be evicted. A purchaser of property, on the other hand, under a valid contract of sale and once title has been recorded in the Land Register for Scotland/General Register of Sasines may do what he wishes with the property (subject, of course, to planning, nuisance, servitude restrictions and any restrictions imposed by the feudal superior, etc.). The tenant has a right to use the subjects, while the owner has full rights both of use and disposal.

3. CREATION OF A RESIDENTIAL LEASE

Basic requirements

1–20   The legal requirements for the creation of residential leases is a fairly well established area of Scots law. There are four basic elements required for the creation of a lease—parties, subjects, rent and duration or termination date (called an "ish").[49] At common law such agreements were personal and enforceable against the landlord and his personal representatives only. However, following the Leases Act 1449, this personal right could be transformed into a real right, enforceable against the singular successors of the landlord, if the tenant took possession of the subjects. This possession must be exclusive.[50]

The parties entering a contract of lease must have the capacity to do so and the general contractual rules govern leases. Although there must be agreement about subjects, these need not remain the same throughout the period of the lease. So long as the parties are agreed as to a mechanism for identifying the subjects these may change and a lease may be created.[51] The court is unable to specify a rent where there is no agreement between the parties.[52] A contract

---

[47] *Pollock v. Assessor for Inverness-shire*, 1923 S.C. 693.
[48] See Chap. 9.
[49] *Gray v. Edinburgh University*, 1962 S.C. 157.
[50] *Millar v. McRobbie*, 1949 S.L.T. 2.
[51] *Brador Properties Ltd v. British Telecommunications plc*, 1992 S.L.T. 490.
[52] *Shetland Islands Council v. B.P. Petroleum Development Ltd*, 1989 S.C.L.R. 48. In *Glen v. Roy* (1882) 10 R. 239 the court appeared willing to supply a "rent" figure, the parties having entered into the relationship of landlord and tenant. However, *Shetland Islands Council* has suggested that the term "rent" was not being used strictly in *Glen* and that it should not be taken as authority for the proposition that a lease may exist in the absence of agreement as to rent.

without rent is not a lease.[53] Where a duration has not been specified, a duration of one year may be inferred. However, this is only appropriate where the parties have come to an agreement about the other elements and the tenant has taken possession of the subjects, or agreement exists that possession is to be taken. [54]

It is common practice in Scotland for leases to specify two durations—for 1–21 example, that a lease is to be for the period of one year and monthly thereafter. It is suggested that this is a perfectly lawful practice even though the contract specifies more than one termination date. At any time during the occupancy of the subjects both parties can be clear about when the lease is due to expire and the courts would wish to give effect to this agreement between the parties. This view is supported by the decision in *Brador Properties Ltd v. British Telecommunications plc*[55] where the issue was whether a lease could exist which allowed for the subjects to be changed during the term of the contract. The Lord Justice-Clerk noted, referring to the decision in *Gray v. Edinburgh University*[56]:

> "If it is open to parties under a lease to stipulate for one of the cardinal elements, namely, rent being fixed by some agreed machinery, I see no reason in principle why they should not be entitled to agree that another cardinal principle, namely the subjects, should not also be determined by some mechanism which they have agreed."[57]

Requirements of Writing

Leases for more than one year's duration must be formally constituted in writing.[58] 1–21A This writing must take a specific form. For leases entered into after July 31, 1995, the form of writing must comply with the Requirements of Writing Act 1995.

Leases before August 1, 1995

Leases entered into before August 1, 1995 must be either probative, holograph, 1–21B or adopted as holograph.[59] To be probative, the lease must be subscribed by the landlord and tenant, with each signature being witnessed by two people. If the documents have failed to meet any of these particular forms of writing, the defect can be cured by the common law doctrines of *rei interventus* and/or homologation. The plea of *rei interventus* would be used where party A, in the full knowledge and acquiescence of party B, has acted (or refrained from acting), because they believe that the contract exists, and party B tries to withdraw from the contract. Homologation prevents a party to the contract from withdrawing from it after they themselves have acted in reliance on the contract. The acceptance of rent, or the allowing of a tenant to take possession of accommodation might be typical actions which could give rise to pleas of *rei interventus* or homologation.[60] These doctrines operate to cure an imperfect contract. The existence of the imperfect

---

[53] *Mann v. Houston*, 1957 S.L.T. 89; *Shetland Islands Council v. B.P. Petroleum Development Ltd*, above.
[54] *Gray v. Edinburgh University*, 1962 S.C. 157; *Shetland Islands Council v. B.P. Petroleum Development Ltd*, above.
[55] 1992 S.L.T. 490
[56] 1962 S.C. 157.
[57] 1992 S.L.T. 490 at 496 K–L.
[58] Paton and Cameron, *Landlord and Tenant* (1967), p. 16; Requirements of Writing (Scotland) Act 1995, s. 1(2) for leases after July 31, 1995.
[59] McBryde, *Contract*, p. 637; Woolman, *Contract* (2nd ed.), p. 60.
[60] See, for example, *Nelson v. Gerard*, 1994 S.C.L.R. 1052.

contract must, therefore, first be proved. This can only be done by writ or oath, *i.e.* by there being some form of writing, or by way of swearing an oath in court that the contract existed.[61] Proving the existence of a contract by oath has been uncommon for a long time, and practically speaking, is unlikely to be used in that it requires the defender in the action to swear that a contract exists (when it is presumably in his interest to deny its existence). Some kind of writing is required, therefore, if proof by oath is not to be used. Writing by only one of the parties should be suffice. This, in combination with subsequent actings of the parties, can point to the existence of the imperfect contract, and can cure it.[62]

Leases after July 31, 1995

1–21C   The rules about the requirements of writing are now much simpler. Leases must simply be subscribed by the landlord (or landlords if there is more than one of them) and the tenant (or tenants if there is more than one of them).[63] A single witness to the signatures will raise the presumption that the signature is in fact that of the landlord or, respectively, the tenant.[64] This makes the lease self-proving.

The 1995 Act sets out a new version of the doctrine of *rei interventus* for certain of the contracts, obligations and trusts covered by its terms.[65] This replaces the former doctrines of *rei interventus* and homologation. Where one of the parties to the contract has acted or refrained from acting in reliance on the contract with the knowledge and acquiescene of the other party, this other party may not withdraw from the contract and the contract will not be regarded as invalid. For the informal contract to be cured in this way, however, there is the requirement that the first party is affected to a material extent by their own actings, and would be materially affected by the other party's withdrawal from the contract.[66] Proof by writ or oath has been abolished.[67]

It is unclear whether the former doctrines of *rei interventus* and homologation remain operable after the 1995 Act.[68] It has also been suggested that rights of lease set up by missives of let alone may be excluded from the application of the new version of *rei interventus*.[69] This would be the case if the missives of let in such a situation are better regarded as creating an interest in land,[70] rather than as being a contract for the creation of an interest in land.[71] The new version of *rei interventus* only applies to the latter and not the former. This, in theory, would mean that imperfect writings could not be cured by subsequent actings, and, accordingly, that a real right in lease would not have been created. However, such an interpretation would be in tension with the terms of the Leases Act 1449 which confers a real right on lessees once in possession of the subjects. It also seems unlikely that Parliament would have intended to take away rights previously enjoyed by lessees prior to the 1995 Act with potentially drastic consequences.

---

[61] See Paton and Cameron, *op. cit.*, pp. 19–28; McAllister, *Scottish Law of Leases*, pp. 19–21.
[62] *Errol v. Walker*, 1966 S.C. 93; *Nelson v. Gerard*, above.
[63] Requirements of Writing (Scotland) Act 1995, s. 2.
[64] *ibid.* s. 3.
[65] *ibid.* s. 1(3)–(5).
[66] *ibid.* s. 1(3) and (4).
[67] *ibid.* s. 11(1) and (2).
[68] For a discussion of this problem, see Reid, *The Requirements of Writing (Scotland) Act 1995* (Sweet & Maxwell/W. Green, 1995).
[69] See Reid, *op. cit.*
[70] Requirements of Writing (Scotland) Act 1995, s. 1(2)(b).
[71] *ibid.* s. 1(2)(a).

Leases of a year or less

Leases of a year's duration or less do not require to be constituted in writing.[72] 1–21D
Verbal leases of such a duration, therefore, are perfectly valid. Where there is a
dispute as the existence of an agreement between parties to create such a lease,
written and parole evidence is permissible.

Tacit relocation

Although one of the cardinal requirements for the creation of a lease is duration, 1–22
this does not mean that the relationship of landlord and tenant automatically ceases
at the expiry of the lease's duration. A presumption is made in law that unless one
of the parties indicates that he/she wants the relationship to end, they intend it to
continue for a further period under exactly the same terms. This presumption is
called the doctrine of *tacit relocation*. A lease will be repeated under this doctrine
for the same duration as the original lease, unless the original duration is for more
than one year. If this is the case, the lease will only repeat in cycles of one year
until the lease is brought to an end by one of the parties.

The required period of notice for leases of more than four months is 40 clear days.
For leases of four months or less, the required period of notice is one-third of the
duration of the let. For residential tenancies, however, the statutory minimum period
of notice is 28 days.[73] Notices to quit for regulated and assured tenancies must contain
prescribed information.[74] If one party to a lease is not given a sufficient period of
notice, then tacit relocation will operate, even if the period is short by a single day.[75]

The doctrine is premised upon the implied consent of all the parties to a lease, so 1–23
the giving of notice by only one of joint tenants is sufficient to prevent *tacit relocation*
from operating.[76] What is required here is the effective communication of one party to
a lease to the other that he wants the lease to end. The usual and safest way to do this
is to serve proper notice on the other party. However, there are *obiter dicta* to the effect
that the actings of one party may be capable, albeit in exceptional circumstances, of
preventing the doctrine from operating.[77] It is suggested that in the context of residential
tenancies such circumstances are particularly unlikely to occur. The court has also
held that it is possible to contract out of the operation of tacit relocation.[78]

Whether a defective notice to quit is capable of preventing the doctrine from
operating is an unsettled point of law.[79] It is suggested, however, that a defective
notice to quit provided it gives the requisite period of notice while being incapable
of founding an action for recovery of possession, is nevertheless capable of
effectively communicating to the tenant that the landlord wishes to bring the
lease to an end, thereby preventing tacit relocation from operating.

---

[72] Paton and Cameron, *op. cit.*, p. 19; Requirements of Writing (Scotland) Act 1995, s. 1(1) and
(7) for leases after July 31, 1995.
[73] Rent (Scotland) Act 1984, s. 112.
[74] Rent Regulation (Forms and Information Etc.) (Scotland) Regulations 1991 (S.I. 1991
No. 1521), as amended by the Rent Regulation (Forms and Information Etc.) (Scotland)
Regulations 1993 (S.I. 1993 No. 647); Assured Tenancies (Notices to Quit Practical
Information) (Scotland) Regulations 1988 (S.I. 1988 No. 2067).
[75] *Signet Group PLC v. C.J. Clark Retail Properties Ltd*, 1996 S.C.L.R. 1020.
[76] *Smith v. Grayton Estates Ltd*, 1961 S.L.T. 38.
[77] *Signet Group PLC v. C. J. Clark Retail Properties Ltd*, above.
[78] *MacDougall v. Guidi*, 1992 S.C.L.R. 167.
[79] G. Paton and J. Cameron, *Landlord and Tenant* (1967), p. 225.

4. SOLE AND JOINT TENANCIES

1–24   Although this is not a common problem for the courts, where property is shared problems can arise relating to the nature of legal status of the occupiers and the impact of the actions of one occupier on another.

Joint tenancies and tenancies in common

1–25   Although the situation where more than one individual leases a single property is normally referred to as a "joint tenancy", it should be noted that, strictly speaking, the parties are likely to be tenants in common. Joint property arises only in the relatively few situations (such as clubs and trusts) where there is a single title held jointly by individuals who do not have separate estates in the property in question.[80] Unless the "joint" tenants in a lease fall within these limited situations where joint title is possible, or unless the lease is conferred on two parties and the survivor of them, the tenants will be tenants in common. Tenants in common have distinct rights to the subjects *pro indiviso* which can be separately transmitted or assigned without affecting the entitlements of the other tenant,[81] provided, of course, that assignation is permitted.[82] For convenience, however, tenants in common will be referred to in this text as "joint tenants".

Absence of one joint tenant

1–26   Each of the joint tenants is liable for performance of the obligations under the lease, including the requirement to pay rent, unless provision is made to the contrary.[83] The fact that one joint tenant is not present in the subjects does not prevent that tenant from being liable for the non-performance of the tenants' obligations by the other tenant.[84]

Renunciation by one joint tenant

1–27   It is not possible for one joint tenant to renounce his entitlement to the joint tenancy and thereby leave the remaining tenant as sole tenant. Renunciation requires the agreement of the landlord and tenant. It would not be possible for a contract of lease involving joint tenants to be converted to a different contract involving a sole tenant by the actions of a single tenant and the landlord.[85] Where assignation is not prohibited, it is possible for one joint tenant to assign his share to the other joint tenant, thereby giving the remaining tenant sole rights as tenant.[86]

---

[80] *Provost, Magistrates and Councillors of Banff v. Ruthkin Castle Ltd*, 1944 S.L.T. 373; K. G. C. Reid, *The Law of Property in Scotland* (1996), p. 20; W. M. Gloag & R. C. Henderson, *The Law of Scotland* (10th ed., 1995), p. 671.

[81] *Coats v. Logan*, 1985 S.L.T. 221 at 225; G. Paton and J. Cameron, *Landlord and Tenant* (1967), p. 60.

[82] See paras 1.56 and 1.57.

[83] G. Paton and J. Cameron, *Landlord and Tenant* (1967), p. 60.

[84] *Sutherland v. Robertston* (1736) Mor. 13979.

[85] See the opinion of Lord Skerrington in *Graham v. Stirling*, 1922 S.C. 90 at 107. A similar point was also made in *Smith v. Grayton Estates Ltd*, 1961 S.L.T. 38 in relation to the question of whether a timeous notice to quit of one joint tenant could have the effect of ending the tenancy of the tenant who gave notice thus leaving the other as sole tenant.

[86] See, for example, *Middle Ward of Lanark District Council v. Marshall* (1896) 24 R. 139.

Notice to quit by one joint tenant to expire at ish

Notwithstanding the fact that one joint tenant cannot renounce his entitlement 1–28
to the tenancy and thereby leave the remaining tenant as sole tenant, tacit
relocation will be prevented from occurring where one joint tenant serves a
notice to quit on a landlord.[87] The doctrine of tacit relocation, as noted above, is
premised upon the implied agreement of all the parties to a lease, through their
silence, to prolong the terms of the lease for a maximum of a further year. If one
joint tenant serves notice on a landlord this signifies the lack of agreement on
his part. A similar approach has been adopted by the House of Lords in the
English case of *Hammersmith LBC v. Monk.*[88]

Notice to quit by one joint tenant prior to ish

The situation in the above section where a tenant serves a notice to quit on the 1–29
landlord which expires at the ish must be contrasted with the situation where a
tenant serves a notice to quit which expires during the term of the lease. Where
the contract of lease provides for it, a tenant may bring the tenancy to an end
prematurely by serving a notice to quit on the landlord. In this situation the consent
of all joint tenants is required. Such is the general rule regarding the management
of common property. In the same way that all joint tenants must agree to continue
a lease for a further term through tacit relocation (that is, by all omitting to serve
a notice to quit), so must all the joint tenants agree to terminate a lease prematurely.[89]

Termination of joint secure tenancies

Secure tenancies must be considered separately. Section 46 of the Housing 1–30
(Scotland) Act 1987 imposes a strict limit upon the circumstances by which a secure
tenancy may be terminated, notwithstanding the terms of the lease.[90] It is suggested
that there is a clear statutory basis for the view that the consent of all joint tenants is
required to terminate a tenancy. Two of the six permitted means of termination
concern us here: first, by written agreement between the landlord and tenant[91]; and
secondly, by four weeks' notice given by the tenant to the landlord.[92] "Tenant" is
later defined for the purposes of this Part of the Act as meaning "in the case of joint
tenants … all the tenants."[93] These provisions in the 1987 Act must be contrasted
with the position in England and Wales where it has been held that a notice to quit
from one joint tenant will have the effect of determining a "periodic" secure tenancy,
thereby leaving the remaining tenant without security of tenure.[94] It has been common
practice in England and Wales for local authorities to advise a spouse who is a joint
secure tenant and has to leave the home because of violence to serve on them a
notice to quit. This means that when the wife and the children are rehoused under
homelessness legislation the council can claim back the other "family-sized" home
where the husband remains. This option is not open to Scottish local authorities.

---

[87] *Smith v. Grayton Estates Ltd,* 1961 S.L.T. 38.
[88] [1992] 1 A.C. 478.
[89] This is also the approach adopted in the English courts. See *Greenwich L.B.C. v. McGrady* (1982) 81 L.G.R. 288, in particular the passage from the judgment of Sir John Donaldson M.R. quoted with approval in *Hammersmith L.B.C. v. Monk* [1992] 1 A.C. 478.
[90] See Chap. 5.
[91] Housing (Scotland) Act 1987, s. 46(1)(c).
[92] *ibid.* s. 46(1)(f).
[93] *ibid.* s. 82.
[94] *London Borough of Greenwich v. McGrady* (1984) 16 H.L.R. 36 at 40.

Effect of notice to quit on security of tenure

1–31   Where a tenancy falls under the terms of the Rent (Scotland) Act 1984 or the Housing (Scotland) Act 1988, the termination of the contractual tenancy would merely have the effect of bringing a statutory tenancy into existence. The security of tenure provided by the above Acts would apply. A landlord in this situation may raise an action for recovery of possession. However, the grounds for possession are discretionary and a reasonableness requirement must accordingly be satisfied.[95] It may prove difficult, then, to persuade the court to grant decree where one joint tenant has served a notice to quit rendering the other remaining "innocent" joint tenant vulnerable to such an action.

Application to court for transfer of joint to sole tenancy

1–32   Where a matrimonial home forms the subjects of lease, there are statutory provisions which allow one joint tenant to apply to the court for the transfer of the joint tenancy into his or her sole name.[96] In deciding whether to grant such an order the court must have regard to the respective needs and financial resources of the spouses; the needs of any child of the family; the extent (if any) to which the matrimonial home is used in connection with a trade, business or profession of either spouse; and whether the entitled spouse offers or has offered to make available to the non-entitled spouse any suitable alternative accommodation. It must also consider the suitability of the applicant to become the tenant and the applicant's capacity to perform the obligations under the lease of the matrimonial home.[97] Compensation may be payable to the spouse who is being divested of his tenancy rights.[98]

Recovery of possession against joint tenants

1–33   It is competent to recover possession against only one of joint *pro indiviso* tenants.[98a] However, this is not possible in relation to secure or assured tenancies by virtue of the fact that 'tenant' is defined in the respective legislation as meaning, in the case of a joint tenancy, all the tenants.[98b] There is no equivalent provision in relation to protected tenancies.[98c] The actions of one joint tenant (for example in causing nuisance) are capable of founding a ground for recovery of possession,[99] and in deciding whether it is reasonable to require a local authority landlord to make other accommodation available to the tenant in such a situation, the court need only concern itself with the joint tenant who was responsible for the nuisance. The circumstances of the other joint tenant are, however, pertinent to whether it is reasonable to grant the decree for recovery of possession.[1]

---

[95] Rent (Scotland) Act 1984, Sched. 2, Case 5; Housing (Scotland) Act 1988, Sched. 5, Ground 10.

[96] Matrimonial Homes (Family Protection)(Scotland) Act 1981, s. 13(9). See Chap. 8.

[97] *ibid.* s. 13(3).

[98] *ibid.* s. 13(9).

[98a] Rankine *Leases* (3rd ed.), p. 520; Paton and Cameron, *Landlord and Tenant*, p. 257.

[98b] Housing (Scotland) Act 1987, s. 82; Housing (Scotland) Act 1988, s. 55(3); see *Aberdeen C. C. v. Drummond*, 1997 Hous.L.R. 116.

[98c] See Rent (Scotland) Act 1984, s. 115(1).

[99] *SSHA v. Lumsden*, 1984 S.L.T. (Sh.Ct.) 71.

[1] *Glasgow D.C. v. Brown*, 1988 S.C.L.R. 679.

Determining legal status in shared property

The sharing of accommodation can create difficulties in establishing what 1–34 legal relationships exist. Sharers of a flat, for example, may be joint tenants of single subjects, or may be sole tenants of individual subjects which are located within a single physical structure. Where there is a single tenant with several known sharers then the latter would be lawful sub-tenants. A problem which occurred in the past where tenancies were not reduced to writing involved changes in either the tenant and/or sub-tenants. Where the principal tenant and the sub-tenants change there may be problems of proof but the new occupiers would be regarded as tenants/sub-tenants. A landlord's claim that such new occupiers were squatters was not successful in 1974.[2]

5. OBLIGATIONS OF THE PARTIES: LANDLORDS' OBLIGATIONS

The common law lays down certain requirements for parties to a lease. It is 1–35 open to landlords and tenants to vary the common law on such issues as what kinds of activities the tenant may carry on in the property. However, statute may limit the changes in relation to protected, assured and secure tenancies, or may impose additional duties on the parties.

Duty to give possession and maintain tenant in possession

The landlord must give possession at the commencement of the lease and 1–36 maintain the tenant in possession throughout the period of the lease.[3] Either party may raise an action for specific implement if the other party fails in their obligations regarding possession.

Although in most cases possession will be given of the whole of the subjects there are circumstances where there may be certain parts of the subjects reserved. In a lease of a country house the landlord reserved possession without notice of a charter room, store room, observatory and spare furniture room and it was held the tenant was not entitled to abandon the lease.[4] In addition, in a furnished house the landlord may lock cupboards, wardrobes, etc.[5] The tenant is also entitled, by implication, to those rights which are essential to the purposes of the lease. Thus where a positive servitude exists in favour of the subjects over neighbouring land (*e.g.* a right to cross the neighbouring land) the tenant will be entitled to keep this right in being by use of the right.

Duty to provide habitable and tenantable subjects

The landlord in a residential tenancy must provide property that is habitable and 1–37 tenantable at common law. The property must be fit for human habitation and under an implied statutory repairs obligation the tenant has a right to have the property kept in repair.[6]

---

[2] *McDougall v. McGinlay*, Glasgow Sh. Ct., June 7, 1974, unreported, *per* Sheriff Middleton.
[3] G. Paton and J. Cameron, *Landlord and Tenant* (1967); A. McAllister, *The Scottish Law of Leases* (1995).
[4] *Webster v. Lyell* (1860) 22 D. 1423.
[5] *Miller v. Wilson*, 1919 S.L.T. 223.
[6] See Chap. 3.

Duty to provide written lease

1–38   The regimes of private sector assured tenancies and public sector secure require that all leases be in writing.[7] If the landlord fails to have a written lease drawn up the tenant can seek to have this omission rectified or the terms varied.[8] However, no such requirement was necessary for tenancies entered into before secure and assured tenancies were introduced. Although local authorities have regularised the position of their tenants by providing them with written leases there are still situations where tenants hold property on agreements which were devised when the provision of a clear outline of rights and obligations was not accorded great weight. These can give rise to unanticipated problems in both the kind of security of tenure a tenant may enjoy[9] as well as other rights to which a tenant may lay claim.[10]

Duty to provide rent book

1–40   Landlords of regulated and assured tenancies and Part VII contracts must provide tenants with a rent book where rent is payable weekly.[11]

Duty to ensure safety of gas appliances

1–41   The Gas Safety (Installation and Use) Regulations 1994[12] impose an obligation on landlords to ensure that all gas appliances and associated pipework are maintained in a safe condition. Safety checks must be made every year by an approved person. Work on appliances can only be carried out by an approved person. Additionally, a safety check record must be kept. Any person in lawful occupation of the premises in question may examine this record by making a reasonable request with reasonable notice. "Relevant premises" are defined as meaning premises (or a part of them) occupied for residential purposes under a lease or licence. The arrangement must involve the payment of money. "Lease" includes a statutory tenancy, but not a lease of seven years or more. Gas appliances supplied by a cylinder are excluded from the terms of the Regulations.

Duty to ensure fire safety of furniture and furnishings

1–42   In certain residential tenancy situations the landlord is under an obligation to comply with Regulations aimed at ensuring that furniture and furnishings comply with fire safety standards. The Furniture and Furnishings (Fire) Safety Regulations 1988[13] were enacted under the terms of the Consumer Protection Act 1987. Where a landlord can be considered to be supplying such "goods in the course of a business"[14] he will be required to ensure that such furniture and fittings comply with the fire safety standards set out in detail in the Regulations.

---

[7] Housing (Scotland) Act 1987, s. 53; Housing (Scotland) Act 1988, s. 30.
[8] Housing (Scotland) Act 1988, s. 30(2); the Housing (Scotland) Act 1987 only envisages a local authority landlord drawing up an unfair lease; ss. 53 and 54.
[9] *Family Housing Association v. Jones* [1990] 1 W.L.R. 779.
[10] See Chap. 9.
[11] Rent (Scotland) Act 1984, ss. 79 and 113; Housing (Scotland) Act 1988, s. 30(4); Assured Tenancies (Rent Book) (Scotland) Regulations 1988 (S.I. 1988 No. 2085).
[12] S.I. 1994 No. 1886, as amended by S.I.s 1996 Nos 550, 551 and 2541.
[13] S.I. 1998 No. 1324.
[14] Consumer Protection Act 1987, ss. 11 and 46(5).

6. OBLIGATIONS OF THE TENANT

Take and maintain possession of subjects

Tenants must take and retain possession of the premises and must not invert 1–43
such possession by using the property for prohibited purposes. The obligation
to possess does not require the tenant to reside personally on the subjects although
this may be specifically agreed between the landlord and tenant in the contract
of lease. Unless it is forbidden in the lease, possession will be possible not only
personally but also through the tenant's servants, family, or other such
representatives or agents. In addition, where a tenant dies and one of the
successors is seeking to take on the lease as a statutory regulated tenant or
statutory assured tenant or a succeeding secure tenant then the survivor must
retain possession of the premises.[15] This requires possession to be personal and
cannot be achieved through representatives.[16]

Duty of Care towards Subjects

At common law the tenant is "bound to use a reasonable degree of diligence in 1–44
preserving [the subjects] from harm."[17] So, for example, traditionally there has been
a duty to keep the subjects fired and aired to prevent dampness.[18] The tenant will be
liable for damage caused by his negligence.[19] This duty was considered in relation
to the risk to the structure of a high-rise block posed by the use of bottled gas.[20] The
Inner House provided guidance for determining whether a tenant has acted in such
a way as to have breached the general duty of care. Four factors must be considered:
(1) the foreseeability of a dangerous event happening; (2) the likelihood of the
dangerous event happening; (3) the potential seriousness of the consequences if the
event happens; and (4) whether there are reasonable precautions which can be taken
to avoid or minimise the danger. The degree of care required increases in parallel
with the gravity of the potential consequences. Where the storage of bottled gas in
a high-rise flat posed the risk of an explosion which may have collapsed the whole
high-rise block, the duty to take reasonable care was held to have been breached
even though the risk of an explosion was low.

Duty to pay rent

There is, at common law, an implied duty to pay rent when due.[21] This will 1–45
invariably be made expressly as a contractual term.

Duty to use the subjects only for the purposes for which they were let

Residential subjects are let with a particular sort of possession in mind and the 1–46
tenant may only possess the subjects for the purpose of a dwelling-house. This may
be made express in the contract and there may be a restriction on the number of
persons who may stay in a property. Where the tenant uses the subjects for purposes

---

[15] See Chap. 9.
[16] *Ronson Nominees Ltd v. Mitchell*, 1982 S.L.T. (Sh.Ct.) 18; *Colin Smith Music Ltd v. Ridge* [1975] 1 All E.R. 290.
[17] Erskine, II,vi, 43.
[18] Rankine, *Leases* (3rd ed.), pp. 249–250.
[19] *Mickel v. McCoard,* 1913 S.C. 896.
[20] *Cumbernauld Development Corporation v. Marsh,* IH, August 28, 1991, unreported.
[21] *Glen v. Roy* (1882) 10 R. 239.

outwith those either expressed or implied, this amounts to inversion, or misuse, of possession. This occurs where there is activity inconsistent with the objects of the lease. What is normally required is more than isolated incidents but rather a course of conduct. For example, where a property is let to a single family to be occupied as a dwelling-house, having another family visit and stay would not amount to inversion. Turning the dwelling into a boarding house, however, would be so inconsistent with the implied purpose of a lease of a dwelling-house as to amount to inversion. The act of suicide by a tenant in the bathroom of his furnished lodging was sufficient to constitute inversion.[22] The landlord may lose the right to complain on inversion either where this is expressly renounced or occurs through acquiescence as where a shop was let as a shop but entered in the Valuation Roll for three years as a dwelling-house and was so used by the tenant.[23] This was regarded as being a "public record" and thus the landlord could be assumed to have notice of the entry therein and knowledge could be reasonably inferred. The appropriate remedy for a landlord would be to seek an interdict to stop such inversion of possession.

Duty to grant access to landlord for repairs

1–47   There is a statutorily implied condition in assured[24] and protected[25] tenancies that landlords will be granted access to the subjects of lease for the purposes of carrying out repairs. This must be read alongside the additional implied condition in all residential leases granted after July 3, 1962 of a duration of less than seven years following the provisions of the Housing (Scotland) Act 1987.[26] This additional condition states that a lessor may enter the subjects of lease at reasonable times of the day to view their condition and state of repair, so long as he has given 24 hours' notice in writing to the occupier.

Duty not to make false or fraudulent representations

1–48   Although this duty relates to the actings of parties prior to the existence of the landlord-tenant relationship, it is worth mentioning here and has recently been considered by the courts.[27] In addition to the statutory requirement not to make false statements or withhold information when applying to a local authority for housing as a homeless person,[28] and the ability of landlords of secure tenancies to apply for recovery of possession where the grant of the tenancy was induced by false statements,[29] there is a general duty in the law of contract to be honest when entering into contracts. Contracts which have been induced by fraud or misrepresentation are voidable.[30] As such they are open to actions of reduction. However, the effect of such a reduction is to "terminate" the contractual tenancy, thereby bringing a statutory tenancy into existence if the lease falls under one of the statutory regimes.[31] The landlord, accordingly, must still raise an action

---

[22] *A v. B's Trs* (1906) 13 S.L.T. 830.
[23] *Moore v. Munro* (1896) 4 S.L.T. 172.
[24] Housing (Scotland) Act 1988, s. 26.
[25] Rent (Scotland) Act 1984, s. 111.
[26] Housing (Scotland) Act 1987, Sched. 10, para. 3.
[27] *Govanhill Housing Association Ltd v. Palmer,* 1997 Hous.L.R. 133; *Shettleston Housing Association Ltd v. Bourke,* 1996 Hous.L.R. 53; *Govanhill Housing Association Ltd v. Malley,* 1996 Hous.L.R. 61; *Govanhill Housing Association Ltd v. Palmer,* 1997 Hous.L.R. 133.
[28] Housing (Scotland) Act 1987, s. 40.
[29] *ibid.* Sched. 3, Ground 6.
[30] W.W. McBryde, *The Law of Contract in Scotland* (1987), para. 10–68.
[31] See, in general, Chap. 2.

for recovery of possession for breach of an "obligation of the tenancy".[32] However, where a housing application form or tenancy agreement contains a statement to the effect that information supplied is true and that information has not been withheld, a summary cause action for recovery of possession in the sheriff court is possible without the prior need to seek a reduction of the contract.

7. REMEDIES FOR BREACH OF OBLIGATIONS

Implement and interdict

The obligations of landlord and tenant may be enforced by an action of implement to compel performance of a duty or of interdict to prevent the commission of a breach of the lease's conditions.　　1–49

Rescission

Where there has been a material breach of contract either party may rescind the contract. Whether or not a material breach of contract has occurred will depend on the individual circumstances of each case. Failure to fulfil a contractual obligation to cultivate and maintain the garden has been held not to constitute a material breach of contract.[33]　　1–50

Recovery of possession

A landlord may, of course, seek to recover possession of the subjects where a condition of the tenancy has been broken. This will usually require the landlord to raise a court action, although summary steps are possible where secure tenancies have been abandoned.[34] The vast majority of actions for recovery of possession by landlords occur because of rent arrears. In the public sector the other ground commonly used is one of nuisance or annoyance to neighbours.　　1–51

Retention and abatement of rent

The common law allows tenants to put pressure on landlords who will not fulfil their obligations by retaining rent.[35] Once the obligation has been complied with, the rent becomes due in full. If there is a counterclaim then it is necessary to raise this issue separately with either an action of damages or through the process of abatement. This right to retain rent is an equitable remedy available generally in respect of mutual contracts.[36] Such a right may then be overridden by express contractual provision.　　1–52

There are two distinct legal concepts where tenants go on "rent strike". It is important to be clear which is involved as they have different implications. Seeking abatement occurs where tenants are taking direct action to make a counterclaim. Claims for rent and counterclaims will often be conjoined.[37] Rent retention is a lever to secure action and does not affect the tenant's liability for

---

[32] *Govanhill Housing Association v. Palmer,* 1997 Hous.L.R. 133.
[33] *Couper v. McGuiness* (1948) 64 Sh.Ct.Rep. 249; Holloway v. Povey (1984) 15 H.L.R. 104 on the position under the Rent Acts.
[34] See Chap. 5.
[35] P. Brown and A. McIntosh, *Dampness and the Law* (1987), p. 68 discuss the practicalities of taking withholding action.
[36] *Stobbs & Sons v. Hislop,* 1948 S.C. 216; 1948 S.L.T. 248.
[37] *Davis v. Edinburgh D.C.* (1991) 1 S.H.L.R. 21; *Glasgow D.C. v. McCrone* (1991) 1 S.H.L.R. 45.

rent. It is important that advisers make clear in a situation where an abatement is sought that the rent is not simply being retained pending remedial action. Rent retention results in full liability on completion of the landlord's contractual obligations and leaves the question of abatement or counterclaim for separate consideration.

1–53   It should be noted, however, that some caution should be exercised when withholding rent, especially where the tenancy has no security of tenure or is an assured tenancy and the landlord may proceed under the mandatory Ground 8 of Schedule 5 (three months rent arrears) for recovery of possession.[38] There is also authority which suggests that the common law right to retain is lost by statutory tenants covered by the Rent Acts.[39] However, this decision applied to "controlled" tenants whose landlords could be deprived of a part of the rent if the property did not meet a certain fitness standard. The old regime of rent control froze rents, but provided for increases for landlords to cover repairs. Where the property was not in good and tenantable repair the landlord could not recover this part of the rent.[40] There is no equivalent right for protected, assured and secure tenants and hence this authority is no longer reliable.

Remedy for breach of maintenance of tenant in possession

1–54   Before the tenant can establish breach of the obligation of maintenance in possession there must be either total or partial eviction. "Eviction" occurs where the tenant is unable to enjoy the use of the premises. If there is partial eviction then an action for damages, usually in the form of a reduction or abatement of rent, is appropriate. Where there is total eviction the tenant will normally be entitled either to restitution or to damages. Where the eviction is not directly at the hands of the landlord but comes about as a result of destruction of the subjects different considerations apply. Where there is no fault of the landlord then the landlord will not be liable for damages.

If, without fault of either landlord or tenant, the subjects are destroyed either directly (*e.g.* by fire or flood) or indirectly (*e.g.* through being requisitioned), the relationship of landlord and tenant will come to an end. The tenant will be entitled to abandon the lease and again claim an abatement of rent but cannot claim damages if the landlord is in no way to blame. Clearly if the subjects were destroyed by the landlord's negligent or reckless actings the tenant would have a civil claim for damages (as well as there being possible criminal proceedings).

Any obligations arising under the lease are thus extinguished as a result of the total destruction of the subjects. However, before a lease can be abandoned there must be more than "considerable inconvenience" and the tenant must give the landlord an opportunity to have the damage repaired. The failure of the landlord to deal with the drains of the rented home over a period of several months allowed a tenant to withdraw from a two-year lease. In this case the tenant's family had been very ill as a result of the defective drains and his daughter had died.[41] There may, in less serious cases, be abatement or reduction of rent.[42]

1–55   There may be instances where there is some form of partial or total eviction which it is not reasonable to expect the landlord to guarantee against, such as supervenient legislation. There is clearly nothing a landlord can do if Parliament changes the law so that there is in effect partial eviction. The tenant could not

---

[38] See D. O'Carroll, "The Right to Withhold Rent", 1993 SCOLAG 188–189.

[39] *Stobbs & Sons v. Hislop*, 1948 S.C. 216; 1948 S.L.T. 248.

[40] See Paton and Cameron, *Landlord and Tenant* (1967), p. 538.

[41] *Scottish Heritable Security Co. v. Granger* (1881) 8 R. 459.

[42] *Allan v. Markland* (1882) 10 R. 383.

plead partial eviction if, for example, there were changes in the legislation relating to overcrowding provisions which limited the number of persons allowed to live in a dwelling. Similarly there is no liability under contract where, without direct legislation, there is a resultant change in the circumstances which materially affects the subjects of the lease. In one case there was a lease of a furnished mansion house for 19 years commencing in 1936. In 1940 the military authorities requisitioned the property. The tenant was held able to abandon the lease on the grounds of constructive total destruction of the subjects of the lease.[43] However, in such cases though the tenant may abandon the lease, there is no liability attaching to the landlord. It would be unreasonable to expect the tenant to remain the tenant of subjects which are, in effect, destroyed by supervenient legislation, but just as unfair to lay the full financial burden at the landlord's door. Thus, while the tenant can give up the lease, as the landlord is not to blame there is no redress in an action against the landlord except by way of a rent refund for the period when the subjects cannot be possessed. The appropriate source of any compensation would be the authorities who in effect "destroy the lease". The major point at issue is likely to be whether the condition of the house is actually caused by a natural disaster or simply through the failure of the landlord to keep the premises tenantable and habitable.[44]

Where a tenant's possession is disturbed by the illegal actings of a third party to which the landlord is not party, such as vandalism, again there is no recourse to the landlord except as indicated to require proceedings to be taken against the third party.[45] There may be a contractual alteration of this right. Thus landlords may well impose on their tenants only responsibility for damage caused by the tenant. This means that any damage caused by a third party is the responsibility of the landlord.[46]

8. ASSIGNATION AND SUB-LETTING

The assignation of a lease is a transfer by the tenant of an interest in the lease to   1–56
another person called the assignee, who becomes the new tenant in place of the tenant. The assignor, sometimes known as the granter or cedent, ceases to have any further interest in the lease and as indicated the assignee steps into the previous tenant's shoes. Here there is just one contract, the parties changing. A sub-lease, on the other hand, is a lease granted by a tenant of all or part of the subjects leased so that the original tenant becomes the landlord of the sub-tenant while remaining the tenant of the original landlord.

Where the tenant in a lease is given an express right to assign or sub-let (as where the contract is granted to the tenant, "his assignees and sub-lessees whomsoever"), this will displace any common-law presumption or statutory prohibition against either assignation or sub-letting. If there is no express clause giving the power to assign or sub-let, the tenants of certain classes of leases may have this power. Tenants of urban unfurnished premises have this right at common law. The basis of the rule is the lack of "solidarity" between landlord and tenant in such leases as compared with furnished leases where the element of personal selection by the landlord of the tenant (*delectus personae*) is strong.

[43] *Mackeson v. Boyd*, 1942 S.C. 56.
[44] See para. 3.22 *et seq.*
[45] *Davis v. Edinburgh D.C.*, (1991) 1 S.H.L.R. 21.
[46] *Edinburgh D.C. v. Laurie*, 1982 S.L.T. (Sh.Ct.) 83.

1–57   The common law position has been altered since the introduction of secure tenancies and assured tenancies in the 1980s for certain kinds of dwelling-house lease. The Housing (Scotland) Act 1987 which deals with secure tenancies in the public sector provides that there shall be no implied assignation or sub-letting without the landlord's consent.[47] This consent must not be unreasonably withheld.[48] Similarly for private sector assured tenancies there is to be no sub-letting nor assignation without the landlord's consent.[49] There is in this situation no requirement as to reasonableness. This was not an oversight.[50] There must not, however, be oppression in the landlord's exercise of this right. This is a familiar notion in English landlord and tenant law[51] but it has yet to be directly considered by a Scottish court in the context of residential property.

---

[47] s. 55.
[48] *ibid.*
[49] Housing (Scotland) Act 1988, s. 23.
[50] *Hansard*, H.C. Vol. 354, col. 727 (February. 16, 1988).
[51] *Bates v. Donaldson* [1896] 2 Q.B. 241; *Lovelock v. Margo* [1963] 2 Q.B. 786.

CHAPTER 2

LEASE CONTRACTS AND STATUTORY CONTROLS

In addition to the common law of lease and the provisions of the Leases Act 2–01
1449, there now exists a substantial body of modern statutory regulation of
residential leases. Statutory intervention in relation to residential tenancies has
principally been concerned with two matters—the control of rents chargeable,
and security of tenure for residential tenants. There are three current statutory
regimes. The Rent (Scotland) Act 1984 governs "protected tenancies" and
"Part VII contracts", the Housing (Scotland) Act 1987 regulates "secure
tenancies", and the Housing (Scotland) Act 1988 governs "assured tenancies".

1. RENT (SCOTLAND) ACT 1984—PROTECTED TENANCIES

"Protected" and "statutory" tenancies

The terminology of the Rent Acts needs to be noted before looking at which 2–02
tenancies are protected. A protected tenancy is a contractual tenancy covered
by the Rent (Scotland) Act 1984. In order to qualify for the benefits of the
legislation it is necessary that the tenancy satisfy both the positive requirements
laid down for a protected tenancy[1] as well as not come within the category of
excluded tenancies.[2] A statutory tenancy is one which arises when a tenant retains
possession of a dwelling-house after the termination of a protected tenancy (*i.e.*
when the contract of lease is brought to an end by one of the parties).[3] It is so
called because the right to be a tenant arises by virtue of the statute rather than
contract.

Definition of "protected tenancies"

Although protected tenancies cannot now be created they still exist where 2–03
the tenancy was entered into prior to January 2, 1989 or pursuant to a contract
entered into prior to that date. Such tenancies cannot be protected unless they
satisfy all the following conditions. The property must be let as a dwelling-
house (which may be a house or part of a house),[4] let as a separate dwelling,[5]
and the rateable value on the appropriate day must not exceed a specified sum.[6]
It should be noted, however, that even if these conditions are fulfilled the tenancy
may still fall outside the Rent Acts since certain landlord and tenancies are
excluded. Almost all tenancies entered into after January 2, 1989 will be either

---

[1] Rent (Scotland) Act 1984, s. 1.
[2] *ibid.* ss. 2, 4, 5 and 6.
[3] *ibid.* s. 3.
[4] *ibid.* s. 1(1).
[5] *ibid.*
[6] *ibid.* s. 1(1)(a).

assured tenancies[7] or secure tenancies.[8] The rest of this section must be read bearing in mind that to qualify as a protected tenancy a tenancy will need to have satisfied this requirement.

Let as a dwelling-house

2–04　　The Rent (Scotland) Act 1984 applies to a house which is "let". The tenant must have the exclusive right to possession. If possession is not exclusive the contract will not be protected. However, there may be a joint tenancy where two or more tenants share exclusive occupancy. Whilst the Rent Act protects a service tenant, it does not protect a service occupier whose occupancy of the dwelling-house is attributable not to any lease but to the contract of service.[9]

　　In general, a "dwelling-house" is any permanent structure either the whole or part of which is capable of being used for all the major activities for which dwelling-houses are used (sleeping, eating, cooking, washing). The dwelling-house need not be a whole house. As far as mobile homes are concerned the question depends on their permanence and that of the services to them.[10]

Let as a separate dwelling

2–05　　A tenant must occupy a specific part of a dwelling with exclusive possession. Landlords have attempted to grant agreements which only give a right to share an unspecified part of a dwelling with others. Where there are a number of separate contracts the aim is that no one party is covered by the Rent Acts as there is no "separate dwelling". Such devices have been accepted in England in the Court of Appeal since 1978.[11] The House of Lords has indicated that where this is a mere sham it will look to the reality of the possession.[12] However, while it has confirmed that it will not accept situations where the paper rights and the practice diverge it has accepted "genuine" sharing arrangements. Typically this occurs where there is a flat with a shifting population of individuals who are not known to each other prior to moving in. If none of the occupiers is responsible for the rents of the others or for voids and has no control over replacements then there is a strong likelihood that the courts in England would accept these agreements.[13] The courts in Scotland have never been required to decide whether or not the concept of the non-exclusive residential occupancy agreement is acceptable under Scots law.

2–06　　The legislation applies to parts of houses so that part of a house may itself be a "dwelling-house" for the purpose of the Act provided it is "let" as indicated above. The letting may be a sub-letting; thus if a house is let by Murdoch to Craig to live in and Craig sub-lets three rooms to Gemmell, Gemmell's rooms form a separate "dwelling-house" and the legislation applies to it.[14]

　　Where rooms are let wholly for residential purposes under a separate lease they constitute a "dwelling-house", provided that there is at least one room. The sharing of facilities such as a kitchen or bathroom does not prevent the

---

[7] See para. 2–25 *et seq.*
[8] See para. 2–63 *et seq.*
[9] See para. 1–17 *et seq.*
[10] *R. v. Rent Officer of the Nottinghamshire Registration Area, ex p. Allen* (1985) 52 P. & C.R. 41 at 44.
[11] *Somma v. Hazelhurst* [1978] 1 W.L.R. 1014.
[12] *Street v. Mountford* [1985] A.C. 809.
[13] *A. G. Securities v. Vaughan* [1988] 3 W.L.R. 1205.
[14] s. 19.

rooms forming a "separate dwelling-house" to which the Act applies.[15] This situation must be distinguished from "sharing a house" where the tenant shares a living room with the landlord: in this case the protection given for contracts entered into prior to January 2, 1989 was "Part VII protection".[16] The Housing (Scotland) Act 1988 removed any protection beyond the contract from those who shared with their landlords.[17]

There is no protected tenancy where the property consists of a number of separate units of habitation being sub-let by the tenant. Typically excluded is property used as a college hall of residence,[18] as well as the situation where a dwelling-house contains units of accommodation which are to be occupied separately.[19]

The Act applies to buildings let partly for residential and partly for other 2–07 purposes (*i.e.* premises used as a shop or for business, trade, or professional purposes with a dwelling-house attached, except licensed premises) as far as the dwelling-house is concerned only.[20] The Act does not apply to purely business premises though it will apply where the intention of the tenancy is that the premises are let for residential purposes even if not so used. In the absence of any specified purpose the use will determine whether the premises are let as a dwelling-house or not. Where the Tenancy of Shops (Scotland) Act 1949 and 1964 apply to a tenancy, the premises are thereby excluded from the Rent Act, even where the use of premises as a shop is only partial.[21]

Rateable value

The rateable value on the relevant day or on first appearance on the roll 2–08 thereafter must not exceed the sum laid down by order by the Secretary of State for Scotland. Originally this was fixed in the Rent Act 1965 at £200 and was revised in 1978 to £600 and in 1985 to £1,600.[22] The 1984 Act provides that where there are alterations to the valuation roll made after the appropriate day then they are to be treated as if they were backdated to the appropriate day. The rateable value to be applied is to be the amended valuation.[23]

Excluded tenancies

The legislation provides that a tenancy is not a protected tenancy in certain 2–09 other circumstances.[24] These are detailed below.

Rent payable and not less than two-thirds of the rateable value[25]

The rent means the total sum payable to the landlord. This covers houses let 2–10 at a nominal rent or situations where no rent is paid, which thus do not come

---

[15] Rent (Scotland) Act 1984, s. 97.
[16] See para. 2.18.
[17] Housing (Scotland) Act 1988, s. 12 and Sched. 4, para. 9.
[18] *St. Catherine's College v. Dorling* [1980] 1 W.L.R. 66.
[19] *Horford Investments Ltd v. Lambert* [1976] Ch. 39.
[20] Rent (Scotland) Act 1984, s. 10(1).
[21] *ibid.* s. 10(2).
[22] *ibid.* s. 1(1)(a), (2) (as amended by the Protected Tenancies and Part VII Contracts (Rateable Value Limits) (Scotland) Order 1985 (S.I. 1985 No. 314)).
[23] Rent (Scotland) Act 1984, s. 7(4).
[24] *ibid.* ss. 2, 4, 5, 6 and 10.
[25] *ibid.* s. 2(1)(a).

within the provisions of the Rent Act. This reflects the goals of the Rent Acts—
to prevent exploitation stemming from the undersupply of houses in the market.
The level of low-rent premises is fixed in relation to the rateable value of the
premises. The rent paid must not be less than two-thirds of the rateable value on
the appropriate day.[26]

Lodgings and service lettings

2–11   A tenancy is not a protected tenancy if, under the tenancy, the dwelling-
house is let in good faith, at a rent which includes payments in respect of board
or attendance.[27] If any board is provided the let is not protected. However, it is
possible for a protected tenancy to exist in some situations where attendance
is provided. For the exemption from protection to apply, the amount which is
fairly attributable to attendance, having regard to its value to the tenant, must
form a "substantial part" of the whole rent. No fixed percentage is laid down.
For some years the only modern authority cited both north and south of the
border was a Scottish sheriff court decision from Edinburgh where a continental
breakfast was accepted as amounting to board.[28] This notion that a single meal
amounts to board has been accepted by the House of Lords.[29] A decision in
Paisley Sheriff Court suggested that not only was it necessary for there to be
substance in the provision of board but that there should be a service. Providing
vouchers for cafes or boxes of groceries was not sufficient.[30]

Lettings entered into prior to January 2, 1989 with provisions of services,
although not protected tenancies, are nevertheless subject to rent control and
limited security of tenure by virtue of Part VII of the Rent (Scotland) Act 1984.
The provision of services, however, should be contrasted with the provision of
board, which includes the provision of food. Where accommodation is provided
for a rent, a substantial proportion of which comprises payment for board, such
contracts do not qualify for Part VII protection.[31]

Student tenancies granted by a specified educational institution[32]

2–12   Educational institutions successfully obtained exemption from this part of
the Rent Acts in 1974. The exemption applies only to those bodies covered by the
regulations made by the Secretary of State. These cover universities, institutions
such as Glasgow School of Art, colleges of education and further education.[33]
Direct lettings by private landlords to students are not exempted, nor are
lettings by educational bodies to those who are not pursuing courses of study
at their institution. The latter, however, are subject to a mandatory possession
ground.[34]

---

[26] March 23, 1965, and for subjects first appearing on the roll thereafter, the date of the first
    appearance.
[27] 1984 Act, s. 2(1)(b).
[28] *Holiday Flat Co. v. Kuczera*, 1978 S.L.T. (Sh.Ct.) 47.
[29] *Otter v. Norman* [1988] 2 All E.R. 897.
[30] *Gavin v. Lindsay*, 1987 S.L.T. (Sh.Ct.) 12.
[31] See para. 2.16 *et seq.*
[32] 1984 Act, s. 2(1)(c).
[33] Protected Tenancies (Exceptions) (Scotland) Regulations 1974 (S.I. 1974 No. 1374) and the
    Protected Tenancies (Further Exceptions) (Scotland) Regulations 1982 (S.I. 1982 No. 702).
[34] See para. 5.91.

Holiday lets

Where the purpose of the let is to confer on the tenant the right to occupy the 2–13 dwelling-house for a holiday there can be no protected tenancy.[35] The onus is on the tenant to establish that an agreement which purports to be for a holiday is not in fact really let as holiday accommodation.[36] The concept of the working holiday has been accepted.[37]

Land let with land exceeding two acres[38]

The legislation provides that any land or premises is to be treated as part of 2–14 the dwelling-house unless it consists of agricultural land exceeding two acres.[39] Where a dwelling-house is let with land exceeding two acres it is exempt from the protection of the Rent Acts.[40]

Excluded landlords

Also, certain additional landlords were exempted from being able to confer 2–15 protected tenancies. Where the landord's interest belonged to the Crown, no protected tenancy could be created.[41] This is also the case in relation to public sector landlords,[42] resident landlords,[43] and where the premises in question are licensed for the sale of alcohol for consumption on the premises, or where the premises are used as a shop.[44]

2. Rent (Scotland) Act 1984 — Short Tenancies

Short tenancies were introduced by the Tenants' Rights Etc. (Scotland) Act 1980 2–15A and are now governed by the 1984 Act.[45] Similar to the purpose of the short assured tenancy, it was designed to provide a guarantee of recovery possession at the termination of the contractual term, provided certain steps were taken. The number of short tenancies still in existence are likely to be very few.

Definition of short tenancy

The short tenancy is a special kind of protected tenancy. They could only be 2–15B created after November 30, 1980 and it has not been possible to create them since the Housing (Scotland) Act 1988 came into force.[46] The minimum duration of let is one year, the maximum five years.[47] A written notice in specified form[48]

---

[35] 1984, Act, s. 2(1)(d).
[36] *Buchmann v. May* [1978] 2 All E.R. 99.
[37] *McHale v. Daneham* (1979) 249 E.G. 969.
[38] 1984 Act, s. 2(1)(e).
[39] Rent (Scotland) Act 1984, s. l(3).
[40] *ibid.* s. 2(l)(e).
[41] *ibid.* s. 4.
[42] *ibid.* s. 5, as amended by the Local Government etc. (Scotland) Act 1994, Sched. 13.
[43] *ibid.* s. 6.
[44] *ibid.* s. 10.
[45] *ibid.* s. 9.
[46] *ibid.* s. 9(1)(c)
[47] January 2, 1989.
[48] Short Tenancies (Prescribed Information) (Scotland) Order 1980 (S.I. 1980 No. 1666).

must be served on the prospective tenant prior to the creation of the tenancy. In order to protect protected tenants from being induced to enter into new contracts with reduced security of tenure, it was not possible for short tenancies to be created where the tenant was a standard protected tenant immediately prior to the creation of the tenancy in question.[49] Short tenancies must have a registered fair rent.[50]

The landlord of a short tenancy can recover possession[51] on the termination of the lease provided that he has given written notice to the tenant that he intends to apply for possession. This notice can be given before the expiry date of the contract, or up to three months after it. Possession may then be applied for no earlier than three and no later than six months following the notice.[52] If the landlord fails to serve such notice in time, the short tenancy will continue for a further year. A notice to quit is still required for to bring the contractual tenancy to an end. Possession is effective against sub-tenants, assignees and statutory tenants who have succeeded to the short tenancy.[53]

3. Rent (Scotland) Act 1984—Part VII Contracts

Introduction

2–16   Part VII of the 1984 Act provides a degree of security of tenure and rent control for certain residential occupiers, but one which is less than that of a full protected tenancy. Part VII is a remnant of a distinction which traditionally was made between occupiers who leased unfurnished accommodation as a separate dwelling, and those who were provided with services and/or furniture in addition to their accommodation. Traditionally it was thought appropriate to offer such occupiers a lesser form of protection under the Rent Acts. The Rent Act 1974 eliminated the distinction between furnished and unfurnished accommodation. Part VII, accordingly, covers the remaining situations where residential occupiers are provided with services as part of their rent. In addition to these residual cases special provision was made for "resident landlords" to be covered by Part VII also.

These contracts were left under the jurisdiction of the Rent Tribunal as opposed to the Rent Officer/RAC system. This jurisdiction was transferred to the Rent Assessment Committees (RACs) by the Tenants' Rights Etc. (Scotland) Act 1980 as far as rent fixing is concerned. For contracts entered into before December 1, 1980 the RACs still deal with the issue of security of tenure; for later contracts this matter is dealt with by the sheriff.[54]

2–17   Part VII was based on the assumption that whereas most agreements will simply create tenancies covered by the joint furnished/unfurnished code of the Rent Act, there will be a number of contracts where a right to occupy would have been given in circumstances where it is reasonable to assume that less than full security of tenure is appropriate. As indicated, the political perception of the value of security of tenure shifted during the 1980s to such an extent that since 1989 people in such situations may not be entitled to any security beyond the contractual term. For contracts entered into on or after January 1989 involving

---

[49] Rent (Scotland) Act 1984, s. 9(1)(a).
[50] *ibid*. s. 9(1)(e).
[51] Under Sched. 2, Pt II, Case 15.
[52] Rent (Scotland) Act 1984, s. 14(2).
[53] *ibid*. s. 13(3).
[54] *ibid*. s. 76.

either resident landlords or contracts which are less than leases, there is only protection against illegal eviction and harassment along with any rights given in the contracts themselves.[55]

Effectively, Part VII only relates to old contracts. Since the Housing (Scotland) Act 1988 came into force on January 2, 1989, Part VII contracts can no longer be created. There is also a transitional provision whose effect is to speed up the termination of protections in this area. It is provided that where the rent of a Part VII contract is varied after January 2, 1989 then such an occupancy ceases to be a Part VII contract.[56]

Definition of Part VII contracts

The contracts covered by Part VII of the Rent (Scotland) Act 1984 are those 2–18 which are not covered by the protected tenancy regime and not specifically excluded from this part of the legislation. The equivalent contracts in England were known as Part VI contracts and, since the consolidation of the English Rent Act in 1977,[57] as "restricted contracts". They cover situations where "one person grants to another person, in consideration of a rent which includes payment for the use of services, the right to occupy as a residence a dwelling-house."[58] The second person has to have exclusive possession of some part of the house though this may involve sharing other accommodation with other tenants as well as with the landlord.

"Services" are defined as including attendance (*e.g.* removal of refuse), the provision of heating and lighting, the supply of hot water, and any other privilege or facility connected with the occupancy of a dwelling-house,[59] but not a privilege or facility required for access, cold water supply, or sanitary accommodation. The sums paid for occupation of the dwelling-house, use of furniture, and services are aggregated to form the "rent", to prevent evasion by charging separate sums for these.[60] Services may also include board.

There are, accordingly, three situations where a Part VII contract as opposed to a protected tenancy will exist, provided that situation does not fall within the category of excluded contracts.

Substantial attendance

Where the rent includes a substantial amount attributable to attendance such a 2–19 contract will not be a "protected tenancy". Hence, since the right to occupy is given it will fall under Part VII of the Act. Attendance means "service personal to the tenant performed by an attendant provided by the landlord ... for the benefit ... of the individual tenant."[61] Such services will include changing and providing bedlinen, providing heating or lighting, supplying hot water, or any other facility connected with the dwelling (other than those services relating to either access, such as cleaning the common stairs, or providing cold water or sanitary accommodation).

Less than substantial board

As indicated above, where a right to occupy is given in return for a rent, a 2–20 substantial proportion of which comprises payment for board, this does not

---

[55] P. Brown, "Resident Landlords" (1990) 13 S.H.L.N. 21.
[56] Housing (Scotland) Act 1988, s. 44(2)(a).
[57] Rent Act 1977 (c. 42).
[58] Rent (Scotland) Act 1984, s. 63(1).
[59] *ibid.* s. 81(1).
[60] *ibid.* s. 81(3).
[61] *Palser v. Grinling* [1948] A.C. 291.

qualify for Part VII protection. However, if the board provided is not enough to bring a property into the category of an hotel or guest house then, provided the *de minimis* rule is satisfied, the contract may come under Part VII (*i.e.* provided more than a cup of tea is given). In addition, a student letting by an educational institution with furniture and services will be a Part VII contract, although exempted from the Rent Act.

Dwelling-houses with resident landlord

2–21   If there is a resident landlord, a tenancy is not a protected tenancy.[62] However, such tenancies are subject to the control in respect of rent and security of tenure contained in Part VII[63] where the tenant has exclusive occupation of any accommodation and this involves sharing some accommodation with the landlord or with the landlord and others. Where the dwelling-house is a whole flat in a purpose-built block of flats then the normal full protection applies.[64]

Excluded contracts

Substantial board

2–22   Although, as noted above, "services" may include the provision of board, Part VII protection will not apply to contracts where the value of the board forms a substantial proportion of the whole rent (*i.e.* in hotels and genuine boarding houses).[65]

Exempt landlords

2–23   Certain landlords may not provide Part VII contracts. These are local authorities, new town development corporations, Scottish Homes, housing associations, housing co-operatives and housing trusts.[66] Part VII contracts also may not be granted over Crown property,[67] unless the property is managed by the Crown Estate Commissioners.[68]

Holiday accommodation

2–24   Where a dwelling-house is occupied for a holiday this will not be regarded as the occupation of a residence and Part VII will not apply.[69]

4. HOUSING (SCOTLAND) ACT 1988—ASSURED TENANCIES

2–25   Any contracts entered into after the commencement of Part II of the Housing (Scotland) Act 1988 on January 2, 1989, will not be regulated tenancies. Most private sector tenancies are likely to be assured tenancies although some tenancies will be excluded.[70] The 1988 Act brings into Scots law a version of the original

---

[62] Rent (Scotland) Act 1984, s. 6(1).
[63] *ibid.* s. 96.
[64] *ibid.* s. 6(1)(a)
[65] *ibid.* s. 63(3(c).
[66] *ibid.* s. 63(4), as amended by the Local Government etc. (Scotland) Act 1994, Sched. 13.
[67] *ibid.* s. 63(3)(a).
[68] *ibid.* s. 63(5).
[69] *ibid.* s. 63(6).
[70] See para. 2.32 *et seq.*

assured tenancy which was introduced into England and Wales by the Housing Act 1980.[71] This was essentially a market-rent tenancy with a degree of security of tenure. This was originally confined to newly built property but was extended to cover converted property in the Housing and Town Planning Act 1986.[72] The key features of the Scottish assured tenancy are that it lessens the degree of security of tenure whilst also abolishing any direct method of regulating the rents landlords charge other than the operation of supply and demand.

Definition of "assured tenancy"

The definition of an "assured tenancy" requires that there be four elements[73] as well as requiring that the tenancy does not come within the category of one of the excluded tenancies laid down in Schedule 4. An assured tenancy must be one under which a house is let as a separate dwelling where the tenant (or at least one of the tenants) is an individual and occupies the house as his/her only or principal home.   2–26

Tenancy

The word "tenancy" is defined to include a sub-tenancy.[74] In Scots law there are four necessary elements for the creation of a tenancy. These are that there be parties, subjects, rent, duration or termination date (called an "ish").[75] An individual who has a tied house—sometimes referred to as a service occupancy— is not covered where the occupancy rights stem from the employment contract[76] not a tenancy contract.   2–27

House let as a separate dwelling

Unlike the Rent (Scotland) Act 1984, the Housing (Scotland) Act 1988 talks only of a "house" as opposed to a "dwelling-house". However, this is of limited significance as the house must be let as a dwelling.   2–28

"House" includes both a part of a house[77] and a flat.[78] Agricultural, shop and licensed premises are excluded from being assured tenancies.[79] Combined residential and business use has not prevented premises being covered by the Rent Acts in the past.[80] Apart from the express prohibitions mentioned, where a house is partially used for business purposes it remains a house.[81] The premises must be let as a single dwelling rather than as a tenancy of separate units.[82] Rooms let together need not be a physical unit provided they are let for use as one dwelling.[83]

---

[71] Housing Act 1980.

[72] Housing and Planning Act 1986, s. 12.

[73] Housing (Scotland) Act 1988, s. 12.

[74] *ibid.* s. 55(1).

[75] *Gray v. University of Edinburgh*, 1962 S.C. 157; see para. 1–20.

[76] *Pollock v. Assessor for Inverness-shire*, 1923 S.C. 693; *MacGregor v. Dunnett*, 1949 S.C. 510.

[77] 1988 Act, s. 55(1).

[78] *Langford Property Co. Ltd v. Goldrich* [1949] 1 K.B. 511; see also *Assessor for Lothian Region v. Viewpoint Housing Association Ltd*, 1983 S.L.T. 479.

[79] Housing (Scotland) Act 1988, Sched. 4.

[80] *Ashbridge Investments Ltd v. Minister of Housing and Local Government* [1965] 1 W.L.R. 1320.

[81] *British Land Co. Ltd v. Herbert Silver (Menswear) Ltd* [1958] 1 Q.B. 531.

[82] *St Catherine's College v. Dorling* [1980] 1 W.L.R. 66.

[83] *Langford Property Co. v. Goldrich* [1949] 1 K.B. 511.

The purpose of the letting must be as a dwelling.[84] The property must be let as a separate dwelling. However, where a tenant occupies some accommodation exclusively but shares living accommodation with others (not including the landlord), the exclusively occupied accommodation is treated as a separate dwelling for the purposes of the Act and will be deemed to be let on an assured tenancy.[85]

Tenant must be an individual

2–29   Assured tenancies can only be held by individuals. There was no formal requirement that a protected tenancy be held by an individual and such business tenants could and can apply for registration of a fair rent.[86]

Only or principal home

2–30   This phrase is not defined in the Housing (Scotland) Act 1988. However, it appears elsewhere in the 1988 Act and in the Housing (Scotland) Act 1987 in relation to succession to tenancies.[87] In considering the question of succession to a secure tenancy, the phrase "only or principal home" has been interpreted to a broadly purposive effect.[88] The question of whether or not a home has ceased to be a "principal home" is also pertinent to the recovery of possession of secure tenancies.[89]

Where a person is temporarily absent from a property, he will nevertheless be regarded as occupying it if there are physical signs of occupation and an intention to return to the property.[90] A property will be considered to be someone's principal home if they have such a real, tangible and substantial connection with it that, rather than any other place of residence, the property in question can properly be described as being the only or principal home.[91]

The term "only or main residence" is found in taxation legislation. In *Frost v. Feltham*[92] a publican rented a public house and lived on the premises spending two or three days a month in a house he owned in Wales. He was able to claim that the property in Wales, which was the only house he owned, was his only or main residence.

2–31   One area where a similar phrase was interpreted was in the law dealing with the community charge. In deciding whether a person was required to pay the standard community charge for second homes the Community Charge Registration Officer had to decide whether the house in question was the "sole or main residence" of the individual. The decided cases looked at a variety of different situations. They accepted the main residence of a woman as being the house she occupied at weekends only with her husband.[93] Another woman who spent only her holidays in a house was accepted as having her main residence in that house,[94] whereas a merchant seaman away for six months and then spending two months back in Scotland was not deemed to have his sole or main residence in Scotland.[95]

---

[84] *Horford Investments Ltd v. Lambert* [1976] Ch. 39.
[85] Housing (Scotland) Act 1988, s. 14.
[86] *Ronson Nominees Ltd v. Mitchell,* 1982 S.L.T. (Sh.Ct.) 18.
[87] Housing (Scotland) Act 1988, s. 31(1); Housing (Scotland) Act 1987, ss. 44(1) and 52(2); see para. 9.29.
[88] *Monklands D.C. v. Gallagher,* Airdrie Sh. Ct, Feb. 22, 1988, unreported, cited in (1988) 6 S.H.L.N. 49.
[89] Housing (Scotland) Act 1988, Schedule 3, Ground 5; see para. 5.114.
[90] *Beggs v. Kilmarnock and Loudon D.C.,* 1995 S.C.L.R. 435.
[91] *Roxburgh D.C. v. Collins,* 1991 S.C.L.R. 575; see para. 9–29
[92] [1981] 1 W.L.R. 452.
[93] *McVean v. C.C.R.O. for Dumfries and Galloway Region,* 1990 S.C.L.R. 320.
[94] *Oswald v. Wood,* 1990 S.L.T. (Sh.Ct.) 28.
[95] *Cameron v. C.C.R.O. for Grampian Region,* 1990 S.C.L.R. 329.

Excluded tenancies

Certain kinds of tenancies are excluded from coming within the assured 2–32
tenancy framework. There are 14 categories of excluded lettings and they are
detailed in Schedule 4 to the Housing (Scotland) Act 1988.

Tenancies entered into before January 2, 1989

This category was designed to prevent the kind of activity termed "winkling" 2–33
by unscrupulous landlords as happened after the introduction of the Rent Act
1957.[96] The aim is to limit the incentives for landlords to replace protected
tenants with assured tenants with significantly fewer rights. Assured tenants do
not have the right to have "fair rents" fixed by the Rent Registration Service in
terms of the Rent (Scotland) Act 1984 nor do they have the benefit of full security
of tenure available under the 1984 legislation.

Tenancies at low rent

This exemption parallels the exemption in the protected tenancy code where 2–34
the rent is less than two-thirds of the rateable value. The level will be determined
by statutory instrument made by the Secretary of State for Scotland. The rent is
the sum payable for the accommodation; sums payable for services, repairs,
maintenance or insurance are to be ignored. There is no equivalent to the high
rateable value exemption found in the English legislation. Different "low rent"
figures can be specified for different kinds of houses or different areas. The
current figure is £6 per week.[97]

Shops

Certain kinds of tenancies are covered by the Tenancy of Shops (Scotland) 2–35
Act 1949. This covers any premises where any retail trade or business is carried
on and has been interpreted as covering a sub-post office as well as an optician.[98]
The legislation allows the tenants of such premises on being given notice of
termination of their tenancy to serve a notice on the sheriff for a renewal for up
to a year. The 1949 legislation was made permanent in 1964. Such tenancies
are exempted from the coverage of protected tenancies.[99] If the tenant lawfully
sub-lets part of such premises then the sub-let premises can constitute an assured
tenancy provided that the basic requirements indicated in section 12 of the
Housing (Scotland) Act 1988 are fulfilled.

Licensed premises

Premises which consist of a dwelling-house licensed for the sale of alcoholic 2–36
liquor for consumption on the premises are exempt from the coverage of the
legislation as they have been in previous Rent Acts.[1] Off-licences are not
affected.

---

[96] D. Nelken, *The Limits of the Legal Process* (1983); Milner Holland Report, Cmnd 2805 (1965);
and S. Green, *Rachman* (1979).
[97] Assured Tenancies (Tenancies at a Low Rent) (Scotland) Order 1988 (S.I. 1988 No. 2069).
[98] *Craig v. Saunders & Connor Ltd,* 1962 S.L.T. (Sh.Ct.) 85.
[99] Rent (Scotland) Act 1984, s. 10(2).
[1] *ibid.* s. 10(1).

Agricultural land

2–37   Where a house has in the past been let along with the agricultural land exceeding two acres then the property is exempt from the controls which apply to protect occupiers of residential property from eviction.[2] "Agricultural land" is to be interpreted using the definition in the Rent (Scotland) Act 1984, that is:

> "Land used only for agricultural or pastoral purposes or used as woodlands, market gardens, orchards, allotments or allotment gardens and any lands exceeding one-quarter of an acre used for the purpose of poultry farming, but does not include any lands occupied together with a house as a park, garden or pleasure ground or any land kept or preserved mainly or exclusively for sporting purposes."[3]

Agricultural holdings

2–38   There are distinct sets of rules regulating security of tenure and rent levels for those involved in agriculture. A house is exempt from the coverage of the assured tenancy regime if it is part of an agricultural holding in terms of the Agricultural Holdings (Scotland) Act 1991. This does not include private gardens, pleasure grounds and land kept mainly for sport or recreation.[4]

Student lettings from specified educational bodies

2–39   The Secretary of State may make regulations specifying that certain educational institutions are exempt from the assured tenancy regime. These have been made and currently cover universities, central institutions, designated institutions,[5] further education colleges and the Royal College of Surgeons of Edinburgh.[6]

Holiday lettings

2–40   Where the purpose of the letting is to provide a holiday home for the tenant rather than a permanent home there can be no assured tenancy. The holiday let had been developed as a device by landlords following the closing of furnished tenancy loophole by the Rent Act 1974. That Act gave furnished tenants the same rights as unfurnished tenants. However, a tenant who claimed that the "holiday let" was a device to avoid the Rent Acts was required positively to establish that there was an element of deception and that the documents were obtained by some form of deception.[7] Indirect encouragement to use this device was given in an English county court case[8] where the notion of the working holiday was accepted.[9] A "realist" approach in tune with the House of Lords' approach to shams in *Antoniades v. Villiers*[10] was applied in Bloomsbury and Marylebone County Court in *Francke v. Hakmi*.[11]

---

[2] Rent (Scotland) Act 1984, s. 1(3)—protected tenancies; Housing (Scotland) Act 1987, Sched. 2, para. 6—secure tenancies.
[3] s. 115(1).
[4] B. Gill, *The Law of Agricultural Holdings in Scotland* (3rd ed., 1997); C. Agnew of Lochnaw, *Agricultural Law in Scotland* (1996).
[5] Within the meaning of s. 44(2) of the Further and Higher Education (Scotland) Act 1992.
[6] Assured Tenancies (Exceptions) (Scotland) Regulations 1988 (S.I. 1988 No. 2068) as amended.
[7] *Buchmann v. May* [1978] 2 All E.R. 993.
[8] *McHale v. Daneham* (1978) 249 E.G. 969.
[9] See also *R. v. Camden London Borough Rent Officer, ex p. Plant* (1981) 257 E.G. 713.
[10] [1988] 3 W.L.R. 1205 [*sub nom. A.G. Securities v. Vaughan*].
[11] [1984] C.L.Y. 1906. Discussed by T. Lyons in "The Meaning of 'Holiday' in the Rent Acts" (1984) Con. 286.

Resident landlords

The position of resident landlords has been a recurring issue in postwar 2–41 housing policy. Their position has been recognised as requiring different consideration from that of absent landlords as a lesser degree of security of tenure is deemed appropriate. Under the legislation introduced in Scotland in 1949 it became possible for those with the right to occupy, such as those with resident landlords, to apply to the Rent Tribunal to postpone a notice to quit for up to six months. Under the current legislation, Part VII of the Rent (Scotland) Act 1984, this right is still available for contracts entered into before December 1, 1980 although the functions of the Rent Tribunals have been taken over by RACs. This postponement may be sought indefinitely although the committee will be guided by the limited purpose of this protection—that is, to give the occupier time to find fresh accommodation. For any contracts covered by Part VII entered into on or after December 1, 1980 the occupier must apply to the sheriff court where a single postponement of three months can be obtained. In order to prevent abuse of this easier method of regaining property the limitations on those situations which amount to there being a resident landlord letting are dealt with elaborately.

This exemption is modelled on the definition contained in Part VII of the Rent (Scotland) Act 1984. The definition has been refined to avoid excepting landlords of accommodation which is not purpose-built. The definition covers tenancies of houses which form part only of a building and where the tenancy was granted by a person who at the time of the grant occupied another house which forms part of the building. The landlord must occupy the property as his only or principal home. In addition, the ordinary means of access to the tenant's house must be via the landlord's house or the landlord must have to pass through the tenant's house to reach the landlord's property. This would include such things as having a common hallway, but not simply living on the same stair.

Crown tenancies

The assured tenancy regime does not apply where there is a tenancy and the 2–42 interest of the landlord belongs to Her Majesty in right of the Crown or to a government department or is held in trust for Her Majesty for the purposes of a government department. The exemption does not apply where the Crown Estate Commissioners are managing the property.

Public sector tenancies

The bodies who traditionally have granted secure tenancies[12] may not grant 2–43 assured tenancies—local authorities, co-operative housing associations,[13] and urban development corporations. They are joined by Scottish Homes in its role as the successor or to the Scottish Special Housing Association[14] and the Housing Corporation in Scotland.

---

[12] Currently under the Housing (Scotland) Act 1987.
[13] A. Robertson, "Housing Associations" (1991) 10 S.H.L.N. 3; I. Swinney, "Housing Co-operatives" (1991) 10 S.H.L.N. 9.
[14] T. Begg, *50 Special Years — A Study in Scottish Housing — The Scottish Special Housing Association* (1987).

Shared ownership agreements

2–44   Such occupation does not need the protection against eviction offered by an assured tenancy. Provided that the terms of the agreement are complied with such an occupier may not be evicted. This situation was considered in *Langstane (SP) Housing Association Ltd v. Davie*.[15] The Housing Association sought to recover possession because of 'rent' arrears. However, it was held that the action was incompetent on the basis that the relationship between the Housing Association and Davie was not one of landlord and tenant, and that the payments to the Housing Association were not in fact rent. They had the relationship of common owners each owning a *pro indiviso* share in a single property. The appropriate action would then be one of division and sale.

Transitional cases: secure, housing association and regulated tenancies

2–45   These transitional case exemptions should be read with sections 42 to 45 of the Act. Where there already exist protected tenancies or secure tenancies then such tenants continue to hold under such contracts with all the rights that go along with this status. Similarly, existing tenants of housing associations do not become assured tenants as a result of the Housing (Scotland) Act 1988. Only those becoming tenants after the legislation comes into effect on January 2, 1989 are automatically assured tenants.

The transitional arrangements make it clear that the exclusion from the assured tenancy regime applies where the tenancy is granted to a person who immediately before the tenancy was granted was the tenant of the same landlord.[16] Although it was initially a matter of controversy whether these provisions were mandatory or merely permissive, there is now authority to the effect that they are mandatory.[17]

Temporary accommodation for homeless persons

2–46   Under an amendment added by the Housing Act 1988[18] it is provided that there is an exemption from cover where a tenancy is granted expressly on a temporary basis in the fulfilment of a duty imposed on a local authority by Part II of the Housing (Scotland) Act 1987. This brings such temporary accommodation into line with the position of secure tenancies. Under the Housing (Scotland) Act 1987 such temporary accommodation cannot form a secure tenancy even though let out by local authorities.[19]

Short assured tenancies

2–47   This is a quite distinct form of assured tenancy whose main feature is that there is no provision for a right to a continuation of the term of the tenancy beyond the term of the original minimum of six months.[20] This is a version of the "short tenancy" which was introduced into Scotland by the Tenants' Rights Etc. (Scotland) Act 1980. The short tenancy had to be for a minimum of one

---

[15] 1994 S.C.L.R.158 (Notes).
[16] Housing (Scotland) Act 1988, ss. 42–43.
[17] *Milnbank Housing Association Ltd v. Murdoch,* 1994 S.C.L.R. 684.
[18] Housing Act 1988, Sched. 17, para. 90.
[19] Housing (Scotland) Act 1987, Sched. 2, para. 5.
[20] Housing (Scotland) Act 1988, s. 32.

year although the Bow Group proposals on which it was based had suggested six months. It required that a fair rent be registered in return for a guarantee of repossession to the landlord. The new short assured tenancy makes some provision for the fixing of rents which are considered to be excessive. However, as is noted below, the criteria for fixing a rent level are limited to what the going market rent is. In addition, there can only be reference to an RAC where there is a sufficient number of similar houses in the locality let on assured tenancies and the rent being charged is "significantly higher" than could be expected in the market place.[21]

Definition of "short assured tenancy"

A short assured tenancy is one where there is a minimum period of six months 2–48
and where a notice (Form AT5) has been served to the effect that the tenancy is a short assured tenancy. The landlord can regain possession of a short assured tenancy either automatically on giving notice or on any of the assured tenancy repossession grounds.[22] The notice establishing that the tenancy is a short assured tenancy must be served on the prospective tenant before the creation of the tenancy and if there is more than one landlord service by one of them is sufficient. By inference all prospective joint tenants will need to be served the appropriate notice individually. Form AT5 indicates to a prospective tenant that the landlord will be allowed to evict him provided that the proper notice is given and that there is a right to apply to an RAC for a rent determination. The limitations on references—pool of comparable tenancies and significantly higher rent—are not mentioned. There can be no valid short assured tenancy unless this notice is served. If the notice is not served then the tenancy created is an assured tenancy.[23] Although the proposal was not adopted that the notice to be effective would need to be signed and adopted as holograph by the tenant, service would nonetheless be a matter which would need to be established in possession proceedings. Landlords often include a clause in the lease to the effect that the tenant has received the Form AT5 prior to signing the tenancy agreement.

Where at the end of the short assured tenancy it continues by tacit relocation or there is a new contractual tenancy of the same or substantially the same premises then such a tenancy is a short assured tenancy. This applies whether or not the requirements as to length of time of the tenancy and notice apply. The continuation of a short assured tenancy of varying lengths does not apply where the landlord serves a written notice in the prescribed form on the tenant that the continued new tenancy is not to be a short assured tenancy.[24]

5. MISCELLANEOUS TENANCY ARRANGEMENTS UNDER THE HOUSING (SCOTLAND)
ACT 1988

Property rented along with land exceeding two acres

Where property is rented out with other land then whether or not it is covered 2–49
by the assured tenancy regime depends on the main purpose of the letting. If the main purpose of the letting is the provision of a home for the tenant then the

---

[21] Housing (Scotland) Act 1988, s. 34(3).
[22] *ibid.* Sched. 5, Pt 1.
[23] *Mountain v. Hastings* (1993) 25 H.L.R. 427.
[24] Form AT7.

land is treated as part of the house and covered by the Act. Alternatively, where the main purpose is not to provide such a home then the tenancy is not to be covered by the Act.[25] The purpose must be to provide a "home". "Home" is not defined in the Act. Whether premises are in use as a home is a question of fact. It is important that there be a regular degree of personal occupation.[26] In section 12 there is a requirement that it be the "only or principal home" of the individual. It must not only be provided as a home at the commencement of the tenancy but must remain so throughout the tenancy.

"Let together with" does not mean that the land must be attached to the house as long as they are in the vicinity.[27] The let need not be in a single agreement.[28] Whether or not the lease is covered by the Act is to be determined as at the date the status of the tenancy is in question rather than the date the lease began.[29] The exceptions in Schedule 4 relating to agricultural tenancies and agricultural holdings are not affected by section 12.

Sharing accommodation with persons other than the landlord

2–50   As already indicated, although section 12 of the 1988 Act requires property to be let as a separate dwelling for a tenancy to be assured, protection is extended under section 14 to situations where the tenant is granted exclusive use of some accommodation but shares living accommodation with others (not including the landlord). "Living accommodation" is defined (in a rather circular fashion) in terms of what is needed for premises to amount to a "separate dwelling".[30] This would cover the activities of cooking, eating and sleeping.[31] Where rights to shared accommodation are withdrawn or their use made so difficult or impracticable that a tenant would have to leave the separate accommodation this does not prevent a tenant having a "separate dwelling".

While the tenant is in occupation of the separate accommodation there can be no changes in the rights to use that part of the shared accommodation which is living accommodation. Any attempt to terminate or modify the rights to use the part of the shared accommodation is of no effect.[32] There is one exception where there is a provision in the lease which allows the identity of those sharing the shared accommodation to be varied or their number increased.[33] There seems to be no limitation on this right other than what is in the contract.

Sharing accommodation with sub-tenants

2–51   Where an assured tenant sub-lets part of his premises, the tenancy will remain an assured tenancy. No part of the premises will lose this protection by virtue of the fact that it is shared with the sub-tenant or by a number of sub-tenants.[34] This is parallel to the protection available under the Rent (Scotland) Act 1984.[35]

---

[25] Housing (Scotland) Act 1988, s. 13.
[26] *Hall v. King* (1987) 19 H.L.R. 440; *Herbert v. Byrne* [1964] 1 W.L.R. 519.
[27] *Langford Property Co. Ltd v. Batten* [1951] A.C. 223.
[28] *Mann v. Merrill* [1945] 1 All E.R. 708.
[29] *Campbell v. McQuillan*, 1983 S.L.T. 210.
[30] Housing (Scotland) Act 1988, s. 14(4).
[31] *Goodrich v. Paisner* [1957] A.C. 65; *Thomson v. City of Glasgow D.C.*, 1986 S.L.T. (Lands Tr.) 6.
[32] See also s. 21 on the right of the sheriff to restrict or terminate the right to use shared non-living accommodation.
[33] Housing (Scotland) Act 1988, s. 14(3).
[34] *ibid.* s. 15.
[35] Rent (Scotland) Act 1984, s. 99.

Although the rationale for repossession of the tenant's part of the property may not relate to the part shared with the sub-tenant, the property, nonetheless, is to be treated as a whole for such purposes. If, for example, there is a deterioration of the house or common parts and repossession follows then the sub-tenant would on the face of it also be covered by such a possession order.[36] The fact that there could be an eviction of an "innocent" sub-tenant would presumably be a factor which would be drawn to the attention of the sheriff and would be weighed as a relevant issue in assessing whether it is reasonable to grant an order.[37] The respective rights of tenant and sub-tenant are not affected by this provision allowing eviction of sub-tenants. Although this has not been a major feature of landlord–tenant relations in the past, it is open to sub-tenants to sue for losses incurred as a result of their eviction where this stems from the failure of the other party. For example, antisocial activities by one party could result in the bringing of a possession action by the superior landlord. This remedy is also available where there is more than one tenant or sub-tenant. The implication of *City of Glasgow District Council v. Brown*[38] would seem to be that sub-tenants would need to be made party to the possession proceedings.

6. EVASION OF PRIVATE SECTOR STATUTORY CONTROLS

Methods of evading the statutory controls on tenancies in the private sector have 2–52 already been referred to above in brief. However, it is worth examining the main methods of evasion in a single section. Some of these methods have been rendered obsolete by the enactment of the Housing (Scotland) Act 1988, but are nevertheless still pertinent to pre-existing arrangements under the Rent (Scotland) Act 1984. The evasion techniques can be categorised as those which seek to prevent the arrangement in question from being one of lease, and those which seek to prevent tenancies from enjoying security of tenure under the statutory regimes.

Avoiding the existence of a lease

No fixed subjects of let

One way in which landlords have sought to avoid the statutory control over 2–53 their provision of accommodation is to prevent a tenancy from existing. Such attempts are common in the supported accommodation sector.[39] The attempt is made by providing in an "occupancy agreement" that the landlord reserves the right to change the accommodation of which the occupier is granted exclusive use. The written agreement, for example, may provide that the occupier can be moved to a different bedroom within a supported hostel. The rationale here is that there are no fixed subjects of let and that, accordingly, no lease can exist. It is suggested, however, that such attempts at evasion may fail. The Inner House has held that it is not fatal to the creation of a lease that the subjects of let change during the period of let, provided that there is agreement between the parties about the mechanism for making such a change.[40]

---

[36] 1988 Act, Sched. 5, ground 14.
[37] *Glasgow D.C. v. Brown,* 1988 S.C.L.R. 679.
[38] 1988 S.C.L.R. 679.
[39] A. Mina Coull, "Housing Agreements in Supported Accommodation in Scotland" (Shelter, 1997).
[40] *Brador Properties Ltd v. British Telecommunications plc,* 1992 S.L.T. 490.

Deferred purchase agreements (or rental purchase)

2–54   Purchase by instalments, particularly for cheaper property, is a well-established
form of straightforward sale, but it has been used as a method of avoiding the
Rent Acts. Sellers/landlords tended to use leonine bargains which stated that the
property was not transferred until the final payment was made, and that upon
default all payments would be treated as payment towards occupancy of the
property. As a purchaser, of course, the occupier has security of tenure and, if
expressed in writing, the financial commitment is fixed. However, it was often a
way of shifting repair obligations on to the shoulders of the purchasing occupier.
In practice there would be high turnover of occupiers who would never complete
the purchase and would cost the "landlord/seller" nothing in repair. This kind of
operation was highlighted by the media in 1988 in the north-west of England.
Purchasers in default found themselves with no property and no redress for their
outlay. The lenders in such operations strenuously proclaimed their intention to
sell, but the evidence in support of such a view was not strong.
      A more recent version of this device is the sale at a grossly inflated price. The
seller contracts to sell the property and agrees to take the price by way of, say, 12
monthly instalments with the final balance payable in a single lump sum at the
end of the period. The monthly payments are in reality rent since the price is fixed
at such a high price that there is no genuine intention by the seller to dispose of
the property. However, it seems that the seller does not have to meet the repair
obligations which a landlord owes a tenant. It also means that the occupier can be
evicted easily as there is no security of tenure for a defaulting purchaser.

Preventing leases from enjoying security of tenure

Holiday lettings

2–55   Out-of-season lettings, not exceeding eight months, of holiday property allow
the landlord to recover possession automatically provided notice is given to the
tenants at the start of the lease.[41] This method has been used by some landlords
in Glasgow to ensure that at the end of the academic year students can be speedily
removed. It often runs in conjunction with sham holiday agreements.
      Initially it seemed from the approach taken by the English Court of Appeal,
that the approach to such sham agreements was to assume that they represent
the intentions of the parties until some specific evidence can be brought to
show that they are in some way misleading. What the Court of Appeal seemed
to suggest in *Buchmann v. May*[42] was that if the agreement said it was a holiday
agreement, then that was how the courts would treat it. The obvious difficulty
in separating real holiday agreements from devices by landlords to avoid totally
the restrictions of the statutory control as to rental and security of tenure might
have led one to expect the Court to enquire beyond the document into the
circumstances of the case. The Court of Appeal took a narrow view that a sham
involved deception; but observed further that where the bargain is merely leonine
the fact that the landlord in a situation of acute housing scarcity is able to dictate
one-sided terms to the tenant, depriving him of the protection of the Rent Acts,
is only to be expected, and in these circumstances the Court will not intervene.
Broadly, if landlords could find loopholes in the Rent Acts then the courts do
not seem keen to strike these down as being against the spirit of the Acts.

---

[41] Rent (Scotland) Act 1984, Sched. 2, Case 13; Housing (Scotland) Act 1988, Sched. 5, Ground 3.
[42] [1978] 2 All E.R. 993.

The House of Lords in *Antoniades v. Villiers*[43] preferred an approach to shams 2–56
which looked at shams and devices from the point of view of the reality of the
situation. It should be noted that almost all the case law in this area stems from
England (more specifically London) and such issues are untested in Scotland.

Company lets

Whilst letting to companies did not prevent the "tenant" applying to have a fair 2–57
rent set under the protected regime[44] the requirement for an assured tenancy that the
tenant be an individual[45] means that company lets take such arrangements outside
the coverage of assured tenancy protection.[46] There is some evidence that the courts
may be willing to consider the possibility of these as shams[47] but this is limited.[48]

Bed and breakfast

Lets are excluded from the protected tenancy regime under the Rent (Scotland) 2–58
Act 1984 where board or substantial attendance is provided.[49] Such arrangements
would be Part VII contracts. In the 1920s the view was expressed in an *obiter*
statement in the Court of Appeal that board implied more than merely providing
a sandwich to the tenant. However, two practices emerged at the end of the
1970s in Scotland which appear to provide a lucrative loophole for the landlords
involved.

First, it was accepted that in these days of the European Union a landlord can
provide a continental breakfast and thereby avoid the Rent Acts. An Edinburgh
sheriff in *Holiday Flat Co. v. Kuczera*[50] explained that it would probably be
pedantic (particularly since the British entry into the European Economic
Community) to deny the continental breakfast the status of a meal sufficient to
constitute board. He held that by supplying a breakfast consisting of tea or
coffee, toast, butter and marmalade the landlord was providing board.

Secondly, a rather more elaborate approach was adopted in Glasgow, with
landlords providing breakfast at a central dining area for those tenants who
wished to avail themselves of the service. This often involved a journey of up to
two miles, and while the breakfasts were substantial they attracted a very small
proportion of the tenants. In order to cover possible objections the landlords
offered, at a substantial extra charge, to deliver breakfasts to the door. Other
landlords provided a box for breakfast foods each week or month in order to
come within the bounds of providing board or made arrangements for tenants
to obtain breakfast at local cafes.

These practices have been looked at in some details in two cases. In *Gavin v.* 2–59
Lindsay[51] Sheriff Kearney proposed a double test of substance and service on
the premises. He suggested that both elements needed to be present for a proper
bed and breakfast arrangement otherwise the agreement was no more than a

---

[43] [1988] 3 W.L.R. 1205.
[44] *Ronson Nominees Ltd v. Mitchell*, 1982 S.L.T. (Sh.Ct.) 18.
[45] Housing (Scotland) Act 1988, s. 12(1)(a).
[46] *Hilton v. Plustitle* [1988] 3 All E.R. 1051.
[47] *Navinter SA v. Pastoll*, CA, Mar. 21, 1989 unreported; (1989) 10 S.H.L.N. 24 on the possibility
   of distinguishing *Hilton v. Plustitle*.
[48] See more recently *Browns South Molton Street Ltd v. Cap M Securities Ltd*, CA, Mar. 6, 1990,
   unreported.
[49] Rent (Scotland) Act 1984, s. 2.
[50] 1978 S.L.T. (Sh.Ct.) 47.
[51] 1985 S.L.T. (Sh.Ct.) 12.

tenancy covered by the Rent Acts. The House of Lords considered the question
of the extent of meals required to amount to board in *Otter v. Norman*[52] and was
satisfied that a single meal sufficed. Unfortunately it did not seem to have had
the opportunity to consider the issues raised in *Gavin v. Lindsay*.

Non-exclusive occupation agreements

2–60   It has already been pointed out that there is a substantial volume of case law
in England and Wales regarding the distinction between leases and licences.[53]
Concerted attempts were made south of the border to prevent leases from existing
by providing that the residential occupier did not have exclusive occupation of
his accommodation. The aim was to create mere licences, thereby avoiding the
full protection of the Rent Acts. We saw above that the Inner House has warned
against looking towards English law to determine the lease-licence question in
Scotland.[54] The concept of lease in Scots law is broader than its counterpart in
England and Wales and lack of exclusivity of possession is not fatal to the
existence of a lease, but is necessary for the conversion of the lessee's personal
right to a real right.[55] However, the exclusivity of possession will have a bearing
on whether a lease is an assured or protected tenancy. Under both regimes
exclusivity of possession over at least some accommodation is required.[56] An
examination of attempts to provide "non-exclusive occupation agreements" and
the reaction of the English courts to these attempts is, therefore, appropriate.

It should be noted, however, that following the introduction of short assured
tenancies which have no security of tenure, there is now less need for private
landlords to adopt such a complex device. Further, in the supported
accommodation sector where concern may now be greatest to avoid any statutory
protection, research has indicated that most residential occupiers are granted
exclusive occupation of a bedroom.[57]

This method of evading statutory protection is simple if legalistic. The would-
be occupiers sign non-exclusive occupancy agreements in which they agree
that they do not have exclusive possession of the property involved. The landlord
retains the right to stay there or to insert any other third party into the dwelling.
The Court of Appeal upheld this device in a series of cases, but were also prepared
to strike down agreements where there was an element of deception involved.
Even though the occupiers were, in effect, prepared to sign anything to obtain
the accommodation, the Court of Appeal did not feel that this merited rejection.

2–61   The Court of Appeal accepted the non-exclusive agreement in principle in
Somma v. Hazelhurst[58] where a student and his girlfriend were given the use of
one room in a flat with the proviso that the landlady could introduce any third
party into the flat at any time. The landlady explained that she did not really
intend to do this and that she would always make sure that such a person, if ever
introduced, was compatible with the present occupiers. The Court of Appeal
was prepared to let the terms of the agreement operate to deprive the occupiers

---

[52] [1988] 2 All E.R. 897.
[53] See paras 1–11 to 1–16.
[54] *Brador Properties Ltd v. British Telecommunications plc,* 1992 S.L.T. 490.
[55] *Millar v. McRobbie,* 1949 S.L.T. 2.
[56] Rent (Scotland) Act 1984, s. 1; Housing (Scotland) Act 1988, s. 12.
[57] A. Mina Coull, "Housing Agreements in Supported Accommodation in Scotland" (Shelter, 1997).
[58] [1978] 1 W.L.R. 1014.

of rental and security rights. The same line was taken in a similar case three months later in *Aldrington Garages v. Fielder*.[59] The Court did not feel that it was having the wool pulled over its eyes in interpreting two separate agreements entered into by a couple with the landlords as totally separate, despite the fact that they went to rent the flat together. Only in blatant cases of duplicity were the courts prepared to reject such agreements. In *Demuren and Adefope v. Seal Estates*[60] two Nigerian students, recently arrived in London, rented a flat under the impression that the agreement was a straightforward lease. The actions of the landlord's agent, however, in sweeping aside any of the technical problems stemming from the signing of the non-exclusive agreements backfired on him, and the Court held that there was a prior oral agreement which created a joint tenancy.

This kind of blatant situation was dealt with by the House of Lords in *Street v. Mountford*[61] where exclusive possession was in fact granted. Their Lordships indicated that where exclusive occupancy was granted then the occupier was either a tenant or, if services were provided, a lodger. This was confirmed in *Antoniades v. Villiers*[62] where the occupiers had a double bed and a small sitting room where there was convertible settee. It was written into the individual agreements that the landlord had a right to introduce either a third party or himself to the flat. There was in fact accommodation which could have been occupied. This was rejected as "an attempt to disguise the true character of the agreement which it was hoped would deceive the court and prevent the appellants enjoying the protection of the Rent Acts."

Landlords' professional advisers noted that this principle might not be applicable where there was sharing between strangers and where the agreement did not give landlords the right to claim rent unpaid by one occupier from fellow occupiers. A variety of Court of Appeal cases were heard after *Street* from which a confused message emerged. The matter seemed to have been clarified by the House of Lords in two cases heard together dealing with these kinds of agreement. In *Antoniades v. Villiers*,[63] noted above, the House of Lords was prepared to regard as a sham an agreement whereby the landlord had the right to introduce a third party or himself. On the other hand, in *A. G. Securities v. Vaughan*[64] there were occupiers who came to the property at different times; they paid different rents; they had no control over the filling of vacancies; they were not liable for the costs of defaulting occupiers nor when there were vacancies. This was accepted by the House of Lords as a "sensible and realistic arrangement to provide accommodation for a shifting population of individuals who were genuinely prepared to share the flat with others introduced from time to time who would, at least initially, be strangers to them." 2–62

However, the matter is far from settled in the English courts. Since *A. G. Securities* there have been further cases before the Court of Appeal which reveal a degree of confusion amongst the judiciary about the nature of licences and leases. The problem has centred around what is the appropriate approach to sharing agreements. Where agreements confer exclusive occupation but do not require sharers to pay more than their proportion of the rent they have not been treated

---

[59] (1979) 37 P. & C.R. 461.
[60] (1978) 249 E.G. 440.
[61] [1985] A.C. 809.
[62] [1988] 3 W.L.R. 1205.
[63] *ibid.*
[64] *ibid.* at 1207.

as leases.[65] However, the courts have accepted agreements as leases where they are satisfied that the intention is to grant exclusive possession at a rent no matter what the agreement actually says.[66] Obviously suspect devices have been struck at,[67] but for the future a realistic assessment was made in the Court of Appeal in *Hadjiloucas v. Crean*[68]:

> "The legal problems [in cases of sharers] are much more complex than in the case of sole occupation ... Given the informality of many sharing situations, and the obvious contemplation that they may terminate earlier than expected, the problems of fitting an essentially fluid arrangement into the structure of a tenancy for a term may be formidable indeed."[69]

7. HOUSING (SCOTLAND) ACT 1987—SECURE TENANCIES

2–63   There are two major ways in which local authorities are involved in the provision of housing accommodation. They are involved indirectly through the obligation of their building control and environmental health departments to ensure that the standards of all housing, private or public, owner-occupied or rented, are maintained. They also have a direct obligation to consider the housing conditions in their area and the needs of their area for the provision of further housing accommodation. They can be required by the Secretary of State for Scotland to prepare and submit proposals for the provision of housing accommodation.[70] They may then use their powers to provide accommodation to meet the needs disclosed by their inspection.[71]

Definition of "secure tenancy"

2–64   Since the passing of the Tenants' Rights Etc. (Scotland) Act 1980, public sector tenants occupy as secure tenants provided that the dwelling-house is let as a separate dwelling. In order to count as a separate dwelling what is required is the occupation of a property which is used for the major activities of residential life, for example, cooking, eating and sleeping. Whether or not a property constitutes a separate dwelling will turn on the individual facts of the case in question. Where living activities are carried out in accommodation which is not part of the subjects of let, but which the tenant has a right to use in common with others, the court is unlikely to regard the subjects as a separate dwelling.[72]

The tenant must also be an individual and use the dwelling-house as his or her only or principal house. The landlord must be one of the following bodies[73]:

(a)   a local authority;
(b)   a development corporation;
(c)   Scottish Homes;
(d)   a registered housing association (until the Housing (Scotland) Act 1988);

---

[65] *Stribling v. Wickham* (1989) 21 H.L.R. 381; *Makeover Ltd v. Brady* [1989] 3 All E.R. 618.
[66] *Nicolaou v. Pitt* (1989) 21 H.L.R. 487; *Duke v. Wynne* [1989] 3 All E.R. 130.
[67] *Aslan v. Murphy* (No. 1) [1989] 3 All E.R. 130—denial of occupation by landlord for 90 minutes per day.
[68] [1987] 3 All E.R. 1008.
[69] *ibid. per* Mustill L.J. at 1022.
[70] Housing (Scotland) Act 1987, s. 1(3).
[71] *ibid.* s. 2.
[72] *Curl v. Angelo* [1948] 2 All E.R. 189; *Thomson v. City of Glasgow D.C.,* 1986 S.L.T. (Lands Tr.) 6.
[73] s. 44(2) and s. 61(2)(a) as amended by the Local Government etc. (Scotland) Act 1994, Sched. 13.

(e)   housing co-operative;

(f)   housing trust.

Excluded tenancies

The following tenancies are specifically excluded from the ambit of secure   2–65
tenancies under Schedule 2 to the Housing (Scotland) Act 1987.

Service tenancies/tied accommodation

These occur where the tenant is an employee of the landlord and the contract   2–66
of employment requires the tenant to occupy the house for the better performance
of his duties.[74] This covers implied or express contracts and, if express, whether
it is oral or in writing.

Temporary letting to person seeking accommodation

This occurs where a landlord expressly lets a house on a temporary basis to   2–67
a person moving into an area in order to take up employment there and for the
purpose of enabling him to seek accommodation in that area.[75]

Development and temporary letting

Letting of this type occurs where it is expressly provided that the let is temporary   2–68
pending development affecting the house—typically, short-life property.

Decant property let temporarily

In this type of let a house is let while works are being carried out on the   2–69
original dwelling-house and the original house is a secure tenancy and the tenant
is entitled to return there after the works are completed either because of
agreement or by order of the sheriff.[76]

Homeless persons' temporary accommodation

In this category a house is let expressly on a temporary basis to a homeless applicant   2–70
under the homeless persons' legislation—as where inquiries are being made or where
a priority need exists, but the applicant became homeless intentionally. This section
has been abused by some authorities providing "temporary" accommodation on a
long-term basis to avoid problems in any subsequent action for repossession.

Agricultural and business premises

A property is not a secure tenancy where a house: 2–71

(a)   is let together with agricultural land exceeding two acres;

(b)   consists of premises used as a shop or office for business, trade or
professional purposes;

(c)   consists of premises licensed for the sale of excisable liquor;

(d)   is let in conjunction with either business or licensed trade.

---

[74] See paras 7–11 to 7–14 on the right-to-buy issues arising from the exemption.

[75] See para. 7–15.

[76] Housing (Scotland) Act 1987, s. 48(5).

Police and fire authority property

2–72   A further exception is where the landlord is a police authority in Scotland
and the tenant is a constable of a police force occupying rent-free. Also excluded
is the situation where the landlord is a fire authority in Scotland and the tenant is
a member of the fire brigade who requires to live in close proximity to a particular
fire station or where the house is expressly let on a temporary basis pending it
being required for the purposes of such a fire brigade.

Houses part of, or within the curtilage of certain other buildings

2–73   This exception occurs where the house forms part of or is within the curtilage
of a building which mainly is held by the landlord for purposes other than the
provision of housing accommodation and consists of accommodation other than
housing accommodation. Typically this provision covers school houses joined
on to the school buildings.[66]

---

[77] See n. 66 and paras 7–16 and 7–17.

CHAPTER 3

REPAIR AND HABITABILITY OF DWELLING-HOUSES

1. BACKGROUND

The renting of property involves a contract with obligations on both sides. The 3–01
tenant has to pay rent and the landlord in turn has to provide accommodation in
repair and which is fit to be occupied by the tenant. There is a range of different
remedies with different rules applicable. These remedies co-exist and there is no
hierarchy of importance. In this section we look at each remedy separately. This
may seem to involve an element of repetition. It is important because, although
the import of the various standards is broadly the same, the details are different.
Tenants may seek remedies either under the specific terms of their contract, under
the common law obligation of habitability and tenantability, under the statutory
implied repairing obligation, under the statutory requirement that property be fit
for human habitation or under the procedure for the removal of nuisance under
environmental protection legislation. It may not be clear at the outset which of the
different remedies is likely to be most effective in securing a house in good repair.
The law in each sector has developed in a haphazard fashion. For the most part
the obligations apply to public sector landlords as to those in the private sector.
There are, however a number of crucial differences which are discussed below.[1]

Which remedy is adopted by those affected by insanitary or unacceptable 3–02
living conditions will depend on a variety of factors. These include the
availability of finance and whether legal aid is likely to be obtained. There may
be the possibility of "direct action" with the cost of the repair being met from
the rent where this is feasible. In addition for certain tenants there are statutory
and, occasionally contractual rights to have repairs carried out independently
of the landlord. The likelihood of using nuisance procedures may also depend
on how quickly the local Environmental Health Department respond to
complaints as well as whether financial recompense is an important part of the
claim since a separate action for this would need to be raised in addition to the
nuisance action. Finally it should be noted that EHOs have traditionally been
unwilling to act against the local authority as landlords.[2]

2. GENERAL PRINCIPLES OF REPAIR

Introduction

In addition to the question as to what form of remedy may be sought and 3–03
what criteria are relevant there are two central issues which must be addressed.

---

[1] See para. 3–92.
[2] As to whether it is possible for an local authority to act against itself see below at para. 3–55 *et seq.*

First it is necessary to distinguish between repair and improvement since the landlord is obliged to effect repairs as opposed to improvements. In addition the obligation of the landlord is to repair on notice rather than to act as an insurer of the property's condition.

Repair distinguished from improvement

Introduction

3–04   According to Rankine repair signifies "such operations on the subject let as are necessary to put and maintain it in a condition fit for the purpose for which it was let".[3] Everything beyond this is simply improvement and cannot be claimed by the tenant under the lease. A problem arises, however, where the repair requires the replacement of a dilapidated item with something new. It might then be expected that tenants would not benefit if there is an element of improvement. The vast majority of the case law on this issue comes from England and must be treated with some caution. However, since the initial approach of the Court of Appeal has been cited with approval, the extensive case law is discussed on the basis of its likely acceptance in Scotland.

Replacement does not constitute improvement

3–05   The basic approach of English law was expressed by Lord Denning in a discussion of the replacement of a 60-year-old drainage system with a modern equivalent.[4] He indicated that if the work which was to be done was the provision of something new for the benefit of the occupier, that was an improvement; but if it was only the replacement of something there, which had become dilapidated or worn out, then albeit that it was a replacement by a modern equivalent, it came within the category of repairs and not improvements.

Fhis distinction between repair and improvement has been accepted into the law of Scotland where it has been stated that the criterion was "correctly laid down" in *Morcom* when discussing how the Rent Acts should treat the replacement of a w.c., basin, sink unit and fireplace with modern fittings.[5] The Rent Acts made allowance for tenants' improvement to be ignored in the rent-fixing exercise where a tenant had made such improvements. However, this particular work was not to be treated as anything more than a mere repair (albeit one which the tenant was not obliged to carry out).

3–06   In a subsequent interpretation of how one replaces a defective item the English authorities have seemed to recognise the crucial interest of tenants to have repairs carried out. In a case involving a lease of commercial property where the tenant was liable for repairs[6] it was decided that remedying an inherent design defect amounted not to an improvement but a repair. In the *Ravenseft* case a building in concrete had not included expansion joints because it had not been realised that they were essential. Remedying this required the removal of the building's cladding. It was stated to be a matter of degree whether an inherent defect was work of repair as opposed to an improvement. In this instance since no competent

---

[3] *Leases* (3rd ed., 1916), p. 240.
[4] *Morcom v. Campbell-Johnstone* [1956] 1 Q.B. 106.
[5] *Stewart's J.F. v. Gallacher,* 1967 S.L.T. 52, *per* L.P. Clyde at 53.
[6] *Ravenseft Properties Ltd v. Davstone (Holdings) Ltd* [1980] Q.B. 12.

professional engineer would allow the cladding to be replaced without the addition of expansion joints then this was the only way that the building could be repaired and the work was not an improvement. The question then may well be the subject of expert professional opinion as to what is involved in putting property into a state of proper repair.

Similar questions about repairs as opposed to improvements arose where a tenant rented a property to which there was a "jerry-built" extension at the back of the property which, whilst it seemed sound at entry, in due course collapsed. The tenant was not bound to rebuild since this would have involved the landlord getting back an edifice different from the unstable jerry-built structure which the tenant had leased.[7] The notion was also accepted in a case involving the need to put in a damp-proof course where this has been omitted in the original building work.[8]

Replacing an inherent defect

As far as rental housing is concerned the same principle has been accepted 3–07 where the local authority was faced with an inherent defect problem.[9] There was a need to rectify condensation stemming from the lack of insulation round the concrete lintels, sweating from the single-glazed metal-framed windows and inadequate heating. The local authority were ordered to replace the metal window frames and face the lintels under the statutory implied repairs obligation.[10] The landlords successfully took their case to the Court of Appeal on the basis that the implied repairs provision talked of keeping in repair and thus there needed to be disrepair before its remedying could be discussed. Lord Justice Lawton explained that there must be disrepair before any question arose as to whether it would be reasonable to remedy a design fault when doing the repair. In this particular instance there was no evidence that the single-glazed windows and lintels were in any different state at the date of the trial from what they had been in when the tenant first became a tenant. However, the importance of *Quick v. Taff-Ely Borough Council* was its enunciation of the principle that where disrepair arose from an inherent defect whose curing required improvement of the property the tenant was entitled to have the improvement/ repair carried out provided this did not give the tenant something wholly different from what had been originally rented.

In *Stent v. Monmouth District Council*[11] just such a problem arose where a 3–08 door failed to carry out one of its functions, namely keeping out water. In a tenancy starting in 1953 various steps were taken by the landlords to solve the problem over the years. These included fitting a new door in 1979. Finally in 1983 a new aluminum door sealed door unit was fitted. The tenant sued for damages for carpet damage and loss of amenity due to water ingress. He was successful in the county court and the Court of Appeal indicated the appropriate approach. They suggested that the repair obligation had to be carried out so that not only was the obviously damaged door repaired but so that continual future repairs to the door would not be required.

---

[7] *Halliard Property Company v. Nicholas Clarke Investments* (1984) 269 E.G. 1257.
[8] *Elmcroft Developments Ltd v. Tankersley-Sawyer* (1984) 15 H.L.R. 63.
[9] *Quick v. Taff-Ely B. C.* [1985] 3 All E.R. 321; see also *Staves and Staves v. Leeds C.C.* (1991) 23 H.L.R. 107.
[10] See para. 3–42 *et seq.*
[11] 19 H.L.R. 269; (1987) 54 P. & C.R. 193.

Patching and improvement

3–09   These matters often are dependent on the effectiveness of "patching" rather than renewal. Thus in a case a few months after *Stent* the Court of Appeal applied the repair/improvement principle to a defective roof. The roof of an Edwardian property had been repaired over a six-year period on some half a dozen occasions. While it was accepted that at some point a roof might reach a stage where it required replacement, this point had not been reached in this instance. In *Murray v. Birmingham City Council*[12] the tenant failed because, while the roof was capable of being repaired by renewal, it could also be dealt with by replacement and renailing of the defective and slipped slates. The problem, however, was more serious in an eviction case involving an old alms house complex and the tenants were provided with suitable alternative accommodation.[13]

3–10   A Scottish case on this point was heard in Airdrie Sheriff Court in 1988.[14] A claim was made for repair work to a steel house erected in the 1940s. The complaints included allegations of gaps in the construction of the house, lack of insulation, external walls and roof which conducted heat rather than retained it. The claim was unsuccessful and the sheriff referred to the issue of repairs as opposed to improvement. It was the sheriff's view that the tenant's primary purpose in bringing this action was to force the district council to modernise his home. The tenant had, according to Sheriff Boyle, apparently mistakenly equated the desire for modernisation with a belief that the council had failed in its common law obligations.[14a]

        Even if this "patching" approach is adopted in Scotland it does not mean that there is no remedy for tenants of houses with design deficiencies. Housing must be tenantable and habitable at common law.[15] There is also an implied contractual term under statute that the landlord will keep the property in repair.[16] It must also be fit for human habitation under statute[17] and the living conditions must not amount to a nuisance.[18]

3. OBLIGATION OF NOTIFICATION

Introduction

3–11   Their general repair obligation[19] obliges landlords at their own cost to repair any defect through which the premises may become or have become less than wind and water tight when such defect is brought to their attention. However, it was pointed out that there is no obligation on a landlord to carry out periodic inspections "to see what their condition is when he has no reason to suspect or believe that they are other than they should be".[20]

        This means that, assuming a landlord puts the property into repair at the start of the tenancy then that landlord does not become liable until notice is given of

---

[12] (1988) 20 H.L.R. 39.
[13] *Trs of the Dame Margaret Hungerford Charity v. Beazely* (1993) 26 H.L.R. 269.
[14] *Traynor v. Monklands D.C.* (1988) 6 S.H.L.N. 52, *per* Sheriff John S. Boyle.
[14a] *McDougall v. Easington D.C.* (1989) 21 H.L.R. 310.
[15] See para. 3–22 *et seq.*
[16] Housing (Scotland) Act 1987, s. 113 and Sched. 10, para. 3.
[17] See para. 3–43 *et seq.*
[18] See para. 3–59.
[19] *Hampton v. Galloway & Sykes* (1899) 1 F. 501.
[20] *ibid.* at 505.

any alleged defect.[21] This approach was neatly summed up by the then Master of the Rolls, Sir John Donaldson who stated that the golden rule is: "Tell your landlord about the defects".[22]

Implied notice

In Scotland it should be noted that the principle of notice was not noted by   3–12
Rankine who took the view that the landlord in letting property impliedly guaranteed that the property was fit for human habitation. There is some modern support for the obligation resting on the landlord to be aware of some obvious defects without the need for the tenant to notify. The view has been expressed[23] that there may be cases in which a landlord would be liable for failure to repair a defect of which he had no actual knowledge but of which he ought reasonably to have known before it could be discovered by the tenant.[24] This statement, however, was incidental to the principle governing the decision. In addition Lord Dunpark did not explain what circumstances he had in mind as to when this principle of assumed knowledge would apply. Obviously knowledge from ownership of adjacent property would be covered and a landlord with actual personal knowledge of a defect would be barred from claiming that the tenant had not told him. So, for example, where the landlord owned an upper flat and lower flat and knew of a defect in the upper flat resulting in water seeping into the lower flat, the landlord's liability under contract would emerge at the moment of knowledge rather than when notified by the tenant of the lower flat. By the same token where, for instance, a landlord's workforce inspected property in connection with the obligation to ensure the safety of gas appliances and noted that there seemed to be problems with the system but nothing was done then liability would arise in the event of system failure occurring within the space of a couple of months.

Reasonable time to effect repairs

Landlords will normally require notification during a lease that there is a repair   3–13
required.[24] At common law they have a reasonable period of time to effect repairs once notified of them. How long the landlord will get to carry out the repair depends on the seriousness of the repair. In the event of the landlord failing to carry out the repairs, there are various options open to a tenant. The tenant may leave and claim damages; alternatively, the tenant may stay and seek a rebate of rent for inconvenience and/or the cost of repair carried out by tenant.

The Victorian cases in this area tended to revolve around tenants shifting within the private rented sector. Nonetheless the principles are applicable today where tenants may not have an effective option to move but will be suing for damages and/or implement.

Staying a reasonable time

Tenants are not expected to remain beyond a reasonable time if the landlord   3–14
is unable to effect the necessary repairs.[25] Dr Granger rented a house for six years from 1876 with a break in 1880. He took entry and in 1879 complained

---

[21] See para. 3–41.
[22] *McGreal v. Wake* (1984) 13 H.L.R. 107 at 109.
[23] *Golden Casket (Greenock) Ltd v. BRS (Pickfords) Ltd,* 1972 S.L.T. 146.
[24] *ibid.*
[25] *Scottish Heritable Security Co. (Ltd) v. Granger* (1881) 8 R. 459.

about the drains. He entered into negotiations to lease the house at a reduced rent and this was agreed in February 1880. In that month his family became ill with typhoid fever and the youngest child died. Dr Granger made inquiries and concluded that the drains were the cause. He left the property for two months while the landlord dealt with the drains. The landlord sought the full half year's rent from the tenant. The court accepted that the landlord's failure to provide him with a habitable house for two months entitled him to give up the lease with no rent due for the period after he left.

3–15   In another Victorian case[26] the tenant was held entitled to give up the lease of property because the house was not in a tenantable condition. Due to debris and rubbish beneath the house it was damp and foul-smelling. The health of the tenant's wife was badly affected. The landlord denied that the house was in an insanitary condition and failed to respond to the complaints except to instruct the fitting of "a few extra gratings" to allow a stronger current of air under the floor. The tenant had taken the house from May 1898 to May 1899 but left in October 1898. The landlord sued for the return of the tenant's furniture and rent for the whole year as agreed. The failure of the landlord to meet the tenant's complaints entitled him to treat this as a material breach of contract and leave without penalty and without the need to pay the rent.

It should also be noted that the complex rules about the voluntary acceptance of risk need to be borne in mind where a tenant remains in the face of a patent danger.[27]

4. EXPRESS CONTRACTUAL RIGHTS

Introduction

3–16   The starting point for any discussion of what rights the tenant may have as against the landlord starts with the contract which they have entered. Traditionally landlords and tenants could put whatever conditions they chose into the contract other than the normal prohibition against illegal or immoral contracts. Leases could be as short and simple or as long and complex as the parties chose. There was no limit on the length of the lease. Short leases did not need to be in writing. The situation for commercial property continues to be simple. The parties are free to make any bargain they choose.

There are now requirements for landlords of secure and assured tenancies to provide written leases. The legislation does not, however, require these landlords to indicate the extent of the obligations of the landlord towards the tenant as far as the condition of the property is concerned. Landlords may lawfully provide minimal information on these issues. It should be emphasised, of course, that landlords may not avoid their repairing obligations. Social landlords have for some years had the opportunity of good practice guidance from the Scottish Federation of Housing Associations. They produce various documents covering assured and short assured tenancies.

The current version of the SFHA Model Secure Tenancy Agreement reflects the implied statutory obligations. It explains, for instance, that the landlord will "keep in repair the structure and exterior of the house and keep it fit for human habitation".[28]

---

[26] *McKimmie's Trustees v. Armour* (1899) 2 F. 156.
[27] See paras 3–100 to 3–104; *Proctor v. Cowlairs Co-operative Society Ltd,* 1961 S.L.T. 434.
[28] cl. 7.

It then replicates the relevant part of Schedule 10,[29] adding that the landlord will "make good damage caused by acts of vandalism/criminal activity provided they have been notified to the police within 24 hours of occurring, or as soon as is reasonably practicable by the Tenant or by someone acting on the tenant's behalf".[30]

The writers have examined a range of leases in the private rented sector. 3–17 These vary from very simple clauses which state that the landlord is responsible for "keeping the subjects of the let wind and water tight, and the exterior decoration thereof in good order" to much more elaborate clauses incorporating the terms of the statutory implied repairs provision.[31] A number of leases also borrow from the SFHA model and include an obligation on the landlord to make good damage caused by acts of vandalism provided that these have been notified by the tenant to the police within 24 hours of occurring. There are also leases which make no direct mention of the landlord's obligations to repair nor of its extent. Repair is here only discussed in terms of the need for tenants to give access for repairs to be carried out. It is important to note that the absence of express agreed repair rights does not affect the tenant's rights to repair under common law or statute. Silence does not absolve the landlord from responsibility.

Interpretation of lease terms

Introduction

The terms of leases will be interpreted according to the general rules of 3–18 interpretation. Repairs rights derived from statute cannot be displaced by contract.[32] The lease's terms can displace the provisions of the common law such as the right to withhold rent[33] although this is seldom encountered in practice. It is, however, expressly provided that the statutory implied repairs provision may not be displaced by contract.[34]

Presumption in favour of tenant

According to the normal rules of interpretation, any ambiguity or doubt in a 3–19 document drawn up by one party will be interpreted in favour of the other party. It is assumed that the author of the document is in a better position to provide self-protection and will have done so.[35] This is sometimes referred to as the *contra proferentem* rule. It only applies where an ambiguity actually exists.[36] The general presumption has been applied to allow a tenant to claim damages where he had to abandon his property due to flooding caused by the actions of local vandals. The tenancy agreement indicated that the landlord would restore essential services and make the premises secure within 24 hours of such repairs being notified. Upon notification by the tenant the landlord failed to secure the property and the tenant suffered loss of his possessions when the flat was set on

---

[29] See paras 3–43 to 3–49.
[30] cl. 7(x).
[31] Housing (Scotland) Act 1987, Sched. 10, para. 3.
[32] Housing (Scotland) Act 1987, Sched. 10, para. 5.
[33] *Skene v. Cameron,* 1942 S.C. 393.
[34] See para 3–50.
[35] *Evans v. Glasgow D.C.,* 1978 S.L.T. 17.
[36] *City of Glasgow Council v. Murray,* 1997 Hous.L.R. 105.

fire.[37] The question as to whether this principle applies where documents have been drawn up by solicitors on both sides was left unresolved in a case involving missives for the purchase of a house.[38]

Express inclusion of one obligation implies exclusion of obligations not mentioned

3–20   If the lease states that a tenant is liable for one particular obligation then it is to be inferred that the tenant is not liable for obligations of a similar character. Lawyers sometimes refer to this as *expressio unius, exclusio alterius*.

In one case the lease dealing with the statutory implied repairs obligation[39] provided that the Council's obligation was restricted to keeping in repair the structure and exterior of the house and keeping in repair and proper working order the installations for the supply of water, gas and electricity and for sanitation, space heating and water heating.[40] The tenant was responsible for all other repairs. Any repair which was necessary as a result of improper use of the premises by the tenant was stated to be the tenant's responsibility. John Laurie, the tenant, had a window broken by vandals. He claimed the cost of repair from his landlords. The sheriff principal explained that by stating that the tenant's specific obligation related to their improper use of the premises the lease overrode the suggestion that the tenant was responsible for all "non-statutory" repairs. The implication of the relevant sentence was that the tenant was not to be responsible for any repair which was necessary as a result of improper use by someone other than the tenant.

Presumption against alteration of the common law

3–21   One of the fundamental rules of Scots law is that in the absence of specific and unambiguous language the common law should not be altered. This was confirmed in a case where a window was broken by vandals and the tenant sought to recover the replacement cost from the landlords, the district council.[41] The landlords argued that the common law rule that landlords were not liable for the actions of third parties applied and was not altered by the statutory implied repairs provision. Sheriff Ireland, however, noted that the statute specifically exempted from the repairs obligation, owed by the landlord, damage caused by either the tenant's negligence or acts of nature. He explained that there was no trace of the common law exception "the act of a third party". He inferred from this omission that, whatever the reason may have been, it was not intended to include it among the exceptions. Thus the obligation on the district council to keep the window in repair was not subject to the qualification that it ceased to apply where damage was caused by vandals. The language of the statute here was clear and unambiguous.[42]

---

[37] *Murdoch v. City of Glasgow Council*, 1998 Hous.L.R. 30.
[38] *Taylor v. MacLeod*, 1990 S.L.T. 194.
[39] See para. 3–50 *et seq.*
[40] *City of Edinburgh D.C. v. Laurie*, 1982 S.L.T. (Sh.Ct.) 83.
[41] *Hastie v. Edinburgh D.C.*, 1981 S.L.T. (Sh.Ct.) 61.
[42] *ibid.* at 64.

5. Rights Implied at Common Law

Introduction

There is a body of common law rights which have been built up by the courts   3–22
over the years which determine the relationship of landlord and tenant. In the
absence of express terms or statutory alterations which take away or add to
these rights then tenants are entitled to these rights. The rights granted by the
common law are both direct and indirect as far as the standard of the
accommodation is concerned. However, it is standard practice for the majority
of commercial leases to be full repairing and insuring leases. The landlord shifts
the obligations on to the tenant. It is possible to shift the onus of repair on to the
tenant in commercial tenancies.

As we noted above,[43] landlords must give possession of the subjects leased;
they must normally give full possession of the subjects; they must maintain
tenants in possession and restore possession where this is lost. If it is not possible
to put a tenant back in possession then a claim for damages will arise. There are
a number of exceptions where either the subjects are destroyed or where the
tenant had lost possession through his own fault or as a result of actings outwith
the control of the landlord such as natural disaster, third party actings, or
supervening legislation.

The common law obligation as to the fitness of the subjects, where not   3–23
excluded, sits alongside the statutory implied repairs provision and statutory
regulation of housing conditions. Which path a tenant seeking remedies chooses
is often a matter of personal choice. There are, as indicated, sometimes good
reasons for pursuing contractual remedies in preference to statutory or common
law nuisance since this allows damages to be sought as well as rectification of
the defect in a single action. If a nuisance action is pursued a separate action for
damages must also be raised since the statutory nuisance procedure makes no
provision for damages. On the other hand, the identification and policing of
statutory nuisances is provided as part of the services of the local authority at
no direct cost to the complainer.

The principle of fitness of leased subjects

The early Scottish institutional writers wrote mainly of the law of leases as it   3–24
affected leases of agricultural land. In these there was an obligation that the
subjects be fit for the purpose let. In terms of urban subjects (*i.e.* artificial
structures such as buildings) then the common law rule was, according to Erskine,
that they be in a habitable condition at the time of entry and be kept in tenantable
repair during the lease.[44] Bell suggests that the rented subjects in general must
be fit for the purpose for which they are let.[45]

This obligation is paralleled by legislation stemming from concern over public
health and hygiene which applies to dwelling-houses as well as other buildings
and property. There are situations where the more general common law obligation
of the landlord is a valuable adjunct to statutory provisions.

---

[43] See para. 1–35 *et seq.*
[44] Erskine, *Inst.,* II, vi, 43.
[45] Bell, *Prin.,* s. 1253.

3–25   The guarantee or warrandice as to the fitness of such urban artificial structures as housing is that they be reasonably fit for the purpose for which they are let. According to older authorities this obligation may vary according to the value and rent of the subjects.[46] In effect, the more valuable the premises the more onerous the duty of the landlord. This is unlikely to operate today to deny tenants of poorer housing their rights to tenantable and habitable dwellings. It is more likely to mean that a house should be suitable for the climatic conditions in the area in which it is situated. A house which is habitable for a tenant in Dumfries may not be so for someone living in an exposed headland in Lewis.[47] It is also worth noting that tenants of large and expensive properties may well have leases beyond the seven-year period specified in the statutory implied repairs provision.[48] Their rents may also exceed the weekly level laid down in relation to "reasonably fit for human habitation".[49] At the luxury end of the market where scarcity of supply has not traditionally been a problem one would expect that any such tenant who experienced unacceptable living conditions would find landlords keen to rectify these matters if only to protect their capital investment. Hence, although they might be outwith statutory control this might be one situation where market forces could provide adequate protection.

The fitness principle as it relates to housing

3–26   In the case of housing Bell suggests that the landlord is bound to provide the lessee with a habitable house.[50] This has commonly been expressed in two major ways. Property must be either tenantable and habitable or wind and water tight.

Tenantable and habitable

3–27   The writer of the most extensive and authoritative text on the Scots law of landlord and tenant, Rankine, expressed the obligation thus: "The rule of common law, as applied to urban tenements (i.e. buildings) is that they shall be put into habitable or tenantable condition by the landlord at entry".[51] He explained further that this obligation extends throughout the duration of the lease. "The landlord of an urban tenement is further bound at common law and unless it be otherwise stipulated, to uphold it in a tenantable or habitable condition during the course of the lease".[52]

The question of whether a property is tenantable or habitable is a matter of fact to be decided on proof. Some assistance may, in the future, be derived from the interpretation of the statutory implied obligation that rented houses be "fit for human habitation"[53] now that the Housing (Scotland) Act 1988 has widened the application of that legislation to almost all houses in Scotland. Until the 1988 Act the scope of the obligation had been allowed to diminish over the years since it only applied to houses below a certain fixed rent. This figure had last been adjusted back in 1923 and since then inflation had had a major impact on the number of houses covered by the legislative protection.

---

[46] *Mechan v. Watson,* 1907 S.C. 25.
[47] Paul Brown and Angus McIntosh, *Dampness and the Law* (SHELTER, 1987), p. 13.
[48] See paras 3–50 to 3–54.
[49] See paras 3–43 to 3–49.
[50] Bell, *Prin.,* s. 1273.
[51] Rankine, *Leases* (3rd ed.), p. 241.
[52] *ibid.*
[53] Housing (Scotland) Act 1987, Sched. 10, para. 1.

There is older English authority on the meaning of "fit for human habitation"   3–28
which may offer some assistance as to what standard property must reach to be
tenantable[54] although the problem of a small and declining amount of houses being
covered by a fixed statutory figure has been noted in England in the mid 1980s[55]
and late 1990s.[56] There has been no equivalent of the expansion of the fitness for
human habitation coverage by statutory instrument in England and Wales.

Wind and water tight

The phrase "wind and water tight" has also been used to indicate what   3–29
amounted to a habitable or tenantable condition. The classic statement of the
law was expressed by Lord President Dunedin:

> "By the law of Scotland, the lease of every urban tenement is in default of
> any specific stipulation, deemed to include an obligation on the part of the
> landlord to hand over the premises in a wind and water tight condition,
> and if he does not do so there is a breach of contract and he may be liable
> in damages. He is also bound to put them into a wind and water tight
> condition if they become not so ."[57]

In looking to see exactly what was covered, his Lordship went on to explain
that the expression "wind and water tight" itself meant "wind and water tight
against what may be called the ordinary attacks of the elements, not against
exceptional encroachments of water due to other causes."[58] The case of *Gunn v.
National Coal Board*[59] accepted that this applied to rising damp. This appears
to have rejected what Angus McAllister refers to as the "rather strange decision"[60]
in *McGonigal v. Pickard*[61] that wind and water tight did not apply where the
tenant descended to the basement in her bed one morning when the rotted floor
joists gave way.

The fitness principle in practice

This has been held to cover a variety of different complaints. Again, there is   3–30
no restriction on other inadequacies which can be pursued successfully as long
as they can be shown to contribute to the unfitness of the subjects.

Rain/snow penetration

Flooding of a house was caused where the construction of the roof was such   3–31
that it would not deal with a fall of snow.[62]

Rising damp

In one case a ground floor flat was rented by the National Coal Board. The   3–32
house was damp. This was caused by rising damp which resulted in the premises

---

[54] See paras 3–43 to 3–49.
[55] *Quick v. Taff-Ely B.C.* [1985] 3 All E.R. 321 at 323.
[56] *Issa v. Hackney London B.C.* [1997] 1 All E.R. 999 at 1007—the equivalent English sections
were described as being "completely dead letters".
[57] *Wolfson v. Forrester,* 1910 S.C. 675 at 680.
[58] *ibid.*
[59] 1982 S.L.T. 526.
[60] *Scottish Law of Leases* (1995), p. 35.
[61] 1954 S.L.T. (Notes) 62.
[62] *Reid v. Baird* (1876) 4 R. 234.

not being in a habitable condition. The tenant was able to recover damages for damage to clothing, aggravation of health and inconvenience. Lord Mayfield stated:

> "[T]he landowner of the dwelling-house is under a general obligation to uphold it in a habitable condition … In my view the rising damp present in the house and notified after about a month amounts to a breach of a general obligation. The presence of that rising damp … made occupation of the bedroom impossible".[63]

This would seem to call into question the earlier authority that wind and water tight does not cover rising damp.[64] It should also be noted that this authority was decided prior to the emergence of the issue of condensation dampness.

Condensation dampness

3–33   After a series of cases during the 1980s mainly involving Glasgow District Council it has now been established that claims of the existence of condensation dampness could not simply be met with a blanket rejection by landlords.[65]

Councils had until these decisions relied on the argument that the tenants' lifestyles had contributed to the dampness. The argument was backed up by evidence of the use of paraffin heaters, and the blocking up of flues and windows. The contention had been accepted in some cases.[66]

It was decided in the *McArdle* case that while there may be problems in technical evidence, nonetheless condensation dampness is clearly covered by the common law obligation to provide fit subjects.[67] Despite frequent complaints and redecoration the property continued to be damp and have mould growth. The tenants sued and the sheriff pointed out that landlords had a responsibility to respond realistically to unfitness when it was caused by the combination of inadequate heating, ventilation and insulation and that the landlords had been too ready to blame this chronic problem upon some failure on the tenants' part to heat or ventilate the houses properly.

3–34   The problem here has revolved around who is responsible for the dampness. The Scottish Affairs Committee set the tone for the modern approach when they stated:

> "It is unreasonable to blame tenants for problems which arise because their living habits are those common in society generally, or because they cannot afford to pay for heating or because their homes are badly designed or built. Nonetheless many tenants do not appear to understand the nature of condensation as well as they might."[68]

This notion of how condensation dampness comes about through the interaction of heating ventilation and insulation has been discussed in the Court of Session[69] as well as in the sheriff court.[70]

---

[63] *Gunn v. National Coal Board*, 1982 S.L.T. 526.

[64] *McGonigal v. Pickard*, 1954 S.L.T. (Notes) 62.

[65] *Gunn v. Glasgow D.C.*, 1997 Hous.L.R. 3; *Fyfe v. Scottish Homes*, 1995 S.C.L.R. 209.

[66] *Maguire v. Glasgow D.C.*, 1983 S.H.L.R. 1.

[67] *McArdle v. Glasgow D.C.*, 1989 S.C.L.R 19.

[68] *Report on Dampness in Housing* (1984), Summary of conclusions and recommendations—cl. 11.

[69] *Gunn v. Glasgow D.C.*, 1997 Hous.L.R. 3 at 5; *Guy v. Strathkelvin D.C.*, 1997 Hous.L.R. 14 at 18.

[70] *McCarthy v. City of Glasgow D.C.*, 1996 Hous.L.R. 81; *Fyfe v. Scottish Homes*, 1995 S.C.L.R. 209; *Quinn v. Monklands D.C.*, 1996 Hous.L.R. 86; *Burns v. Monklands D.C.*, 1997 Hous.L.R. 34; *McGuire v. Monklands D.C.*, 1997 Hous.L.R. 41.

The limit to heating and ventilation. As one leading activist in this area has 3–35
pointed out "if you can afford sufficient heat, a tent at the North Pole" will
suffice to solve problems of condensation.[71] It is clear from decided cases that
the tenant is not expected to take wholly unreasonable action "curing" damp by
ventilation.[72] In *McArdle* it was stated that if persons were to be housed on the
exposed twenty-first floor of a tower block, it would not always be practical to
have windows open, particularly in inclement weather. Nor would the tenant be
expected to heat the house come what may and there was a limit to the effort
and money which it was reasonable to expect from a tenant to overcome a
severe condensation problem.[73] The same approach was taken in *Fyfe v. Scottish
Homes*[74] where it was stated that simply by applying large amounts of heat and
incurring inordinate heating bills a house did not thereby become habitable.[75]

It should, however be noted that in some of the early Glasgow dampness
cases some sheriffs took the view that the problem of heating and ventilating
houses rested squarely upon the tenant[76] and stated that, whilst tenants are often
unwilling or unable, because of the high cost, to heat bathrooms adequately, or
indeed to heat adequately any rooms in the house which are not in constant use,
nonetheless the responsibility to heat and ventilate a house was clearly on the
tenant, not on the landlord. Recent cases, culminating in the Inner House decision
in *Gunn*,[77] favour the line of responsibility resting with landlords.

In *Gunn* the Second Division explained that where the landlords wished to attribute 3–36
damage to the tenant's failure to heat or ventilate the premises they had to specify in
their pleadings sole fault or contributory negligence supported by relevant averments.
They had to explain, in essence, in what ways the tenant had failed.

The proportion of income to be devoted to heating. Remarks made in earlier 3–37
cases have been expanded on to indicate what level of expenditure is reasonably
required from tenants. The question which has been raised is whether or not the
lifestyle of the tenant is likely to give rise to condensation problems because it
is outwith the spectrum of lifestyles which the local authority could reasonably
expect its tenants to follow.[78] In *Burns v. Monklands District Council*[78a] the
view was expressed that the landlords required to indicate the tenant's lifestyle
in so far as it potentially affected condensation and the range of lifestyles
reasonably to be expected by the landlords. This extent of the spectrum of
lifestyles is of great significance: if the most impecunious tenant can afford to
pay only, say, 50p per week on heating, he would be at one of the anticipated
spectrum of styles and it might be difficult for the landlord to establish that the
pursuer/tenant's lifestyle was outwith that spectrum, at least so far as
underspending on heating goes. Translating the spectrum into reality, in *McGuire v.
Monklands District Council*[79] the sheriff accepted 7.5 per cent of the tenant's
income as being reasonable expenditure.

---

[71] Jonathan Mitchell, quoted in *McArdle v. City of Glasgow D.C.*, 1989 S.C.L.R. 19 at 23.
[72] *McArdle v. City of Glasgow D.C.*, 1989 S.C.L.R. 19.
[73] *Miller v. City of Glasgow D.C.* (Dec. 1, 1987) (1991) 1 S.H.L.R. 143.
[74] 1995 S.C.L.R. 209.
[75] *ibid.* at 212.
[76] *e.g. McGuire v. Glasgow D.C.* (March 4, 1983) (1991) 1 S.H.L.R. 1.
[77] 1992 S.C.L.R. 1018; 1997 Hous.L.R. 3.
[78] *Quick v. Taff-Ely B.C.* [1986] Q.B. 809.
[78a] 1997 Hous.L.R. 34.
[79] 1997 Hous.L.R. 41 at 44.

Inadequate drains and water supply

3–38   This principle has been held to cover inadequate water supply and drains.[80] In the *Tennent's Trustees* case it was agreed that the landlord would put the water and drains in thorough order. A report indicated that extensive repairs were required for these and the tenant was not able to occupy the house on time. He successfully retained rent to cover this period.

Infestation of vermin/insects

3–39   An early example of the problems of vermin and insects established that such additional residents in a house would mean it was uninhabitable.[81] In *Kippen*, beetles and cockroaches were present in the property, particularly at night, and the tenant was entitled to give up the tenancy. It should be noted that many of the nineteenth century cases centred around whether the contractual obligations were at an end. Since over 90 per cent of housing was private rental housing the preferred remedy for tenants was to move. Each removal term there was a turnover of about 10 per cent of tenants.[82]

Anything likely to endanger the tenant in the premises

3–40   If there is anything which is likely to cause harm to the tenant then this would clearly mean that the premises were not habitable through lack of safety. In one case a woman was injured in a fall following an epileptic fit.[83] She struck her head on the fire which, not being secured, tipped forward spilling burning coal on to her. The previous tenant had installed the fire. According to Lord Grieve tenantability included seeing that there was no part of the subjects in a condition likely to endanger the tenant.

When is the fitness principle applicable?

3–41   The landlord must put the subjects into a fit condition at entry and maintain them in this condition during the tenancy. According to Erskine: "[I]n the lease of a dwelling-house, the landlord must deliver the subject set (*i.e.* let) to the tenant in an habitable condition".[84] This was expressed by Lord Grieve as requiring[85] landlords to carry out an inspection of the premises prior to the entry by tenants in order to satisfy themselves that there was nothing in the state of the premises which was likely to endanger tenants when they took up occupation.

        This obligation sits uneasily alongside the landlord's defence that a defect was obvious at the commencement of the lease.[86] Indeed it seems to be a direct contradiction. However, neither of the cases which are cited in this context have ever been formally overruled. Nonetheless, it would, in the authors' view, be surprising if the doctrine of "defect obvious at time of commencement of lease"[87] in *Mechan*[88] and *Davidson*[89] was accepted by a modern court.

---

[80] *Tennent's Trs v. Maxwell* (1880) 17 S.L.R. 463.
[81] *Kippen v. Oppenheim* (1847) 10 D. 242.
[82] W. W. Kelso, *Sanitation in Paisley* (1920).
[83] *Lamb v. Glasgow D.C.*, 1978 S.L.T. (Notes) 64.
[84] Erskine, *Inst.*, II, vi, 43.
[85] *Lamb v. Glasgow D.C.*, above.
[86] See para. 3–105.
[87] *ibid.*
[88] 1907 S.C. 25.
[89] 1909 S.C. 566.

Introduction

The Housing of the Working Classes Act 1885 was the first instance of tenants 3–42
being given the specific protection of minimum standards of buildings. This
was complemented by the introduction in 1962 of a statutory implied repairs
provision. Since then it has not been possible for a landlord to shift the burden
of repairs on to most residential tenant. There are in fact two distinct sources of
statutory rights. Property must meet a minimum standard of habitability as an
implied condition of the contract. It must be reasonably fit for human habitation.
In addition, certain repairs are the responsibility of landlords and these cannot
be avoided by contract.

Reasonably fit for human habitation

General scope

The Housing (Scotland) Act 1987 as amended by the Housing (Scotland) 3–43
Act 1988 provides that: "[T]here shall be implied a condition that the house is
at the commencement of the tenancy, and an undertaking that the house will be
kept by the landlord during the tenancy, in all respects reasonably fit for human
habitation".[90] Although almost all leases are covered, whether or not the statutory
standard applies depends on the rent level and length of lease.

Rental level

This applies to houses rented out at a rent of less than £300 per week.[91] This 3–44
new level of application has applied since January 2, 1989 and revives a piece
of legislation that had become largely defunct. The annual rent level originally
provided in the Housing of the Working Classes Act 1890 was raised in 1909
and 1923 but thereafter remained at £26 per annum. This excluded the vast
majority of tenancies by the 1980s. This has now been reversed with a very
high proportion of tenancies covered since the phrase "house" includes part of
a house. This means that if a six-bedroomed property were rented out at £70 a
week for each room it would still be covered since each contract would be a
contract for letting a house.[92]

Length of lease

This condition is not to be implied where the house is let for a period in 3–45
excess of three years and there is an obligation on the tenant to put the property
into a condition reasonably fit for human habitation. What counts here is the
length of the lease being at least three years. It is immaterial if on a shorter
lease the tenant spends in excess of three years relying on tacit relocation of
the shorter lease. This is, however, an area where the writer has come across
tenants being unable to use the protection because the lease was for a period
well in excess of three years. They still, of course, have the protection of the

---

[90] Sched. 10, para. (3).
[91] The Landlord's Repairing Obligations (Specified Rent) (Scotland) (No. 2) Order 1988
(S.I. 1988 No. 2155) as specified in Sched. 8 to the Housing (Scotland) Act 1988.
[92] See para. 2–28.

common law, discussed above. In such longer term arrangements one would expect some kind of agreement as to compensation for works carried out by the tenant.

Definition of "reasonably fit for human habitation"

3–46   In considering whether a house is fit for human habitation regard must be had to the extent to which the house falls short of the provisions of the building regulations in operation in the district by reason of disrepair or "sanitary defects" in the house.[93] This is an important development the impact of which has yet to be tested in modern case law.[94] The expression "sanitary defects" is defined as including lack of air space or of ventilation, darkness, dampness, absence of adequate and readily accessible water supply or of sanitary arrangements or of other conveniences, and inadequate paving or drainage of courts, yards or passages.

The definition of "fitness for human habitation" contained in the Housing (Scotland) Act 1966 required regard to be had when deciding such issues as whether to demolish, close or improve properties to a range of matters. These were the general state of repair, structural stability, freedom from dampness, natural lighting, air space, ventilation, adequacy and accessibility of water supply, adequacy and accessibility of sanitary and other conveniences, drainage, condition of paving and drainage of courts, yards and passages, and facilities for storage, preparation and cooking of food and for the disposal of waste water.[95]

That standard has now been superseded for the purposes of local authorities deciding how to take action on an area basis through the Improvement Order or Housing Action Area procedure. Since 1969 a slightly different standard has operated called the "tolerable standard". This is now found in Part IV of the Housing (Scotland) Act 1987.[96]

Interpretation of "reasonably fit for human habitation"

3–47   Since the fitness for human habitation has not been a "live issue" for the past 50 years in Scotland and England[97] the modern case law specifically on the meaning of "unfit for human habitation" comes from older cases interpreting equivalent English legislation. As indicated, the notion of "fitness for human habitation" continues to be part of the law of England and Wales. Two cases from England are worthy of particular note and have been followed in Scotland in the Outer House of the Court of Session. The classic statement of the law in England was made by Lord Justice Atkin in the Court of Appeal in *Morgan*:

> [I]f the state of repair of a house is such that by ordinary user damage may naturally be caused to the occupier, either in respect of personal injury to life and limb or injury to health, then the house is not in all respects reasonably fit for human habitation".[98]

---

[93] Sched. 10, para. 1(4).
[94] *Cameron v. Glasgow D.C.*, (1991) 1 S.H.L.R. 5 on water byelaws.
[95] The Housing Act 1985, which is the equivalent statute for England and Wales, operates the standard of "unfit for human habitation" and it requires regard to be had to similar matters as the Scottish legislation: s. 604.
[96] s. 86.
[97] See para. 3–28.
[98] *Morgan v. Liverpool Corporation* [1927] 2 K.B. 231.

This approach was approved by the House of Lords in *Summers*[99] where a window sash cord broke and was reported to the landlords. Meanwhile, when Mrs Summers was cleaning the window the other sash cord broke trapping her hand. She was injured and sued for damages for personal injury based on the landlord's failure to provide accommodation "fit for human habitation". Lord Wright explained: "human habitation is in contrast with habitation by pigs, horses or other animals, or with use as warehouses and the like, but I think it also imports some reference to what we call humanity or humaneness".

Lord Milligan applied both *Morgan*[1] and *Summers*[2] in a subsequent case   3–48 north of the border but pointed out that the overall question was whether the specific defect rendered the house as a whole unfit for human habitation: "in order to saddle the [landlords] with responsibility for the repair of the pane of glass, the [tenant] must establish that with the pane in its cracked condition the house was not 'in all respects reasonably fit for human habitation".[3]

The Court of Appeal in 1997 confirmed this approach when they discussed whether it was correct to look at each item or at the cumulative effect of individual disrepair.[4]

Developments in the 1990s

The alteration of the financial limit now means that tenants' cases can be   3–49 brought using the slightly more general language of paragraph 1 of Schedule 10. This has been done successfully in the case of a house with high levels of dampness resulting from the introduction of sealed double-glazed windows.[5] It has also seen a successful claim reduced through the application of the principle of contributory negligence where the tenant refused to allow the landlords to carry out remedial dry-lining work following an extensive dispute about a damp and mouldy house.[6] The tenant was not at fault, however, in refusing to accept an anti-condensation device which would have been costly to run and whose efficacy was in doubt.

It is important to note, in addition, that the question of whether premises are reasonably fit for human habitation is to be looked at in terms of the extent to which the house falls short of the provisions of the current building regulations.[7]

Rights to repair implied by statute

General scope

The Housing (Scotland) Act 1987 also includes an implied provision that the   3–50 landlord will keep certain parts of the rented premises in repair. The landlord must:

> "(a) keep in repair the structure and exterior of the house (including drains, gutters and external pipes); and

---

[99] [1943] A.C. 283.
[1] [1927] 2 K.B. 231.
[2] [1943] AC 283.
[3] *Haggerty v. Glasgow Corporation,* 1964 S.L.T. (Notes) 95.
[4] *Dover D.C. v. Sherred and Tarling,* [1997] 29 H.L.R. 864.
[5] *Burns v. Monklands D.C.,* 1997 Hous.L.R. 34.
[6] *Kearney v. Monklands D.C.,* 1997 Hous.L.R. 39.
[7] *Fyfe v. Scottish Homes,* 1995 S.C.L.R. 209; see also *Quinn v. Monklands D.C.,* 1995 S.C.L.R. 393.

(b) keep in repair and proper working order the installations in the house—
  (i)   for the supply of water, gas and electricity, and for sanitation (including basins, sinks, baths and sanitary conveniences but not, except as aforesaid, fixtures, fittings and appliances for making use of the supply of water, gas or electricity), and
  (ii) for space heating or water heating".[8]

Any provision that the tenant will repair the premises or will paint, point or render the premises (or pay money to the landlord in lieu of such repairs) are to be of no effect in so far as they relate to the items mentioned in (a) and (b). Nor is a landlord permitted to limit his obligations as landlord or impose on the tenant any penalty, disability or obligation when the tenant tries to enforce or rely on the implied repairs provisions.[9] The obligation is to carry out the repair within a reasonable time so that a landlord is not in breach until a reasonable time has elapsed.[10]

Exceptions to the repair obligation

3–51   Although the repair obligation provides valuable rights there are certain situations where the statute expressly states that the obligation does not apply. It is limited to leases of less than seven years granted on or after July 3, 1962. This includes any shorter lease where the tenant has the option to extend the lease beyond seven years.[12] It does not cover defects caused by the tenant,[13] defects caused by destruction or damage by fire, or by tempest, flood or other inevitable accident[14] and does not apply to fittings and fixtures removable by the tenant.[15] Agreements to contract out specifically may be approved by the sheriff on the grounds that it is reasonable having regard to the other terms and conditions of the lease and to all the circumstances of the case.[16] There are no reported instances of this having happened or as to how the criteria might be applied in practice. One situation which has been drawn to the writers' attention involved landlords unwittingly (apparently) avoiding being responsible for repairs. An estate was purchased which included properties lawfully occupied by individuals who paid no rent but who were, in return, responsible for maintaining the premises in good repair. One can see why a sheriff might approve such an arrangement, which appears on the face of it to fall foul of the proscription on shifting the repairs onus on to the tenant. As was noted when discussing the nature of tenancies, it would be the cost of doing the repairs which constituted this arrangement as a tenancy.[17] It is not an arrangement that is likely to be encountered with great frequency.

---

[8] Sched. 10, para. 3.
[9] *ibid.*
[10] *Calabar Properties Ltd v. Stitcher* [1984] 1 W.L.R. 287.
[11] This contrasts with the period covered in relation to fitness for human habitation: see para. 3–45.
[12] Sched. 10, para. 4. Leases in excess of seven years have been encountered by the writers in a dispute about the fitness of the subjects as a dwelling-house. The protection of this part of Schedule 10 was, accordingly, unavailable to the tenant.
[13] *ibid.* para. 3(2)(a).
[14] *ibid.* para. 3(2)(b).
[15] *ibid.* para. 3(2)(c).
[16] *ibid.* para. 5.
[17] *Scottish Residential Estates Development Co Ltd v. Henderson,* 1991 S.L.T. 490.

Notice of disrepair to landlord and implied notice

The general common law principle about notice has been applied where there   3–52
is an implied statutory repairs obligation.[18] However, it has been pointed out
that while the tenant is best advised to tell the landlord[19] there are situations
where the landlord may be assumed to have notice of a defect. For example, in
McGreal[20] it was implied that notice from the tenant might not be strictly
required. The Court of Appeal interpreted the implied repairs obligation to "keep
in repair" as being much more onerous than if it were simply worded "repair on
notice".

In addition, in a number of situations the landlord is assumed to have notice
of the existence of a defect without express notice. Thus where the tenant
complained to the landlord about water-hammering in the water supply system
and the landlord's plumber found the tank to be discoloured, the inspection was
sufficient to be equated with notice to the landlord of the defect which resulted
in the tank bursting some six weeks later.[21] Similarly, where the landlord had
actual knowledge through a surveyor's report obtained by the tenant in
connection with a possible purchase, this amounted to notice of serious and
significant repairs.[22] Notice was also inferred from a solicitor's letter outlining
why the tenant had not been paying rent, sent in response to a notice to quit for
rent arrears.[23]

Interpretation of repair obligation

General. The Housing (Scotland) Act 1987 specifically requires that in   3–53
determining the impact of the implied repairs provision regard must be had to
various factors,[24] specifically the age, character, prospective life of the house
and the locality in which it is situated.

"Structure and exterior" The court have interpreted some of the specific
words of the statutory implied repairs provision. In one case[25] it was determined
that the word "window" fell within the phrase "structure and exterior". Sheriff
Ireland was of the view that a window was not part of the "structure" of the
building because the structure of a house is that part of it which gives it stability,
shape and identity as house. The essentials were the foundations, walls and
roof. Windows did not contribute to the stability, shape nor identity of the
building. The window aperture was part of the structure of the building, but
the glass which was inserted into it was not. However the sheriff looking at
the question of the "exterior" decided that the exterior of the house was the
part of the house which lay between what was outside the house and what
was inside the house. It was the part of the house which you could see if you
looked at it from the outside.

---

[18] *O'Brien v. Robinson* [1973] A.C. 912; *Morris v. Liverpool Corporation* (1988) 20 H.L.R. 498.
[19] *McGreal v. Wake* (1984) 13 H.L.R. 107.
[20] *ibid.*
[21] *Dinefwr B.C. v. Jones* (1987) 19 H.L.R. 445.
[22] *Hall v. Howard* (1988) 20 H.L.R. 566.
[23] *Al Hassani v. Merrigan* (1988) 20 H.L.R. 238.
[24] Sched. 10, para. 3(3).
[25] *Hastie v. Edinburgh D.C.*, 1981 S.L.T. (Sh.Ct.) 61.

In general, the terms are to be given their ordinary everyday meaning.[26] In interpreting the equivalent English legislation[27] the Court of Appeal has also held that structure and exterior extends to door frames, window sills and lintels.[28]

Cost of alternative accommodation. The English courts have also looked at the English legislation[29] on this issue, and the Court of Appeal held that the tenant was entitled to damages for the cost of alternative accommodation where it was necessary for the work to be completed.[30]

3-54 **Cost of redecoration**. After the landlord has completed repairs under the implied repairs provision, the additional cost of redecoration must be borne by the landlord, according to the English Court of Appeal.[31] This principle has been accepted in Scotland at sheriff court level.[32] However, it should be noted that where the landlord has effected improvements rather than repairs then the tenant may not recover the cost of redecoration, according to the Court of Appeal in *McDougall v. Easington District Council*.[33] Here the local authority had carried out an extensive "enveloping" scheme and their Lordships noted that the tenants had had works worth over £10,000 carried out on their premises increasing the value from £10,000 to £18,000 and, accordingly, the "repair plus redecoration" principle from *Bradley*[34] was not applicable.

7. STATUTORY REGULATION OF REPAIR

Introduction

3-55 There are two statutes which directly make provision for the standard of repair to be dealt with by orders from the public authorities rather than through the enforcement of contract. The major difference as a mechanism for obtaining a house which is capable of being lived in for the tenant is that these mechanisms do not contain provisions for damages. Damages would need to be sued for separately, under either the express terms of the lease or its implied terms, whether they be the habitable and tenantable standards implied at common law or the statutory implied repairs provisions of Schedule 10 to the Housing (Scotland) Act 1987.

Whether or not the tolerable standard laid down in the Housing (Scotland) Act 1987 gives rise to a right of action against the local authority is a controversial matter on which there is conflicting case law in the Sheriff court and which has yet to be resolved in a higher court.[35] Similarly, the English approach taken on enforcement has not been tested in the Scottish courts.[35a]

It should also be noted that it is possible for tenants to make use of the nuisance provisions which exist at common law—these parallel the statutory nuisance

---

[26] *Douglas-Scott v. Scorgie* [1984] 1 All E.R. 1086—here covering a roof repair.
[27] Housing Act 1961, s. 32 (now the Landlord and Tenant Act 1985, s. 11).
[28] *Quick v. Taff Ely B.C.* [1985] 3 All E.R. 321.
[29] Landlord and Tenant Act 1985, s. 11 (formerly the Housing Act 1961, s. 32).
[30] *McGreal v. Wake* (1984) 13 H.L.R. 109.
[31] *Bradley v. Chorley B.C.* (1985) 17 H.L.R. 395.
[32] *Little v. City of Glasgow D.C.* (Glasgow Sh. Ct., May 12, 1988) (1991) 1 S.H.L.R. 195 and *McCarthy v. City of Glasgow D.C.* (Glasgow Sh. Ct., April 29, 1988) (1991) 1 S.H.L.R. 181.
[33] (1989) 21 H.L.R. 310.
[34] *Bradley v. Chorley B.C.* (1985) 17 H.L.R. 395.
[35] See para. 3–83.
[35a] *R. v. Cardiff C.C., ex p. Cross* (1984) 16 H.L.R. 1.

procedure but, like the contractual matters mentioned before, require action to be taken by the tenant rather than through the local authority. In addition, tenants injured by dangerous premises may be able to take action in terms of the Occupiers' Liability (Scotland) Act 1960 as well as Part V of the Housing (Scotland) Act 1987 relating to repair notices. It is also possible to refer problems stemming from maladministration to the Local Ombudsman in terms of the Local Government (Scotland) Act 1975. Although this is a process which should take months rather than years, the likely financial settlements tend not to be high[36] and, of course, the system is voluntary.[37]

The relevant repair regulation statutes are: 3–56

(1) Environmental Protection Act 1990—statutory nuisance procedure;
(2) Civic Government (Scotland) Act 1982—procedure for bringing building into a reasonable state of repair;
(3) Housing (Scotland) Act 1987—tolerable standard requirement on local authorities (according to some of the case authorities);
(4) Housing (Scotland) Act 1987—repair notices.

Environmental Protection Act 1990

Introduction to statutory nuisance procedure

Public Health inspectors were introduced on a national basis by the Public Health 3–57
Act 1867. Their role was made non-optional in the Public Health (Scotland) Act 1887. This was in due course replaced a decade later with legislation and formed the basis in Scots law for a good deal of the work carried out by the Environmental Health Department until 1996 when the relevant sections of the 1990 Act came into force. The legislation applied is now the same in England and Wales as in Scotland.

Inspection

It is the duty of every local authority to cause its area to be inspected from 3–58
time to time to detect any statutory nuisances.[38] In addition the authority must take such steps as are reasonably practicable to investigate any complaint of a statutory nuisance made to it by a person living within its area.[39]

Statutory nuisances

The following matters constitute statutory nuisances where they are prejudicial 3–59
to health or a nuisance:

(a) any premises in such a state;
(b) smoke emitted from premises;
(c) fumes or gases emitted from premises;
(d) any dust, steam, smell or other effluvia arising on industrial, trade or business premises;
(e) any accumulation or deposit;
(f) any animal kept in such a place or manner;

---

[36] Case No. 1196, *West Dunbartonshire Council* (Mar. 26, 1997), 1997 Hous.L.R. 54.
[37] For further details of this system, see Robson and Poustie, *Homeless People and the Law* (Butterworths, 1996).
[38] Environmental Protection Act 1990 (hereafter "1990 Act"), s. 79(1).
[39] *ibid.*

(g)   noise emitted from premises;
(h)   noise emitted from or caused by a vehicle, machinery or equipment in a road;
(i)   any other matter declared by any enactment to be a statutory nuisance.

This list covers both specific issues like smoke and noise nuisance as well as containing general matters. Certain kinds of smoke do not constitute nuisance—smoke emitted from a chimney of a private dwelling within a smoke control area; dark smoke emitted from certain boiler or industrial plant chimneys; smoke emitted from a railway locomotive steam engine or dark smoke emitted from industrial or trade premises.[39a] Prejudicial to health means injurious, or likely to cause injury, to health.

Entry

3–60   If the local authority or a proper officer of the authority have reasonable grounds for believing that a nuisance exists on any premises, they may demand entry and, if refused, may obtain a warrant to do so. They are also entitled to make such tests as are necessary on condition that, if no nuisance is found, they must restore the premises to their former condition.

Notice

3–61   Where a local authority is satisfied that a statutory nuisance exists or is likely to occur or recur, in the area of the authority, the local authority must serve a notice called an "abatement notice".[40] This must be served on the person responsible for the nuisance.[41] If, however, the nuisance arises from any defect of a structural character the abatement notice must be served on the owner of the premises.[42] If the person responsible for the nuisance cannot be found, notice must be served on the occupier or owner of the premises.[43]

The notice imposes all or any of the following specified requirements:

(a)   the abatement of the nuisance or prohibition or restriction of its occurrence or recurrence;
(b)   the execution of such works and the taking of such other steps as may be necessary to abate the nuisance and prevent it occurring or recurring.[44]

The abatement notice must specify the time or times within which the requirements of the notice are to be complied with, although it has been held that, in the absence of a stated time for compliance, a notice came into effect at midnight following the day of service: *Strathclyde Regional Council v. Tudhope*.[45]

Non-compliance with notice

3–62   If a person on whom an abatement notice is served without reasonable excuse contravenes, or fails to comply with any requirement or prohibition imposed by the notice, that person is guilty of an offence. They are liable on summary

---

[39a] 1990 Act, s. 79(3).
[40] *R v. Carrick D.C., ex p. Shelley* [1996] Env.L.R. 273.
[41] 1990 Act, s. 80(2)(a).
[42] *ibid.* s. 80(2)(b).
[43] *ibid.* s. 80(2)(c).
[44] *R. v. Fenny Stratford Justices, ex p. Mann (Midlands)* [1976] 1 W.L.R. 1101 at 1106.
[45] 1983 S.L.T. 22.

conviction to a fine not exceeding level 5 on the standard scale. If, however, there is a statutory nuisance committed on industrial, trade or business premises, the fine is a figure not exceeding £20,000. "Reasonable excuse" does not appear to have any specified meaning in the legislation. Lack of finance has been held not to amount to a reasonable excuse.[46]

The defence of "best practicable means" is available for certain kinds of nuisance. It covers those committed on industrial, trade or business premises rather than residential premises. It applies where the offender is able to prove that the best practicable means were used to prevent, or to counteract the effects of, the nuisance. "Practicable" means reasonably practicable having regard among other things to local conditions and circumstances, to the current state of technical knowledge and to the financial implications.[47] The test is to apply only so far as compatible with any duty imposed by the law and with safety and safe working conditions and subject to any emergency or enforceable circumstances.[48] In the case of noise nuisance, any codes of practice produced under section 71 of the Control of Pollution Act 1974 are relevant.[49]

Where an abatement notice has not been complied with the local authority 3–63 may, irrespective of whether there is a prosecution for breach, abate the nuisance and do whatever may be necessary in execution of the notice.[50] Any expenses reasonably incurred by the local authority in abating or preventing the recurrence of the nuisance may be recovered from the person by whose act or default the nuisance was caused.[51] These costs may be apportioned by the court as they consider fair and reasonable.

Failure to act by the local authority

If the local authority fail in their duty in regard to nuisances, there is a direct 3–64 means for individuals to take proceedings. This is less restrictive than the 10 ratepayers or procurator fiscal mechanisms which were available under the Public Health (Scotland) Act 1897. A person who is aggrieved by the existence of a statutory nuisance may bring a summary application before the local sheriff.[52] If the sheriff is satisfied that the alleged nuisance exists or is likely to recur, he must make an order either of abatement or prohibiting recurrence. Where any works are necessary to secure the abatement or prevent the recurrence, these shall be specified.[53]

Where the sheriff is satisfied that the alleged nuisance exists and renders the premises unfit for human habitation, there may be an order prohibiting the use of the premises for human habitation until the premises are rendered fit.[54]

---

[46] *Saddleworth UDC v. Aggregate and Sand* (1970) 114 S.J. 931.
[47] 1990 Act, s. 79(9)(a); see also *Wivenhoe Port v. Colchester B.C.* [1985] J.P.L. 175 (aff'd [1985] J.P.L. 396).
[48] 1990 Act, s. 79(9)(d).
[49] *e.g.* Control of Noise (Code of Practice for Construction Sites) (Scotland) Order 1982 (S.I. 1982 No. 601).
[50] 1990 Act, s. 81(3).
[51] *ibid.* s. 81(4).
[52] *ibid.* s. 82(1).
[53] *ibid.* s. 82(2).
[54] *ibid.* s. 82(3).

Prior to bringing proceedings before the sheriff, the aggrieved party must give a notice in respect of the nuisance, giving not less than 21 days' notice in most instances. Only three days notice is required for noise nuisance.[55]

Contravention of any requirement of prohibition is an offence punishable by a fine not exceeding level 5 together with a further fine of an amount equal to one-tenth of that level for each day the offence continues after conviction.[56]

The defence of best practicable means is available only where industrial, trade or business premises are concerned. The defence is not available where premises are rendered unfit for human habitation.[57]

3–65   The sheriff may, after conviction for an offence and hearing the local authority, direct the authority to do anything which the convicted person was required by order to do. There is also provision for compensation to the person bringing proceedings to cover their expenses.[58] Where neither the person responsible for the nuisance nor the owner or occupier of the premises can be found, the sheriff may, after giving the local authority an opportunity to be heard, direct the authority to do anything which would have been ordered against the person responsible for the nuisance.[59]

Interpretation of statutory nuisance in the courts

3–66   As there have not been many cases under the 1990 legislation, it is still helpful to refer to cases interpreting the pre-1996 law where the wording and tests are not significantly different.

3–67   **Nuisance or injurious to health**. Action may be taken in respect of dwelling-houses affected by damp or condensation or in respect of a house not served by an efficient drainage system. Premises must either be of such construction or in such a state as to be prejudicial to health or to constitute a nuisance. It would seem that it must be established that there is some danger to health, or a nuisance of the common law type (*i.e.* there is some interference with the enjoyment or use of neighbouring property), for there to be a statutory nuisance. It is not enough simply to establish that certain conditions exist without linking this to either it being prejudicial to health or it amounting to a nuisance. The same sort of link was required under the previous Public Health (Scotland) Act 1897. In one instance the court held that the fact that a house had defective windows and gutters did not mean that there was a statutory nuisance.[60] There was no evidence of prejudice to the health of the occupants and the court took the view that the word "nuisance" as used in the legislation had to be given the same meaning as it has at common law. There was therefore no nuisance in this case as the neighbours were not, of course, affected at all by these defects.[61]

3–68   There may well be difficulties in forecasting how different problems will be treated. For example, there has been a problem of interpretation regarding the treatment of inert rubbish. There is English authority under the old Public Health Act 1936 that an accumulation of inert matter such as builders' rubble will not

---

[55] 1990 Act, s. 82(7).
[56] *ibid.* s. 82(8).
[57] *ibid.* s. 82(10).
[58] *ibid.* s. 82(12).
[59] *ibid.* s. 82(13).
[60] *National Coal Board v. Thorn* [1976] 1 W.L.R. 543.
[61] See the Civic Government (Scotland) Act 1982 at paras 3–77 to 3–80, for a remedy where other bodies might be affected in due course.

amount to a statutory nuisance.[62] The Divisional Court took the view that the English Public Health Act 1936 struck at the threat of disease, vermin, etc. and not at the danger of injury to persons coming on to land by inert matter or the visual impact of such an accumulation. In *Cartwright* there had been indiscriminate tipping on a vacant unfenced plot of land of scrap iron, building materials, broken glass, tin cans and household refuse. A complaint that these amounted to a statutory nuisance was unsuccessful on appeal to the Queen's Bench Division, even though it was claimed that such a dump could encourage rodent infestation close to an infant school. It should be noted that the authority periodically removed the household refuse but left the other materials alone. However, the same view was not taken in a Scottish sheriff court case where Sheriff Kelbie decided that an accumulation of asbestos amounted to a nuisance.[63]

Application to other property used for human habitation. Previously, 3–69 impermanent structures such as any tent, van, shed, or similar structure used for human habitation which is in such a state as to be a nuisance or injurious or dangerous to health or is so overcrowded as to be injurious to the health of the inmates amounted to a nuisance liable to be dealt with summarily under the now repealed 1897 Act.[64]

For standard housing there are alternative powers available to local authorities under Part VII of the Housing (Scotland) Act 1987.

Premises and "block repairs". There is no reason why "block repairs" should 3–70 not be covered by the 1990 legislation.

There is English authority under the Public Health Act 1936 to support the proposition that a nuisance order must be used with care where the aim is to secure comprehensive repairs.[65] The Divisional Court did not rule out the possibility of "block" repairs. They felt it was possible to envisage in a block of flats a prejudice to health which is not confined to any one constituent unit in the block, and which could only be related to the entire block. In that event, providing the evidence of nuisance is sufficiently compelling, the court might well be driven to making a comprehensive order, rather than individual orders for separate premises.

Condensation dampness and nuisance

Condensation is discussed in some detail above in the context of unfitness for 3–71 human habitation.[66] There is nothing to prevent it being dealt with by way of the statutory nuisance procedure and in the past tenants have successfully used the Public Health (Scotland) Act 1897. In 1998 a campaign was mounted to clarify more precisely the nature and extent of the duty under the modified 1990 legislation.[67]

Condensation dampness occurs where the combination of available heating, insulation and ventilation is mismatched. There can be inadequacies in all three departments. Tenants have some control over two of the elements—heating

---

[62] *Coventry City Council v. Cartwright* [1975] 2 All E.R. 99.
[63] *Clydebank D.C. v. Monaville Estates,* 1982 S.L.T. (Sh.Ct.) 2.
[64] 1897 Act, s. 73.
[65] *Birmingham City D.C. v. McMahon* (1987) 86 L.G.R. 63.
[66] See paras 3–33 and 3–34.
[67] *Anderson v. Dundee City Council* — Mike Dailly of the Legal Services Agency is taking this case on behalf of SHELTER.

and ventilation—but little over insulation. The question of responsibility has become a fraught one both in Scotland and England. The question centres around how the condensation dampness is caused.

Condensation dampness accepted as a nuisance

3–72   Tenants successfully used the statutory nuisance provisions formerly available under the 1897 legislation in relation to damp houses. As with the common law test of habitability and tenantability and the implied repairs provision discussed above,[68] the problem here has revolved around who is responsible for the dampness. The Scottish Affairs Committee set the tone for the modern approach when they stated:

> "It is unreasonable to blame tenants for problems which arise because their living habits are those common in society generally, or because they cannot afford to pay for heating or because their homes are badly designed or built. Nonetheless many tenants do not appear to understand the nature of condensation as well as they might."[69]

This notion of how condensation dampness comes about through the interaction of heating ventilation and insulation was accepted in the Court of Session.[70] Lord McCluskey noted that the insulation factor is the factor which determines whether extra artificial heating is required. However, the question of responsibility was not raised in the action before him.

The need to use heating

3–73   The role of heating was raised in two cases where the English Courts laid down principles which one might well expect to be applied by Scottish courts. The Divisional Court accepted that where tenants suffered from condensation dampness, but did not use the heating provided, the condensation which resulted was partly a result of the increase of water vapour in the house caused by the tenants using paraffin or calor gas heaters. The tenants' rationale for not using the heating was that the electric underfloor system supplied was too expensive.[71] It was thus decided that there was no responsibility on the landlords where the tenants did not use the system provided.

The need to supply heating

3–74   The requirement to use heating was modified in a later similar case.[72] However, there was a distinction in that in the later case the landlords had removed the original means of heating, namely an open solid fuel fire, by blocking up the flues and had instead provided one storage heater. This was inadequate and was later removed and the tenant used three oil fires and an electric fire. Their Lordships took the view that the landlords, the Greater London Council, were responsible for the nuisance and explained that landlords were required to apply their minds to the necessity of ventilation and, if need be, to insulation and heating. Landlords had to provide a combination of these factors to make a house habitable for the tenant. However, once the landlord had provided facilities, the tenant must use them.

---

[68] At paras 3–27, 3–28 and 3–43 *et seq.*
[69] *Report on Dampness in Housing* (1984), Summary of conclusions and recommendations—cl. 11.
[70] *Renfrew D.C. v. McGourlick,* 1987 S.L.T. 538, *per* Lord McCluskey.
[71] *Dover D.C. v. Farrar* (1980) 2 H.L.R. 32.
[72] *Greater London Council v. London Borough of Tower Hamlets* (1983) 15 H.L.R. 57.

The limit to heating and ventilation

It is, however, clear from Scottish sheriff court cases that the tenant is not 3–75 expected to take wholly unreasonable action in "curing" damp by ventilation.[73] In *McArdle* it was stated that if persons were to be housed on the exposed twenty-first floor of a tower block, it would not always be practical to have windows open, particularly in inclement weather. Nor would the tenant be expected to heat the house come what may and there was a limit to the effort and money which it was reasonable to expect from a tenant to overcome a severe condensation problem.[74] Traditionally some sheriffs took the view that the problem of heating and ventilating houses rested squarely upon the tenant[75] and stated that responsibility to heat and ventilate a house clearly rested on the tenant, not on the landlord. More recent cases, culminating in the Inner House decision in *Gunn*,[76] favour the line of responsibility resting with landlords, although the concept of *volenti* may apply.[77]

Relationship between other local authority duties and statutory nuisance procedures

Whether or not a house meets the tolerable standard under the housing 3–76 legislation is quite a different matter from whether or not the premises constitute a nuisance or a danger to health under the 1990 Act.[78] In a House of Lords case the local authority had declared certain areas as clearance areas but subject to a postponement of demolition.[79] One of the occupiers brought an action against the authority for abatement of the nuisance of dampness, defective sanitary fittings, leaking roof, defective drainage, etc. This was successful. It seems that whilst these separate codes have similar goals they are to be interpreted independently of one another. Thus, while in *Salford City Council v. McNally*[80] the authority attempted to use their powers under the Housing Acts to postpone demolition of unfit housing to provide short-life accommodation, it was still open to those affected to require them to remove any statutory nuisance still remaining.

This independence is seen even more clearly in *R. v. Kerrier District Council, ex parte Guppys (Bridport) Ltd*[81] where two tenanted houses were unfit for human habitation in terms of the English housing legislation. They also constituted statutory nuisances. However, where there was an obligation on authorities to act through a closure order where they were satisfied that a house was not fit for human habitation it was not open to them to prefer the statutory nuisance procedure. The landlords had objected as the statutory nuisance procedure seemed to involve them in lesser obligations towards their tenants. The tenants, though, have no place in the decision as to which course of action the local authority must take.[82]

---

[73] *McArdle v. City of Glasgow D.C.*, 1989 S.C.L.R. 19.
[74] *Miller v. City of Glasgow D.C.* (Dec. 1, 1987) (1991) 1 S.H.L.R. 143.
[75] *e.g. McGuire v. Glasgow D.C.* (Mar. 4, 1983) (1991) 1 S.H.L.R. 1.
[76] 1992 S.C.L.R. 1018; 1997 Hous.L.R. 3.
[77] *Kearney v. Monklands D.C.*, 1997 Hous.L.R. 39.
[78] *Salford City Council v. McNally* [1976] A.C. 379.
[79] *ibid.*
[80] *ibid.*
[81] (1976) 32 P. & C.R. 411.
[82] *R v. Maldon D.C., ex p Fisher* (1986) 18 H.L.R. 197.

Civic Government (Scotland) Act 1982

Introduction

3–77   Prior to this legislation there existed local statutes which enabled local authorities to take action in the area of repairs and the same concept of a tenant making representations to the local authority applies. There was provision in local legislation regulating housing conditions for Aberdeen, Dundee, Edinburgh and Glasgow. The uniform procedure which replaced these local Acts allows local authorities to take swift action against property owners whose property is in poor condition and where this is likely to affect neighbours. Tenants who are affected may seek to have the local authority take action under this legislation.[83]

Reasonable state of repair

3–78   The local authority may give notice to the owner of any building in their area to rectify such defects as are required to bring the building into a reasonable state of repair. In determining what is a reasonable state of repair regard must be had to the age, type and location of the property.

Emergency procedure

3–79   Where it appears to the local authority to be necessary, in the interests of health or safety or to prevent damage to any property, to repair any property, they should repair immediately a building in their area and they can rectify such defects without prior notice to the owners. Under this procedure they may recover the expenses of the repair from the owner of such a building. The authority have the power to apportion the cost where there is more than one owner and they have discretion as to how this should be done. This would seem to imply that where a block of flats has been affected by an unattended problem stemming from one flat only then it would be expected that the authority would not simply divide the bill equally. However, there is no case law directly on this point.[84] Clearly, although the local authority is given discretion in the legislation, any decision would be open to challenge through judicial review on the grounds of perversity, *i.e.* it was a decision which no authority directing itself properly could have reached.[85]

Appeal

3–80   There is provision for appeal to the sheriff provided this is done within 14 days of receipt of the notice. This covers both the service of the notice as well as the cost sought by the local authority.[86–87]

Housing (Scotland) Act 1987, Pt IV

3–81   This legislation covers the "tolerable standard". There is a difference of opinion within the Scottish judiciary as to whether or not it is possible for a tenant to sue the local authority for their failure to bring a standard up to the tolerable standard.

---

[83] s. 87.
[84] *City of Edinburgh D.C. v. Gardner,* 1990 S.L.T. 600.
[85] J. St Clair and N. Davidson, *Judicial Review in Scotland* (W. Green & Son, 1986).
[86–87]   *ibid.*

Cases from the 1980s give clear authority for the view that the tolerable standard is simply a guideline for local authorities and does not allow tenants to sue for breach of that standard[88]:

> "section 14 does not impose any duty on the defenders but specifies the situation in which a duty arises under section 13 of the Act. That section imposes a duty on the defenders not as landlords of houses let by them, but as the local authority in respect of all houses in the district which do not meet the standard as defined in section 14. It has nothing to do with the standard of maintenance required of them as landlords".[89]

There is support for the alternative view that it is perfectly possible for a tenant to successfully take action for failure of the local authority to enforce the tolerable standard:[90]

> "[S]ection 13 of the 1974 Act [now Housing (Scotland) Act 1987] lays a duty upon every local authority to secure that all the houses in their district which do not meet the tolerable standard are closed, demolished or brought up to the tolerable standard within such period as is reasonable in all the circumstances. This duty is not enforceable with criminal sanctions, nor can it readily be said to have been created only for the benefit of the community which the local authority serves, as a whole. It seems to me that the duty created by the 1974 Act also laid upon the Local Authority an obligation towards each and every tenant of the houses in question."[91–92]

As sheriffs do not bind other sheriffs this makes taking action on this ground   3–82 something of a lottery at the time of writing. The practical impact is unlikely to be major given the overlapping between the matters in the common law landlord's obligation, the obligation to provide housing which is reasonably fit for human habitation, the statutory implied repairs provision and statutory nuisance. As has been pointed out, there is a strong resemblance between the issues involved in deciding what amounts to fitness for human habitation and the tolerable standard.

Housing (Scotland) Act 1987, Pt V

The 1987 Act makes provision for local authorities to serve repairs notices on   3–83 individual properties where property is in a state of serious disrepair. Local authorities have discretion as to whether they respond to complaints from the general public about alleged serious disrepair.[93] It is, however, open to any member of the public including tenants to bring such a state of affairs to the attention of the local authority with a view to a repair notice being served, although financial criteria may cause an authority to take the view that the financial costs do not justify repairs and that closure or demolition is appropriate.[94]

---

[88] *Campbell v. City of Glasgow D.C.* (Aug. 5, 1987) (1991) 1 S.H.L.R. 105; *Miller v. City of Glasgow D.C.* (Dec. 1, 1987) (1991) 1 S.H.L.R. 120; *Freeman v. City of Glasgow D.C.* (Mar. 10, 1988) (1991) 1 S.H.L.R. 175.

[89] *Campbell v. Glasgow D.C.* (1991) 1 S.H.L.R. 105, *per* Sheriff Mowat at 110.

[90] *Davis v. Edinburgh D.C.* (Apr. 30, 1984) (1991) 1 S.H.L.R. 21; *Sutherland v. City of Glasgow D.C.* (Feb. 19, 1988) (1991) 1 S.H.L.R. 142; *McEachran v. City of Glasgow D.C.* (Feb. 19, 1988) (1991) 1 S.H.L.R. 149.

[91–92] *Davis v. Edinburgh D.C.*, (1991) 1 S.H.L.R. 21, *per* Sheriff Thomson at 31.

[93] *R. v. Kerrier D.C., ex p. Guppys (Bridport) Ltd* (1976) 32 P. & C.R. 411.

[94] *R v. Maldon D.C., ex p. Fisher* (1986) 18 H.L.R. 197—note that this involved the interpretation of Pt II of the Housing Act 1957 (now Pts VI and IX of the Housing Act 1985).

Introduction

3–84   As indicated dissatisfied tenants have a range of options. They may sue under
the terms of their contract using both its express terms and its implied common
law or statutory terms. They may alternatively claim damages under the law of
reparation where fault can be established or use the Occupiers' Liability
(Scotland) Act 1960.[95-96] They may also use the statutory nuisance procedure:
this allows for the premises to be dealt with but has limited provisions as regards
recovery of sums of money.

Rights of tenants of unsatisfactory premises

3–85   Tenants who notify their landlords have various rights in the event of a failure
by the landlord to meet the standards required either by the express terms of the
lease or implied by common law or statute.[96] In general, after landlords receive
notice of the defect, they are then entitled to a reasonable time in which to
repair the defects complained of. What amounts to a reasonable time depends
on the actual existing circumstances: that is to say, a sagging ceiling will require
a swifter response than a cracked sink. Of course, there is no such thing as a
reasonable period of time in the abstract and there is precious little authority
from the private rented sector. However, where the problem clearly requires
swift action then the courts have rejected delays. In one sheriff court case[97]
there was a flooding from an unoccupied upstairs flat at 8 o'clock in the morning.
The local authority were informed immediately and a water department official
arrived at about 8.45 a.m. He telephoned the appropriate district council office
at about 9 a.m. No one arrived to deal with the leak until about 4.15 p.m. The
sheriff discussed the question of whether this was an unreasonable delay and
found it to be so, while accepting that some defects may permit longer delay
than others before negligence can be inferred. However, where the defect
involves water penetration of a dwelling-house, such defect demands prompt
attention if not immediate attention.

          As indicated, the tenant has the choice of various remedies and will need
to seek advice as to which is most feasible or suitable for the particular
situation. A major difficulty facing tenants has been how to quantify the
damage suffered (*e.g.* it may not be easy to store damaged carpeting or
produce bills for wallpaper and paint from previous decoration) although
some sheriffs have been prepared to take a "broad axe" approach to such
issues.[98]

Implement

3–86   Where the tenant is still forced to live in premises which are the subject of a
complaint, he will seek to obtain rectification of defects along with a claim for
past damage. The landlord will then be given a period of time to complete the
work. Typically in dampness cases,[99] councils have been given six months to

---

[95-96] *Scott v. City of Glasgow Council*, 1997 Hous.L.R. 107.
[97] *Bolam v. Glasgow D.C.* (Dec. 18, 1984) (1991) 1 S.H.L.R. 40.
[98] *McArdle v. Glasgow D.C.* 1989 S.C.L.R. 19.
[99] *Nugent v. City of Glasgow D.C.* (Jan. 12, 1988); (1991) 1 S.H.L.R. 132 and *McGourlick v. Renfrew D.C.*, 1982 SCOLAG 151.

sort out the condensation dampness which was the basis of the tenant's successful action. The question of how the conditions can best be remedied may be remitted to a person of skill. The 1993 Sheriff Court Rules specifically provide that a remit to a person of skill, made by joint motion or with the consent of all parties shall be final and conclusive with respect to the subject-matter of the remit.[1] One problem, identified by Sheriff Bell, was whether seeking such a remit was competent where it was opposed by the other side. In *Welsh v. City of Glasgow District Council* it was held to be incompetent in view of the opposition of the defenders to this procedure.[2]

Whilst implement tends to be an issue of competing technical views as to how best the defects can be remedied, the major legal development in this area has been the suggestion in one case that implement of obligations can be resisted by landlords on the grounds of lack of finance.[3] Sheriff Principal Caplan was of the view that the tenant had not established that the time taken by the landlord to effect repairs was unreasonable. The landlords had instigated a repair programme in 1980 for their high rise blocks following a long period of problems starting in 1967. Thus, while it would have been "practicable physically to organise the major repair affecting the (tenant's) flat a year sooner than was done" the question of whether this was not done within the "reasonable time" specified in the tenancy agreement had to be looked at in the context of the situation facing the parties. He stated that such provisions were to be construed so as to impose upon the landlord no higher an obligation than would be reasonable and that must mean having some regard to the actual situation facing the parties. In this case the pursuer had contracted with a local authority. Therefore the pursuer was aware that she was contracting with a landlord which had responsibilities to tenants other than herself, had a public duty to act fairly to all its tenants and which in the public interest had to budget for and exercise some control over its spending.

The decision is controversial. It does not sit happily with more recent authority 3–87 from the English Divisional Court in similar fields where it has been decided that a local authority could not lawfully plead lack of finance because of ratecapping as an excuse for failing to meet its statutory duty. In *Gillan*[4] the authority was providing an inadequate service for homeless people and the court was not satisfied that the shortage of money resulting from ratecapping could properly be described as an adequate excuse. Central government, however, fared somewhat better in a challenge concerning its failure to meet the statutory requirement that it deal with housing benefit claims within 14 days.[5] Which approach will dominate in the future must remain a matter for conjecture, although it would be surprising if this issue did not resurface in the courts.

Damages

The kinds of items covered include damages for loss of property (wallpaper, 3–88 furniture, carpets and clothing), lost wages and the costs of services and alternative accommodation. Typically damage to clothes, carpets and furniture

---

[1] Act of Sederurnt (Sheriff Court Ordinary Cause Rules) 1993 (S.I. 1993 No. 1956), r. 29.2.
[2] 1990 S.L.T. (Sh.Ct.) 12 at 15.
[3] *McLaughlin v. Inverclyde D.C.*, Nov. 4, 1986; (1988) 6 S.H.L.N. 25.
[4] *R. v. Camden L.B.C., ex p. Gillan, The Independent*, Oct. 13, 1988.
[5] *R. v. Secretary of State for Social Services, ex p. Child Poverty Action Group, The Times*, Feb. 15, 1988.

requires these items to be retained. Their original cost and the cost of replacement are strictly necessary to found a claim. This is not always the first thought when damp ruins a carpet. Most people do not have facilities for storing mouldy water damaged goods. The problem led to a "broad axe"[6] approach—where none of the damaged items had been retained, the figure the sheriff struck upon was based on the guesstimates of the tenants and the need to protect landlords from specious unproven claims. According to the English Court of Appeal, the items for which a tenant is entitled to claim include the cost of redecoration after the landlord has completed repairs under the implied repairs provision.[7] This principle has been accepted in Scotland at the sheriff court level.[8]

Damages for suffering (solatium)

3–89   As regards sums for suffering or *solatium* (as it is called in Scots law), the courts recognise the misery of having to live in damp and unhygienic conditions. The awards vary depending on the time and seriousness of the problem, as the case law demonstrates:

- *Gunn v. NCB,* 1982[9]—£300 for 10 months in conditions stemming from inadequately treated rising damp;
- *Gunn v. City of Glasgow District Council,* 1997[10]—£400 for one year's loss, damage and inconvenience in a flat with condensation dampness and rainwater penetration between April 1984 and March 1985;
- *McArdle v. City of Glasgow City Council,* 1989[11]—£750 for about five years' insect infestation and dampness which the landlords failed to treat effectively;
- *Campbell v. City of Glasgow District Council,* August 5, 1987[12]— £1,000 for persistent mould for a period of more than 10 years but including in the final two years seepage from a waste pipe;
- *Miller v. City of Glasgow District Council,* December 1, 1987[13]— £1,500 for three years of severe condensation dampness (after receiving *ex gratia* dampness payments for pre-1981 dampness);
- *McEachran v. City of Glasgow City Council,* February 19, 1988[14]— £1,950 for three years of dampness from water penetration through roof and gutters;
- *Sutherland v. City of Glasgow District Council,* February 19, 1988[15]— £1,500 for a family's inconvenience from condensation damp over a three-year period;
- *Tosh v. City of Glasgow District Council,* August 23, 1990[16]—£2,400 for inconvenience from rising damp over six-year period;

---

[6] *McArdle v. City of Glasgow D.C.,* 1989 S.C.L.R. 19, *per* Sheriff Jardine.
[7] *McGreal v. Wake* (1984) 13 H.L.R. 107; *Bradley v. Chorley B.C.* (1985) 17 H.L.R. 305.
[8] *Little v. City of Glasgow D.C.,* Glasgow Sh. Ct., May 12, 1988; (1991) 1 S.H.L.R. 195 and *McCarthy v. City of Glasgow D.C.,* Glasgow Sh. Ct., April 29, 1988; (1991) 1 S.H.L.R. 181.
[9] 1982 S.L.T. 526.
[10] 1997 Hous.L.R. 3.
[11] 1989 S.C.L.R. 19.
[12] (1991) 1 S.H.L.R. 105.
[13] (1991) 1 S.H.L.R. 120.
[14] (1991) 1 S.H.L.R. 149.
[15] (1991) 1 S.H.L.R. 142.
[16] (1991) 1 S.H.L.R. 222.

- *Morrison v. Stirling District Council,* February 13, 1991[17]—£10,000 for wife (50) and £3,000 for daughter (13) where dampness in house was a material factor in bringing about death of husband;
- *Quinn v. Monklands District Council,* December 1994[18]—£2,500 for inconvenience and general depression, aggravated by three years living with condensation dampness—worse in the winter months;
- *Burns v. Monklands District Council,* 1997[19]—£500 solatium for each year of living in flat with condensation dampness between February 1992 and August 1995—£1,600 in total;
- *McGuire v. Monklands District Council,* 1997[20]—dampness from March 1991 to September 1995—solatium at £500 per year totalling £2,250;
- *Kearney v. Monklands District Council,* 1997[21]—solatium for condensation dampness from March 1989 to June 30, 1994 totalling £3,200; £700 for year from June 1994 to 1995 subject to 60 per cent reduction for failing to mitigate loss by accepting landlord's offer to dry-line walls.

Refusal or renunciation of lease

This was a technique more widely practised in nineteenth-century cases, where   3–90 some 90 per cent of housing was rental housing and where it was relatively easy for the better-off tenants to obtain fresh rental accommodation.[22] However, more recently where commercial premises were destroyed, the Court of Session[23] confirmed the old rule that destruction of the premises ends the lease.[24] Given the obligation to rebuild included in most feus this principal is of doubtful applicability.

Withholding rent

This operates in two ways. First, it is recognised as an acceptable lever to   3–91 force landlords to respond to complaints. In such a situation the rent becomes payable when the defect is dealt with. This was graphically illustrated in a case where a tenant withheld £1,439.61 of rent over a two-year period because the house he rented suffered from severe damp and the district council's remedial measures were ineffective.[25] Withholding rent needs to be distinguished from a counterclaim where the tenant refuses to pay rent because of the problems and formally meets a claim for rent with a claim for damages. For example, this occurred[26] where a district council sued for an action for recovery of possession for non-payment of rent amounting to £1,600. The tenant raised an action for £1,000 for loss and damage suffered as a result of occupation of the damp and frequently flooded house, with blocked drains. The landlords did not obtain possession and the tenant was awarded the full amount of £1,000 permitted under the summary cause procedure in operation at that time.

---

[17] (1991) 1 S.H.L.R. 246.
[18] 1996 Hous.L.R. 86.
[19] 1997 Hous.L.R. 34.
[20] 1997 Hous.L.R. 41.
[21] 1997 Hous.L.R. 39.
[22] *McKimmies Trustees v. Armour* (1899) 2 F. 156; *Scottish Heritable Security Co. v. Granger* (1881) 8 R. 459.
[23] *Cantors Properties (Scotland) Ltd v. Swears and Wells,* 1980 S.L.T. 165.
[24] *Allan v. Markland* (1882) 10 R. 383.
[25] *City of Glasgow D.C. v. McCrone,* Jan. 3, 1985; (1991) 1 S.H.L.R. 54.
[26] *Davis v. Edinburgh D.C.,* Apr. 30, 1984; (1991) 1 S.H.L.R. 26.

There is some evidence that the introduction of the Small Claims procedure has led to cases being raised by tenants[27] and this also occurs in the English system.[28]

The statutory scheme for small repairs

Introduction

3–92   New rights were introduced for secure tenants only as from October 1, 1994 in relation to minor repairs.[29] The legislation entitles secure tenants of prescribed landlords[30] to have qualifying repairs carried out to the house. There is also provision for housing associations to operate a parallel voluntary scheme on the same lines. Regulations prescribe the maximum amount which will be paid in respect of a qualifying repair.[31] The regulations provide that only certain repairs below a specified financial ceiling are covered. The current ceiling is £250.[32] The regulations lay down the following matters:

    (a) qualifying repairs;
    (b) approved contractor;
    (c) procedure;
    (d) time-limit;
    (e) access;
    (f) compensation.

Qualifying repairs

3–93   The regulations lay down the following matters as being qualifying repairs[33]:

One-week repairs
- blocked flue to open fire or boiler;
- blocked or leaking foul drains, soil stacks or toilet pans where there is no other toilet in the house;
- blocked sink, bath or basin;
- loss of electric power (total);
- insecure external window, door or lock;
- leaks or flooding from water or heating pipes, tanks or cisterns;
- loss of gas supply (total or partial);
- loss of space or water heating where no alternative heating is available (total or partial);
- toilet not flushing where there is no other toilet in the house;
- unsafe power or lighting socket or electrical fitting;
- loss of water supply (total);

Three-week repairs
- loss of water supply (partial);
- loose or detached banister or hand rail;

---

[27] *Small Claims* (1990) 10 S.H.L.N. 15 ; Strathclyde University/Dundee University, Report for Scottish Office, 1991.
[28] *Joyce v. Liverpool City Council* (1995) 27 H.L.R. 548.
[29] Leasehold Reform, Housing and Urban Development Act 1993, s. 146.
[30] Secure Tenants (Right to Repair) (Scotland) Regulations 1994 (S.I. 1994 No. 1046), reg. 4 Scottish Homes and councils.
[31] Secure Tenants (Right to Repair) (Scotland) Regulations 1994.
[32] *ibid.* reg. 3(2).
[33] *ibid.* reg. 5 and Sched., col. 1.

- unsafe timber flooring or stair treads;
- loss of electric power (partial);

Seven-week repairs
- mechanical extractor fan in internal kitchen or bathroom not working.

Approved contractor

A list must be maintained by the landlord of contractors who are prepared to 3–94 carry out qualifying repairs including the usual contractor.[34] Secure tenants must be made aware of these regulations and the landlord must provide written details once a year of same along with a list of contractors prepared to carry out qualifying repairs.[35]

Procedure

Finally, where the tenant makes an application for prescribed repairs the 3–95 landlord must respond by either visiting the property forthwith to ascertain if the repair is a qualifying repair or indicate whether the repair is a qualifying repair.

Where the landlord accepts that the repair is covered by the scheme the tenant must be told the maximum time within which the repair is to be completed, the last day of the maximum time, arrangements for access and details of at least one other listed contractor. If the matter is a qualifying repair then a works order must be issued to the usual contractor. This must specify the nature of the repair, the maximum time within which the repair is to be completed and the last day of the maximum time as well as the arrangements for access.[36]

Where the usual contractor has not started the qualifying repair by the last day of the maximum time the secure tenant may instruct another listed contractor to carry out the qualifying repair.[37] This contractor must in due course inform the landlord of his instructions and is entitled, on request, to a copy of the works order from the landlord[38] as well as an indication of the number of working days in the maximum time.

Time-limits

The aim of the scheme is to improve the service delivery to tenants from 3–96 public sector landlords. To this end the regulations specify a range of time-limits between one week and seven weeks.[39] The maximum time starts on the first working day after the date of receipt of notification of the repair to the landlord or date of inspection by the landlord where the landlord decides that it is necessary to inspect to decide whether the complained of matter is indeed a qualifying repair.[40]

The running of the maximum time is to be suspended for so long as there are circumstances of an exceptional nature, beyond the control of the landlord or

---

[34] Secure Tenants (Right to Repair) (Scotland) Regulations 1994 (S.I. 1994 No. 1046), reg. 6.
[35] *ibid.* reg. 13.
[36] *ibid.* reg. 7.
[37] Provided that no guarantee for work done or materials supplied available to the landlord is infringed — *ibid.* reg 10(4).
[38] *ibid.* reg. 10.
[39] reg. 9 and col. 2 of Sched.
[40] Where the landlord considers it necessary to inspect the house to ascertain whether the repair is indeed a qualifying repair: reg. 7 (a).

the contractor carrying out the repair, and these prevent the repair being carried out. This power to suspend appears to lie with the landlord as the landlord must inform the secure tenant where the running of the maximum time is suspended.[41]

Access

3–97   Where the tenant fails to give access, either to allow the landlord to decide if the matter complained of is a qualifying repair or to carry out an agreed repair then the application of the regulations ceases to apply.

Compensation

3–98   Where the usual contractor has failed to carry out the qualifying repair by the last day of the maximum time the landlord must pay the secure tenant a sum of compensation. This is a sum between £10 and £50. A basic sum of £10 is payable plus £2 for every working day in excess of the original maximum specified time.[42] One issue which has emerged has been the practice of some landlords to leave the question of claiming to tenants rather than automatically to instruct payment or at least the sending out of claim forms where they have knowledge that the time-limits have not been met.

9. RESTRICTIONS ON RIGHTS OF TENANTS

3–99   There are a number of limitations on what may be obtained by the tenant depending on how the tenant and landlord act in relation to defects. It should be noted that some of these exceptions do not seem to be in accord with the spirit of increased statutory protection for tenants in the twentieth century but they have not been abolished and they may be still be accepted by the courts.[43]

Voluntary acceptance of the risk

Background

3–100   This doctrine which is found in Scots law is sometimes known by the Latin brocard *volenti non fit injuria*. The defence may, under certain circumstances, be open to a landlord whose tenant is injured as a result of a defect which is not attended to. In effect where the landlord does not carry out his duty to repair after due notice of defect then the tenant must after a reasonable time leave the premises. If tenants stay they accept the risks of injury and so, although the landlord is initially in breach, the tenants, by staying, have taken the risk upon themselves unless they receive either assurances of safety or promises of repair.

Full knowledge of the risk

3–101   Where the tenant remains in occupation of the subjects in full knowledge of the defect any injury sustained as a result of the defect will be the tenant's own responsibility as where a tenant took possession of a house at Whitsunday which had steps leading up to it. These were worn. She remained in the house for nine

---

[41] reg. 12.
[42] reg. 11.
[43] *Steel v. Ramage,* Dunoon Sh. Ct., Feb. 1992—discussed at paras 3–102 and 3–105. For a modern overview, see *Neilson v. Scottish Homes*, 1988 Hous.L.R. 52.

months with the stairs in this worn state although she complained to the landlord's factor. By staying, the Court considered that this was tacit acceptance of the risk of injury and her remedy was, "after a reasonable time", to abandon the lease and seek to bring an action of damages for inconvenience against the landlord.[44]

This general principle was reaffirmed reluctantly in 1961 by Lord Kilbrandon[45] where the tenant died after falling on a defective common stair leading to his flat. He was held to have voluntarily accepted the risk as he did not move after his complaints to his landlord failed to achieve any repairs after his wife injured her ankle on the worn stairs. The judge accepted that the doctrine of *volenti* might seem "socially unrealistic" but said that nevertheless it was still the law in the twentieth century.[46]

In a subsequent housing case in the sheriff court where the defence of 3–102 voluntary acceptance of a risk was put forward the sheriff was able to avoid the implications of following *Webster*. Here the tenant sued in terms of reparation rather than contract and the need for the landlord to provide premises free from danger in terms of the Occupiers' Liability (Scotland) Act 1960 was met with a *volenti* claim. However, Sheriff Gordon limited the application of the defence.[47] where a young girl aged two caught her hand in a toilet bowl which was broken when her parents took the tenancy. Its state was communicated in writing to the landlords who had not attended to the repair two years later when the accident occurred. The sheriff explained that he accepted that there was a specific known risk, but that the landlords had not shown that in all the circumstances the tenant "willingly" accepted the danger.

In 1992, however, a tenant who suffered from windows which were not weatherproof and a defective chimney had her damages reduced because of the application of the *volenti* doctrine by the sheriff.[48] Also, as has been noted above, damages have been reduced under contributory negligence where the tenant refused to allow the landlord to take further remedial work.[49]

Landlord's promises/assurances

Where the landlord has given an assurance that the repairs will be carried out 3–103 at once, again the landlord cannot plead *volenti* as where the pursuer complained about a ceiling which was cracked and the landlord agreed to repair this in February. Despite frequent repetition of the complaint nothing was done until the ceiling fell injuring the tenant in November. The landlord was bound by his undertaking to repair the defect and was liable for damages.[50]

Where the premises are declared safe by the landlord, particularly where a degree of skill in judgment is required to assess danger, then the landlord may not plead *volenti* against a tenant who remains on his assurance of safety—for example, where there was a cracked ceiling which the landlord assured the tenants was safe and which subsequently fell injuring the tenant and family.[51a] It is unreasonable to expect tenants to appreciate the danger of some item like a

---

[44] *Webster v. Brown* (1892) 19 R. 765.
[45] *Proctor v. Cowlairs Co-operative Society,* 1961 S.L.T. 434.
[46] *ibid.* at 435.
[47] *Hughes' Tutrix v. Glasgow D.C.,* 1982 S.L.T. (Sh.Ct.) 70.
[48] *Steel v. Ramage,* Dunoon Sh. Ct., *per* Sheriff J. Irvine Smith.
[49] *Kearney v. Monklands D.C.,* 1997 Hous.L.R. 39.
[50] *Shields v. Dalziel* (1897) 24 R. 849.
[51a] *Caldwell v. McCallum* (1901) 4 F. 371.

ceiling though more obvious dangers such as worn stairs might still allow in *volenti* as requiring less expertise and being more a common sense issue.[51]

3–104   Two cases illustrate the difference between where a landlord makes a clear promise and the danger is not obvious and where the tenant should have appreciated that the defect was potentially dangerous and avoided using that part of the premises or quit the premises. In the first case[52] the tenant was injured when she caught her foot in a hole in the wash-house floor. She could have avoided this danger, the court felt, and had received no assurances about its repair. However, noting the proverb that "a creechy door hangs long",[53] Lord President Inglis and the First Division of the Court of Session accepted that it was reasonable for the tenant to continue to use a wooden staircase which had become loose where the landlords had assured her it would be fixed.

Defect obvious at the time of commencement of lease

3–105   Where the tenant is injured because of some defect which was patently obvious to any tenant then this will preclude or prevent a claim against the landlord in the event of subsequent injury arising therefrom. Thus, where a child fell through a railing on the common stair it was held that the injury was a result not of the landlord's negligence but of the design and construction of the building. Accordingly the tenant had the opportunity both to observe and complain about this and his action of damages failed.[54] Similarly, where a child was burned to death as a result of a low-slung gas lamp on a stair setting fire to her nightdress it was held that this danger was one which the tenant had accepted and was not caused by any act of negligence by the landlord.[55] These cases illustrate a variation on *volenti non fit injuria*. Here, although the tenants are not being provided with safe and tenantable premises, this is "obvious" at the beginning of the tenancy. The effect is to dissolve the landlord's duty. The Courts take the view that the landlord is not "in the position of an insurer of the safety of his tenant".[56]

This is not to say that it may not be possible to sue in terms of reparation. The question here revolves around reasonable foreseeability. In addition, whilst the defences of voluntary acceptance and contributory negligence are still available to landlords it is a matter of some doubt whether the courts would want to apply these socially harsh doctrines today. Professor T. B. Smith suggested in 1955 that this was unlikely.[57] Despite the setback in *Proctor*, he retained the same view in 1962.[58] The limitation on *volenti* was taken up by Sheriff Gordon in *Hughes' Tutrix*[59] but the concept was approved by Sheriff Irvine Smith in *Steel v. Ramage*[60] and in *Kearney v. Monklands District Council*.[60a]

---

[51] *Caldwell v. McCallum* (1901) 4 F. 371.

[52] *McManus v. Armour* (1901) 3 F. 1078.

[53] *Mullen v. Dunbarton County Council*, 1933 S.C. 380.

[54] *Mechan v. Watson*, 1907 S.C. 25.

[55] *Davidson v. Sprengel*, 1909 S.C. 566.

[56] For a full discussion of these defences as they developed between 1850 and 1915, see Peter Robson, *Housing and the Judiciary* (1979, University of Strathclyde).

[57] T.B. Smith, *The United Kingdom: The development of its laws and constitution—Scotland* (Stevens, 1955), p. 1093.

[58] T.B. Smith, *United Kingdom: The development of its laws and constitution—Scotland* (Stevens, 1962), p. 705.

[59] 1982 S.L.T. (Sh.Ct.) 70.

[60] Duworn Sh.Ct, Feb. 1992.

[60a] 1997 Hous.L.R. 39.

Natural disaster

Where there is a pure accident, although as we have seen the tenant may 3–106
claim an abatement of rent for loss of possession or even abandon the lease
where there is total or constructive total loss, the landlord is not liable for damages
for the destruction. Landlords are not to blame for an "Act of God" and, as they
have no control over such things as storms, explosions and so on, no liability
attaches. They are not obliged to repair or rebuild at common law.

Tenant's own negligence

There will be no claim if the defect is itself due to the tenant's own negligence, 3–107
as where a tenant left property unoccupied for a month during the winter without
turning off the water and draining the cisterns.[61] In the past decade this has been
encountered most frequently in the defence of landlords to claims involving
condensation dampness. Although there were instances in the early 1980s where
the courts stated that tenants' lifestyles meant that they should receive no
damages, this line has generally been displaced by more recent authorities.[61a]
The more recent approaches seem to suggest that there is a limit to the effort
and money which it is reasonable to expect a tenant to expend to overcome a
severe condensation problem.[62]

Actions of third parties

The landlord will not be responsible where a defect arises from third party 3–108
actings — for example, where as a result of careless use of the drains a drainage
system becomes blocked and the resultant overflow damages the tenant's
property.[63] Where the landlord has failed to take reasonable steps to limit the
likelihood of the effects of vandalism there may be liability under delict.[64] The
position is, however, less than clear.[65] In addition, if the express terms of the
lease require tenants only to repair damage which they personally cause, this
does not mean they are liable for the actions of vandals.[66]

---

[61] *Mickel v. McCoarsl*, 1913 S.C. 896.
[61a] Contrast *McGuire v. Glasgow D.C.*, Mar. 4, 1983; (1991) 1 S.H.L.R. 1; *City of Glasgow D.C. v. McShane,* Sep. 5, 1985; (1991) 1 S.H.L.R. 64 and *Nicol v. Glasgow D.C.*, Nov. 30, 1990; (1991) 1 S.H.L.R. 269 with *Barrie v. Glasgow D.C.*, Oct. 31, 1986; (1991) 1 S.H.L.R. 98; *Sutherland v. City of Glasgow D.C.*, Feb. 19, 1988; (1991) 1 S.H.L.R. 168 and *Miller v. City of Glasgow D.C.,* Dec. 1, 1987; (1991) 1 S.H.L.R. 143.
[62] *Gunn v. City of Glasgow D.C.*, IH, July 31, 1992, *per* Lord Morison.
[63] *NB Storage Co. v. Steele's Trs*, 1920 S.C. 194.
[64] *Maloco v. Littlewoods Organisation,* 1987 S.L.T. 425.
[65] Contrast *Davis v. Edinburgh D.C.*, (1989) 1 S.H.L.R. 26 at 33, *Evans v. Glasgow D.C.*, 1978 S.L.T. 17 and *King v. Liverpool City Council* [1986] 3 All E.R. 544.
[66] *Hastie v. Edinburgh D.C.*, 1981 S.L.T. (Sh.Ct.) 92; *Edinburgh D.C. v. Laurie,* 1982 S.L.T. (Sh.Ct.) 83.

CHAPTER 4

RENTS

1. BACKGROUND

4–01 Rent, as has been noted, is one of the requirements for the existence of a tenancy. Landlords and tenants were able to negotiate freely in the market over the level of rent. Inability to pay the contracted rent could result in eviction. There was no defence on the grounds that the tenants had nowhere else to go or that circumstances beyond their control resulted in non-payment. There have, however, been controls over what landlords may charge their tenants since the first Rent Act legislation introduced in 1915. This was introduced directly as a response to profiteering by landlords during wartime. The notion of landlords being able to make a profit out of a human necessity is one which those on the political left have had difficulty in coming to terms with.[1] The responses have ranged from providing an alternative through municipal housing charging affordable rents to encouraging ownership of property. The problem of what to do with private rented housing has been chronic. Solutions have included the prevention of price exploitation through control, the orderly run-down of existing renting as well as municipalisation. The most recent shifts back to setting rents through the mechanism of the market recognise that widespread removal of protection to existing tenants would be likely to produce serious social stress and so existing tenants' rights are not affected by the new system introduced in the Housing (Scotland) Act 1988. This means that several regimes co-exist and the position as to what rent may be charged will depend on what kind of tenancy there is.

Although the likelihood of intervention is much limited under the Housing (Scotland) Act 1988, such tenancies form the majority of tenancies likely to be encountered in practice. It is, however, crucial to bear in mind that older tenancies continue to exist and there is also a discussion of the rules affecting them later in this chapter.[2]

2. ASSURED TENANCIES

Introduction

4–02 The central feature of the regime introduced by the Housing (Scotland) Act 1988 is that there is a minimal role for intervention in the contract entered into between the parties. The parties are assumed to have agreed to a rent which

---

[1] "The plain fact is that rented housing is not a proper field for private profit": Harold Wilson in a speech to Leeds Labour Party, Feb. 9, 1964.
[2] See para. 4–45.

suits both parties. This position has its roots in the personal subsidy available for individual tenants through rent allowances and housing benefit since 1972 rather than through restricting returns on classes of property.

Provision for Involvement of the Rent Assessment Committee

The Housing (Scotland) Act 1988 makes provision for the determination of a market rent by the Rent Assessment Committee where there is a statutory assured tenancy after a contractual tenancy has been terminated.[3] There is no equivalent of the application *during* the tenancy on the grounds that the rent is too high as is found in protected tenancies[4] or short assured tenancies.[5]   4–03

Declining Jurisdiction

Rent Assessment Committees have declined jurisdiction to look at the rent in a variety of situations: 4–04

- where a contractual tenancy exists and the landlord has taken no steps to bring this to an end[6];
- where there has been a purported notice to quit served but this is defective in its form. Typically this occurs where the landlord fails to enclose the information prescribed by statutory instrument[7] and as required by the statute informing tenants of their rights[8];
- where the minimum period of notice provided in the notice is not given[9];
- where the tenancy cannot be within the 1988 regime as it is a regulated tenancy created prior to January 2, 1989[10];
- where the tenancy agreement includes a rent increase provision which complies with section 24(5), avoiding the use of section 25.[11]

Non-jurisdiction

Rather more controversially, a Certificate of Non-jurisdiction has been issued where the tenancy agreement copied to the Committee has not met the requirements of section 30 of the Act that the lease document be properly drawn up and executed. Whilst protection of tenants' rights is to be welcomed, it should be noted that there is a separate remedy available to the tenant where the landlord has failed to draw up a document reflecting the terms of the tenancy.[12] On   4–05

---

[3] 1988 Act, s. 24.

[4] Rent (Scotland) Act 1984, s. 46.

[5] Housing (Scotland) Act 1988, s. 34.

[6] The issue is discussed at some length in a Statement of Reasons in respect of 10 Main Street, Dalmeny Village, dated July 16, 1993; see also Certificates of Non-Jurisdiction in respect of Rooms B and C, 75/2 Bangor Road, Edinburgh, dated Oct. 21, 1993; Certificates of Non-jurisdiction in respect of 3 and 4 Crown Terrace, Glasgow, dated Jan. 25, 1994.

[7] Assured Tenancies (Notices to Quit Prescribed Information) (Scotland) Regulations 1988 (S.I. 1988 No. 2062), reg. 2.

[8] Certificate of Non-jurisdiction in respect of the Stables Cottage, Culross, dated Nov. 26, 1993.

[9] Certificate of Non-jurisdiction in respect of 196 Castlemilk Road, Glasgow, dated Nov. 12, 1993.

[10] Certificate of Non-jurisdiction in respect of 1 Hilltown Terrace, Dalkeith, dated Aug. 30, 1993.

[11] Certificate of Non-jurisdiction in respect of 28 First Street, Newtongrange, dated Aug. 30, 1993.

[12] Housing (Scotland) Act 1988, s. 30(2). (Subsequent references refer to the 1988 Act unless otherwise indicated.)

summary application by a tenant the sheriff must draw up such a document and, where this is done, it is deemed to have been duly executed by the parties.[13]

Role of the Rent Assessment Committee (RAC)

4–06   There is a range of distinct roles for the Rent Assessment Committee under the assured tenancy regime. However, under the 1988 legislation they are the first port of call rather than providing an additional layer beyond the Rent Officer, as under the Rent (Scotland) Act 1984.

Fixing the terms of statutory assured tenancies by RACs

4–07   Where an assured tenant relies on the rights of security of tenure[14] and remains in the property after the original contract has been terminated, then provision is made for the adjustment both of the terms of rent and of terms other than rent.[15] If there is no rent increase mechanism then, where the tenancy reaches its termination date and there is no notice to quit, the whole tenancy relocates including the original rent. The landlord, therefore, must formally serve a notice to quit to bring the tenancy to an end and a statutory assured tenancy is created. Not later than the first anniversary of the termination of the former tenancy the landlord may serve a notice of variation of terms on the tenant. The variation may not affect specific rights given in the Act covering the prohibition on assignation without consent[16] and the requirement that there be access for repairs.[17] The right to have the RAC involved can be exercised by either landlord or tenant on the termination of an assured tenancy. Either landlord or tenant may serve a notice on the other party proposing new conditions for the tenancy other than those relating to rent. They may also propose new rental terms to take account of the changes in the conditions.[18] Any proposed changes must be served in the form prescribed by the Secretary of State[19]—Form AT1(L) for landlords and Form AT1(T) for tenants. The forms detail the proposed changes and draw the attention of the recipients to their rights to have the proposals referred to a rent assessment committee.[20]

Referral to the Rent Assessment Committee

4–08   Where a notice is duly served, the recipient—whether landlord or tenant—has three months from the date of service to refer this proposal to the RAC. If there is no referral to a rent assessment committee then the terms proposed become the terms of the agreement.[21] The reference to the rent assessment committee must also be in the prescribed form—Form AT3(T) for references by tenants and Form AT3(L) for references by landlords.[22]

---

[13] s. 30(2)(b).
[14] s. 16.
[15] ss. 17, 24 and 25 .
[16] s. 23.
[17] s. 26.
[18] s. 17(2)(b).
[19] Assured Tenancies (Forms) (Scotland) Regulations 1988 (S.I. 1988 No. 2109).
[20] s. 17(3)(a).
[21] s. 17(3)(b).
[22] Assured Tenancies (Forms) (Scotland) Regulations 1988 (S.I. 1988 No. 2109).

General framework for RAC work on assured tenancies

In the event of a reference to the RAC their task is to assess the proposal in   4–09
terms of what might reasonably be expected to be found in a contractual assured
tenancy granted by a willing landlord to a willing tenant. The date is to be for an
agreement commenced at the same time as the newly extended tenancy. The
task of the RAC is not simply passive as they may put forward and approve
terms other than those proposed, provided these deal with the same subject-
matter as the changes in the notice.[23] The Rent Assessment Committee have
discretion to adjust the rent where they approve proposals to change the tenancy
conditions. This includes changes proposed by the committee themselves.[24] In
their deliberation on the proposed new rent, the RAC must ignore the fact that
the tenant is a sitting tenant.[25]

The terms set by the RAC are to apply to the tenancy and the rent shall be
that set by the committee. However, there is provision for the parties to agree
otherwise.[26] Any rent figure determined by the RAC is not to be backdated
beyond the date when the notice was referred to the committee.[27] Rent is defined
as including any sums payable for the use of furniture or services whether or
not these sums are separated out from the sum payable for the occupation of the
premises or are payable under separate agreements. [28]

Withdrawal of reference

The RAC do not have to carry on and make a determination if the tenancy is   4–10
brought to an end by a possession order or if the landlord and tenant give written
notice that they no longer require the rent fixing.[29] The Rent Registers in Glasgow
and Edinburgh show that in almost a quarter of instances in Scotland an initial
reference has been withdrawn.

Determining rent where no provision has been made for increase in the rent agreement

The underlying principle behind the Housing (Scotland) Act 1988 is an attempt   4–11
to revive the private rented housing sector by allowing market forces to operate.
Rents are to be fixed in the market by what landlords are able to charge to
willing tenants. If a landlord, however, fixes a rent for a tenancy and fails to
make provision for a rent increase, then the RAC cannot be used until that
tenancy reaches its end. A general reference to the rent being reviewed will not
be enough to allow the RAC to exercise jurisdiction.[30] However, in certain
specified circumstances there is provision for the RAC to have a role.

Rent increase proposals

Tenancies have a finite life. As noted, if there is no rent increase mechanism   4–12
then where the tenancy reaches its termination date and there is no notice to

---

[23] s. 17(4).
[24] s. 17(5).
[25] s. 17(6).
[26] s. 17(7).
[27] s. 17(7)(b).
[28] s. 25(3).
[29] s. 17(8).
[30] The issue is discussed at some length in a Statement of Reasons in respect of 10 Main Street, Dalmeny Village, dated July 16, 1993.

quit, the whole tenancy relocates including the original rent. However, where the negotiated rent period comes to an end and the landlord seeks to increase the rent, the RAC may be involved in making a determination of the rent.[31] This includes referrals by tenants. A landlord seeking an increase of rent at this time must serve a notice on the tenant in the form prescribed by the Secretary of State as well as an NTQ preventing tacit relocation. Tenants cannot initiate the referral procedures themselves, as they can under the fair rent system. It is assumed that they find the initial rent level acceptable. The fact that the rent level may not be accepted by the local authority for housing benefit purposes was drawn to the Government's attention but was not regarded as a problem.[32]

Where a landlord wishes to secure a rent increase a notice must be served on the tenant in the form prescribed by the Secretary of State[33]—Form AT2. The rent increase cannot take effect until a minimum period of time passes after this notice.[34] The minimum period of time is six months where the assured tenancy is for six months or more—for tenancies of less than six months the minimum period is the length of the tenancy or a month, whichever is the longer.[35]

Preventing the proposed increase

4–13   The advisory notes to Form AT4 which tenants will need to fill in when considering referring an increase to a rent assessment committee suggest that tenants might find it helpful to discuss the matter with the landlord before going ahead. Where there are joint tenants all will need to be party to the referral or new agreement. Where there has already been either an increase or a RAC determination and there is a new notice of increase, the proposed new rent takes effect no earlier than one year from the date of the previous increase or RAC determination.[36]

There are three situations which can prevent the increase going ahead as proposed.[37]

4–14   **Referral to RAC by tenant.** The tenant can refer the notice to a RAC by returning Form AT4. There is no specific time-limit mentioned in the section other than the need to refer to the RAC before the date on which the new rent is due to take effect.

4–15   **Agreement on increase.** The landlord and tenant can agree to a change in the rent different from that in the notice.

4–16   **Agreement on no change.** The landlord and tenant may agree that there should be no change in the rent.

Determination of rent by RAC

Criteria for fixing the rent

4–17   Where a tenant refers a notice of increase to a RAC they must fix a rent which they consider the house would let for in the open market by a willing

[31] s. 24.
[32] *Hansard*, H.C., First Scottish Standing Committee, col. 728, February 16, 1988.
[33] Assured Tenancies (Forms) (Scotland) Regulations 1988 (S.I. 1988 No. 2109).
[34] s. 24(1).
[35] s. 24(2).
[36] s. 24(4).
[37] s. 24(3).

landlord.[38] There are no detailed criteria as found in the fair rent formula. Relevant issues could include the capital value of the property, the extent of past and likely capital appreciation, levels of alternative investments and their capital growth potential. In addition, the state of repair of the property and its age, character and locality should provide guidance as to what constitutes a reasonable rent in relation to the property in question. The expected body of rents has failed to materialise in any meaningful way.

Assumptions

The RAC are to make certain assumptions.[39]   4–18

Period of cover. It is to be assumed that the determination covers the period   4–19
when the notice is to take effect.

Conditions. It is further to be assumed that the non-rent conditions are   4–20
unchanged.

Notice. Where relevant, the RAC are to assume that the appropriate notice has   4–21
been given to bring into effect the mandatory grounds 1 to 5 of Schedule 5
(landlord's former only or principal home; property subject to pre-tenancy
mortgage; off-season holiday let; non-student letting by approved educational
institution of student accommodation; minister or full-time lay missionary
occupancy).

Disregards

The RAC are also to disregard the effect of certain factors.[40]   4–22

Sitting tenant. The RAC are to disregard the fact that a tenancy was granted to   4–23
an individual who was already a sitting tenant. The effect of giving up rights in an
existing regulated tenancy in exchange for the benefits of a sub-market rent
might initially appeal to a tenant. The difficulty is that this advantage would be
short-lived as the RAC would not be allowed to take that factor into account
and the tenant would not be protected from the impact of market forces. Given
the effective bargaining power of landlords in situations of inadequate supply
of housing such forms of "winkling" can easily be imagined, although this has
not been reported as an issue by housing advisers.

Voluntary improvements. The tenant's "voluntary" improvements are not to   4–24
be counted against tenants in their rent although repairs would not be relevant.
If tenants have expended money on improving the landlord's property they are
not expected to pay for the privilege. A similar feature is found in the Rent
(Scotland) Act 1984.[41] The question of where repair ends and improvement
starts is a complex issue.[42]

---

[38] s. 25.
[39] s. 25(1).
[40] s. 25(2).
[41] s. 48 (3)(b).
[42] *Stewart's J.F. v. Gallagher* 1967 S.C. 59; *ACT Construction Ltd v. Customs and Excise Commissioners* [1981] 1 All E.R. 324; *Quick v. Taff Ely B.C.* [1985] 3 All E.R. 321 and other cases noted at para. 3–04 *et seq*.

4–25 **Damage or harm**. Tenant's damage or harm to the landlord's property is not to be taken into account in the rent-fixing process. This is the mirror of the previous issue. Just as tenants do not have to pay for their improvements, so it is reasonable that they should not benefit from their misdeeds. If tenants have caused the property to deteriorate they cannot expect to obtain a lower rent as a result of their failing to abide by the conditions of the tenancy. Again, this has an equivalent in the Rent (Scotland) Act 1984.[43] It should also be noted that such actions might well amount to grounds for eviction.[44]

4–26 **Rates**. The fact that rates are paid by the landlord is to be ignored. This issue was of only passing interest with the replacement of rates for heritable property with the poll tax under the Abolition of Domestic Rates Etc. (Scotland) Act 1987. With the introduction of the council tax an amendment has been made to the legislation.[44a]

Changes in terms and rent level

4–27   They may be situations where there is a reference to an RAC where changes in terms are proposed running concurrently with a reference under the statutory increase section. In these circumstances the RAC can, provided that the periods of the tenancy overlap, hear the references together. In these circumstances the determination in relation to the initial determination is to be taken first; thus any reference to the terms of a tenancy is to be taken as a reference to the terms as varied by the RAC.[45]

The rent shall be the amount as determined by the RAC from the date specified in the notice unless the landlord and tenant agree otherwise or the RAC consider that this would cause undue hardship to the tenant. In such a case the RAC may postpone the date when the new rent is to commence up until the date of the decision.[46]

Discontinuation of consideration of rent determination

4–28   A RAC may discontinue consideration of a rent determination in two distinct situations.[47]

Tenancy ended

4–29   If the tenancy is brought to an end by the order of a sheriff, in such circumstances it might be considered inappropriate for the RAC to spend time on a hypothetical exercise.

Notice from landlord and tenant

4–30   If the landlord and tenant give notice in writing that they no longer require a determination the RAC may also decide not to proceed with the exercise. One would expect that they would need to be satisfied that the tenant was a genuinely willing party to the intimation. This might be achieved in like manner to the

---

[43] s. 48(3)(a) .
[44] See para. 5–37.
[44a] s. 25B, inserted by S.I. 1993 No. 658.
[45] s. 25(5).
[46] s. 25(6).
[47] s. 25(7).

granting of "consent to a dealing" under section 6(3) of the Matrimonial Homes (Family Protection) (Scotland) Act 1981 by having such statements notarially executed, expressing an understanding of the implications of the document.

RACs and rent fixing

There is limited information from which to make an assessment regarding 4–31 how RACs operate the statutory increase mechanism. All the determinations of the committees in Scotland under the Housing (Scotland) Act 1988 have been examined by the authors. The number of applications is not extensive. In the first eight years of the operation of the legislation 114 applications have been dealt with. Rent increases were successfully sought in just under 50 per cent of cases. As indicated, the major problem encountered by landlords centred around absence of jurisdiction.

Those statements of reasons which have been issued indicate certain 4–32 guidelines for those debating what amounts to a market rent:

- registered fair rents are not regarded as relevant[48];
- comparables from either the Register of Assured Tenancies or actual agreed rents will be regarded as best evidence[49];
- some evidence of a market rent level is required rather than a view that a higher rent would be unfair[50] (unless neither side produces any evidence)[51];
- general information as to rent levels in an area will be viewed as having less significance than actual rents agreed[52];
- a market rent may involve fixing a rent at a higher level than that sought by the landlord[53];
- the level of the market may come from evidence of landlords seeking bids from potential tenants[54];
- information as to the size and nature of the properties being suggested as comparable will usually be required[55];
- the state of repair of the property is relevant in deciding what amounts to a market rent[56];
- capital value return will only by resorted to in the absence of good comparable rent evidence[57];
- where return on capital is argued the Committee prefer actual sales rather than guesstimates.[58]

There seems to be a differing approach between committees as to whether they are required "[to reach] their decision ... strictly on the basis of the evidence

---

[48] GWR.A.9 dated Sept 16, 1992 and RAC/A39 dated June 2, 1993.
[49] GW.A.0003 dated May 15, 1992 and GW.A.7 dated Aug. 6, 1992.
[50] GW.A.0004 dated May 12, 1992; GWR/A/13 Mar. 24, 1993 and RAC/A6 dated May 12, 1992.
[51] RAC/A39 dated June 2, 1993.
[52] RAC/GWR/A/14 dated Apr. 15, 1993.
[53] RAC/A27 dated Dec. 19, 1992.
[54] GWR.A.9 dated Sept. 16, 1992; RAC/A/6 dated May 12, 1992 and RAC/A/13 dated May 12, 1992.
[55] RAC/GWR/A/14 dated Apr. 15, 1993.
[56] GWR/A/13 dated Mar. 24, 1993; RAC/A/26 dated Oct. 21, 1992 and RAC/A/31 dated Oct. 21, 1992.
[57] GW.A.7 dated Aug. 6, 1992.
[58] GWR/A/13 dated Mar. 24, 1993.

led and canvassed at the hearing"[59] as opposed to drawing on the knowledge and experience of the committee[60] or supplementing the failure of either party to produce evidence of market rents.[61] The statements of reasons of those committees based in the Glasgow office tend to make it clearer what factors have led them to fix on the figure determined. Those from Edinburgh based committees[62] tend to follow the more oblique approach preferred by Lord Widgery.[63]

4–33   A couple of cases are a reasonable reflection of what has occurred. Extensive statements of reasons were issued in two applications by tenants of the Western Heritable Investment Company. In January 1990 there was a reference by a statutory assured tenant who had succeeded to her mother's tenancy in March 1989. The fair rent had been £1,356 p.a. The landlords proposed a phasing of the rent from the fair rent up to what they considered to be the market level. This was to be £1,920 for the first year, followed by a year at £2,520 and then £3,120. The Committee indicated they were not empowered to make such a staged rental determination and fixed the rent at £3,120. Their reasoning was interesting. The tenant, on the basis of some general enquiries in the Cathcart area, suggested that the general level of rents was in the region of £65 per week (£3,380 p.a.). The landlords submitted a figure of £3,380 and indicated that their source came from offers for two other unfurnished lettings advertised by them in the *Glasgow Herald* and *Evening Times*. They were closely similar to the property under consideration except for internal decoration. These each yielded seven offers of between £2,600 and £3,380. They had duly been rented out at the higher figure. The Rent Assessment Committee noted that there had been only one offer at the higher level of £3,380 for each property, but that there were two offers at £3,120. Their conclusion was that: "[I]t could therefore be argued that the market demand at that rental had been satisfied. It did however recognise that on the basis of the tenders there was a market demand of £3,120 from a further two prospective tenants".[64]

4–34   The same kind of situation concerning a daughter succeeding to a tenancy in a West End Glasgow tenement occurred three months later. The property consisted of a first floor flat in a three-storey brick and roughcast tenement built in approximately 1930 consisting of kitchenette, two public rooms, two bedrooms and bathroom. The property had new PVC windows, had been recently rewired and was in good order. The landlords again proposed a phased rent increase from the fair rent of £1,428. The first year was to be £1,920, followed by £2,520 and finally £3,120. The tenant offered no evidence other than that the majority of houses in the vicinity were owner-occupied and those similar to hers sold for about £40,000. The landlords suggested this as the capital value and produced comparables from a variety of four-in-a-block houses each with its own front door. They took the view that the properties were in different markets, with the West End enjoying popularity because of Glasgow University and various other further education establishments, whereas Croftfoot was an area where people would be seeking family accommodation. The Committee

---

[59] GW.A.0003 dated May 15, 1992.
[60] GWR.A.9 dated Sept. 16, 1992.
[61] RAC/A39 dated June 2, 1993.
[62] Typically, RAC/A/25 dated Sept. 3, 1992 and RAC/A/32 dated Oct. 8, 1992.
[63] *Guppys Properties v. Knott (No. 1)* [1978] E.G.D. 256.
[64] Glasgow Rent Assessment Committee Statement of Reasons at 2—GW.A. 90.001 dated March 9, 1990.

approved the approach taken by the previous Committee in relation to the advertisements and noted an advert for a Byres Road flat at £2,600 in the paper on the day of the hearing. They also noted that the premises under consideration were a tenement flat and not a house with its own front door and decided that the market rent was £3,000 p.a.

Avoiding the statutory rent increase mechanism

Original position

Landlords in assured tenancies can avoid the role of RACs by providing for a 4–35 rent increase either by a specified sum or by a percentage of the rent.[65] When the legislation was originally introduced one view expressed was that the wording of the 1988 Act prevented the landlord specifying anything other than a fixed amount or fixed percentage. Others took the view that there was no reason why the term "specified sum" could not be related to some external method of measurement such as changes in the Retail Price Index or a similar factor. Which view would have prevailed is unlikely to be resolved. The section was altered to remove any doubt and to clarify the intention of Government that the parties were to be given a free hand to reach whatever contractual arrangements they chose.

1990 amendment

The amended section provides that the statutory mechanism does not affect 4–36 the operation of any term of a contractual tenancy which makes provision for an increase in rent (including provision whereby the rent for a particular period will or may be greater than for an earlier period). Nor shall the existence of statutory increase provisions prevent increases in rent by an amount or fixed by reference to factors specified in the tenancy contract or by a percentage specified therein or fixed by reference to factors specified in the contract of the rent payable under the tenancy.[66] The factors referred to must be factors which, once specified, are not wholly within the control of the landlord.[67] In addition they must be such as will enable the tenant at all material times to ascertain without undue difficulty any amount or percentage falling to be fixed by reference to them.[68] These could presumably include changes in the Retail Price Index or be tied to the value of a major currency. In a couple of references the RAC have declined jurisdiction because the tenancy agreements specified a rent increase mechanism outwith the control of the landlords.[69] Unfortunately they did not specify the nature of the mechanism in question.

Landlords may well choose, as Western Heritable Investment Company have done, to keep to simple percentage increases[70] to avoid complicated litigation where limited guidelines are provided. However, the Model Assured Tenancy Agreement provided for housing associations by the Scottish Federation of

---

[65] s. 25(5).
[66] s. 25(5).
[67] s. 25(6)(a).
[68] s. 25(6)(b).
[69] See paras. 4–03 to 4–05.
[70] In two references in January 1990 and May 1990 the Western Heritable Investment Co. indicated that they were letting advertised properties with tenancy agreements providing for an automatic increase of 9% p.a. on the rent—GW.A. 90.001; Glasgow Rent Assessment Committee dated Jan. 24, 1990 and GW.A. 90.002; Glasgow Rent Assessment Committee dated May 11, 1990.

Housing Associations includes a rent increase clause which states that the rent "will be reviewed in accordance with the Association's rental policy".[71]

3. SHORT ASSURED TENANCIES

Introduction

4–37   There is a limited role for the RAC provided that certain criteria are satisfied.[72] The tenant can have the rent decided by a rent assessment committee. The criterion they must apply is what rent the landlord might reasonably be expected to obtain under a short assured tenancy. The fact that housing benefit is not available to cover the full rent is not a relevant question.[73] There appears to be an element of circularity in the suggestion that the rent for a short assured tenancy should be what a landlord might reasonably expect to obtain under a short assured tenancy. That is presumably what has been charged and accepted by the tenant. In reality the tenant may not have had much choice in a situation of undersupply of rented housing. Tenants may be under the mistaken impression that housing benefit will cover whatever housing costs.[74] In addition, during the debates on the Bill it was explained that it was expected that those occupying under less secure shorthold assured tenancies would have to pay lower rents than the market assured tenancy rents.[75]

Non-determinations under Short Assured Tenancies

4–38   Rent Assessment Committees have reached non-determination decisions in about one-third of applications covered by the Glasgow office and in one-fifth of those covered by the Edinburgh office.[76]

Avoiding duplication

4–39   Although tenants of short assured tenancies have the right, like those with regulated tenancies, to apply to the RAC for a rent determination, they must satisfy the RAC on two distinct matters before the RAC go on to consider the level of rent.[77] They must be satisfied that a rent has not already been fixed by an RAC for a short assured tenancy and that a rent has not already been fixed in terms of section 25.[78] The aim is to avoid duplication of work already done.

Pool of Comparables

4–40   The RAC can test the level of the rent only if they have information with which to work. The statute requires that there be a pool of comparable rented

[71] cl. 5A of the Scottish Federation of Housing Associations, Model Tenancy Agreement, July 1997 available from SFHA, 38 York Place, Edinburgh EH1 3HU.
[72] s. 34.
[73] Glasgow Rent Assessment Committee, Statement of Reasons, dated Apr. 19, 1990, GW.S. 90.001.
[74] Tenants' submissions outlined in the Glasgow Rent Assessment Committee Statement of Reasons, February 5, 1991, GW.S. 0003.
[75] *Hansard*, H.C., First Scottish Standing Committee, col. 819, February 18, 1988.
[76] Data from the Rent Assessment Committees in Glasgow and Edinburgh who kindly gave us access to their records.
[77] s. 34 (2).

properties to which to look for a yardstick.[79] The statute does not make it clear whether the responsibility of establishing that the pool of comparables exists is the tenant's or whether there is an assumption that the RAC will be taken to have knowledge and experience of such a factor. This has always been assumed in relation to the operation of regulated tenancies in England and Wales.[80] However, in Scotland the equivalent statute had to be changed to reverse the Court of Session's decision in *Albyn Properties v. Knox*.[81] This decision had favoured landlords in that as they would employ professionals as representatives in the rent-fixing process, these professionals would have access to information supporting their contention, whilst tenants would be less likely to be able to draw on equivalent information. This inequality was rectified by the changes introduced in 1980 to the fair rent section of the Rent (Scotland) Act 1971.[82] Rent Assessment Committees were required to have regard to their own knowledge and experience of current rents of comparable properties. The fact that the tenant might not know whether or not the landlord's evidence was a full and complete picture was no longer an issue. The RAC could be expected to go not only on the evidence presented but also on that which *could* have been presented.

The problem with the pool of comparables

The need for a pool of comparables presents problems to short assured tenants 4–41 since there is no reference to the knowledge and experience of the RAC. The question is whether they would follow the English approach or require tenants to establish a pool of comparables. The authors' original gloomy forecast on this issue[83] has some support from the limited information available. In the one case in Glasgow on the Register of Non-Determinations under Short Assured Tenancies the RAC took the view that they were confined "to forming its opinion solely on the basis of rental comparisons". They explained that whilst the Act gave no guidance as to what number might be sufficient, "the solitary example produced by the tenants which was the only relevant information before them", was "clearly insufficient".[84] This suggests that if the information is not produced the RAC will not draw on their own knowledge and experience. However, this is a limited base from which to draw firm conclusions. It should be said that the landlord's submission was not based on this point but simply related to the level of the rent.

Significantly higher rent

The RAC must not make a rent determination even where there are sufficient 4–42 comparables unless the rent paid by the tenant is significantly higher than the rent which the landlord might reasonably expect to be able to obtain judging by rents charged for similar houses in the locality.[85]

---

[78] See above — this section relates to the role of RACs in fixing rents for *statutory* assured tenancies.

[79] s. 34(4)(a).

[80] *Metropolitan Properties v. Lannon* [1968] 1 W.L.R. 815 at 831; *Crofton Investment Trust Ltd v. Greater London Rent Assessment Panel* [1967] 2 Q.B. 955 at 967.

[81] 1978 S.C. 41.

[82] Now repealed and re-enacted in s. 48 of the Rent (Scotland) Act 1984.

[83] *Housing (Scotland) Act 1988* (1989), p. 46.

[84] Glasgow Rent Assessment Committee, Statement of Reasons dated Feb. 2, 1991, GW.S. 0003.

[85] Housing (Scotland) Act 1988, s. 34(3)(b).

There are no criteria provided in the legislation as to how much is "significantly higher". The assistance from the Register of Rents Determined under Short Assured Tenancies is limited. In the first decided case in this area from April 1990 the rent of a second floor flat of kitchen, 3 rooms and bathroom with adequate furniture in the West End of Glasgow was reduced from £608 per month to £520 per month.[86] The four tenants submitted information from one neighbouring flat along with information from an advert in a newsagent's window of another flat, plus the cost of single and shared bedsits. The landlords provided evidence of nine other short assured tenancies which they had rented in the immediate neighbourhood with rents between £520 and £694 as well as information from Glasgow University lets in the same street at £540 per month. The RACs decision about "significantly higher" was that looking to the level of rents in the same street drawn to their attention by the landlord at between £520 and £540 per month, "the Committee considered that the rent payable under the short assured tenancy under consideration was significantly higher than the rent which the landlord might reasonably be expected to obtain under the tenancy having regard to the level of rent payable in the locality for similar houses."

In November 1990 the rent of a short assured tenancy of second floor flat in a three storey stone built flat from the early nineteenth century in Stirling was reduced from £65 per week to £50. The furniture was poor in quality and the flat comprised a livingroom/kitchen, bedroom with shower room/toilet off.

Coming into effect of the determination

4–43   Where a rent has been fixed by the RAC, it is to take effect as from the date set by the committee.[87] However, it cannot be backdated to before the date of application.

The excess is not to be recoverable by the tenant. The rent determination lasts for one year from the date when it comes into operation. The previous private sector rents fixed under the Rent (Scotland) Act 1984 lasted for three years, although the English Rent Act 1977, dealing with protected tenancies since 1980, provides for two-year intervals.

Abolition of the RAC function

4–44   The Secretary of State is given the power by statutory instrument to abandon the rent determination provisions applied to short assured tenancies in relation to certain kinds of tenancies or geographical areas.[88] Such a power exists in the Rent (Scotland) Act 1984[89] to cover a situation where there is an adequate supply of rented housing and the need to protect the tenant from the vagaries of the market might disappear. No such order was made under the 1984 legislation nor its 1965 and 1971 predecessors. It is not clear in what circumstances the limited role of the rent assessment committees indicated in section 34 could be superfluous given the distinction between assured and short assured tenancies as far as security of tenure is concerned.

---

[86] Actually expressed in the decision as £7,296–£6,240 p.a.
[87] s. 34 (4).
[88] s. 35.
[89] s. 95.

4. Protected Tenancies

Background

Those private tenancies in existence at January 2, 1989 continue to be governed by 4–45 the Rent (Scotland) Act 1984 so far as rent fixing is concerned. This involves the fair rent and the Rent Officer and RAC procedure set up originally by the Rent Act 1965.

A rent may be registered voluntarily at the behest of landlord or tenant, or both. Landlords may themselves apply to have rents registered, as this will avoid later difficulties with dissatisfied tenants. If rent levels can be predicted then the landlord can plan future expenditure and investment without the fear of a significant downturn in income. Applications by landlords are particularly common for reviews of property already registered at the end of the three-year period covered by the initial fixing.[90] Indeed, this is currently the major source of applications to the Rent Officers.[91]

In addition, landlords were able to apply for a "Certificate of Fair Rent" for property which they were considering letting out in the future.[92] Such a certificate allowed the landlord to see how rents were moving. The process was criticised in the Francis Report[93] since, in determining the rent for an empty property the Rent Officer or RAC only hear one side of the story, and there is no-one to challenge the landlord's submissions directly.

Initially applications by the tenant provided most of the work for Rent Officers, but in the 1980s it had fallen away considerably.[94] Just as with a landlord application, there is an opportunity for the tenant, in addition to suggesting a figure for the rent, to support this with both written and oral submissions. Even where landlords and tenant both join together to suggest a commonly agreed fair rent, there is still an obligation on the Rent Officer to consider the figure on its merits and determine whether or not this does indeed represent a fair rent.

Procedures for rent registration

Background

The machinery for rent-fixing set up under the 1965 Act comprised two tiers— 4–46 Rent Officers, who dealt with initial rent fixing and Rent Assessment Committees (RACs), who were available to reconsider any rents where either or both parties were not happy with the Rent Officer's decision. Although the RACs are not strictly an appeal body, their decisions supersede those of the Rent Officers and carry more weight with other RACs as evidence of comparable fair rents, when this is relevant. The subsequent amendments to the legislation have left the status and relationship of these rent-fixers as originally specified in the Rent Act 1965.

Rent Officers

Originally, when the 1965 Act was introduced, it was envisaged that a separate 4–47 independent body of men and women could engender a spirit of co-operation between landlord and tenant in coming to a mutually agreed fair rent. Rent

---

[90] *Housing and Construction Statistics,* 1979–1989, Table 11.7 (HMSO, 1990).

[91] *ibid.* Tables 11.4 and 11.6.

[92] s. 47—still available but the purpose would be unclear as post-1988 tenancies would be "assured".

[93] Francis Committee, Cmnd. 4609 (1971) at 66.

[94] *Housing and Construction Statistics,* above.

Officers are appointed by the Secretary of State for Scotland[95] and are part of the Civil Service.[96] Their current work is split between continued fair rent work in terms of the Rent (Scotland) Act 1984, both private sector and housing association tenancies and assessments about the level of rents in terms of the housing benefit legislation.[97]

RACs

4–48　　Whilst Rent Officers are full-time officials, those who deal with the querying of their decisions are part-time professionals and lay persons. The Secretary of State for Scotland draws the members of RACs from a panel of lawyers, valuers and laymen.[98] The legislation also provides for the appointment of a president of the RACs, who along with a vice-president exercises overall supervision of RACs.[99]

　　Rent Assessment Committees sit in panels of three, and deliver their decisions without dissenting notes although this was possible in the early days.[1] RACs have been criticised for their strong professional and business connections with landlords and property companies. Since many of the panel members are valuers in firms of surveyors or lawyers generally working for landlords, there may be some substance to this complaint.

Rent Officer procedure

Background

4–49　　The first individual with whom a tenant or landlord comes in contact during the rent-fixing process is the Rent Officer.[2] Once the application is lodged the Rent Officer will arrange to visit the property and examine the accommodation. On an initial application this will involve measuring up the property and noting its physical characteristics as well as other amenities. Normally on that same afternoon the Rent Officer will arrange for a meeting between landlord and tenant to discuss the proposed rent. This meeting was originally intended to "take some of the steam" out of the landlord/tenant relationship, by showing both sides that their problem was being dealt with by a professional expert disinterested party. This aspect of the rent scheme does not appear to have been an unqualified success. Since neither party is required to attend many landlords do not turn up, which limits the conciliatory nature of the exercise and leaves the Rent Officer explaining his job to the tenant alone. Rent Officers regard it as a useful part of the process whereby they come to a decision as to what rent figure is "fair", as their first figure will be provisional.

Written notification of decision

4–50　　Following the meeting with the parties, the Rent Officer will then inform them in writing of the figure fixed upon, although only minimal information is

---

[95] s. 43(3).
[96] Transfer of Functions (Minister for Civil Service and Treasury) Order 1981 (S.I. 1981 No. 1670).
[97] Housing Benefit (General) Regulations 1987 (S.I. 1987 No. 1971), reg. 11.
[98] s. 44 and Sched. 4.
[99] Sched. 4, paras 4 and 5.
[1] *Picea Holdings Ltd v. London Rent Assessment Panel* [1971] 2 Q.B. 216.
[2] Sched. 5, Pt 1.

available to the parties as to the factors deemed relevant by the Rent Officer. Rent Officers, unlike RACs, are not required to give reasons for their decisions. This, in part, explains the lower status accorded to Rent Officers by RACs and landlords.

Register of Rents

In the publicly available Register of Rents and in the notice received by the 4–51
parties, the information is sparse. The Rent Officer comments on areas—whether or not each is considered good, fair, poor, etc. There is also information on the state of any furniture provided and the nature and extent of any services provided.

RAC procedure

Background

There is space on the form which notifies the Rent Officer's decision for 4–52
either party to require the RAC to consider the rent, if either party is dissatisfied. This must be done within 28 days of service of the notification of the Rent Officer's decision.[3] Technically this is not an appeal nor like a judicial review, in that the RAC do not concern themselves with the data deemed relevant by the Rent Officer nor the process whereby the Rent Officer reached the fair rent figure being challenged. What is involved is, in fact, a fresh hearing of the whole issue.

The RAC, too, visit the property in question and, where possible, speak to the parties involved at the "locus".[4] Thereafter a hearing is normally held, again generally on the same day as the visit while the property is fresh in the minds of the RAC members. It is not obligatory for there to be a hearing, although this is almost always the case. Since the RAC can not only confirm or reduce the Rent Officer figure but also raise it, it is normally felt to be in the interests of all parties to attend.

The hearing is relatively informal and runs on standard tribunal lines laid 4–53
down by statutory regulations.[5] The RAC call on the objecting party to explain why the figure is felt to be inappropriate, and then on the other party to make any comments which will be helpful. In practice, depending on the RAC personnel, a high degree of informality is found in these procedures. Evidence is not required to be formally presented. Before this stage or at the hearing, either party may, in addition to an oral presentation, produce a written submission in support of their contentions.

Most landlords' cases are characterised by a degree of professionalisation, with "comparables" and "capital values" and "return" figures prominent. Tenants face rather special problems in their presentations in the light of the criteria for "fair rents".

Normally the RAC let the parties know of their decision by post but it is not unknown for a decision to be given there and then. As a tribunal under the Tribunals and Inquiries Act 1971, the RAC are required to state their reasons for their decisions when requested so to do.[6] This obligation led to a number of

---

[3] Sched. 5, para. 6.
[4] Rent Assessment Committee (Scotland) Regulations 1980 (SI 1980 No. 1665) as amended by Rent Assessment Committee (Scotland) Regulations 1982 (S.I. 1982 No. 259), reg. 6.
[5] *ibid.*
[6] *ibid.* regs 7 and 7A.

problems in Scotland with the Court of Session taking the view that these reasons must be such as to "explain how their figures of fair rent were fixed".[7] This contrasted markedly with the approach of the Divisional Court in England in such cases as *Guppys Properties v. Knott (No.1)*.[8] The law in England is the same although contained in different statutes. There is one minor change between the wording of the English and Scottish legislation stemming from rather different approaches taken to the role of tribunals as expert bodies. The English approach has been preferred and this has led to changes in the law in Scotland which are discussed below.[9]

The assessment of rents

4–54 **Introduction.** The formula for determining rents introduced in the Rent Act 1965[10] remains almost unchanged in the current legislation, the Rent (Scotland) Act 1984.[11] The corresponding English provisions are in the Rent Act 1977[12] and the wording is identical except for one matter.

The legislation requires Rent Officers and RACs to have regard to certain factors and ignore others in coming to a fair rent figure as well as making one crucial assumption.[13] Despite the apparent clear direction given by the Act, a number of problems of interpretation have been encountered over the years.

4–55 **Matters which RACs must have regard to**. In determining a fair rent the rent fixers—the Rent Officers or RACs—have a duty to have regard to certain matters. They must specifically have regard to all the circumstances and, in particular, they must apply their knowledge and experience of current rents of comparable property in the area.[14] The latter direction is the only difference between the Scottish and English legislation. It was introduced to bring Scottish practice into line with the English approach following litigation in the late 1970s.[15] The English approach allowed RACs flexibility in making their decisions and in giving reasons. The Scottish approach tied them to the evidence presented. This favoured those with professional advisers and the solution was seen as this requirement for Committees to pay regard to their own knowledge and experience. That meant that even if evidence was not presented it could be taken into account by the Committee.

In addition RACs are required to have regard to the age, character and locality of the dwelling-house and its state of repair.[16] Where there is furniture involved the state of this furniture as regards its quantity, quality and condition must be looked at.

4–56 **Matters to be disregarded.** The thinking behind the disregards is that there should be an element of equity in the rent-fixing process. The tenant should not benefit from failing to abide by the terms of the tenancy agreement and causing

---

[7] *Albyn Properties v. Knox*, 1977 S.L.T. 41.
[8] [1978] E.G.D. 255.
[9] See paras 4–65 to 4–67.
[10] s. 27.
[11] s. 48.
[12] s. 70. This replaces Rent Act 1968, s. 46.
[13] s. 48.
[14] s. 48(1).
[15] Peter Robson and Paul Watchman, "Determining Fair Rents" (1978) N.L.J. 1209.
[16] s. 48.

the property or the furniture to deteriorate. Similarly the landlord should not benefit from improvements to the property which have been paid for by the tenant. These are issues that should normally be raised during the visit to the property by the parties.

Personal circumstances. The legislation requires that in looking at all the 4–57 circumstances this is not to include personal circumstances.[17] Thus, whether the tenant can afford the rent or whether the landlord is already well-off is irrelevant. The rent fixed is for the property. The fact that a tenant has security of tenure and his presence limits the capital value of the property is a personal circumstance which the rent fixer must not take account of.[18]

Any disrepair which stems from the tenant failing to abide by the terms of the 4–58 *lease.* A tenant cannot ask for a reduction on account of the house being in a bad state of internal repair if the tenant has been the cause of the disrepair.[19]

Tenant's improvements. Any improvement or replacement of fittings and fixtures 4–59 by the tenant should not benefit the landlord in the form of an enhanced rent except where the lease so provides.[20] This also covers replacement of furniture. It applies to work carried out by the tenant or any predecessor in title such as an assignee or successor and means during the current tenancy so that improvements carried out by a tenant under a previous tenancy could be taken into account in fixing the fair rent. However, where a tenant chose to use her own furniture in a tenancy rather than that provided by the landlord, this was held to be no bar to the RAC fixing a rent for the house as a furnished property.[21]

In *Stewart's Judicial Factor v. Gallagher*[22] the Court of Session decided that where work was done by way of repair it did not fall to be regarded as improvement and so was not to be disregarded. The specific issue in this case has been amended but the principle remains applicable. The case was concerned with the replacement of a w.c., sink unit and fireplace with new fittings—these are now to be disregarded in the rent-fixing process.

Deterioration in condition of furniture. If furniture is provided, any deterioration 4–60 in the condition of the furniture due to ill-treatment by the tenant, or any person residing or lodging with the tenant or any sub-tenant must be disregarded.[23]

Assumption of equilibrium of supply and demand. The principle behind the 4–61 introduction of the fair rent formula was that tenants in a situation of scarcity of supply should be protected from market forces. In order to achieve this end the legislation requires that it be

> "assumed that the number of persons seeking to become tenants of similar dwelling-houses in the locality on the terms (other than those relating to rent) of the regulated tenancy is not substantially greater than the number

[17] s. 48(1).
[18] *Mason v. Skilling,* 1974 S.L.T. 42.
[19] s. 48(3)(a).
[20] s. 48(3)(b).
[21] *R. v. London Rent Assessment Panel, ex p. Mota* (1987) 20 H.L.R. 159—using the Landlord's inventory to assess the value of the Landlord's furniture.
[22] 1967 S.C. 59.
[23] s. 48(3)(c).

of such dwelling-houses in the locality which are available for letting on such terms".[24]

It involves an active process rather than merely passively assuming that such a set of affairs actually exists. This passive approach was the somewhat unusual thinking behind the majority decision in *Western Heritable Investment Co. v. Husband*.[25] The approach threatened to undermine the rationale of the fair rent procedure. On appeal to the House of Lords, it was rejected by their Lordships. As Lord Fraser of Tullybelton explained:

> "[T]hey seem to have read the proviso in s. 42(2) that 'it shall be assumed that the number of persons seeking to become tenants ... is not substantially greater than the number of ... dwelling-houses' as creating a irrebuttable presumption of fact that there is no scarcity, whatever the true facts may be. With the utmost respect that impresses me as a most improbable construction of the subsection".[26]

4–62   The procedure involved in operating this assumption is normally described as the "scarcity deduction". A percentage of the rent is deducted from the market rent as representing the impact of scarcity on the level of rents. This varies from 20 per cent to 50 per cent and seems to be based on common-sense notions of the extent of local scarcity. Thus at the height of the Aberdeen oil boom in the mid-1970s scarcity deductions of 40 per cent to 50 per cent were being accepted.

4–63   **Fair rents in practice.** During the first 15 years of the fair rent legislation there was considerable litigation by landlords on how fair rents should be fixed. There were two elements in these cases. First, there was the simple motive of income maximisation. Landlords were keen that the courts would sanction the approach which brought them the highest level of profit. In addition there was the related aim of trying to try establish a clear, consistent pattern which would allow them to plan subsequent investment by knowing what levels of income could be expected.

4–64   **Original goals.** When he introduced the legislation in 1965, Richard Crossman deliberately avoided requiring rent fixers to follow some kind of mathematical formula. Rather he saw the fair rent procedure as a mechanism to weed out unscrupulous profiteering landlords.

> "At first sight it does seem an extraordinary thing that we have done. What we have said is that we would not try to define a fair rent by any normal method and we wouldn't relate it either to a fair return on the landlord's money or a standard rent or anything else. What Arnold Goodman has in fact said to me is, don't try to invent a formula. Get the right people and let them do the job of setting a series of precedents in the early decisions."[27]

This consequent lack of clear statutory direction meant that there have been various challenges to the approaches taken by RACs—since Rent Officers do not give reasons for their figures their practice has not been subject to such challenge in the courts. In 1971, the Francis Committee found that there were

---

[24] s. 48(2).
[25] 1983 S.L.T. 578 *per* Lord Kincraig at 581.
[26] *ibid.* at 582.
[27] Richard Crossman, *The Diaries of a Cabinet Minister* (1975), Vol. 1, p. 187 (March 24, 1965).

three methods used in calculating fair rents—comparables; market rents where there is no scarcity rents; conventional valuation methods.[28]

Comparables method. The comparables method has been favoured in England 4–65
and Wales since the legislation came into force. In *Crofton Investment Trust v. Greater London Rent Assessment Committee* Lord Widgery stated, just as Crossman had indicated, that fair return on capital was rarely an accurate guide to the fair rent.[29] Subsequently Lord Parker went on to suggest that the comparables approach was preferable because of the question of uniformity:

> "It must surely be the essence of this whole scheme that there should be uniformity, and no doubt as the volume of registered fair rents increases in the future no one will go to the market rent less scarcity, they will go straight to the enormous volume of fair rents that have been registered."[30]

There are two problems with comparables. First, there is no reason why the first batch of comparable rents used as a yardstick for subsequent fair rents is intrinsically fair.[31] Secondly, there is a problem for non-professionals in obtaining access to information as to what rents are being charged in an area. This is more likely to affect tenants but could be a problem for landlords with limited property portfolios. The solution to this inequity of information is to be found in the publicly available Register of Rents. These registers provide information as to when previous "fair rent" figures were set and some limited information as to responsibility for any services as well as, on occasion, a comment on the nature of the area and property.

Capital return. Despite the intentions of Crossman and the perspective of the 4–66
English judiciary there has been extensive pressure from landlords to have the capital return method endorsed as a method of fixing rents. This has been approved as one legitimate way for rent fixers to determine a fair rent although not the only one which may be used.[32] It involves making allowances for management costs, repairs and a return on the capital value of the property.[33]

The approach after assured tenancies. Subsequently, however, in *Albyn* 4–67
Properties v. Knox[33a] concerning how a RAC should operate the fair rent legislation, the Court of Session came to a very different decision from the English courts. They decided that a committee must make clear the basis on which they had reached their decision. This included indicating what evidence they accepted and what they rejected. The decisions were to be reached only on the evidence led. This favoured landlords and the use of capital return computations and seemed to allow no possibility of the Committee using their own knowledge and experience gleaned from their day-to-day work. The legislation was altered to allow particular regard to be had to the Committee's "knowledge and experience of current rents of comparable property in the area".[34]

---

[28] Francis Committee, Cmnd. 4609 (1971) at 58.
[29] [1967] Q.B. 955.
[30] *Tormes Property Co. Ltd v. Landau* [1970] 3 All E.R. 653 at 655.
[31] P. Robson "Fair for Whom?" (1974) 118 S.J. 307.
[32] *Learmonth Property Investment Co. v. Aitken,* 1971 S.L.T. 349; *Skilling v. Arcari's Exrs,* 1974 S.L.T. 46.
[33] See, *e.g. Western Heritable Investment Co. v. Husband,* 1983 S.L.T. 578 at 590.
[33a] 1997 S.L.T. 41.
[34] Rent (Scotland) Act 1984, s. 48(1).

The changes effected in response to the *Albyn* decision with the emphasis on "current rents of comparable property" mean that these are likely to be the best indication of what the fair rent should be. In England the Court of Appeal have accepted the significance of assured tenancy rents.[35] In Scotland, however, the Court of Session have taken a rather different view in *Western Heritable Investment Co. Ltd v. Johnston.*[36] They were of the view that since such major adjustments would require to be made to take account of the scarcity factor there was no compelling reason, in normal circumstances, to depart from the comparables in the Register of Rents.[37]

4–68 **Amount to be registered as rent.** The amount to be registered as rent is to include any sums payable by the tenant to the landlord for the use of furniture or for services. These are to be noted in the Rent Register whether or not they are separate from the sums payable for the occupation of the dwelling-house.[38] There is to be a separate note if the amount attributable to the use of furniture or the provision of services is 5 per cent or more of the registered rent.[39] Thus, costs such as cleaning or the provision of door entry systems have been entered on the Register.

4–69 **Increase of rents**. Once fixed, fair rents are valid for the next three years.[40] There may be a fresh application before the expiry of the three years where there has been a change in the condition of the dwelling-house. The change may be for the worse or can include the making of any improvement. There may also be an early reference back if there is a change in the terms of the tenancy. Finally, the rent may be looked at again where there is a change in the quantity or deterioration in the quality or condition of any furniture provided for use, other than fair wear and tear.[41]

Controls over the phasing of increases is included in the legislation,[42] although there is power to repeal such limitations.[43] The current regulations as to phasing limit increases to the greatest of the following amounts: £104; one-quarter of the previous rent limit; half the difference between the previous rent limit and the registered rent.[44]

4–70 **Excess charges.** A landlord is not entitled to recover from the tenant more than the registered rent[45] and if the tenant has been charged more than the registered rent this may be recovered by the tenant from the landlord.[46] No amount which a tenant is entitled to recover is recoverable after two years from the date of payment.[47] This period is calculated from the time when the claim is intimated

---

[35] *Spath Holme Ltd v. Greater Manchester and Lancashire Rent Assessment Committee, The Times,* July 13, 1994; *Curtis v. London Rent Assessment Committee* [1997] 4 All E.R. 842; *Northumberland and Durham Property Trust Ltd v. London Rent Assessment Committee (No. 2)* [1998] 24 E.G. 128.

[36] 1997 S.L.T. 74.

[37] *ibid.*

[38] s. 49(1).

[39] s. 49(2) and (3).

[40] s. 46(3).

[41] s. 49(3).

[42] Rent (Scotland) Act 1984, s. 33.

[43] Housing (Scotland) Act 1988, s. 41—this power had not been exercised at the time of writing.

[44] Limits on Rent Increases (Scotland) Order 1989 (S.I. 1989 No. 2469).

[45] s. 28.

[46] s. 37.

[47] s. 37(3).

rather than when a court action is commenced.[48] Any other result would penalise a tenant who attempted to negotiate.[49]

5. Part VII Contracts

Although as indicated[50] there are unlikely to be many Part VII contracts in   4–71 existence, the fact that tenants choose to have the rent determined in terms of the Rent (Scotland) Act 1984 does not affect their rights to continue as Part VII tenants. These rights are likely to be limited.[51]

The RACs deal with the matter of fixing rents and some residual security of tenure matters. As has been noted, the RAC has three members—two professional and one lay. They are drawn from a panel of lawyers, valuers and laymen by the Secretary of State for Scotland.

Where the Act is in force, either party to the contract or the local authority may refer the contract to the local RAC.[52] The RAC may then require the landlord to furnish them with information about the contract of tenancy under penalty of a fine.[53] The contract referred to the RAC must be in force at the time of referral (though it will not affect the RAC's deliberation that it has ceased by the time they consider the reference).

The RAC shall make such inquiry as they think fit, and give to each party to   4–72 the contract an opportunity for reasonable representations. They may approve the rent payable, reduce or increase it or dismiss the reference.[54] There is no guidance given to the RAC as to the principles to be applied in fixing the rent other than that they are to be satisfied that it is reasonable.[55] Both parties and the local authority must be informed of the RAC's decision, together with the reasons for it if requested. The RAC shall keep a register of rents available for inspection showing the rents as approved, reduced, or increased.[56]

Where a rent has been registered for any dwelling-house, it shall not be lawful to charge more than this registered rent.[57] There is provision for a fine or imprisonment, or both, for contravention.[58] Excess rent may be recovered. There is no time-limit on the recovery. In addition, the court may order recovery of excess.[59] Normally the rent determination lasts for three years.[60] This may be shortened if there is a change in the condition of the dwelling-house, the furniture or services provided or the terms of the contract or any other circumstances taken into account in the rent-fixing process.[61] There is no time-limit if the reference is a joint one of landlord and tenant.[62] Again, the rent may be reduced, increased, or kept the same on an early reference.

---

[48] *North v. Allan Properties (Edinburgh)*, 1987 S.L.T. (Sh.Ct.) 141.
[49] *ibid. per* Sheriff Principal O'Brien at 143.
[50] See paras 2–18 to 2–21.
[51] See paras 2–16 and 2–17.
[52] s. 65.
[53] s. 65(3)—fine not exceeding level 3 on the standard scale .
[54] s. 66(1).
[55] s. 66(1)(b).
[56] s. 67.
[57] s. 69(1).
[58] s. 69(4).
[59] s. 69(4).
[60] s. 66(4).
[61] *ibid.*
[62] s. 68.

6. SECURE TENANCIES

4–73   A local authority may fix such reasonable rents as they may determine for the houses rented out by them.[63] They must review their rents periodically.[64] When fixing their standard rents authorities must not take account of the personal circumstances of the tenants.[65] This means that rents may differ between different classes of houses but not be lowered because of an individual's poverty or wealth. Thus an authority may fix the rent for a two-apartment property in a certain area at £x for anyone living there whilst in another area a similar size of house would be £x+5. There is no direct provision for rent fixing by any body external to the landlord authority where local authority secure tenancies are involved. However, the fear that local authorities would court electoral popularity by fixing low rents[66] has been countered by the financial control central government has exercised over local government.

Until the 1970s governments were by and large content to leave these issues to local authorities.[67] However, they have a variety of powers to control the level of rent payable. This is done directly through the fixing of the level of the central government grant for housing. The way this has operated since 1980 has, in effect, ended local rent-fixing autonomy.[68] Thus the direct limitation on local authority rents comes through the financial subsidy regimes[69] rather than any rent-fixing tribunal. There is provision for rent allowances for low income secure tenants. The local authority has a certain limited discretion to affect the level of allowance given through the mechanism of housing benefit and rent allowance.[70]

However, for secure tenancies rented from housing associations the fair rent mechanism is prescribed.[71] This applies to housing association tenancies granted after the Tenants' Rights, Etc. (Scotland) Act 1980 and prior to the Housing (Scotland) Act 1988—between December 1, 1980 and January 1, 1989.

7. CONTRACTUAL TENANCIES

4–74   For those tenancies which are not within the coverage of the Rent (Scotland) Act 1984 or the Housing (Scotland) Act 1988 there is no provision for their rents to be externally assessed. Rent increases are governed by whatever the contract provides. In the event that no rent increase mechanism is written into the contract, in theory this would need to be terminated to prevent tacit relocation on the same terms and conditions, including rent.

---

[63]   Housing (Scotland) Act 1987, s. 210(1).
[64]   *ibid.* s. 210(2).
[65]   *ibid.* s. 210(3).
[66]   Royal Commission on the Housing of the Industrial Population of Scotland, Rural and Urban, Cd. 8731 (1917) (Minority Report).
[67]   Stephen Merrett, *State Housing in Britain,* (RKP, 1979).
[68]   For a very clear discussion, see Chris Himsworth, *Housing Law in Scotland,* (Butterworths Planning Exchange, 1994).
[69]   Housing (Scotland) Act 1988, s. 70—housing benefit levels are fixed by Rent Officers in terms of the Rent Officers (Additional Functions) (Scotland) Order 1990 (S.I. 1990 No. 396).
[70]   See the current edition of the CPAG *National Welfare Benefits Handbook*—published in April every year.
[71]   See para. 4–45 *et seq.*

CHAPTER 5

RECOVERY OF POSSESSION

1. SECURITY OF TENURE

Introduction

From the earliest intervention in the private rental market in 1915 the controls over   5–01
rent were complemented by limitations upon when a landlord could evict once the
tenancy had been brought to an end. There is little point in being able to have the
rent limited if the landlord can intimidate his tenants and get them to leave through
fear of the consequences. The security of tenure provisions attempt to ensure that
the landlord is barred from ending the tenancy arbitrarily or merely on whim. The
principle which is incorporated in the legislation is that a landlord can evict a tenant
only for an approved reason even after the tenancy has been brought to an end.

Again, as in the various statutory rent-fixing processes, a tenant is under no
obligation to use the security of tenure rights which the legislation affords. Nor
would there seem to be an obligation on a landlord to obtain a court order for
possession if the tenant voluntarily quits the premises. The security of tenure
provisions only come into play if the tenant is unwilling to leave when the
landlord purports to bring the contract of lease to an end.

Tacit relocation

The Scottish rule of tacit relocation in the law of leases means that, even   5–02
where a contract of lease reaches the date of termination specified in the contract,
it is automatically continued until one of the parties gives notice of termination.
If a tenant gives notice of termination she cannot be compelled to continue in
the tenancy. If, however, a tenant were to attempt to leave before the term of the
lease there would be liability for the contractual obligations. Normally landlords
cover themselves for this eventuality by taking both rent in advance and a deposit.
Although this is often actually taken to cover breakages, it is typically applied
to cover other forms of loss to the landlord—a questionable practice.

Notice

The amount of notice landlords must give depends on the length of the lease.   5–03
For leases of more than four months the period of notice is 40 days. The period
of notice for leases for less than four months must be one-third of the duration
of the let. In the case of dwelling-houses there is a statutory minimum of not
less than four weeks from the day on which it is to take effect.[1] The Rent Acts
prescribe the information which must accompany such a notice to quit.[2]

---

[1] Rent (Scotland) Act 1984, s. 112.
[2] See para. 5–49.

Types of Tenancy

5–04   There are three major distinct legal tenancy regimes under which tenants may be occupying their properties and enjoying security of tenure under statute. It is important to establish whether the tenancy is protected, assured or secure. Each regime has different grounds of repossession. However, there are clear similarities between some of these as well as important differences in wording. Accordingly it will usually be worth checking the case law in another regime as it may have a bearing on the case in question. In order to assist in this initial sifting process it is worth consulting SCOLAGs broad guide which indicates some of these differences and similarities.[3]

5–05   Originally, there was an additional category which covered furnished leases and other agreements from 1943.[4] These contracts were referred to as "Part VII contracts" after the part of the Rent Act 1965 dealing with furnished leases. There was an amalgamation of furnished and unfurnished tenants' rights in the Rent Act 1974. After 1974 furnished leases ceased to be Part VII contracts and were specifically incorporated into the protected tenancy regime. This left a residual category covering principally situations where there were resident landlords. Such tenancies are specifically excluded from the protected, secure and assured regimes. They were covered by the residue of Part VII contracts but since their demise in the Housing (Scotland) Act 1988 they have ceased to have any protection. Part VII protection was abolished by the Housing (Scotland) Act 1988 and anyone commencing such an arrangement on or after January 2, 1989 has no security of tenure beyond the terms of their contract and, where it operates, tacit relocation.

        It was largely to avoid the security of tenure provisions of the various Rent Acts that landlords developed the various avoidance mechanisms discussed above.[5]

2. ASSURED TENANCIES

Introduction

5–06   The same general principle is retained in relation to assured tenancies as has operated in relation to Rent Act tenancies in the past, namely that of security of tenure. The contractual tenancy must first be lawfully brought to an end. This cannot occur until either the ish date or there is an alleged breach of the terms of the tenancy. Notice to quit must be served along with the prescribed information.[6] Notices to quit do not explain the reason for termination: this is provided for in the notice of proceedings for possession, which must also be served on the tenant.[7]

Statutory assured tenancies

5–07   Occupation as a statutory assured tenant is allowed after the contractual tenancy has been terminated by notice to quit. So long as the tenant retains possession there is a statutory right to stay in the property.[8] The tenant who

---

[3]   Peter Robson, "Security of Tenure", (January) 1990 SCOLAG 10.
[4]   Introduced following exploitation of tenants in Scotland during the Second World War.
[5]   See para. 2–52 *et seq.*
[6]   Assured Tenancies (Prescribed Information) (Scotland) Regulations 1988 (S.I. 1988 No. 2067).
[7]   See para. 5–49.
[8]   s. 16.

retains possession is entitled to the benefits of all the terms and conditions of the original contract of tenancy. By the same token such a tenant is obliged to abide by the terms of the original contract.[9] This can only be brought to an end with an order from the sheriff.[10] The sheriff may only make an order for possession on the grounds laid down in Schedule 5 to the Housing (Scotland) Act 1988.[11] These grounds are either mandatory or discretionary.

The major difference between the grounds of possession for assured tenancies and for protected tenancies is the greater scope for landlords in the automatic grounds for repossession under the assured regime. In operating the mandatory possession grounds there is no overall discretion vested in the sheriff to refuse an order on the grounds of reasonableness.[12]

Security of tenure

Security of tenure is applicable where certain statutory conditions are satisfied, namely[13]:

(1)   an assured tenancy existed;
(2)   the contract has been terminated;
(3)   the tenant retains possession of the house.

5–08

Until a landlord seeks repossession through the sheriff court, the occupying tenant continues to have all the rights and obligations of the original agreement except for any relating to termination by the landlord. In these circumstances where the tenant relies on the statute to remain in the property, this is termed a "statutory assured tenancy".

Joint tenancies

The word "tenancy" covers a joint tenancy so that any one of the joint tenants will be able to claim the protection of the Act.[14] There is a fuller discussion of joint tenancies above.[15–16] The practical problem which joint tenants will normally encounter is that their liability for rent will normally and contractually be joint and several. This has the effect that whilst one or more joint tenants may quit the property, the remaining joint tenant(s) will be obliged to meet the whole of the rent bill. The landlord is not obliged to accept substitute tenants and this may have the effect of rendering the remaining joint tenancy rights of limited value. Joint and several liability for the rent implies rights to the property for which the remaining tenant is contractually bound to pay.

5–09

Retaining possession of the property

A statutory assured tenant who gives up possession loses the benefit of the Act. The possession must be exercised either personally or through the tenant's spouse. Spouses automatically obtain rights in the property of their partner

5–10

---

[9]   s. 16(1)(b).
[10]   s. 18.
[11]   See para. 5–12 *et seq.*
[12]   s. 18(3).
[13]   s. 16(1).
[14]   s. 55(3).
[15–16]   See para. 1–24 *et seq.*

under the Matrimonial Homes (Family Protection) (Scotland) Act 1981,[17] except
where the property was obtained other than as a matrimonial home.[18] In addition
it is possible for a non-tenant cohabitee to seek a grant of occupancy rights
where a couple are living together as husband and wife.[19] The right to hold is
not lost by a temporary absence such as holiday or business trips. There is no
provision in the Act equivalent to the abandonment procedure for secure
tenancies[20] nor any ground for repossession for absence without reasonable cause
for a continuous period in excess of six months.[21] Although to create an assured
tenancy it is necessary that the property be the "only or principal home" of the
tenant, this could still allow temporary subsidiary purposes such as letting to
summer visitors.[22] As the Act states, however, that assured tenancies cannot be
assigned or sub-let without express written permission,[23] it would be necessary
for such an activity to be specifically approved by the landlord as well as
consistent with the retention of possession. Assured tenants can only be
individuals so that the question of whether a company let is a "sham" or not is
less likely to be encountered.[24] However, landlords wishing to rent out for periods
of less than six months without providing any security of tenure to their tenants
still continue to utilise these avoidance techniques.[25]

Quitting the premises without further notice

5–11   Often a rental agreement contains a clause or clauses purporting to take away
the rights of the assured tenant in relation to security of tenure and requiring the
tenant to quit the premises without any further order at the end of the contract.
Such statements are of no effect and are overridden by the express requirement
in the legislation that a tenancy cannot be brought to an end except through an
order by the sheriff.[26] Provided that the landlord is able to persuade a sheriff
that he is entitled to a possession order, then this overrides any other requirement
in the rental agreement concerning notices to quit.[27] Sheriffs will need to be
satisfied that the tenant has received proper notice of the possession proceedings
in order to provide an opportunity to challenge them.[28]

3. GROUNDS FOR RECOVERY OF POSSESSION

Introduction

5–12   One of the major aims of the rent legislation in Scotland since the Leases Act
1449 has been to provide a level of security of tenure to those occupying property.
The current statute retains the concept of security of tenure but extends those

---

[17] s. 1.
[18] Law Reform (Miscellaneous Provisions) (Scotland) Act 1985, s. 13(10).
[19] s. 18 (as amended by the Law Reform (Miscellaneous Provisions) (Scotland) Act 1985, s. 13(9)).
[20] Housing (Scotland) Act 1987, ss. 49, 50 and 51.
[21] Housing (Scotland) Act 1987, Sched. 5, Ground 5.
[22] *Stewart v. Mackay*, 1947 S.C. 287.
[23] s. 23.
[24] *Ronson Nominees v. Mitchell*, 1982 S.L.T. (Sh.Ct.) 18.
[25] *Hilton v. Plustitle* [1988] 3 All E.R. 1051; correspondence with various solicitors post-1989.
[26] s. 18 and Sched. 5.
[27] s. 16(3).
[28] This has an equivalent in s. 15(5) of the Rent (Scotland) Act 1984.

situations where landlords can have tenants evicted. Under the assured tenancy regime, as with protected tenancies under the Rent (Scotland) Act 1984 and secure tenancies under the Housing (Scotland) Act 1987, there is a requirement that possession orders only be given on one or more of the grounds specified in the legislation. There are two sets of requirements—grounds for possession must be established and proper notice given.

Grounds for possession must be established

The sheriff has no power to make an assured tenancy possession order in   5–13
any circumstances other than those laid down in Schedule 5 to the 1988 Act. One or more of the grounds for possession must be established. There are two situations which can exist when a possession order is sought. Under the discretionary grounds the sheriff has discretion and must be satisfied not only that the conditions in the ground are satisfied but also that it is reasonable to grant the order for possession. In situations where mandatory grounds are being invoked, if the ground is satisfied there is no element of discretion and the order must be granted. As well as giving a notice to quit, proper notice of proceedings for possession must be served before there can be an order for possession.

Necessity for inclusion of grounds in tenancy agreement

The legislation also provides that there can be no possession order while the   5–14
contract runs under certain grounds unless the tenancy agreement specifically makes such provision.[29] This seems to have the effect that where a short, perhaps amateur, lease agreement merely states the premises, term and rent, then during the contractual term the landlord may not use these grounds. The landlord would need to terminate the contractual tenancy at its term and would then be able to use one of the grounds in Schedule 5. This requirement to incorporate the possession ground in the tenancy agreement is in addition to the need for a separate written notice of intention required for the certain grounds.[30] The grounds which must be specified in terms of section 18(6) are as follows:

(1) mortgage repossession;
(2) rent three months in arrears;
(3) persistent delay in paying rent;
(4) rent in arrears;
(5) breach of terms of tenancy (other than rent);
(6) deterioration of house or common parts;
(7) nuisance or illegal or immoral purposes;
(8) deterioration of condition of furniture.

4. MANDATORY GROUNDS FOR POSSESSION

Introduction

Where the ground which is established is listed in Part I of Schedule 5, the   5–15
sheriff must grant a possession order. In addition, some of the grounds may

[29] s. 18(6).
[30] See para. 5–15 *et seq.*

only be available after the specified time laid down in the Schedule—off-season holiday lets and lettings of student accommodation by specified educational institutions.

The sheriff may not adjourn an action if it is a situation where the landlord is using one of the mandatory grounds of possession or if it is a "short assured tenancy".[31]

Where a possession order is granted for one of the appropriate grounds noted, such an order brings to an end the contractual rights of the tenant. In addition, if "statutory assured tenancy" rights have come into effect a possession order ends these too. They come to an end on the day that the possession order takes effect without the need for additional notice to quit.[32]

Reasonable to dispense with notice

5–16   The test applied under the Housing (Scotland) Act 1988 is one of reasonableness rather than the "just and equitable" test previously applied in notice cases in the Rent Acts.[33] The Court of Appeal have examined the provision in the Housing Act 1988 covering England and Wales in a case involving landlords who rented out property on a short assured tenancy. The landlords' plan was to work from their small country cottage. This turned out not to be feasible. Unfortunately, although this case gives an indication of the factors currently deemed relevant, the test in the Housing Act 1988 is "just and equitable". No Scottish decisions are known to the authors.

Landlord wants property for his own home [Ground 1]

5–17   This ground occurs where the landlord or one of the joint landlords occupied the house as his only or principal home and wants possession of the property. It should be noted that there is no need for the landlord to establish any need for the property provided that written notice is given at the commencement of the tenancy that possession might be recovered on this ground. "Require" does not imply any element of necessity nor that it is reasonable to regain the property.[34]

Alternatively, this ground is available where the landlord or one of the joint landlords requires the house as his or his spouse's only or principal home. Again there must be written notice at the start of the tenancy. This ground is not available to those who become landlords by purchase after the start of the tenancy. There is no requirement that the landlord "reasonably" require the premises. It has been accepted that occupation of a dwelling as an only or principal home not for a reasonable period but only until it could be sold is permissable.[35]

---

[31] s. 20(6).
[32] ss 16(3) and 18(7).
[33] Rent (Scotland) Act 1984, ss. 9 and 11 and Sched. 2. Contrast the Court of Appeal cases of *Fernandes v. Parvardin* (1982) 5 H.L.R. 33; *Bradshaw v. Baldwin-Wiseman* [1985] 1 E.G.L.R. 123; and *Boyle v. Verrall* [1997] 1 E.G.L.R. 25. These cases deal with the failure to give notice in relation to the owner-occupier mandatory ground of possession under the English equivalent of the Rent (Scotland) Act 1984 and the Housing (Scotland) Act 1988.
[34] *Kennealy v. Dunne* [1977] Q.B. 839 at 849.
[35] *Lipton v. Whitworth* (1994) 26 H.L.R. 293.

Dispensing with Notice

The sheriff can dispense with the need for notice if it is considered reasonable 5–18 to do so. As noted the test is whether it is reasonable to dispense with the notice. Dealing with the equivalent English legislation the Court of Appeal looked at the position of owner-occupier landlords who purported to rent out on a short assured tenancy[36] but failed to serve the necessary formal notice that the tenants' rights were limited.[37] Thinking that the tenants had no security of tenure the landlords did not, of course, serve a Ground 1 notice. The Court of Appeal were of the view that it was "just and equitable" to dispense with this notice looking to all the circumstances.[38] These included informal conversations about the landlords re-occupying the rented property and early written notice that the property would be required. Also of relevance were the respective needs of the parties— the landlords' alternative accommodation was not really satisfactory for someone who needed to work in London. The tenants, for their part, had no particular need to live in that particular area of London and their lack of income would be met by housing benefit wherever they stayed, in the view of the Court of Appeal.

Mortgage default [Ground 2]

This ground is available where a heritable security over the house existed 5–19 before the creation of the tenancy and where the property is being repossessed following default by the debtor. The tenant must have been given written notice that possession might be recovered under this ground although the sheriff has the power to dispense with this requirement where he considers it reasonable. Problems have arisen where lenders are keen that Housing Associations should incorporate this ground into their agreements whilst the Associations are not keen to do so.

This is an example of a case where the contractual rights of the tenant may not be fulfilled because of the owner losing his/her rights due to the lender repossessing. Where the landlord has unlawfully leased property without the written consent of the creditor, it is likely that a sheriff will dispense with the requirement for notice.[39] Where a creditor recovers possession against a defaulting landlord only to find that an unauthorised tenancy exists, the creditor has two options. It can raise an action to have the unlawful tenancy reduced, or it can raise an action for recovery of possession under this ground.

Off-season holiday property [Ground 3]

This is designed for properties rented out "between seasons" which aims to 5–20 guarantee that the property will be available for renting out for the next season. It is available where property is rented out for a period not exceeding eight months and was at some time within the 12 months prior to the start of the tenancy occupied for a holiday. The same conditions as regards notice at the

---

[36] Actually the equivalent under the Housing Act 1988—a shorthold assured tenancy.
[37] See paras 2–47 and 2–48.
[38] *Boyle v. Verrall* (1997) 1 E.G.L.R. 25; approved in *Mustafa v. Ruddock* (1997) 30 H.L.R. 495.
[39] *Tamsoui v. Clydesdale Bank plc*, 1997 S.L.T. (Sh.Ct.) 20.

commencement of the tenancy apply here too but may not be dispensed with by the sheriff. This means that the landlord must start out using the property as a holiday let prior to renting out in the off-season to be in a position to take advantage of this ground.

For the purposes of this ground the tenancy is treated as not exceeding eight months if it can be terminated at the option of the landlord before the expiry of eight months from the start of the tenancy. Where there are options for renewal by the tenant which if added to the original length of the tenancy exceed eight months then such an agreement is regarded as exceeding eight months. The term "holiday" has been interpreted flexibly in relation to Rent Act evasions and is discussed above.[40]

Educational body non-student tenancies [Ground 4]

5–21   This ground is more restricted than simply student tenants. It covers rentings to those not exempted by Schedule 4. This took tenancies rented to students by recognised educational institutions outwith the scope of the 1988 legislation. Educational institutions, in addition, are encouraged to rent out out-of-term. If they have been renting out accommodation in the previous 12 months to a student then they may rent out to a non-student and rely on the mandatory ground to gain repossession. Such a tenancy must not exceed 12 months. As indicated the landlord must be one of the educational institutions specified in the Act.[41] The non-student tenant must be given notice at the commencement of the tenancy. There is no provision here for the sheriff to waive the requirement if the landlord fails to provide proper notice to the tenant.

Minister/lay missionary property [Ground 5]

5–22   The interests of clerical personnel to have access to convenient accommodation are reflected in this ground. It arises where the property is held for occupation by a minister or full-time missionary as a residence from which to perform the duties of the religious office and where the property is required for occupation by a minister or missionary. There must be written notice to the tenant that possession might be recovered on this ground.

Demolition or reconstruction work [Ground 6]

5–23   This ground was originally rather less specific. Its main use was expected to be by housing associations. Before the 1988 Act housing associations had experienced some problems in this area with tenants in decants.[42] It is available where the landlord intends to demolish or reconstruct or carry out substantial works[43] on the house or building of which it forms part and the proposals are likely to be hampered by the tenant. This ground is only available to landlords who owned the property before the tenancy was created. The landlord must establish that he cannot reasonably carry out the intended work without the tenant giving up possession of the property. This ground may be brought into play by a landlord where the work can be carried out only if the tenant accepts a variation in the terms of the tenancy or accepts an assured tenancy of part of

---

[40] See paras 2–55 and 2–56.
[41] Sched. 4, para. 7 and the Assured Tenancies (Exceptions) (Scotland) Regulations 1988 (S.I. 1988 No. 2068).
[42] *Charing Cross and Kelvingrove Housing Association v. Kraska,* 1986 S.L.T. (Sh.Ct.) 42.
[43] *Bath v. Pritchard, The Times,* August 11, 1989.

the house or both of these and the tenant refuses to accept such a change. In addition the ground is available where the work cannot be carried out even if the tenant accepts a variation in the terms of the tenancy or an assured tenancy of only part of the house or both.

Tenancy inherited under a will or on intestacy [Ground 7]

Where under the will of the tenant or where there is no will, on intestacy, the 5–24 tenancy passes to another party the landlord may get the property back provided that proceedings are started not later than 12 months after the death of the former tenant. The sheriff may direct that this 12-month period be computed from the date when the landlord became aware of the former tenant's death. There is no indication as to what criteria should be used by a sheriff in making such a decision and it will be up to the landlord to establish the circumstances in which he failed to be aware of the tenant's death. The statute specifies that acceptance of rent from a new tenant is not to be regarded as creating a new tenancy unless the landlord agrees in writing to a change in the amount of rent, the period of the tenancy, the premises which are let or any other terms of the tenancy—as compared with the tenancy prior to the death.

Three months' rent arrears [Ground 8]

Possession may be recovered where the tenant is at least three months in 5–25 arrears with the rent at both the date of service of the notice and at the date of the hearing. The original wording in the Bill was changed to make it clear that a full three months' arrears was required rather than what was originally proposed which was simply "some rent lawfully due ... more than 3 months in arrears". Solicitors have indicated that they have not used this ground with any confidence that possession will be secured since it is always vulnerable to the tenants reducing the arrears prior to the court appearance. McAllister suggests that tenants will have limited room for manoeuvre as they will receive only a section 19 notice of two weeks.[44] Where, however, the lease does not specifically provide for the tenancy automatically terminating in this situation, a notice to quit will be required which must give at least four weeks' notice or more.[44a] It is suggested in any case that this would be the prudent course of action.

In addition, in many instances of large arrears there is a dispute about the level of services or quality of the accommodation behind the non-payment rather than simply wilful refusal to pay In such circumstances the tenant could hardly be regarded as being in arrears of rent "lawfully due".

5. Discretionary Grounds

Introduction

The discretion of the sheriff is a positive one. The sheriff must be satisfied 5–26 about overall reasonableness before granting a possession order under one of the grounds in Part II of Schedule 5. It involves taking into account every relevant circumstance affecting the interests of the parties such as their conduct and any possible hardship which might result if the order were to be made as a well as the interests of the public.[45] The question of the possibility of the tenant obtaining other accommodation is relevant as well as any rights under statute such as

---

[44] *Scottish Law of Leases* (2nd ed.), p. 216.
[44a] See para. 5–50.
[45] *Minchburn Ltd v. Fernandez* [1986] 2 E.G.L.R. 103.

legislation for homeless persons. The steps to be followed before a case comes to court and the various procedural issues are outwith the scope of this text and are covered by Jonathan Mitchell's *Eviction and Rent Arrears*.[46]

Alternatives available to the court

5–27   The Housing (Scotland) Act 1988 makes provision for the sheriff to adjourn, sist, suspend or postpone possession.[47] Where the landlord is seeking possession under one of the discretionary grounds the action can be postponed or sisted.[48] Even where a possession order is granted it is possible for the sheriff to postpone the date when the eviction is to take place. Alternatively conditions can be set concerning payment of rent arrears or about any other conditions.[49]

Postponing execution of a possession order

5–28   The sheriff can exercise the option to halt execution of the possession order or postpone the date. The sheriff also decides how long the period of these postponements is to last. Most postponements are for up to one month.[50] Conditions are also frequently imposed as to rent payments and arrears in this context.[51] In practice it may be that if the tenant keeps to any other conditions imposed the possession order may not be operated and the assured tenancy continues. Typically this would occur where a schedule of repayments of arrears of rent is fixed and the tenant keeps to this.[52]

Imposing conditions in adjournments or postponements

5–29   When adjourning any possession action or postponing the operation of possession the sheriff is required by the Act to impose conditions where tenants are in arrears or there are payments due for occupation after the end of the tenancy. There is an exception if the sheriff considers that to impose conditions would cause exceptional hardship or would otherwise be unreasonable. The sheriff has discretion to impose any other conditions which he thinks fit such as concerning behaviour or treatment of the premises where the tenant's past behaviour or treatment of the premises is the ground for possession.[53]

Cancelling a possession order

5–30   The sheriff may cancel a possession order in the same way as under the Rent (Scotland) Act 1984 if the tenant abides by the conditions which they have imposed.[54] This would apply where either rent arrears are cleared or where a tenant whose

---

[46] Shelter Scottish Housing Law Service (1995), section 5.
[47] s. 20—this is similar to powers that exist in relation to protected tenancies under the Rent (Scotland) Act 1984, s. 12 and secure tenancies under the Housing (Scotland) Act 1987, s. 48.
[48] s. 20(2).
[49] s. 20(3).
[50] Some 70% of successful possession orders are suspended for up to one month and 14% for over one month—*Housing and Construction Statistics* 1979–1989 (HMSO, 1990), p. 146, Table 11.10.
[51] In England and Wales this occurs in some 20% of possession orders made in county court recovery of possession actions—*Housing and Construction Statistics* 1979–1989, *op. cit.*
[52] *Thompson v. Elmbridge B.C.* (1987) 131 S.J. 128.
[53] s. 20(3).
[54] s. 20(4).

actions caused a nuisance is able to show that there has been a change in behaviour.

Rights to sists and postponements of spouses/cohabitees

If there is a spouse or cohabitee with occupancy rights living in the premises 5–31 when possession proceedings are started that spouse/cohabitee has the same rights to get sists (temporary discontinuations) or postponements in the possession action.[55] No distinction is made between spouses and cohabitees in the legislation. The view has been adopted that the occupancy rights of spouses are the same as the rights of cohabitees to apply to have their rights determined by the courts.[56] Whilst this appears to be a somewhat doubtful proposition, since it is accepted by the Government it can be assumed that if their confidence was to be misplaced an amendment would be forthcoming.

Suitable alternative accommodation [Ground 9]

Although the availability of alternative accommodation is less likely in the 5–32 private sector than in social housing this ground is encountered from time to time as the case law indicates. Landlords may regain their property where they are able to offer accommodation broadly equivalent to the existing tenancy or where generally satisfactory conditions are on offer. The details of what amount to suitable alternative accommodation are covered in Part III of Schedule 5 and are dealt with later.

Tenant withdraws a notice to quit [Ground 10]

There may be a number of very good reasons why tenants might give a notice 5–33 to quit such as where a job offer falls through or family circumstances change. The ground applies where the tenant has given notice to quit but stays on after this has expired in either the whole or part of the premises. In addition proceedings for possession must have been started by the landlord within six months of the expiry of the tenant's notice to quit as well as there not being a new tenancy either expressly or impliedly entered into.

Persistent delay in rent payment [Ground 11]

This was a ground new to the Rent Acts in 1988 and was originally to have 5–34 been one of the mandatory grounds of possession. No assistance can be gained from the business tenancy sector since the element of discretion given to sheriffs in this ground has no parallel in commercial leases. In the debates on the ground it was suggested that persistently meant "repeatedly" or "over a long time".[56a]

It is not necessary that the rent be in arrears when the proceedings are begun. However, one of the problems which has bedeviled the rental market since its introduction has been the delays and difficulties experienced by tenants since housing benefit was introduced by the Social Security and Housing Benefits Act 1982. Drawing a parallel with the treatment of like issues under the homeless persons legislation, such a problem, being outwith the control of tenants, would not amount to persistent delay. It lacks the conscious element implied. Landlords

---

[55] s. 20(5).
[56] Lord McDonald in *McAlinden v. Bearsden and Milngavie D.C.,* 1986 S.L.T. 191.
[56a] *Hansard*, H.L., First Scottish Standing Committee, col. 704, February 16, 1988.

in the private sector, as Jonathan Mitchell points out,[57] do, however, have the option to insist on direct payment of housing benefit where there are rent arrears of at least eight weeks.[58] The authority have the discretion to pay direct where there are either no arrears or less arrears. Such a decision can be reviewed within six weeks of its notification by either landlord or tenant.[59]

Nor would the ground cover non-payment by tenants done in pursuance of legal rights. This occurs where tenants use their right to withhold rent to put pressure on landlords to carry out repairs or as a tactic in a dispute over the obligations of the parties under the lease.

Rent due [Ground 12]

5–35   This was treated as part of the breach of tenancy obligations under the Rent (Scotland) Act 1984 but was separated out for assured tenancies. Two elements are required in this ground of possession. Rent must be unpaid at the date when the action for recovery is started and be in arrears at the date of service of notice. The need for this second element is, of course, not necessary where the sheriff dispenses with the need for service of the notice of proceedings for possession.

Breach of obligations of tenancy [Ground 13]

5–36   Establishing that there has been a breach is the first step in this two-stage process which involves, significantly, looking at reasonableness. It comes into play where any obligation of the tenancy has been broken or not performed. Breach needs to be material, involving something more than a triviality. A condition banning any pets would, for instance, be breached by a tenant having a dog in the premises but a goldfish would be dismissed as irrelevant. The presence of a parakeet or budgie, however, would be of significance for a landlord looking to evict on breach. The fact that a dog had been purchased for the protection of the tenant's wife during the Yorkshire Ripper's years of activity did not assist a tenant whose tenancy agreement forbade such animals—the court did note that the Ripper had been imprisoned and that the tenant and his wife had divorced.[60] The absence of an equivalent to the special repossession head in the public sector has led housing associations to use this head of possession when tenants have given false or misleading information to obtain tenancies with mixed success.[61] This is likely to be used rather than reduction since following an Outer House decision, the landlord would still need to satisfy a sheriff in terms of the Schedule that the granting of possession order was reasonable.[62] The reduction of the lease would simply have the effect of giving rise to a statutory assured tenancy.

[57] *Eviction and Rent Arrears*, p. 49.
[58] Housing Benefit (General) Regulations 1987 (S.I. 1987 No. 1971), reg. 93—exceptionally it may be held that it is in the overriding interest of the tenant that the benefit be retained by the authority under reg. 95.
[59] reg. 79(2); for further details see Mitchell, p. 49.
[60] *Green v. Sheffield City Council* (1994) 26 H.L.R. 349.
[61] Contrast *Shettleston H.A. Ltd v. Bourke,* 1996 Hous.L.R. 53 (misinformation about tenant's housing history) (granted) with *Govanhill H.A. Ltd v. Malley,* 1996 Hous.L.R. 61(applied for housing with boyfriend/fiance who turned out to be applicant's uncle—allocated two-bedroom rather than three-bedroom accommodation) (not granted due to personal circumstances including illness).
[62] *Govanhill Housing Association Ltd v. Palmer,* 1997 Hous.L.R. 133—see the comments at 140.

The breach must also be a term of the tenancy rather than a breach of a collateral personal agreement. The kind of term found in commercial tenancies that the existence of a breach is in the sole judgment of the landlord is not conclusive in so far as the sheriff still requires to be satisfied as to the reasonableness of granting a possession order.

Condition of house deteriorated [Ground 14]

Many of these grounds have their origins in earlier legislation. This ground 5–37 appeared in the first emergency Rent Act in 1915 and there is a modified version covering protected tenancies.[63] It was expanded to take in an issue which was introduced when public sector tenants were given security of tenure in the Tenants' Rights, Etc. (Scotland) Act 1980, namely common parts such as stairways, lifts and halls. Establishing deterioration in connection with individual houses may be possible on failure to use a reasonable degree of diligence to preserve the property from harm such as damp by heating the property. One would expect the problem for the future increasingly to centre around putting this notion into practice.[64] There are real problems involved in heating and ventilating property with poor thermal qualities as expressed in the U-value. Since the *McGourlick*[65] and *Gunn*[66] decisions in the Inner House and *Guy* in the Outer House,[67] the landlord can no longer simply blame the tenant as some public sector landlords tried to do in the past. *Gunn* goes further in making it clear that landlords who blame the tenant must specify exactly how the tenant's actions have caused the condition of the property to deteriorate.[68]

As for common parts, in the absence of effective control through door-entry systems one could imagine landlords experiencing evidential problems in convincing sheriffs that the poor condition of common stairs is caused by specific tenants.

Nuisance, annoyance and illegal/immoral use of premises [Ground 15]

Losing one's tenancy as the result of nuisance or annoyance was also a feature 5–38 of the 1915 Rent Act. As this is the same as the ground found in the Rent (Scotland) Act 1984 and the Housing (Scotland) Act 1987 for regulated and secure tenancies the precedents which have emerged are relevant.[69] The first point to be made is that the courts have in the past taken the view that the tenant is responsible for all the activities of other occupants of the premises. Tenants have been evicted where they failed to control their families while living in the property,[70] whilst in prison[71] or when they were physically incapable of restraining the nuisance behaviour.[72] The protection for joint tenants is that the sheriff must be satisfied as to overall reasonableness.[73]

---

[63] Ground 3 in Sched. 2 to the Rent (Scotland) Act 1984.
[64] See Chap. 5 at 00.
[65] *Renfrew D.C. v. McGourlick*, 1988 S.L.T. 127.
[66] *Gunn v. Glasgow D.C.*, 1992 S.C.L.R. 1018 (Notes).
[67] *Guy v. Strathkelvin D.C.*, 1997 S.C.L.R. 405.
[68] See para. 3–36.
[69] See above.
[70] *R v. Salford City Council, ex p. Davenport* (1984) 82 L.G.R. 89; *Glenrothes Development Corporation v. Graham*, Dec. 14, 1994, discussed at length in O'Carroll & Collins, pp. 108–109.
[71] *R v. Swansea City Council, ex p. Thomas* (1982) 9 H.L.R. 66.
[72] *R v. Swansea City Council, ex p. John* (1982) 9 H.L.R. 58.
[73] *City of Glasgow D.C., v. Brown*, 1988 S.C.L.R. 679.

Where there are criminal activities going on in the premises the precedents suggest that a wide interpretation on this head of possession. Frequent or continuous use is not required, but a single conviction would probably be insufficient—although where the issue involved, say, drug-pushing as opposed to individual use, this might result in the exercise of the discretion against such a tenant.[74] Where the tenant argues that the landlord has forfeited the right to seek repossession through acquiescence in the conduct or that this has been condoned, such a claim must be clearly demonstrable. It is not enough simply to indicate that there has been acceptance of rent after the alleged conduct.

Deterioration of furniture [Ground 16]

5–39 This ground was introduced into rent legislation when previously unprotected tenants of furnished property were given the same protection as tenants of unfurnished property in the Rent Act 1974. There is little evidence of its use in the past which may stem from practical considerations. Landlords do not always provide an inventory of what furniture is provided in furnished premises. If they do there may be no indication as to its condition. In cases of deterioration—often known as "wear and tear"—as opposed to destruction establishing ill treatment rather than fair wear and tear may be a problem.

Ex-employee tenant [Ground 17]

5–40 This ground appears as a discretionary ground rather than as a mandatory one in the legislation. It allows individuals who have taken a tenancy as part of the terms of employment with their landlord in essence to argue that it is not reasonable for the landlord to obtain a possession order. The landlord will have to indicate why the property is required and a possession order would, presumably, not be granted simply without a good reason being given such as rehousing a relative. The availability of properties to landlords for their own or a spouse's use is dealt with in ground 1 above. It is not necessary that there be a new employee requiring to be housed by the landlord.

It has been suggested that where occupancy derives from a contract of service rather than a lease such occupiers are not tenants and hence are not covered by the Rent Acts. It is not easy to see how this statement is compatible with the existence of ground 17. The case authority for the service occupancy proposition does not appear to be in point.[75]

The National Health Service and Community Care Act 1990 specified that tenancies entered into on or after April 1, 1990 were no longer to be treated as exempt from the coverage of the Housing (Scotland) Act 1988.[76] This applies to many doctors and nurses working for the National Health Service.

6. SUITABLE ALTERNATIVE ACCOMMODATION

Introduction

5–41 The legislation also provides for landlords being able to offer different accommodation to their tenants. It must be stressed, again, that this is a ground

---

[74] *Schneiders & Sons v. Abrahams* [1925] 1 K.B. 301; *Abrahams v. Wilson* [1971] 2 Q.B. 88—see para. 5–111.
[75] *Cairns v. Innes*, 1942 S.C. 164; *MacGregor v. Dunnett*, 1949 S.C. 510; *Cargill v. Phillips*, 1951 S.C. 67.
[76] 1990 Act, Sched. 8, para. 11.

which requires the sheriff's satisfaction as to reasonableness. There is little evidence that it is an option available to many landlords and it appears to be seldom encountered in practice.

The criteria for landlords regaining their property when they provide the sitting tenant with suitable alternative accommodation are on the same lines as those provided in the Rent (Scotland) Act 1984 and the Housing (Scotland) Act 1987. This can stem either from a local authority certificate of suitability or from being deemed by the sheriff to be suitable.

Local authority certificate[77]

Although conclusive evidence of suitability, these certificates are rarely used 5–42 in the authors' experience, although they have been encountered in the case law.[78] If the public authority where the premises are situated certifies that suitable alternative accommodation will be provided for the tenant, this is conclusive proof that such accommodation will indeed be available. It applies to local authorities and Scottish Homes. The court must then determine whether or not the alternative accommodation offered is similar to the accommodation in the certificate provided by the local authority in respect of similar sized families.[79]

Deemed suitable by sheriff[80]

Alternatively, the sheriff must be satisfied as to the level of security of tenure 5–43 being offered. If there is no certificate from the local authority or Scottish Homes then accommodation is to be regarded as suitable as far as security of tenure is concerned if it consists of either separate premises let on an assured tenancy (with certain important exceptions mentioned below) or a short assured tenancy or a tenancy which the sheriff considers will give the tenant reasonably equivalent security of tenure to the assured tenancy mentioned here. The assured tenancies which are excluded from this paragraph are those covered by the mandatory grounds of possession 1–5 where notice has to be given to the tenant:

(a) property is the landlord's former principal home;
(b) mortgage on the property before the lease;
(c) off-season let of holiday property;
(d) lease by educational body to non-student;
(e) lease to minister or full-time lay missionary.

Criteria for suitability[81]

The sheriff must be satisfied that the accommodation is reasonably suitable 5–44 to the needs of the tenant and his family. Three issues have to be addressed. First, the question of proximity to work must be considered. This must be satisfied along with one of two additional tests. The initial issue, which has never been encountered by the authors is whether the tenancy is similar as regards rental to equivalent public sector housing. The alternative test is whether the accommodation is reasonably suitable to the means and needs of tenant. Given that most post 1988 tenancies in the private rented sector have been short assured

---

[77] para. 1.
[78] *Trustees of the Dame Margaret Hungerford Charity v. Beazely* (1993) 26 H.L.R. 269.
[79] *Jones v. Cook* (1990) 22 H.L.R. 319.
[80] para. 2.
[81] para. 3.

tenancies there has been no case law emerging under the 1988 Act on suitable alternative accommodation and the provisions of the pre-1988 regime are relied on.[82]

Proximity to place of work

5–45   This is determined by looking to the reality of the situation and the practicability of travelling between home and work.[83] Where a person has a number of places of work to visit in the course of his work there will be difficulties in deciding which is the place of work. The issue of doing some work at home will also be factor in deciding whether the proposed alternative accommodation is suitable as regards proximity to work.[84]

Similar as regards rental and extent to the accommodation

5–46   This is looked at in terms of what is offered in public sector housing (local authority, or Scottish Homes) in the neighbourhood to persons whose needs are similar as regards extent of accommodation in the view of the sheriff. In order to decide whether or not property is similar to that provided by a public authority a certificate from that body as to the extent of accommodation provided for a given size of family and the rent charged is conclusive of these facts. Again this is a test which has not been encountered in the case law nor in the experience of the authors.

Reasonably suitable to the means of the tenant and to the needs of the tenant and his family as regards extent and character

5–47   This is the main issue which has been litigated under the Rent Acts and an objective test has emerged. Suitability goes beyond mere size of accommodation.[85] It does not, however, cover lifestyle.[86] The standard of housing is judged rather than ancillary personal interests or "fads, fancies and preferences".[87] If a landlord offers accommodation which is overcrowded this cannot be deemed suitable to the needs of the tenant and his family.[88] The test for overcrowding is found in Part VII of the Housing (Scotland) Act 1987.[89]

7. PROCEDURAL ISSUES

Introduction

5–48   In addition to establishing that the substantive grounds exist, to justify a possession order it is necessary that the landlord establish that the tenant has received the proper notice. This involves both a notice to quit and a notice of proceedings for possession. Once the relevant notices have been served the case comes before the sheriff court, where the Sheriff Court Rules determine the appropriate procedure to be followed.[90]

---

[82]   *Laimond Properties Ltd v. Al-Shakarchi (No. 2), The Times*, Feb. 23, 1988.
[83]   *Yewbright Properties v. Stone* (1980) 40 P. & C.R. 402 at 411.
[84]   *ibid.*
[85]   *Redspring v. Francis* [1973] 1 All E.R. 640.
[86]   *Hill v. Rochard* [1983] 1 W.L.R. 478.
[87]   *Christie v. Macfarlane,* 1930 S.L.T. (Sh.Ct.) 5.
[88]   para. 4.
[89]   See para. 10–10 *et seq.*
[90]   See Mitchell, at section 5.

Notice to quit

For all tenancies in the private sector the Rent (Scotland) Act 1984 specifies 5–49
that no notice to quit any premises let as a dwelling-house is valid unless it is
in writing, contains information which may be prescribed and is given not less
than four weeks before the date on which it is to take effect.[91] Secure tenancies
are a statutory creation whose methods of termination are specified in the
Housing (Scotland) Act 1987.[92]

The requirement for a notice to quit specified in the Rent (Scotland) Act 1984
applies to assured tenancies and nothing in the Housing (Scotland) Act 1988
alters this. Regulations concerning the additional information to accompany
notices to quit have been issued which require tenants to be informed of their
rights—that the court can only grant a possession order on the grounds laid out
in the legislation and that in the event of uncertainty the tenant can obtain advice
from a solicitor.[93]

Minimum periods for notices to quit

The minimum periods for notices to quit are laid down in the Sheriff Courts 5–50
(Scotland) Act 1907.[94] Where the lease is for more than four months the period
of notice is 40 days, while it is one-third of the duration of the let for leases less
than four-months. This is subject to the four week statutory minimum indicated
in the Rent (Scotland) Act 1984.[95]

Notice of proceedings for possession

Before sheriffs can consider granting a possession order they must be satisfied 5–51
that the landlord has given notice that he intends to raise proceedings for
possession.[96] This is modelled on the approach to termination of secure tenancies
in the Housing (Scotland) Act 1987.[97] Sheriffs can dispense with the need for
notice if they consider it reasonable to do so. Such a waiver is not available in
relation to the secure tenancy regime. A notice of proceedings for possession is
effective whether or not it is served on a tenant occupying the property under
the original contract or someone holding under the statute, *i.e.* a person exercising
their rights of security of tenure.[98]

Dispensing with the notice of proceedings for possession

This necessary preliminary to the possession action must be served by the 5–52
landlord in the proper form.[99] The sheriff may allow the landlord to do without
such a notice if he considers it reasonable[1] except where the landlord is seeking

---

[91] s. 112 (1).
[92] See para. 5–100 *et seq.*
[93] Assured Tenancies (Notices to Quit Prescribed Information) (Scotland) Regulations 1988 (S.I. 1988 No. 2067).
[94] ss. 34–38.
[95] s. 112(1).
[96] s. 19.
[97] See paras 5–108 and 5–109.
[98] s. 19(6).
[99] s. 19(1)—form AT6 in terms of the Assured Tenancies (Forms) (Scotland) Regulations 1988 (S.I. 1988 No. 2019).
[1] s. 19(1)(b).

possession on the grounds that the rent is three months in arrears.[2] The test of reasonableness differs from the "just and equitable" test found in the Rent (Scotland) Act 1984 in relation to notice for retirement property, short tenancies, and temporarily absent owner-occupiers and service personnel.[3] The "just and equitable" test has been retained, however, in the part of the Housing Act 1988 applying to England and Wales on this matter.[4]

Contents of the notice of proceedings for possession

5–53   The current notice is the form AT6.[5] The ground and particulars of it are specified in the notice under this section. The grounds specified in the section 19 notice may be altered or added to with the leave of the sheriff.[6] It should be made clear to the tenant what actions need to be done to put matters right.

The section 19 notice must inform the tenant that the landlord intends to raise proceedings for possession on the grounds indicated in the notice. In addition it must indicate that the proceedings will not be started until either two weeks or two months have expired from the date of service of the notice. The appropriate time depends on the kind of ground on which the possession order is based.[7]

Minimum period of notice of proceedings for possession

5–54   Minimum periods are laid down depending on the ground of possession on which repossession is being sought:

(a)   two months—
    (i)   landlord's former home (ground 1);
    (ii)   mortgage repossession (ground 2);
    (iii)   minister/lay missionary (ground 5);
    (iv)   demolition/reconstruction (ground 6);
    (v)   inherited tenancy (ground 7);
    (vi)   suitable alternative accommodation (ground 9);
    (vii)   ex-employee tenancy (ground 17);

(b)   two weeks—in any other case.

"Life" of notice of proceedings for possession

5–55   Notices have a "life" of six months after the date on which the action could have been started.[8] Part 4 of form AT6 requires the landlord to calculate when the six-month period commences. In calculating the six-month period during which proceedings have to be raised, some assistance can be obtained from the interpretation of the same issue under the Housing (Scotland) Act 1987 in relation to secure tenancies—proceedings are raised on the date when an initial writ is served on the tenant rather than the date when it is warranted.[9]

---

[2] s. 19(5).
[3] See para. 5–87 *et seq.*
[4] Sched. 2, Pt IV, paras 8(1) and (2).
[5] s. 19(3) as amended by the Housing Act 1988, Sched. 17, para. 85(b).
[6] s. 19(2) as amended by the Housing Act 1988, Sched. 17, para. 85(a).
[7] s. 19(4).
[8] s. 19(7).
[9] *Edinburgh D.C. v. Davis,* 1987 S.L.T. (Sh.Ct.) 33.

Requirement for both notice to quit and notice of proceedings for possession

Where recovery of possession is being sought against a statutory tenancy, no notice to quit is required. However, where possession is being sought during the currency of a contractual tenancy on one of the permitted grounds[10-11] it is suggested that the service of a notice to quit in addition to the section 19 notice is a prudent course of action, despite the fact that it may not be technically necessary where a lease provides that a contractual tenancy will automatically terminate if one of the grounds included in section 18(6) is satisfied.

5–56

8. SHORT ASSURED TENANCIES

Introduction

The tenant of a short assured tenancy has no defence to a properly based possession action.[12] The landlord may seek possession on the ground that the termination date has been reached. This option exists in addition to the mandatory and discretionary grounds available for all assured tenancies,[13] since the short assured tenancy is a form of assured tenancy.

5–57

Requirements for an automatic grant of possession

Where there is a short assured tenancy the sheriff must grant an order for possession if satisfied that four matters are established. They are that the tenancy has reached its ish; no tacit relocation is operating; no further contractual tenancy is in existence; and a notice has been served on the tenant indicating that the landlord requires the premises. Each element must be present.

5–58

Tenancy has reached its ish

The automatic repossession is only available where the tenancy has reached its termination date. Hence in the common situation of a one-year or two-year short assured tenancy the landlord cannot use this ground until the expiry of the period. Where the tenancy is for a six-month initial period and monthly thereafter, this ground is available to the landlord only once the initial period is reached. In such circumstances the normal periods laid down for valid notice to quit would need to be satisfied.[14]

No tacit relocation operating

Where neither party gives the relevant minimum period for a notice to quit then such a tenancy will relocate, *i.e.* be deemed to have been renegotiated for either the period of the original term of the lease or one year—whichever is the

5–59

[10-11] Housing (Scotland) Act 1988, s. 18(6).
[12] s. 33.
[13] s. 33(1).
[14] See para. 5–50.

shorter period. Hence if a two-year short assured tenancy reaches its termination without either party taking any steps to terminate the agreement, it carries on for a further year. If the agreement was for six-months, the agreement would carry on for another period of six months.

No further contractual tenancy is in existence

5–60   If the initial tenancy has been superseded by a fresh agreement between the parties, the automatic ground of possession is not available since the tenant is entitled to rely on the terms of the new contract to remain in the property.

Section 33 notice

5–61   The final requirement is that the landlord must have given notice that he requires possession of the house. This is rather different from the question of whether the landlord "reasonably requires" the house "for occupation as a residence" as occurs under the Rent (Scotland) Act 1984.[15] The short assured tenancy requirement is formal and does not involve the landlord satisfying any test of necessity. It is for the landlord to decide if he requires possession of the property and it does not seem to be open to the sheriff to consider whether the landlord has an objective need for the property.[16] There is no form laid down for the notice and the equivalent for the assured tenancy[17] requires considerable adaptation. Written notice is not specified and is probably not required. The leading commentator on the equivalent English legislation suggests that while the requirement is not that notice be "served" but "given" supports this view. He suggests, however, that "there is safety in writing".[18] Mitchell takes the same view.[19] There is no authority on the subject as landlords have, in the authors' experience, always provided written notices.

The period of notice given to the tenant indicating that the landlord requires possession must be either two months or such period in excess of two months as the tenancy agreement provides.[20] The fact that there is no formal style provided has led to a suggestion that such notice could be included in the tenancy agreement itself. This strikes the authors as highly doubtful. There is no formal "life" to the notice that the landlord requires the property back. However, one can reasonably assume that sheriffs will not be keen to allow proceedings to be based on old notices nor on notices contained in the tenancy agreement.

Requirement to serve AT6 notice?

5–62   There has been considerable discussion amongst housing lawyers in the past couple of years as to whether it is also necessary to serve a section 19 notice of proceedings for possession. In favour of the service is the fact that a short assured

---

[15] Sched. 2, grounds 7 and 8.
[16] *Kennealy v. Dunne,* [1977] Q.B. 837.
[17] Assured Tenancies (Forms) (Scotland) Regulations 1988 (S.I. 1988 No. 2019), Form AT6.
[18] R.E. Megarry, *The Rent Acts* Vol. 3 Andrew Arden, *Assured Tenancies* (1988), p. 164.
[19] Eviction and Rent Arrears, section 5.9.
[20] s. 33(2).

tenancy is a form of assured tenancy. The 1988 Act specifies that "a sheriff shall not entertain proceedings for possession of a house let on an assured tenancy unless" an AT6 notice is served.[21] When one looks, however, at the form specified under the prescribed regulations the wording is singularly inappropriate and misleading. Landlords are required to specify the grounds under Schedule 5. They are also required to indicate the reasons why the grounds have arisen. This is not really feasible in a short assured tenancy where the only reason the landlord has is that the statute allows automatic repossession. There is, however, a reference to the two-month notice required for a short assured tenancy in the Notes to Part 3 of the AT6 form. The general consensus at present is that no harm is done by serving this notice. Tenants might be forgiven for feeling confused at receiving a notice to quit, a notice under section 33(1)(d) and section 19 notice—the burden of all these being that the landlord no longer wants them.

Date of service of notices

The landlord does not have to wait until the termination date of the tenancy 5–63 to serve the notice that he requires possession of the house. The notice period can form part of the time that the tenancy runs although, of course, it cannot lawfully shorten the agreed tenancy.[22] The legislation also provides that where a tenant has stayed on after the termination date of the original tenancy agreement and a sheriff subsequently grants a possession order under this section then any statutory assured tenancy which has arisen is to come to an end on the day when the possession order takes effect.[23]

9. PROTECTED TENANCIES

Introduction

Although no new tenancies can be entered into under the Rent (Scotland) 5–64 Act 1984 it is likely that these will continue to be part of legal practice for some considerable time to come. The crucial date to remember is January 2, 1989. If the tenant was in occupation before that date then the basic rule of thumb is that the protected code applies. Under the 1984 Act, where the landlord gives the appropriate notice to quit [24] this must also be accompanied by certain prescribed information.[25] However, despite the wording of the notice to quit, as the information makes clear, the tenant in a protected tenancy does not have to leave. The tenant can stay on in the property, relying on the provisions of the Rent (Scotland) Act 1984, as a statutory tenant. In order to take advantage of statutory rights of security of tenure it is necessary that any tenant occupies the dwelling-house.[26] The question is whether the tenant has given up occupation. Occupancy can be exercised either personally or through a spouse. It does not cover property tenanted by a spouse where the property is acquired other than

---

[21] s. 19(1).
[22] s. 33(3).
[23] s. 33(4) .
[24] See para. 5–49.
[25] Rent Regulations (Forms and Information etc) (Scotland) Regulations 1991 (S.I. 1991 No. 1521).
[26] s. 3(1)(a).

as a matrimonial home.[27] This would nowadays almost certainly include a cohabitee since in all respects of succession and statutory occupancy rights their position is treated as broadly that of the spouse.

Occupying the property

5–65   There is no requirement that the property be occupied as the tenant's residence as stated in the equivalent English legislation.[28] One problem which has been encountered over the years has been that of the tenant with two houses. In considering the English legislation, the House of Lords decided that the crucial question was whether the tenant was occupying the property in dispute as his residence.[29] In *Hampstead Way Investments Ltd v. Lewis-Weare*[30] a tenant bought a house elsewhere in which the rest of his family lived but because of his working hours as general manager of a night club, he spent five nights a week sleeping in his rented flat. His stepson actually lived full-time in the flat but it was deemed not to be the tenant's residence. However, looking to the terms of the Rent (Scotland) Act 1984, he would no doubt have satisfied the less exacting Scottish test of simple occupation. In fairness, the English test has been applied fairly loosely in some instances where the level of possession has not been extensive.[31] As for the question of those who intend to return, this is looked at along with the facts of physical occupation. A tenant who initially lived away for seven years and then after proceedings used his property as a furniture store for three years and only physically returned to take up occupancy when court proceedings commenced was unsuccessful in persuading the court that he had not ceased to reside in the property.[32]

Discretionary and mandatory grounds of possession

5–66   Where the tenant chooses to exercise his statutory rights of security of tenure the onus is on the landlord to show that the tenant should leave for one of the approved reasons.[33] Such reasons fall into one of two categories—discretionary or mandatory—depending on whether the sheriff may or must otherwise terminate the tenancy.[34] At the time of writing the legislation in relation to protected[35] and secure[36] tenancies requires the court to be satisfied whilst in the assured[37] code the requirement is that the sheriff be satisfied. This led to decisions being made by sheriff clerks rather than sheriffs since rule 18 stated that a first calling and any continuation thereof may be before the sheriff clerk.[38] The summary cause rules have been amended in relation to recovery of possession of secure tenancies.[38a]

[27] *Hall v. King* [1987] 2 E.G.L.R. 121.
[28] Rent Act 1977, s. 2(1)(a).
[29] *Hampstead Way Investments Ltd v. Lewis-Weare* [1985] 1 E.G.L.R. 120.
[30] *ibid.*
[31] *Brickfield v. Hughes* [1988] 1 E.G.L.R. 106—retired teacher living in rural Lancashire who did not visit his rented London flat for nine years. His children occupied the London flat and he considered it his home where he would probably return if he became a widower.
[32] *Duke v. Porter* [1986] 2 E.G.L.R. 101.
[33] Rent (Scotland) Act 1984, s. 15.
[34] s. 11.
[35] Rent (Scotland) Act 1984, s. 11.
[36] Housing (Scotland) Act 1987, s. 48.
[37] Housing (Scotland) Act 1988, s. 18.
[38] (1990) 13 S.H.L.N. 2.
[38a] S.I. 1991 No. 821.

Voluntary termination of tenancy by tenant

In principle, the Rent Acts are permissive rather than mandatory in their 5–67 effect: that is to say, no tenant is required to insist on staying beyond the contractual term if they do not choose to so long as the tenant gives the required notice. A related issue which has exercised the courts in England and Wales has been how to treat formal agreements where the tenant agrees to give up statutory rights and then has a change of heart since there is always the danger that such a decision is less than voluntary.[39] In *Blackburne*[40] a tenant and landlord who were in dispute about rent arrears and failure to repair came to an agreement whereby the landlord paid some £11,000 for the tenant to give up his tenancy. A consent order was made by the county court judge. The tenant changed his mind a week later and the Divisional Court quashed the order giving possession. This was confirmed by the Court of Appeal.

Discretionary grounds for possession

Sheriffs have discretionary powers in most of the cases which come up before 5–68 them. This means that the sheriff must normally be satisfied not only that the situation falls within the terms of the specific ground of possession, but also that to grant the order for possession would be reasonable.[41] The Rent (Scotland) Act 1984 makes provision for the sheriff to adjourn, sist (temporarily halt), suspend or postpone possession.[42] Where the landlord is seeking possession under one of the discretionary grounds the date of the action can be adjourned for such period as the court thinks fit.[43] Even where a possession order is granted it is possible for the court to postpone the date when the eviction is to take place.[44] Alternatively conditions can be set concerning payment of rent arrears or about any other conditions.[45] The sheriff may not adjourn an action if it is a situation where the landlord is using one of the mandatory grounds of possession or if it is a "short assured tenancy".[46]

Options available to the sheriff

The court has a variety of options. These allow the sheriff temporarily to halt 5–69 the order becoming operational or to postpone this date. The court can decide how long these postponements are to last. Most postponements are for a period of up to one month.[47]

When adjourning any possession action or postponing the operation of possession the court may impose conditions where tenants are in arrears or there are payments due for occupation after the end of the tenancy. The sheriff

---

[39] *R v. Bloomsbury and Marylebone County Court, ex p. Blackburne* [1985] 2 E.G.L.R. 157.
[40] *ibid.*
[41] s. 11(1).
[42] s. 12 .
[43] s. 12(1).
[44] s. 12(2).
[45] s. 12(3).
[46] s. 12(5).
[47] Some 70% of successful possession orders are suspended for up to one month and 14% for over one month—*Housing and Construction Statistics 1979–1989* (HMSO 1990), Table 11.10, p. 146.

has discretion to impose any other conditions which he thinks fit such as providing compensation to the owner for loss of possession.[48]

The court may discharge or rescind any possession order if the tenant abides by the conditions which have been imposed.[49] This would apply where either rent arrears have been cleared or where a tenant whose actions have caused a nuisance is able to show that there has been a change in behaviour.

Transitional protection

5–70   Protected tenants are entitled to the benefit of the transitional arrangements of the Housing (Scotland) Act 1988.[50] This allows protected tenancies to be entered where they are granted to a person who was the protected tenant or the statutory tenant of the same landlord. In addition, where the court is involved in approving suitable alternative accommodation, the legislation provides that such a tenancy may be a protected tenancy.[51] Of course, these transitional arrangements were treated as permissive. There is nothing to stop a tenant deciding to accept an assured or even a short assured tenancy. This would be most likely in situations where landlords are providing financial inducements. In addition, there may well be situations where it is convenient to consolidate a protected tenant's rights into a more rational agreement. This can occur where there has been a protected sharing tenancy which is protected and one of the tenants is leaving. Rather than have protected and assured tenants in the same property with resulting complications, a landlord might wish to consolidate these into a single common regime. It is not possible for any new post-January 1989 tenant to be granted a protected tenancy so that in such circumstances the options would be to continue as protected and assured tenants or as assured tenants. The remaining tenant could not be forced to accept the new assured tenancy with its lesser rights but might be persuaded by financial or similar inducements. As time has passed since the introduction of the 1988 regime, these issues have been encountered on a less regular basis. The possible combinations are myriad and the complex problems which emerge need to be examined according to the facts of each individual case. The view taken in one sheriff court case was that the transitional provisions are, in fact, mandatory.[52]

Suitable alternative accommodation [Pt IV][53]

5–71   If the court is satisfied that suitable alternative accommodation is available for the tenant or will be available for him when the order takes effect then an order for possession may be made.[54] This ground has never been used extensively, although it can arise where a landlord is trying to rationalise a letting operation. It cannot be used simply as an indirect form of harassment, *e.g.* by transferring the tenant from good spacious property into an insanitary slum.

It should be noted that, where the property ceases to be available, either through acquisition by the local authority or because it is a dangerous structure, the landlord is not personally obliged to provide suitable alternative accommodation. In such circumstances the tenant's rights to rehousing would

---

[48] s. 12(3).
[49] s. 12(4).
[50] s. 42.
[51] s. 42 (1)(c)(ii).
[52] *Milnbank Housing Association Ltd v. Murdock*, 1995 S.L.T. (Sh.Ct.) 11.
[53] Sched. II, Pt IV; Suitable Alternative Accommodation.
[54] s. 11(1)(a).

be from the local authority. If requested, the authority in so far as practicable must secure that the tenant is provided with suitable alternative accommodation within a reasonable distance from the tenant's present home.[55]

Local housing authority certificate of equivalence

One of the ways in which a landlord can provide suitable alternative 5–72 accommodation is to obtain a certificate from the local authority. Where a certificate of the local housing authority states that the authority for the district in which the dwelling-house in question is situated will provide suitable alternative accommodation at a date specified in the certificate, then this certificate is conclusive as to alternative accommodation. The certificate must tell the court what the extent of local authority accommodation is.[56] Even when protected tenancies were extensive this option was seldom, if ever, encountered although there is mention of it occurring in one English case from 1993.[57]

Private sector tenancy

Equivalent tenancy. The accommodation must be in the form of an equivalent 5–73 tenancy. Accommodation shall be deemed suitable if the premises are to be let as a separate dwelling which can form a protected tenancy, or which can afford security of tenure reasonably equivalent to a protected tenancy. After the passing of the Housing (Scotland) Act 1988 and the introduction of assured tenancies Shelter reported that some landlords had attempted to persuade tenants to replace their protected tenancies with assured tenancy agreements.[58]

Whilst an assured tenancy would be equivalent as it has broadly similar security of tenure rights, a short assured tenancy, however, carries no security of tenure beyond the term and would not be equivalent.

Similar or reasonably suitable. The accommodation must in addition be similar 5–74 as regards rental and extent to local authority housing in the neighbourhood for families with similar needs. Alternatively it must be reasonably suitable to the means of the tenant and to the needs of the tenant and his family as regards extent and character. Examples of the way in which these criteria are operated can be found in two English cases on the equivalent English legislation. In *Redspring v. Francis*[59] the court considered that in addition to the space requirements and environment, suitability involved a place where a tenant could live in reasonably comfortable conditions suitable to the style of life he leads. This led one tenant to resist a move away from the area where he had his social life and religious connections in *Siddiqui v. Rashid*.[60] The Court of Appeal did not feel that Parliament intended to include such matters as the society of friends or cultural interest in the word "character".

---

[55] Land Compensation (Scotland) Act 1973, s. 36 and the Housing (Scotland) Act 1987, s. 98.
[56] *Jones v. Cook* [1990] 42 E.G. 129.
[57] *Trustees of the Dame Margaret Hungerford Charity v. Beazely* (1993) 26 H.L.R. 269.
[58] Authors' correspondence with Shelter (Scotland) Housing Advice Centres in Aberdeen, Edinburgh and Glasgow.
[59] [1973] 1 All E.R. 740.
[60] [1980] 3 All E.R. 184.

5–75 **Not overcrowded.** The accommodation must comply with the overcrowding provisions of the Housing (Scotland) Act 1987.[61] This means that the number of persons sleeping in a room must not exceed either two persons of differing sexes, 10 years or more in age and not living as man and wife or the permitted number depending on the size of the room and house.

Other discretionary grounds[62]

5–76   When considering these cases the sheriff must be satisfied as to their overall reasonableness, *i.e.* a trifling breach of the tenancy would not be grounds for an order for possession. If, for example, the tenant caused nuisance by having a noisy party on one single occasion during a tenancy, it would be unlikely that the tenancy would be ended on the grounds of breach of tenancy or annoyance to adjoining neighbours.[63] Most possession actions are based on rent arrears.[64]

Rent arrears or the tenant is in breach of the tenancy [Case 1]

5–77   This covers situations where any rent lawfully due from the tenant is not paid. The use of the term "rent lawfully due" means that where there is a counterclaim based on failure by the landlord to provide tenantable accommodation, a landlord would face difficulties if they chose to use this ground for an eviction. Late payment would not allow a landlord to use this ground.[65] Payment after the action has been raised may form part of the argument about the reasonableness of granting an order.[66]

     A breach of the terms has to relate to the tenancy agreement and not to some other personal obligation.[67] The breach must be material rather than a mere triviality. Thus a tenant who deterred prospective purchasers from buying the premises would be covered whilst merely not being in to show such purchasers around the premises would be dismissed as trivial.[68]

Nuisance or annoyance [Case 2]

5–78   There are two aspects to this ground. It applies where the tenant or other resident of the house has been guilty of conduct which is a nuisance or annoyance to adjoining neighbours. Alternatively it may be used where the tenant has been convicted of using the dwelling-house (or allowing it to be used) for immoral or illegal purposes.

     This ground is often combined with a claim relating to rent arrears. Behaviour such as using the property for prostitution is automatically treated as annoying even where the neighbours have not actually complained of annoyance. It has covered excessive noise,[69] persistent loud abuse of the landlord[70] and noisy dogs.[71] "Adjoining neighbours" need to be near enough to be affected.[72]

---

[61] ss. 135–137. See para. 10–08 *et seq.*
[62] Sched. II, Pt I: Cases in which Court may Order Possession.
[63] The numbering of the cases below follows that in Sched. II.
[64] Mitchell, *Eviction and Rent Arrears* (1995), p. 1.
[65] *Bird v. Hildage* [1948] 1 K.B. 91.
[66] *Hayman v. Rowlands* [1957] 1 W.L.R. 317.
[67] *RMR Housing Society Ltd v. Combs* [1951] 1 K.B. 486.
[68] *Chapman v. Hughes* (1923) 129 L.T. 223; 21 L.G.R. 350; 39 T.L.R. 260.
[69] *Florent v. Horez* (1983) 48 P. & C.R. 166.
[70] *Adamson v. Fraser* (1944) 61 Sh. Ct Rep. 132.
[71] *Shepherd v. Braley* [1981] S.C.L. 150—there were 14.
[72] *Cobstone Investments Ltd v. Maxim* [1985] Q.B. 140.

Where the tenant has been convicted of an offence in the house it is necessary that the conviction relate to the premises although a single instance will suffice.[73] Merely being at the scene of the commission of a crime is not enough.[74] The actions of a tenant's family will suffice even where the ability of the tenant to alter their behaviour is limited by incarceration.[75]

Condition of dwelling-house deteriorated [Case 3]

This ground occurs where the condition of the dwelling-house has deteriorated 5–79 owing to acts of neglect or default on the part of the tenant, sub-tenant, lodger or any person residing with the tenant. An example would be failure to take frost precautions in winter[76] or allowing a garden to become overgrown.[77] If the act or neglect was by a lodger or sub-tenant, possession can be granted where the court is satisfied that reasonable steps have not been taken by the tenant to remove the lodger or sub-tenant.

Condition of furniture deteriorated [Case 4]

In this case the condition of the furniture in the dwelling-house has 5–80 deteriorated owing to acts of neglect or default on the part of the tenant, sub-tenant, lodger or anyone residing with the tenant. Where the damage has been caused by someone else residing in the house the tenant must also take reasonable steps to remove the responsible party. Landlords need to provide detailed inventories of furniture to be certain of establishing this ground.

Tenant withdraws a notice to quit [Case 5]

This ground is available where the tenant has given notice to quit and the 5–81 landlord has contracted to sell or let the dwelling-house, and the landlord would in the opinion of the court be seriously prejudiced if he did not obtain possession. This has been held not to apply where the tenant merely left and returned the key.[78] Serious prejudice would arise where the landlord contracts to sell or lease the premises unconditionally[79] but not if the sale depends on the tenant leaving.[80]

Assignation/sub-let of whole house [Case 6]

The tenant who has assigned or sub-let the whole house without the landlord's 5–82 consent can be evicted. The mere fact that the tenancy does not prohibit assignation or sub-letting is not enough.[81] There must be specific consent given although it need not be written and can be inferred from the acceptance of rent in knowledge of the assignation or sub-letting.[82]

---

[73] *S. Schneiders & Sons Ltd v. Abrahams* [1925] 1 K.B. 301.
[74] *Abrahams v. Wilson* [1971] 2 Q.B. 88.
[75] *SSHA v. Lumsden,* 1984 S.L.T. (Sh.Ct.) 71.
[76] *Robertson v. Wilson,* 1922 S.L.T. (Sh.Ct.) 21.
[77] *Holloway v. Povey* (1984) 15 H.L.R. 107.
[78] *Standingford v. Bruce* [1926] 1 K.B. 466.
[79] *De Vries v. Sparks* (1927) 137 L.T. 441.
[80] *Hunt v. Bliss* (1919) 89 L.J.K.B. 174; 122 L.T. 351; 36 T.L.R. 74; 18 L.G.R. 45.
[81] *Dalrymple's Trustees v. Brown,* 1945 S.C. 190; *Regional Properties Co Ltd v. Frankenschwerth* [1951] 1 K.B. 631.
[82] *Hyde v. Pimley* [1952] 2 Q.B. 506.

House reasonably required by the landlord for occupation by a full-time employee [Case 7]

5–83   There may be repossession where the house is reasonably required by the landlord for occupation by a full-time employee, and either the present tenant was a former employee of the landlord and occupied the house as such or the court is satisfied that the person for whose occupation the house is required is employed on work necessary for the proper working of an agricultural holding or estate. The landlord must satisfy the "reasonably required" test but does not need to show necessity[83] and has been able to regain property for an employee who for some years had been living in a house further from his work.[84]

House reasonably required by landlord for occupation as a residence for self or close family member [Case 8]

5–84   This ground is available if the house is reasonably required by the landlord for occupation as a residence for himself[85] or his son or daughter over 18 or his father or mother or father- or mother-in-law, provided he did not become the landlord by purchase after the commencement of the legislation.[86] The interests of sitting tenants are protected from purchasing landlords having this option where they have paid for the property in question.[87]

The court must have regard to all the circumstances, including whether other accommodation is available for the landlord or tenant.[88] It must not make an order for possession if it is satisfied that greater hardship would be caused by granting the order than refusing it.[89] The appropriate date for considering these circumstances is the date of the court hearing.[90]

Whilst it has been stated that in deciding between the competing interests of landlord and tenant it is the latter who must establish the greater hardship[91] there is no reason for landlords not to produce their own evidence.[92] Evidence of hardship must be produced rather than simply be assumed to flow naturally from eviction.[93] The courts take account of such factors as the availability of accommodation under Part II of the Housing (Scotland) Act 1987 (covering homeless applicants[94])

---

[83]   *Aitken v. Shaw* 1933 S.L.T. (Sh. Ct.) 21.
[84]   *Sweeney v. Davis* 1949 S.L.T. (Sh. Ct.) 8.
[85]   *Naish v. Curzon* (1984) 51 P. & C.R. 229.
[86]   Normally, after Mar. 23, 1965; the date for furnished regulated tenancies is after May 24, 1974 and for any dwelling-house tenancy on Nov. 7, 1956 let on or subject to a controlled tenancy after Nov. 7, 1956.
[87]   But see *Thomas v. Fryer* [1970] 1 W.L.R. 845 where a woman, who bought out the inheritance rights of her fellow legatees, was not treated as a purchasing landlord.
[88]   Pt III, Sched. 2.
[89]   *ibid.*
[90]   *King v. Taylor* [1955] 1 Q.B. 150.
[91]   *Manaton v. Edwards* [1985] E.G.L.R. 159 at 160.
[92]   *Bostock v. Tacher de la Pagerie* [1987] 1 E.G.L.R. 104 where the landlord's anorexic daughter provided "strong medical recommendations" that she needed a flat of her own away from her parents' houses; *Thomas v. Fryer* above, where the landlord was able to establish that her mental health would be seriously injured.
[93]   *Alexander v. Mohamadzadeh* [1985] 2 E.G.L.R. 161 at 163.
[94]   *Manaton v. Edwards* [1985] E.G.L.R. 159—the landlord was a ship's cook marrying a Russian woman from Odessa and living in a caravan, while the tenant cohabited with a woman with a six-month-old baby and 15-year-old daughter who visited at weekends; the equivalent legislation for England Wales is Pt III of the Housing Act 1985.

as well as financial[95] and personal[96] factors. On appeal it seems that it will be difficult to overturn a properly expressed finding of greater hardship,[97] but it does occur.[98] This head of possession is not available to joint landlords unless they require the house for all of them.[99]

Excessive rent charged for sub-let [Case 9]

There can be repossession where the tenant has sub-let part of the house as a   5–85 dwelling-house protected by the Act at a rent in excess of the rent recoverable for that part. This would not apply where the landlord shares with someone who does not have separate dwelling and is not covered by the Rent (Scotland) Act 1984. Where a furnished sub-tenancy is granted at a rent greater than the fair rent for an unfurnished tenancy this may well now be covered.[1]

Overcrowded house [Case 10]

Where the dwelling-house is so overcrowded as to be dangerous or injurious   5–86 to the health of the inmates, and the tenant has failed to take reasonable steps to alleviate the situation by removal of any lodger or sub-tenant, this gives grounds for repossession in Scotland. In England and Wales the position is expressed somewhat differently. Where a dwelling-house is statutorily overcrowded then it is stated that nothing in the Rent Acts shall prevent the landlord from obtaining possession.[2] This means, in effect, that it is a mandatory ground in England[3] unlike the position in Scotland where the landlord still requires to show that it is reasonable to give possession. Traditionally Scottish housing has been more densely occupied than that in England and Wales. In deciding what the relevant date for looking at the level of overcrowding, is the Court of Appeal have indicated that the current state of affairs is the test rather than exceptions to it. Thus, the fact that at the time of the court hearing the property was temporarily not overcrowded did not prevent a possession order being made.[4]

Mandatory grounds

If the landlord would be entitled at common law to recover possession of a   5–87 house let on a regulated tenancy, the court must make an order for possession in the following situations.[5] The landlord merely has to state that the property is required. There is difference between this and being "reasonably required". As long as it is genuine and the dwelling-house is sought for the stated purpose then the fact that there are other more reasonable courses which could be pursued is not relevant.[6]

---

[95] *Naysmith v. Maxwell,* 1927 S.L.T. (Sh. Ct.) 4; *Purser v. Bailey* [1967] Q.B. 500.
[96] *Hodges v. Blee* [1987] 2 E.G.L.R. 119 concerned a pensioner tenant living on supplementary benefit (now income support) who smoked and had two Alsatian dogs, and the two homeless sons of the landlord. The tenant lost.
[97] *ibid.*
[98] *Baker v. McIver* [1990] 40 E.G. 123 on the non-availability of rehousing for the tenant.
[99] *Baker v. Lewis* [1947] K.B. 186; but note *Tilling v. Whiteman* [1980] A.C. 1.
[1] *Rakhit v. Carty* [1990] 2 W.L.R. 1107 rejected *Kent v. Millmead Properties* (1982) 44 P. & C.R. 353 which was cited as the authority on this point.
[2] Rent Act 1977, s. 101.
[3] R. E. Megarry, *The Rent Acts* (1988), Vol. 1, p. 486.
[4] *Trustees of Henry Smith's Charity v. Bartosiak-Jentys* (1992) 24 H.L.R. 627.
[5] Pt II, Sched. 2—the numbering continues to follow that in the Schedule.
[6] *Kennealy v. Dunne* [1977] Q.B. 839.

Owner-occupier [Case 11]

5–88   This applies where a person lets property which was occupied as his residence
and where the tenant was given notice that he may require the property back
under this heading. It covers owner-occupiers who rent out their properties during
some temporary absence but not if it has been rented out on a standard regulated
tenancy. It is not necessary that the owner-occupier's prior residence was other
than temporary and intermittent,[7] and the landlord does not need to have lived
in the property immediately prior to the letting.[8] Where there are joint owners
and one of them wishes to repossess this is available.[9]

In addition, since the Tenants' Rights Etc. (Scotland) Act 1980 there are
provisions to cover a number of situations which the original wording did not
cover. Thus, where the owner-occupier has died and the dwelling-house is
required as a residence for a member of his family who was residing with him
at the time of his death, or where an owner-occupier has died and the person
inheriting the house or the owner-occupier has died and the representatives
wish to sell the house with vacant possession then the sheriff must order
repossession.

Similarly, the grounds of automatic repossession are extended to situations where
the house is not reasonably suitable to the needs of the owner-occupier, having regard
to his place of work, and he requires it for the purpose of disposing of it with vacant
possession and using the proceeds to buy a house more suitable to those needs.

Finally, where there is a mortgage over the property, granted before the tenancy
began, the debtor has defaulted and the creditor requires to sell it with vacant
possession, then this is also a ground of repossession although it would not apply
where the sale of the property with a sitting tenant would cover the debt.

Retirement home [Case 12]

5–89   In order to encourage retired people to rent out their properties this ground
was introduced in 1974 where anyone who acquired a dwelling-house for
occupation on his retirement let it before his retirement. Notice of an intention
to use this head of possession must be given to the tenant. There is no prescribed
form of notice. The property must not have not been let on a normal tenancy.
Finally, the court must be satisfied that the owner has retired from regular
employment and requires the dwelling-house as a residence. Alternatively, this
may be used if the retiring owner has died and the residence is required for a
member of his family who was residing with him at the time of his death, or if
the property has been inherited or the personal representatives wish to sell the
property. Finally, it applies where there has been a mortgage default and the
creditor needs to sell to pay off the debt. In addition, the retirement home may
no longer be reasonably suitable for the needs of the owner on retirement. If he
needs to sell it to be able to buy a property more suitable to his needs, then the
tenant may be evicted. It has been suggested, on the strength of *Tilling v.
Whiteman*[10] that this ground would be available to joint owners where only one
of the parties satisfies the test.[11]

---

[7]   *Naish v. Curzon* (1984) 51 P. & C.R. 229.
[8]   Rent (Amendment) Act 1985, s. 1 introduced to counter the impact of *Pocock v. Steele* [1985]
      1 W.L.R. 229.
[9]   *Tilling v. Whiteman* [1980] A.C. 1.
[10] *ibid.*
[11] Jill Martin, *Security of Tenure under the Rent Act* (1986), p. 86.

Off-season holiday let [Case 13]

Again in order to encourage landlords of holiday properties to rent their 5–90
properties out of season, there is a mandatory ground available. It can be used
where a dwelling-house is let for a "specified period" not exceeding eight months
and notice was given by the landlord of intention to recover under this case
provided that in the 12-month period before the relevant date the dwelling-
house was occupied as a holiday residence.

The "specified period" not exceeding eight months exists where the landlord
has the option to terminate before the expiry of the eight-month period, but not
if the tenant has the right to demand renewal and the landlord has no right to
automatic termination or counter-notice. The effect is to enable landlords to
alternate out-of-season and holiday lettings.

Educational body non-student let [Case 14]

Universities and colleges are favoured by being able to rent out their properties 5–91
to non-students and being guaranteed recovery. This requires that the dwelling-
house is let for a "specified period" not exceeding 12 months and for the landlord
to give notice that he intends to recover under this case and applies provided
that at some time within the 12-month period before the relevant date the
dwelling-house was subject to an educational body student tenancy.[12]

The "specified period" not exceeding 12 months exists where the landlord
has the option to terminate before the expiry of the 12-month period, but not if
the tenant has the right to demand renewal and the landlord has no right to
automatic termination or counter-notice.

Short tenancy [Case 15]

Very few short tenancies were ever encountered in the 1980s although there 5–92
is a possibility that they might still exist by dint of tacit relocation. If still in
existence such a short tenancy terminates provided the appropriate notice to
quit is given. Where tenants are quitting and their tenancies are for two years or
less, one month's notice is required and in other cases three months' must be
given. Landlords must serve the appropriate notice for a lease.[13] Failure to serve
notice on time will result in the short tenancy continuing for a further 12 months
from the expiry of the original short tenancy.[14]

Minister/lay missionary property [Case 16]

Where the dwelling-house is for occupation by a minister or a full-time lay 5–93
missionary as a residence from which to perform the duties of that office, and
the tenant is given notice of this in writing, there is no need for the repossession
to be reasonable. Part-time ministers do not seem to be excluded. Whether a
religion and its celebrants are deemed to be "ministers" has not been extensively
canvassed.[15]

---

[12] s. 2(1)(c).
[13] See para. 2–15A *et seq.*
[14] Rent (Scotland) Act 1984, s. 14(3).
[15] *Walsh v. Lord Advocate,* 1956 S.C. (H.L.) 126.

Agricultural worker [Case 17]

5-94   The needs of agriculture and one of the problems of rural housing and labour recruitment are recognised in this head which covers dwelling-houses formerly occupied by a person as part of his job as an agricultural worker. Where this property is later let on standard lease and notice is given that the property might be taken back for use by an agricultural worker, then this results in automatic repossession.

Amalgamation of farms [Case 18]

5-95   Farmers have an additional head of possession where a dwelling-house is occupied by a person responsible for control of farming land prior to an amalgamation under the Agriculture Act 1967 and after amalgamation let on standard lease where notice is given that property might be taken back for use by any person employed on or working land. The court must be satisfied that the person is employed on or working land and that the house is required for such occupation. There is a five-year time-limit for this case following amalgamation approval, reduced to three years after the date of vacation by the person responsible for farmland control or his widow if they continue to occupy after the amalgamation.

Farm occupation [Case 19]

5-96   In addition, there may be repossession of any dwelling-house occupied by a person responsible for control of farmland. This applies whether the occupation was as owner, tenant, servant or agent and also applies to such a person's widow. It covers property which together with the land formed an "agricultural unit" under the Agriculture (Scotland) Act 1948 and the house has been let on a standard lease where notice was given that the property might be repossessed for occupation by a person responsible for farming any of the land. The sheriff must be satisfied that the house is required for such a person or by a person employed or to be employed in agriculture.

Adapted for special needs [Case 20]

5-97   Landlords may get property back where a house is designed or adapted for occupation by a person with special needs and there is no longer a person with special needs in the house and the landlord requires it for occupation by a person who has such special needs. There does not seem to be an equivalent ground in the legislation for England and Wales.

Armed forces personnel [Case 21]

5-98   After the commencement of the 1980 Act a new automatic ground was introduced where the landlord is a member of the regular armed forces, provided written notice is given to the tenant and the dwelling-house is required as a residence for the landlord.

Waiving the notice requirement

5-99   In cases 11 (owner-occupier), 12 (retirement), and 21 (member of armed forces) the court may waive the requirements about notice to the tenant or occupation of the dwelling-house if they consider it "just and equitable" to make an order for possession notwithstanding. The Court of Appeal has indicated that where the tenant had understood the position and had received an oral notice, then it was just and equitable to make the order.[16] However, where there was letting without notice which was never intended to be temporary, it was not appropriate to dispense with the need for notice.[17]

10. SECURE TENANCIES

Introduction

Where premises are sold by a council to a private landlord, the rights of 5–100 tenants change from the secure to the assured regime. This occurs in block transfers, where the tenants are entitled to be consulted[18] but have no right of veto on the sale. It also occurs in individual transfers, where the tenant specifically consents to the new landlord.[19] The major distinction in rights is the retention by the block transfer tenant of the "right to buy".[20]

A secure tenancy may not be brought to an end except in the following circumstances, which may not be varied by the tenancy agreement[21]:

    (a)   death of the tenant where there is no qualified person[22];
    (b)   declining of tenancy by qualified person[23];
    (c)   death of succeeding qualified person[24];
    (d)   written agreement between the landlord and tenant;
    (e)   abandonment of the tenancy[25];
    (f)   possession order from the sheriff court[26];
    (g)   four weeks' notice by tenant to the landlord.

In addition an authority may not use the tenancy agreement to extend the grounds of possession. One district council unsuccessfully attempted to protect themselves from what they regarded as dubious mutual exchanges in this way.[27]

Termination of the tenancy

The approved termination mechanisms are examined in more detail although 5–101 at the time of writing the case law in Scotland is limited and assistance may have to be sought from the interpretation of the equivalent legislation covering secure tenancies in England and Wales.

---

[16] *Fernandes v. Parvardin* (1982) 5 H.L.R. 33.
[17] *Bradshaw v. Baldwin-Wiseman* [1985] 1 E.G.L.R. 123.
[18] Housing (Scotland) Act 1988, Sched. 6A.
[19] Housing (Scotland) Act 1988, Pt III.
[20] Preservation of the Right to Buy Regulations 1992 (S.I. 1992 No. 325); Tom Mullen, "Tenants' Choice and Change of Landlord" (1988) 7 S.H.L.N. 14; Peter Robson, "Selling Estates and the Transfer of Existing Tenancies" (1988) 7 S.H.L.N. 1.
[21] Housing (Scotland) Act 1987 s. 46.
[22] As defined in s. 52.
[23] s. 52(4).
[24] s. 52(5).
[25] s. 50(2).
[26] s. 48(2).
[27] *Monklands D.C. v. Johnstone,* 1987 S.C.L.R. 480.

Death of the tenant

5–102   A qualified person may succeed to a secure tenancy provided they come within the category specified[28]:

(a)   tenant's spouse or living with them as husband and wife where the dwelling-house was the survivor's only or principal home at the time of the tenant's death;

(b)   survivor of joint tenancy where the house was the only or principal home of the survivor at the time of the tenant's death;

(c)   failing these two categories, a member of the tenant's family over the age of 16 where the dwelling-house was that person's only or principal home throughout the period of 12 months immediately preceding the tenant's death.

In the event of there being more than one qualified person the benefit shall go to such person or persons as the qualified persons may all agree or, failing agreement within four weeks of the tenant's death, by the landlord's decision.

Declining secure tenancy by qualified person

5–103   A qualified person entitled to the succession to the tenancy may decline the tenancy[29] by giving notice in writing to the landlord within four weeks of the tenant's death. The house must be vacated within three months thereafter and the declining qualified person is liable only for the rent for occupation after the death.

Death of succeeding qualified person

5–104   Where a qualified person succeeds and later dies the tenancy does not pass a second time,[30] although any person who is a joint tenant is not affected. In addition, anyone who would have been a qualified person may remain for up to six months in the property.[31]

Written agreement between landlord and tenant[32]

5–105   As indicated, this may not be contained within the actual tenancy agreement but if signed voluntarily by a tenant without any duress or deception would operate to terminate a tenancy.

Abandonment of tenancy

5–106   If a landlord has reasonable grounds for believing that the tenant has ceased to reside in the house tenanted, this provides a ground for repossession.[33] The landlord must have reasonable grounds for believing that the dwelling is unoccupied and the tenant does not intend to occupy it as his home. Apart from entering to secure the dwelling against vandalism,[34] the landlord who wishes to take possession of the house must serve on the tenant a notice[35]:

---

[28] s. 52(2); see para. 9–15 *et seq.*
[29] s. 52(4).
[30] s. 52(5).
[31] s. 52(6).
[32] s. 46(1)(c).
[33] s. 49(1).
[34] s. 49(2) and (3).
[35] s. 50(1).

(a) stating that the landlord has reason to believe that the house is unoccupied and that the tenant does not intend to occupy it as his home;

(b) requiring the tenant to inform the landlord within four weeks of service of the notice if the tenant intends to occupy the house as his home; and

(c) informing the tenant that if it appears to the landlord at the end of the four-week period that the tenant does not intend so to occupy the house, the tenancy will be terminated forthwith.

When the notice has been served and when the landlord has made such enquiries as may be necessary to satisfy itself that the dwelling is unoccupied and that the tenant does not intend to occupy it as his home, then at the end of the four-week period a further notice may be served bringing the tenancy to an end.[36] Where these requirements have been complied with there may be repossession without further proceedings. In the event that a tenant is aggrieved by the operation of the abandonment procedure there is provision for a tenant to make a summary application to the sheriff court.[37] There are a number of matters which the sheriff must consider. If it appears to the sheriff that either the landlord has failed to comply with the formal requirements of notice indicated or that the landlord did not have reasonable grounds for finding that the house was unoccupied or did not have reasonable grounds for finding that the tenant did not intend to occupy it as the tenant's home or that the landlord was in error in finding that the tenant did not intend to occupy the house as the tenant's home or that the tenant had reasonable cause, by reason of illness or otherwise, for failing to notify the landlord of intention to occupy the house, then there is redress. The sheriff must make an order that the secure tenancy is to continue where the house has not been let to a new tenant.[38] If the house has been so let the landlord must be directed to make suitable accommodation[39] available.[40]

In one English case the Court of Appeal made it clear that it was not enough merely to assume that vacation of a house with rent owing amounted to surrender of the tenancy. In this case[41] the tenants left owing an unspecified amount of rent. The council did not go through the formal notice procedure as they said the tenants could not be traced. The Court of Appeal stated that there had to be information which would allow the inference to be drawn that there had been a surrender of the tenancy. If it had been shown that the tenants owed a substantial amount and had been absent for a substantial period the inference could have been drawn but not here. The alternative ground of possession for continuous absence is always available but is obviously slower.[42] 5–107

Possession order from sheriff

The landlord must serve a notice on the tenant in the prescribed form and recover the house by summary cause provided that the ground for possession is 5–108

---

[36] s. 50(2).
[37] s. 51(1).
[38] s. 51(2)(i).
[39] See Pt II of Sched. 3.
[40] s. 51(2)(ii).
[41] *Preston B.C. v. Fairclough* (1982) 8 H.L.R. 70.
[42] See para. 5–114.
[43] *Edinburgh D.C. v. Davis,* 1987 S.L.T. (Sh.Ct.) 33.

stated and four weeks' notice of proceedings for recovery of possession is given. At the end of the four weeks' notice a further notice may be served bringing the tenancy to an end. The first notice lapses after six-months unless acted on. The six-month period is calculated from the date when proceedings were raised. This is the date when the writ is served on the tenant rather than the date when the writ is warranted.[43]

The Housing (Scotland) Act 1987 makes provision for the sheriff to adjourn proceedings for possession with or without imposing conditions as to payment of outstanding rent or other conditions.[44]

5–109   The sheriff must make an order if he is satisfied that the landlord has a ground under the first seven heads of possession provided that it is reasonable to make the order. These have been described as the "conduct grounds".[45] Many of these grounds are similar in wording to the private sector grounds and it will be helpful to consult the relevant sections in relation to assured and protected tenancies.

An order must be made where the sheriff is satisfied that the landlord has a ground under heads eight to 15 if it appears to the court that other suitable accommodation will be made available for the tenant when the order takes effect. Himsworth describes these as the "management grounds".[46] In addition, if it appears to the court that the intention of the landlord is that substantial work is to be carried out on the house and the tenant will be returning to the house after the work is completed, an order must be made that the tenant is entitled to return to the house after the completion of the work.[47]

Such an order for repossession shall appoint a date for recovery of possession and shall terminate the tenancy and give the landlord the right to recover possession.[48]

5–110 **Rent unpaid or any other obligation of the tenancy broken [Ground 1].**
The rent must be lawfully due and so there is a defence if the rent has been retained pending repairs.[49] Where breach of obligation is concerned the case law from the private sector is particularly likely to be of assistance,[50] and has included using the premises as car repair base.[51] The courts have also accepted prohibitions against keeping a dog.[52]

5–111 **Immoral or illegal purposes—using the house or allowing it to be so used [Ground 2].**
This head of possession, familiar from private rented housing, is available in public sector property in the same form. Again the immorality must relate to the property so that premises which are merely the locus of a crime such as assault would not come under this head of possession.

The main issue which has been discussed in the courts in the 1990s has been eviction for drug dealing. The courts have been prepared to grant possession

---

[44] s. 48.
[45] Chris Himsworth, *Housing Law in Scotland* (1994), p. 75.
[46] *ibid.* p. 76.
[47] s. 48(5).
[48] s. 50(3).
[49] See para. 3–91.
[50] John Watchman, "Secure Tenancies: Recovery of Possession of Property" (1987) 4 S.H.L.N. 3.
[51] *Mackenzie v. West Lothian D.C.*, 1979 S.C. 433.
[52] *City of Glasgow Council v. Murray*, 1997 Hous.L.R. 105 where the prohibition against "dogs" was held to apply to a single dog.

orders where neighbours have complained[53]as well as where this has not been a feature.[54] The issues which have been considered by sheriffs in 1990s cases have been: (1) public interest; (2) that the defender knew what he was doing; (3) the gravity of the offence; and (4) the consequences of removal. Hence Class A drugs such as heroin would be more seriously regarded than cannabis.

Deterioration of the house owing to acts of waste or neglect or default by the tenant or any resident or lodger [Ground 3].

5–112

Where the deterioration is the fault of one of the lodgers or sub-tenants the tenant is responsible if he has not taken such steps as he ought reasonably to have done for the removal of the lodger or sub-tenant. This applies not just to the house but also to any of the common parts.

Condition of furniture has deteriorated due to ill treatment by tenant or lodger or sub-tenant [Ground 4].

5–113

The same proviso about taking reasonable steps to remove the lodger or sub-tenant responsible for such deterioration also applies. In view of the expansion of this form of housing provision,[55] it may become an issue in the near future.

Absence from the dwelling-house by tenant and spouse without reasonable cause for a continuous period exceeding six months or ceasing to occupy house as principal home [Ground 5].

5–114

This must be contrasted with the abandonment procedure. In ground 5 it is necessary for the landlord to establish that the absence is not reasonable. This might well cover such absences as looking after a sick or aged relative. In *Crawley Borough Council v. Sawyer*[56] the local authority were unable to obtain a possession order under the equivalent ground in the English legislation where a tenant had been living with his girlfriend for over a year until they split up. The Court of Appeal were satisfied with the county court finding that the tenant had not ceased to regard the rented property as his principal home. Where a person is temporarily absent from a property, he will nevertheless be regarded as occupying it if there are physical signs of occupation and an intention to return to the property.[56a] A property will be considered to be someone's principal home if they have such a real, tangible and substantial connection with it that, rather than any other place of residence, the property in question can properly be described as being the only or principal home.[57]

Tenant has induced the landlord to grant the tenancy by a false statement made knowingly or recklessly [Ground 6].

This new head of possession was not in the original 1980 tenants' rights legislation. It was introduced in 1986 and was discussed in one case where the ground was found to be established but possession was not granted because of the tenant's personal circumstances.[57a] Himsworth notes that its possible

5–115

---

[53] *Glasgow D.C. v. Heffron,* 1997 Hous.L.R. 55.
[54] *City of Glasgow Council v. Lockhart,* 1997 Hous.L.R. 99.
[55] John Watchman, *op. cit.,* p. 10.
[56] (1988) 86 L.G.R. 629.
[56a] *Beggs v. Kilmarnoch and Loudon D.C.,* 1995 S.C.L.R. 435.
[57] *Roxburgh D.C. v. Collins,* 1991 S.C.L.R. 575.
[57a] *Falkirk D.C. v. Mclay,* 1991 S.C.L.R. 895.

interpretation was discussed in *Monklands District Council v. Johnstone*.[58] The ground is not available for housing association tenancies granted after January 2, 1989 as these are assured tenancies. Associations have used the breach of tenancy terms with varying success.[59]

Conduct which is a nuisance of annoyance in or in the vicinity of the house and it is not reasonable in all the circumstances that the landlord should be required to make other accommodation available to the tenant [Ground 7].

5–116 This is the first of the conduct grounds and covers situations where the conduct of the tenant is very serious. It covers the same kind of issues that have been used in the private sector repossessions over the years—noise, acts of destruction and acts of violence. It extends beyond the house to the vicinity of the house. The courts have yet to determine how extensively this phrase applies. In England the more restrictive wording has been taken to extend to a broad neighbourhood. The wording, talks in the Housing Act 1985 of "nuisance or annoyance to neighbours".[60]

There is some conflict as to whether or not conduct for which the tenant had no direct responsibility would ground an action for possession. In one case the tenant was evicted for the activities of his spouse while he was in prison[61] whilst in a later decision this line was not taken where only the activities of the husband were the subject of the local authority's, possession claim.[62] These were decisions of different sheriffs principal in neighbouring sheriffdoms. Most recently, a housing association sought to evict a tenant for a single act of aggression against an official from the association. The issue, however, was confused by the different approaches taken by the sheriff and sheriff principal. The sheriff was willing to evict for the single act,[63] whilst the sheriff principal took the view that annoyance needed to cover annoyance to neighbours.[64] The matter was settled extrajudicially.[65]

Conduct which is a nuisance or annoyance in or in the vicinity of the house and in the opinion of the landlord it is appropriate in the circumstances to require the tenant to move to other accommodation [Ground 8].

5–117 Where a particular tenant causes annoyance such as by having small children in a flat above an older tenant then it could well be reasonable to shift the tenant to another location. It might also be used where two tenants do not get on.

Overcrowding [Ground 9].

5–118 This ground applies where the premises are overcrowded in terms of the Housing (Scotland) Act 1987[66] and the overcrowding is not covered by the exemptions available for holidays and temporary visitors.[67]

[58] 1987 S.C.L.R. 480.
[59] See para. 5–36.
[60] *Northampton B.C. v. Lovatt* [1998] 2 F.C.R. 177.
[61] *Scottish Special Housing Association v. Lumsden,* 1984 S.L.T. (Sh.Ct.) 71.
[62] *Glasgow D.C. v. Brown,* 1988 S.C.L.R. 679.
[63] *Govanhill Housing Association v. O'Neill,* Glasgow Sh. Ct., June 18, 1991, *per* Sheriff Eccles.
[64] *O'Neill v. Govanhill Housing Association*, Glasgow Sh. Ct., Sept. 24, 1991 *per* Sheriff Principal MacLeod.
[65] Feb. 9, 1993: the 2nd Division, *per* Lord Ross, adopted the parties' Joint Minute—Mr O'Neill was in rent arrears by this time.
[66] s. 135.
[67] s. 138.

Demolition or substantial work on the building [Ground 10].
Where such work is intended by the landlord within a reasonable time and the 5–119
work cannot reasonably be done without obtaining possession of the house, then
this provides a ground for repossession. The ground is not applicable to decants.[68]

**House designed or adapted for occupation by a person with special needs
[Ground 11].**
Where a person with special needs is no longer occupying the house and the 5–120
landlord requires it for occupation by another person with special needs, then
the property may be repossessed.

**House part of group designed or provided with or located near facilities
for persons in need of special social support [Ground 12].**
Where a person with such a need is no longer occupying the house and the landlord 5–121
requires it for another person with such needs, repossession will be permitted.

**Housing association landlord whose objects are or include housing
persons who are in a special category by reason of age, infirmity,
disability or social circumstances [Ground 13].**
In order to allow such housing associations to fulfil their purposes where a tenant 5–122
is no longer in a special category or the house is no longer suitable for the tenant's
needs and the accommodation is required for someone who is in a special category,
and secure tenancy is involved, this type of repossession is available.

**Landlord's rights have either ended or will do within six months from
raising of possession action [Ground 14].**
This head is appropriate for those situations where the local authority itself 5–123
only has property on a temporary basis and is unable to offer effective security
of tenure. The issue of when proceedings are raised has been discussed in
Edinburgh District Council v. Davis.[69]

Education worker for designated authority [Ground 15].
Where an islands council holds premises which are required for a person who is 5–124
or will be employed by the council for education purposes and a suitable alternative
house cannot be offered, tenant formerly employed in education may be evicted.[70]

Transfer to former spouse or cohabitee [Ground 16].
Originally the Tenants' Rights Etc. (Scotland) Act 1980 provided for transfer at 5–125
the behest of the local authority with the approval of the sheriff. This head was
repealed by the Matrimonial Homes (Family Protection) (Scotland) Act 1981.[71]
This had allowed local authorities to repossess the property on the grounds that
they wished to transfer the tenancy to the spouse or former spouse of the tenant.
This can now be done on application by the spouse (who is not the tenant)
under the 1981 Act, s. 13 but the decision is taken in the sheriff court or Court
of Session on specified grounds.[72] The original transfer ground was restored by
the Housing (Scotland) Act 1986 after local authorities indicated how useful

---

[68] *Charing Cross and Kelvingrove Housing Association v. Kraska,* 1986 S.L.T. (Sh.Ct.) 42.
[69] 1987 S.L.T. (Sh.Ct.) 33.
[70] See para. 7–18.
[71] s. 13(12) .
[72] See para. 8–15.

they had found such a power.[73] The court must be satisfied that suitable accommodation will be made available to the tenant.

Suitability of accommodation.

5–126 Where the landlord is repossessing property and providing alternative accommodation, whether it is suitable is determined by looking to whether there is equivalent security and the needs of the tenant and his family are reasonably met.[74]

Security.

5–127 The house must let as a separate dwelling either under a secure tenancy, a protected tenancy under the Rent (Scotland) Act 1984 or an assured tenancy under the Housing (Scotland) Act 1988.[75]

Suitability.

5–128 In deciding whether a house is reasonably suitable to the needs of the tenant and his family the sheriff must have regard to the following [76]:

    (a) proximity to the place of work of the tenant and other members of his family compared with existing dwelling-house (also includes attendance at an educational establishment);

    (b) extent of the accommodation required by the tenant and his family;

    (c) character of the accommodation offered compared with existing house;

    (d) terms on which accommodation offered compared with those concerning existing house;

    (e) where furniture is provided, a comparison with previously provided furniture;

    (f) any special needs of the tenant or his family.

It was accepted in *Enfield London Borough Council v. French*[77] that a tenant's hobbies are capable of amounting to "special needs".

Four weeks' notice by tenant to landlord

5–129   Tenants may also terminate their tenancies. In practice local authorities tend not to expect that this will be done through formal written notice but rather by the return of keys. This has implications for the occupancy rights position of tenants' spouses and cohabitees.[78]

11. PART VII CONTRACTS

5–130 Legislation introduced in 1946 afforded a limited measure of security of tenure to tenants. Without this protection the rent-fixing provision of the Rent Assessment Committee would be of little value to a "referring" tenant, as they could be evicted if they sought to have their rent reviewed.[79]

---

[73] Institute of Housing/Scottish Homeless Group, *Housing and Marital Breakdown—the Local Authority Response* (1986).

[74] Housing (Scotland) Act 1987, Sched. 3, Pt II.

[75] *ibid.* para. 1.

[76] Housing (Scotland) Act 1987, Sched. 3, para. 2.

[77] (1985) 49 P. & C.R. 223.

[78] See paras 8–10 and 8–11.

[79] See para. 4–71 *et seq.*

Contracts entered into before December 1980

The old Rent Tribunal jurisdiction continues to be exercised by the Rent Assessment 5–131 Committee (RAC). This provides for up to six months' security, extendable on application. If, after the tenant or local authority have referred a contract to the RAC, the landlord serves a notice to quit before the decision of the RAC (or within a period of six months thereafter), the notice to quit shall not take effect for six months. This is subject to the RAC's right to substitute a shorter period of security. This may be done where the tenant has caused annoyance or nuisance to neighbours or used the premises for immoral or illegal purposes as well as generally breaking the terms of the contract, or has caused or allowed the condition of the furniture to deteriorate. The landlord may apply that such a reduction be granted where otherwise the period of six months' security would be granted. Where a reference is withdrawn the notice to quit can take effect seven days from the withdrawal.

In addition, if a tenant receives a notice to quit before he has referred the contract to the RAC, he may still apply to the RAC for an extension of the period in the notice. This may be granted for up to a maximum of six months. A tenant may apply to the RAC for an extension of the period of security where this has not yet expired under the contract or the above provisions, even if the security granted was originally below the six-month period. The point must be emphasised that the six months' security is designed to help the tenant secure accommodation elsewhere. Although the Francis Report found that in the case of one old woman this had extended over some ten years, the normal period was less than a year. This stemmed not so much from a direct policy of the Rent Tribunals formerly and then RACs as from the transitory nature of the tenants.

Contracts entered into on or after December 1, 1980

There is even less security with these contracts. Although the Rent (Scotland) 5–132 Act 1984[80] and the Housing (Scotland) Act 1988[81] make clear that the provisions against harassment of tenants and illegal eviction apply to Part VII contracts, the actual security of tenure provisions now reside with the local sheriff.[82]

Where there is a notice to quit, it may now be referred to the sheriff who may, if he thinks fit, postpone the date of possession for a period which shall not exceed three months. There is no provision for a reapplication for extension of this minimal security. Any postponement may be made subject to such conditions regarding payment of outstanding rent or other conditions as the sheriff thinks fit.

It should be noted that there are to be no new Part VII tenancies created on or after January 2, 1989 unless entered into in pursuance of a pre- 1989 contractual agreement.[83] In addition where there is a change in the rent paid under an existing Part VII contract, this is treated as a new contract[84] and is no longer covered by Part VII.[85] This, however, does not apply where the rent is changed through an increase or reduction in rent under section 66 of the Rent (Scotland) Act 1984.[86]

---

[80] Pt III.
[81] s. 36–40.
[82] s. 55 of the Tenant's Rights Etc. (Scotland) Act 1980.
[83] Housing (Scotland) Act 1988, s. 44(1).
[84] *ibid.* s. 44(2).
[85] *ibid.* s. 44(2)(a).
[86] *ibid.* s. 44(3).

CHAPTER 6

UNLAWFUL EVICTION AND HARASSMENT

1. HISTORICAL BACKGROUND

6–01 The problem of landlords harassing and unlawfully evicting tenants is by no means a new one. During the time when relations between landlord and tenant were governed solely by contract and the common law, landlords complained that the legal system was biased against them[1] and that tenants had excessive rights. Some landlords resorted to repossessing their properties by unlawful means—doors were removed,[2] as were roofs.[3]

Traditionally, tenants enjoyed the limited protection afforded by the common law that "[a] removing (or ejection) is the only legal mode of displacing a sitting tenant. Ejection *brevi manu* is not permissible, even if it be plain that the premises were obtained on lease by fraudulent statements and for improper purposes."[4] Ejection *brevi manu* would give rise to a claim for damages for wrongous ejection[5] in addition to a claim for any damage to possessions and solatium. Non-tenant residential occupiers had only the protection of the terms of their contracts.

Security of tenure was introduced in 1915[6] providing a far more valuable protection for protected tenants. Some landlords have sought to evade its impact through various legal devices.[7] Landlords have also persuaded tenants to leave by less obvious means. They have cut off gas or electricity, they have moved noisy neighbours in. One of the results of the partial relaxation of rent controls when there is vacant possession has been that some landlords have decided to speed up the process of vacant possession so that they can either rent out at full decontrolled rent levels or sell off the property. This occurred when the Rent Acts were relaxed in the 1920s[8] and most notably in the 1950s with the Rent Act 1957.[9]

6–02 The Profumo political scandal of the early 1960s involved spies, sex and housing. One of the crucial ingredients of the investigations was the revelation of the dubious business activities of the landlord Peter Rachman. The media were able to rake over the more salacious aspects of the case since the exploitation

---

[1] Glasgow Landlords Association 1865, quoted in Peter Robson, *"Housing and the Judiciary"* (Ph.D. Thesis, University of Strathclyde, 1979).
[2] *Brash v. Munro & Hall* (1903) 5 F. 1102.
[3] *Bisset v. Whitson* (1842) 5 D. 5.
[4] Rankine, *A Treatise on the Law of Leases in Scotland* (3rd ed.), p. 512.
[5] *ibid.* p. 592.
[6] See Chapter 1.
[7] See para. 2–52 *et seq.*
[8] *Barker v. Hutson* [1929] 1 K.B. 103.
[9] David Nelken, *The Limits of the Legal Process* (1983).

of tenants was the underlying social evil. In 1963 the troubled Conservative administration appointed Sir Edward Milner Holland to chair the Survey into Rented Housing in Greater London. One of the major problems encountered by the Milner Holland Committee[10] in their report was the practice of landlords using various unsavoury ways to persuade tenants to relinquish their contractual rights. They devoted an appendix specifically to Rachman. Their recommendations led to the emergency protection measures of the Protection of Eviction Act 1964. This was quickly followed up by the Rent Act 1965.

The 1965 Act consolidated the security of tenure provisions for protected tenants[11] and provided a statutory basis for the common law rule against the ejection *brevi manu* of non-protected sitting tenants.[12] In addition, moreover, it introduced criminal sanctions against unlawful eviction and harassment.[13] This combination of provisions was retained in the Rent (Scotland) Act 1984 and has been strengthened by amendments contained in the Housing (Scotland) Act 1988 and the Housing Act 1988. These amendments included a provision[14] which, for the first time, provided protection against eviction without due process of law to non-tenant residential occupiers. Also introduced was a statutory method for calculating the quantum of damages for unlawful eviction.

2. INTRODUCTION

Residential occupier

The offences of unlawful eviction and harassment cover actions against 6–03 "residential occupiers".[15] A "residential occupier" is a person who occupies premises as a residence whether under a contract or by virtue of any enactment or rule of law giving him the right to remain in occupation or restricting the right of any other person to recover possession of the premises.[16] This covers a contractual tenant, a statutorily protected tenant, a licensee, lodger or service occupier. It includes a spouse or cohabitee with occupancy rights[17] under the Matrimonial Homes (Family Protection) (Scotland) Act 1981.[18] It also includes a statutory tenant who awaits the lawful enforcement of a decree for the recovery of possession of his premises.[19]

Unlawfully deprive

For the offence of unlawful eviction or harassment to be committed, a person 6–04 must "unlawfully deprive" the residential occupier of premises. There is now, of course, substantial statutory regulation determining the legal requirements

---

[10] Cmnd. 2605 (1965).

[11] Pt I.

[12] s. 32.

[13] s. 30.

[14] s. 39 of the Housing (Scotland) Act 1988 inserted new s. 23(2A) and s. 24(2A) into the Rent (Scotland) Act 1984.

[15] Rent (Scotland) Act 1984, s. 22(1).

[16] *ibid.* s. 22(5).

[17] *McAlinden v. Bearsden and Milngavie D.C.,*1986 S.L.T. 91—Lord McDonald decided that the right to apply for a declaration of occupancy rights amounted to having rights in terms of the homelessness legislation—see P. Robson and M. Poustie, *Homeless People and the Law* (1996), p. 128.

[18] See para. 8–03.

[19] *Haniff v. Robinson* (1994) 26 H.L.R. 386.

of recovery of possession of residential tenancies. Parts II and VII of the Rent (Scotland) Act 1984 deal with protected tenancies and Part VII contracts, Part III of the Housing (Scotland) Act 1987 deals with secure tenancies and Part II of the Housing (Scotland) Act 1988 deals with assured tenancies.[20] As regards common law tenancies, the Rent (Scotland) Act 1984 provides that it is unlawful to recover possession of premises other than by proceedings in court.[21] Since the amendments to the 1984 Act by the Housing (Scotland) Act 1988[22] it has been unlawful to recover possession against all other non-tenant residential occupiers who are lawfully residing in the premises,[23] except for the specific exemptions contained in s. 23A of the 1984 Act. The general prohibition against eviction without due process of law, then, does not apply to those without right or title to occupy, such as squatters, in addition to the statutory exemptions which comprise residence with a resident landlord or member of landlord's family, temporary grants to trespassers and squatters, holiday lettings, and hostel accommodation in the public and housing association sector. However, it should be noted that landlords of tenancies which fall within the exemptions of section 23A, although not being required to raise court proceedings to recover possession, nevertheless must fulfil their contractual obligations.

It is unclear whether an eviction *brevi manu* which has been exempted from unlawfulness by s. 23A of the 1984 Act is nevertheless unlawful at common law. This question has been the source of some debate in recent literature.[24]

3. Unlawful Eviction

6–05   It is an offence for any person unlawfully to deprive the residential occupier of the occupation of the premises or attempt to do so, unless he proves he believed and had reasonable cause to believe that the residential occupier had ceased to reside in the premises.[25] This applies to landlords as well as anyone acting on their behalf. Where evictors claimed not to be acting as agents they would be guilty of the offence but the liability of the landlord for damages could be more problematic.[26]

Unlawful eviction covers both forcible actions moving occupiers out of the premises as well as changing the locks.[27] It can be carried out by any person, which covers not only landlords and their agents, but fellow tenants and partners.[28] The eviction may be extremely brief as long as the occupier believes the exclusion is more than temporary.[29] What is critical is not the

---

[20] For other miscellaneous statutes regulating other tenancies, see the Rent (Scotland) Act 1984, s. 25.
[21] s. 23.
[22] ss. 39 and 40.
[23] Rent (Scotland) Act 1984, s. 23(3).
[24] P. Brown, "Resident Landlords" (1990) 13 S.H.L.N. 21 at 31; M. Dailly, "Ejection *Brevi Manu* and Hostel Dwellings" (1995) 40 J.L.S.S. 435; "Lease or license in Scots Law", 1996 SCOLAG 126; S. Halliday, "Unlawful Eviction and Hostel Accommodation" (1997) 241 SCOLAG, 46.
[25] Pt III of the Rent (Scotland) Act 1984, s. 22(1).
[26] See s. 38 and the section on Damages, below.
[27] See, for example, *Tagro v. Cafane and Patel* (1991) 23 H.L.R. 250.
[28] Part III of the Rent (Scotland) Act 1984 s.22(1).
[29] *Costelloe v. London Borough of Camden* [1986] Crim L.R. 249, DC.

time during which the residential occupier is deprived of occupation, but rather whether the exclusion, however brief, was designed to evict the occupier from the premises. If this is so, the offence would still be committed although the authorities are less than keen to be involved.[30] However, where residential occupiers have been excluded for short periods of time the courts may be more inclined to regard this as constituting harassment rather than unlawful eviction.[31]

4. HARASSMENT

Offences of harassment

There are now two offences of harassment. The first and original offence of harassment is based on the offender intending to cause the occupier to give up occupation or to refrain from exercising any right or pursuing any remedy in relation to the premises.[32] The second offence, subsequently inserted into the 1984 Act,[33] has a more "objective" basis, and does not require the offender to have this intention in doing certain acts. Rather, the offender need only commit acts which are *likely* to interfere with the peace or comfort of the residential occupier, or persistently withdraw services which are reasonably required for the occupation of the premises.

6–06

Both offences apply to "premises" and the meaning of this is wide enough to cover single rooms and caravans. The offence is committed whether or not the deprivation is permanent.[34–35] The offence of harassment can be committed even where there is no breach of the law of contract or reparation. In *R v. Burke*,[36] where a single room was rented out in a large house, the disconnection of the front doorbell and the padlocking of one of the bathrooms in the house did not breach the contractual rights of the tenant. However, since the motive of the landlord was to get the occupier to give up occupation, this amounted to an offence according to the House of Lords. A single act may amount to amount to harassment.[37] Similarly, a course of conduct is capable of comprising harassment.[38]

6–07

Anyone guilty of any of these offences is liable to a fine or imprisonment or both.[39] If there is a summary conviction then the imprisonment is not to exceed six months, whilst on indictment the maximum term is two years.[40]

---

[30] Francis Report, *op. cit.,* Table 41, p. 105; Willie Black, *How to Rent Book: Private Tenants' Rights* (Shelter, 1989) p. 5.

[31] *R. v. Yuthiwattana* (1984) 16 H.L.R. 49; *Costelloe v. London Borough of Camden* [1986] Crim L.R. 249 (DC).

[32] Rent (Scotland) Act 1984, s. 22(2).

[33] *ibid.* s. 22(2A), inserted by s. 38 of the Housing (Scotland) Act 1988, amended by Sched. 16 to the Housing Act 1988.

[34–35] *R. v. Yuthiwattana* (1984) 16 H.L.R. 49 where the landlord refused to supply a replacement key.

[36] [1990] 2 W.L.R. 1313.

[37] *R. v. Evangeles Polycarpou* (1978) 9 H.L.R. 129.

[38] *R. v. Yuthiwattana* (1984) 16 H.L.R. 49.

[39] s. 22(3).

[40] *ibid.*

Intent to cause the occupier to give up occupation

6–08   There are two elements in the first offence[41] which may be committed by "any person". First, there must be the commission of acts calculated to interfere with the peace or comfort of the residential occupier or a member of that person's household, or the persistent withdrawal or withholding of services reasonably required for the occupation of the premises. Second, such acts must be committed with the intention of causing the residential occupier to give up occupation of the whole or part of the premises or to refrain from exercising any right or from pursuing any remedy in respect of the premises.

Threats and intimidation are likely to interfere with the peace and comfort of occupiers and are covered by this section. "Services" covers such items as heat, water and lighting and probably now also telephones. There is a defence if there is another explanation of the actions which the landlord is able to sustain. This has been used successfully where the impact of improvement work resulted in a tenant giving up occupation.[42] Here the landlord persuaded the tenant to vacate a flat for two weeks while works were being done.

Conduct likely to cause the occupier to give up occupation

6–09   This second offence[43] applies only to landlords or their agents. Again there are two elements. First, there must be acts likely to interfere with the peace or comfort of the residential occupier or member of the household or the persistent withdrawal or withholding of services reasonably required for the occupation of the premises. Second, the landlord or agent must know or have reasonable cause to believe that the conduct is likely to cause the residential occupier to give up occupation of the whole or part of the premises or to refrain from exercising any right or pursuing any remedy in respect of the whole or part of the premises. Given the more objective nature of this offence, a defence has been provided to the charge that a person committed harassment by persistently withdrawing services if he can prove that he had reasonable grounds for doing so.[44]

5. DAMAGES FOR UNLAWFUL EVICTION

Introduction

6–10   Damages for wrongous ejection are available at common law.[45] This is in addition to any liability arising under contract or delict. The Housing (Scotland) Act 1988, however, introduced a statutory basis for damages for unlawful eviction.[46] It also provided a method for assessing the quantum of such damages.[47] This statutory formula provides a disincentive to landlords simply calculating the cost of any damages from the profits gained by unlawfully evicting a residential occupier. Where a landlord or anyone acting on his behalf unlawfully deprives a residential occupier of his occupation of the whole or part of his

---

[41] Rent (Scotland) Act 1984, s. 22(2).
[42] *Schon v. Camden London Borough Council* (1986) 84 L.G.R. 830.
[43] Rent (Scotland) Act 1984, s. 22(2A).
[44] s. 22(2B).
[45] See paras 6–01 to 6–03.
[46] Housing (Scotland) Act 1988, s. 36.
[47] *ibid.* s. 37.

premises, the landlord will be liable for statutory damages.[48] This also applies where a residential occupier gives up occupation of premises because the landlord attempted to deprive him of the premises, or did acts likely to interfere with the peace or comfort of the residential occupier or members of the household, knowingly or having reasonable cause to believe that the conduct was likely to cause the residential occupier to give up occupation of the premises or refrain from exercising any right or pursuing any remedy in relation to the premises. Alternatively, statutory damages are available where there is persistent withdrawal or withholding of services reasonably required for the occupation of the premises as a residence.[49] Although the actions which give rise to these statutory damages may be committed by a landlord or any person acting on his behalf, the liability for damages rests with the landlord alone.[50]

As with damages at common law for wrongous ejection, these statutory   6–11
damages are in addition to any liability arising under contract or delict,[51] but cannot be in addition to damages at common law for wrongous ejection.[52] The landlord may avoid this liability under statute, however, if the residential occupier is reinstated in the property before proceedings to recover damages are finally decided or there is an order to this effect from the sheriff.[53] Proceedings to enforce liability are completed when there has been no appeal or leave to appeal sought, or where an appeal is not proceeded with or abandoned.[54] The English Court of Appeal has considered the meaning of "reinstatement" in *Tagro v. Cafane and Patel*.[55] A tenant successfully obtained an injunction to readmit her to her premises following the changing of the lock by her landlord. On return to the premises she discovered that the lock on the front door was broken, her room wrecked and many of her possessions stolen. In an action for equivalent statutory damages the landlord submitted that this constituted reinstatement. The court, however, contrasted "reinstatement" with "readmittance", stressing that "reinstatement does not consist in merely handing the tenant a key to a lock which does not work and inviting her to resume occupation of a room which has been totally wrecked."[56] The court also held that the mere offer of reinstatement does not by itself comprise reinstatement. If an unlawfully deprived occupier refuses such an offer, then reinstatement will not have occurred. The court in this situation, however, has the discretion to reduce the quantum of damages.[57]

Defences to damages action and reduction of quantum

It is a defence if the landlord can prove he believed and had reasonable   6–12
cause to believe that the residential occupier had ceased to occupy the premises when he was deprived of occupation or subjected to the acts complained of.[58] There needs to be a basis for this belief—for example, where the tenant had

---

[48] Housing (Scotland) Act 1988, s. 36(1) and (2)(a).
[49] *ibid.* s.36(2)(b) as amended by the Housing Act 1988, Sched. 17.
[50] Housing (Scotland) Act 1988, s. 36(3); *Sampson v. Wilson* [1995] 3 W.L.R. 455.
[51] Housing (Scotland) Act 1988, s. 36(4).
[52] *ibid.* s. 36(5).
[53] *ibid.* s. 36(6). See, for example, *Murray v. Aslam* (1995) 27 H.L.R. 284.
[54] Housing (Scotland) Act 1988, s. 36(6A), inserted by the Housing Act 1988, Sched. 17.
[55] (1991) 23 H.L.R. 250. See also *Murray v. Aslam* (1995) 27 H.L.R. 284.
[56] Lord Donaldson, M.R. at 255.
[57] Housing (Scotland) Act 1988, s. 36(6B).
[58] *ibid.* s. 36(7)(a).

returned the keys to the landlord or stated that he was leaving on a particular day. As far as services are concerned, the landlord may establish that he had reasonable grounds for withdrawing or withholding such services.[59] This could include a reasonable belief that the property was empty[60] but not where the parties were in dispute and the withdrawal or withholding was part of the bargaining process.

The court may reduce damages where the residential occupier or anyone living with him has been guilty of conduct which leads to the unlawful eviction.[61] Alternatively there may be a reduction where reinstatement has been offered by the landlord before the proceedings were begun.[62] The English Court of Appeal offered the *obiter* remark in *Tagro*[63] that the "proceedings" in question were proceedings for statutory damages and not, for example, emergency proceedings to ensure readmittance after an unlawful eviction. Such a deduction may be applied where the refusal of such an offer is unreasonable or where the occupier has found new premises, provided that the refusal would have been unreasonable had new accommodation not been obtained.[64]

Amount of damages

6–13   The quantum of statutory damages is to be fixed at the difference between the value of the landlord's interest with the residential occupier in occupation and with vacant possession at the time of the cessation of the occupation.[65] In deciding the vacant possession value, it is to be assumed that the landlord is selling on the open market to a willing buyer. Where a landlord is contractually prohibited from sub-letting, it is to be assumed that the "willing buyer" will buy subject to this prohibition, and that the prohibition would not have the effect of reducing the notional value of the vacant premises.[66] There is to be no allowance made for any sitting tenant discount nor for any enhanced value stemming from development of the site.[67] Where, however, a residential occupier has shared property with other occupiers, the level of damages must be arrived at by comparing the interest of the landlord with the residential occupier in occupation with the interest with the residential occupier not in occupation, but the remaining occupiers still there. In other words, the landlord's interest with vacant possession can only be assumed when the residential occupier has been the sole resident of the landlord's property. In *Melville v. Bruton*,[68] statutory damages of £15,000 were awarded at first instance. On appeal, however, this figure was set aside because the damages were calculated with an assumption of vacant possession, despite the fact that there were two other residents left in the shared house. Damages were reduced to £500 accordingly. Where the operation of the statutory formula results in a low or even negative quantum, pursuers should consider suing for damages at common law.

---

[59] Housing (Scotland) Act 1988, s. 36(7)(b).
[60] *Crawley B.C. v. Sawyer* (1988) 86 L.G.R. 62.
[61] Housing (Scotland) Act 1988, s. 36(6B)(a).
[62] *ibid.* s. 36(6B)(b).
[63] (1991) 23 H.L.R. 250.
[64] *ibid.* s. 6B, inserted by the Housing Act 1988, Sched. 17.
[65] Housing (Scotland) Act 1988, s. 37(1).
[66] *Tagro v. Cafane and Patel* (1991) 23 H.L.R. 250.
[67] Housing (Scotland) Act 1988, s. 37(2).
[68] *Melville v. Bruton* (1997) 29 H.L.R. 319.

High levels of damages were reported in the first year of the operation of the   6–14
equivalent English legislation.[69] More recently,[70] however, the courts have shown
some concern over the level of damages. In particular, where the former
residential occupier is the equivalent of a short assured tenant subject to a
six-month tenancy, the court seems willing to regard this "far from irremoveable
status" as a factor which will result in a lower level of damages being calculated.[71]
Where a tenant is effectively evicted by improvement work the courts have
been prepared to award damages to reflect the loss of the property rights and an
element for inconvenience.[72]

---

[69] *Legal Action,* Mar. 1990, p. 16.
[70] For an account of recent awards in the English courts, see N. Madge, "Harassment and Eviction"
(Pts 1 and 2), (1995) N.L.J. 937 and 1060.
[71] *Melville v. Bruton* (1997) 29 H.L.R. 319.
[72] *Cafferty v. Kamaluddin* (1990) 11 S.H.L.N. 27.

CHAPTER 7

LOCAL AUTHORITY HOUSING AND THE RIGHT TO BUY

1. TENANTS' RIGHTS TO BUY RENTED PROPERTY

Introduction

7–01   The Tenants' Rights Etc. (Scotland) Act 1980 introduced the concept of the secure tenancy for public sector tenants. This provided security of tenure for tenants of public sector landlords. In addition, more controversially, tenants were given the right to purchase the properties they were renting in certain circumstances. The coverage was extended by the Housing (Scotland) Act 1986 to tenancies granted by regional councils and housing associations. The law has been consolidated in the Housing (Scotland) Act 1987. In terms of the Housing (Scotland) Act 1988, housing association tenancies granted on or after January 2, 1989 are assured tenancies and these do not carry the right to purchase. Governments have rejected calls for equivalent rights for tenants of private landlords over the years, except where long leases have been involved.[1]

Tenancies covered by the right to buy

7–02   The basic rule is that secure tenancies are covered. The Housing (Scotland) Act 1987 defines a secure tenancy as having three requirements.[2]

Let as a separate dwelling

7–03   An attempt by a man to buy the room he occupied in a district council hostel for single men was unsuccessful.[3] In this instance, the Lands Tribunal looked at all the circumstances of his occupation of a single room in a modern purpose-built Glasgow hostel and concluded that occupying a bedroom with no facilities beyond a bed and sink was not enough to amount to a tenancy of a separate dwelling. The right to buy did not cover a garage let separately to an individual even where this was adjacent to the house,[4] nor property let with agricultural land exceeding two acres.[5]

Tenant's only or principal home of an individual

7–04   The tenant must be an individual and the property must be the applicant's only or principal home. Where there has been an enforced absence such as

---

[1] Long Leases (Scotland) Act 1954; contrast with the Leasehold Enfranchisement legislation for England and Wales.
[2] s. 44.
[3] *Thomson v. City of Glasgow D.C.,* 1986 S.L.T. (Lands Tr.) 6.
[4] *Hannan v. Falkirk D.C.,* 1987 S.L.T. (Lands Tr.) 18.
[5] *Lamont v. Glenrothes Development Corporation,* 1993 S.L.T. (Lands Tr.) 2.

160

imprisonment, and there was evidence of an intention to return, this has been held to satisfy the requirement.[6] Similarly, in the context of the equivalent English legislation a secure tenant was able to live in one place for over 18 months and still retain a secure tenancy elsewhere as his "only or principal home".[7]

The Lands Tribunal have accepted that a man could purchase not only his original flat, but also the adjacent dwelling.[8] A local authority tenant with a large family had obtained a let of a neighbouring house which had been combined with the original rented flat into a single property. The tenant was in principle entitled to purchase the whole property even though there was the possibility of dividing the property back into its original flats and selling them. This was not a relevant matter, since as the tribunal pointed out, "Parliament were clearly aware that a tenant might buy simply to resell at a profit but have dealt with this possibility by providing in the Act itself for repayment of all or part of the discount."

Landlord is one of a specific list of public sector landlords[9]

The relevant public sector landlords are noted below[10] and the principal ones 7–05 are local authorities[11] (formerly regional, islands and district councils) and Scottish Homes.

Secure tenants entitled to purchase

The right to purchase is limited to secure tenants of certain specified public 7–06 sector landlords. In order for there to be a secure tenancy the property must be the tenant's only or principal home.[12] This involves actual occupation of the premises and is unavailable to an applicant who has ceased to occupy.[13] The applicant must be a public sector tenant at the date of application to purchase.[14]

The tenant must have been in occupation of the house or a series of houses rented out by a public sector landlord for not less than two years immediately prior to the date of service of the application to purchase.[15] It is important to note the distinction between those landlords who must sell their property[16] and the tenancies of certain other public sector landlords which count for qualifying occupancy and discount purposes.[17] The latter includes bodies whose property is not subject to the right to buy, such as the prison service and the armed forces, as well as a variety of public sector employers such as the U.K. Atomic Energy Authority.[18]

---

[6] *Beggs v. Kilmarnock and Loudoun D.C.*,1996 Hous.L.R. 28.
[7] *Crawley B.C.v. Sawyer* (1988) 86 L.G.R. 629; but see *Jennings v. Epping Forest D.C.* (1993) 25 H.L.R. 241 and *Taylor v. Newham L.B.C.* [1993] 1 W.L.R. 444.
[8] *Jenkins v. Renfrew D.C.*, 1989 S.L.T. (Lands Tr.) 41.
[9] s. 44(2), list in s. 61(2)(a) and any housing trust in existence on Nov. 13, 1953.
[10] See para. 7–08.
[11] Local Government etc. (Scotland) Act 1994, Sched. 13, para. 152.
[12] s. 44(1)(a).
[13] *McLoughlin's C.B. v. Motherwell D.C.*,1994 S.L.T. (Lands Tr.) 31.
[14] *Lamont v. Glenrothes Development Corporation,* 1993 S.L.T. (Lands Tr.) 2; *McKay v. City of Dundee D.C.,*1996 S.L.T. (Lands Tr.) 9.
[15] s. 61(2)(c).
[16] Housing (Scotland) Act 1987, s. 61(2)(a).
[17] s. 61(11) lists over 20 such bodies and the Secretary of State has authority to add to the list.
[18] s. 61(11)(u).

The rights of relatives to purchase

7–07   The right is not available automatically to relatives of the tenant except spouses, children (over the age of 16), or the spouse of a child, although other family members may be accepted as a matter of discretion.[19] This discretionary element was demonstrated in *Robb v. Kyle and Carrick District Council*[20] where a claim was unsuccessfully made by a person who had been sharing with his wife's brother for a number of years, until the latter moved elsewhere.

Landlords and the right to buy

7–08   The full list of landlords whose property qualifies for the right to buy is specified in the Housing (Scotland) Act 1987.[21] The list includes a number of organisations which have been superseded in local government and other structural reforms and are unlikely to be widely encountered in the future as well as authorities in terms of the Local Government etc. (Scotland) Act 1994[22]:

(1)   an islands or district council, or a joint board or joint committee of an islands or district council or the common good of an islands or district council, or any trust under the control of an islands or district council;

(2)   a regional council or joint board or joint committee of two or more regional councils, or any trust under the control of a regional council;

(3)   a development corporation (including an urban development corporation);

(4)   Scottish Homes or a housing corporation;

(5)   a registered housing association (between 1986 and 1989);

(6)   a housing co-operative;

(7)   a police authority in Scotland;

(8)   a fire authority in Scotland.

The landlord must be heritable proprietor of the house.[23]

Properties exempted from the right to buy

7–09   Some of the properties of the relevant public sector landlords are exempted. Schedule 2 to the Housing (Scotland) Act 1987 declares that certain tenancies are not secure tenancies. The excluded tenancies are:

(1)   premises occupied under a contract of employment;

(2)   temporary letting to a person seeking accommodation;

(3)   temporary letting pending development;

(4)   temporary accommodation during works;

(5)   accommodation for a homeless person;

(6)   agricultural and business premises;

(7)   police and fire authorities accommodation;

(8)   houses which are part of, or within the curtilage of, certain other buildings.

---

[19] s. 61(10)(v.); see *McDonald v. Renfrew D.C.*, 1982 S.L.T. (Lands Tr.) 30.
[20] 1989 S.L.T. (Lands Tr.) 78.
[21] s. 61(2)(a).
[22] Sched. 13, para. 152.
[23] s. 61(2)(b); see *Graham v. Motherwell D.C.*, 1985 S.L.T. (Lands Tr.) 44 where the landlord was a tenant under the 999-year lease and not regarded as a "heritable proprietor".

Most of the case law in relation to the right to buy stems from disputes 7–10
about whether or not property that a public authority has been renting out
falls within these exemptions. The vast majority of the case law before the
Lands Tribunal for Scotland[24] and Court of Session has concerned whether an
employee is occupying for the better performance of duties. There have also
been interesting related issues on whether or not a person has been provided
with temporary accommodation. Since the introduction in 1986 of paragraph
8 there have also been questions arising as to whether or not the house in
question is either part of, or within the curtilage of, another non-housing
property.[25]

Employee as tenant (para. 1)

"A tenancy shall not be a secure tenancy if the tenant (or one of the joint 7–11
tenants) is an employee of the landlord or of any local authority or
development corporation, and his contract of employment requires him to
occupy the house for the better performance of his duties."[26]

There are two distinct aspects to the test which must both be satisfied.

(1) Does the contract of employment require the applicant to occupy the
house?
(2) Is the occupation for the better performance of the applicant's duties?

The approach taken by the Lands Tribunal and the courts has not been without
difficulty over the years. The term of the contract requiring occupation for the
better performance of the duties may be implied into the contract where the
facts warrant such an inference.[27] This has occurred where the employee was
expected to "keep an eye" on the park where he lived.[28] It has also occurred
where another park employee was expected to carry out miscellaneous park-
related duties such as letting out people locked in.[29] It is of significance if in
practice the duties could not be as well carried out if the applicant did not occupy
the property in question.[30] The formal requirement to occupy accommodation
can be displaced where it does not genuinely reflect the reality of the duties
actually carried out.[31]

The typical approach to relatively straightforward cases can be seen in *McKay v.* 7–12
Livingston Development Corporation.[32] This case concerned a farmhouse
surrounded by nursery grounds occupied by a groundsman. Here the conflict
was about whether the applicant was required to occupy the house as well as
whether its occupancy enhanced the performance of his duties. The duties could
not be so well performed if he lived elsewhere and this had been the thinking
behind the offer of the house, and there was no right to buy.

However, some employees' working practices are less clear cut or they change
over time and the assumption by a landlord/employer that no employee tenants

---

[24] s. 71.
[25] Housing (Scotland) Act 1986, s. 10 and Sched. 1, para. 18.
[26] para. 1.
[27] *McTurk v. Fife R.C.*, 1990 S.L.T. (Lands Tr.) 49.
[28] *Douglas v. Falkirk D.C.*, 1983 S.L.T. (Lands Tr.) 21.
[29] *Docherty v. Edinburgh D.C.*, 1985 S.L.T.(Lands Tr.) 61.
[30] *Kinghorn v. Glasgow D.C.*, 1984 S.L.T. (Lands Tr.) 9.
[31] *Gilmour v. City of Glasgow D.C.*, 1989 S.L.T. (Lands Tr.) 74.
[32] 1990 S.L.T. (Lands Tr.) 54.

enjoy the right to buy is not accurate. The point that has been made is that the important factor is not what the contract of employment states, but what the practice is,[33] even if there is a change after the employee's retirement.[34]

7–13   By way of contrast, in one case a manager of a swimming pool whose house was situated close to the pool but separated by a road was successful in his purchase application. The police had contacted him on a number of occasions because of emergencies, but this was on an *ad hoc* basis rather than establishing that he was required to live in the vicinity of the pool. No other swimming pool managers in the department lived near their respective charges.[35]

The point was made in *De Fontenay v. Strathclyde Regional Council*[36] that whilst the tenant did not require any particular house from which to perform his duties "if there was no available accommodation in Tiree … then he would not be able to perform his duties at all." This decision was taken in the context of a very small pool of only 26 local authority houses. It was noted that there might well be serious repercussions for staff recruitment if the authority could not get teachers because of the lack of accommodation.

On appeal[37] the decision was approved and the Court of Session were satisfied that the the the phrase "better performance of his duties" included "any" performance if the duties could not be performed at all without occupancy of the house in question.

7–14   There is a certain conflict between *Gilmour*[38] and *De Fontenay*.[39] The arguments in *De Fontenay* are attractive in that better performance of duties must include being able to perform a job at all. The problem is whether or not the operation of the education service as a whole is a relevant consideration as opposed to the individual service contract of the applicant. The tribunal appeared in *De Fontenay* to choose a community interpretation as opposed to an individualistic one. The distinction may be more pragmatic than principled, depending on the specific circumstances encountered. Hence, in *Jack v. Strathclyde Regional Council*[40] the view was taken that a house on Mull occupied by a head teacher was covered by the right to buy on the grounds that the pressure on housing was less intense than on Tiree. The local authority owned over 260 houses on the island of Mull and there was a reasonably healthy turnover rate of tenancies.

Temporary letting to a person seeking accommodation (para. 2)

7–15   "A tenancy shall not be a secure tenancy if the house was let by the landlord expressly on a temporary basis to a person moving into an area in order to take up employment there, and for the purpose of enabling him to seek accommodation in the area."[41]

---

[33] *Little v. Borders R.C,* 1990 S.L.T. (Lands Tr.) 2.
[34] *Archibald v. Lothian R.C.,* 1992 S.L.T. (Lands Tr.) 75.
[35] *Stevenson v. West Lothian D.C.,* 1985 S.L.T. (Lands Tr.) 9. See also *Fisher v. Fife R.C.,* 1989 S.L.T. (Lands Tr.) 26: houses in the grounds of the outdoor centre occupied by instructors but no express clause in employment contract requiring occupancy. Right to buy confirmed.
[36] 1990 S.L.T. 605.
[37] *ibid.*
[38] 1989 S.L.T. (Lands Tr.) 74.
[39] 1990 S.L.T. 605.
[40] 1992 S.L.T. (Lands Tr.) 29.
[41] para. 2.

The question of whether or not a tenancy is exempt on this ground relates to the question of providing employees with accommodation in the interim while they look for a permanent place to stay and the care taken by authorities in drawing up the relevant occupancy contract. The issue was exacerbated by the fact that when many of the relevant contracts were drawn up the right to buy did not cover the property of regional councils.

The proper approach was outlined by the First Division of the Court of Session in *Campbell v. Western Isles Islands Council.*[42] Mrs Campbell was offered a teaching post by the islands council and had to move into the area to take it up. She and her husband applied for a council house. They were offered a schoolhouse. The offer was made in a letter which explained that the offer was for a two-year period and that no secure tenancy was granted. This letter explained that the tenancy was of temporary accommodation only. The actual tenancy agreement itself contained no restrictions and was a standard form of letting missive. The Campbells in due course sought to purchase the schoolhouse. The First Division upheld the Lands Tribunal decision that the Campbells were entitled to buy the schoolhouse.

> "What is required, in our opinion, is that the missives or contract of lease shall state explicitly that the dwelling house is let on a temporary basis for the defined purpose, so that the tenant will be in no doubt from the outset that he will not enjoy the statutory right to purchase which effeirs to a lessee under a statutory tenancy in certain circumstances."[43]

The impact of this case, as indicated in the Court of Session, was considerable. In the Western Isles Islands Council area alone there were in existence some 20 other tenants in the same position as the Campbells with virtually identical missives and covering letters.

House is part of, or within the curtilage of, non-housing property (para. 8)

In order to remedy the effects of one of the early sell-off cases[44] the scope of 7–16 exemptions was extended. Protection is now afforded to public sector landlords where it would be inappropriate to have housing sold off because it is part of other property or within its grounds. This exemption states that a tenancy is not a secure tenancy:

> "if the house forms part of, or is within the curtilage of a building which mainly —
> (a) is held by the landlord for purposes other than the provision of housing accommodation; and
> (b) consists of accommodation other than housing accommodation."

This problem has mainly revolved around houses kept for various members of staff in educational establishments. There are two distinct issues which have arisen, usually where the need for the janitor or teacher ceases. First, there is the question of whether the house forms part of the building. Although, of course, cases depend very much on the particular layout of the buildings concerned, it is possible to obtain useful guidance from the way the Tribunal has weighed the

---

[42] 1989 S.L.T. 602.
[43] *ibid.* at 604.
[44] *Hill v. Orkney Islands D.C.,*1983 S.L.T.(Lands Tr.) 2.

various issues presented to it. This indicates that whereas detached dwelling-houses may be secure tenancies,[45-46] a flat arrangement will be much harder to deal with. In *Murray v. Strathclyde Regional Council*[47] the right to buy was rejected. The school premises were on the ground floor at one end with a two-floor house attached. Two of the bedrooms of the house were built over the original schoolroom. The house had its own defined garden with pedestrian, but not vehicular access. A servitude right to carry out maintenance would have been required in the event of the house being split off.

7–17   The second issue is whether or not property is within the curtilage of other non-housing property. In *Walker v. Strathclyde Regional Council*[48] this issue was raised. The Lands Tribunal considered whether the property was within the curtilage of the school. While this was not a term of art in Scots law it broadly meant land adjoining a building necessary for the comfortable enjoyment of the latter.[49] The subjects which the applicant was seeking to buy included a lean-to shed at the rear of the house. There was no integral access to the lean-to shed and a specific right of access would have been necessary. For this reason the Lands Tribunal were of the view that this brought the schoolhouse within the curtilage exception.

The occasionally bizarre consequences for the community can be seen in *Shipman v. Lothian Regional Council*[50] which concerned the former home of the chief administrator of an old folks' home which was on an island site and could only be approached through the grounds of the former home. The Lands Tribunal felt it was not within the curtilage, looking to the broad nature of the home with a group of buildings on a 60-acre site. In the opinion of the Tribunal the ordinary meaning of the words used signified a small area of ground attached to a building or perhaps a composite building.

Educational purposes and islands properties

7–18   The 1987 Act gave "an islands council" power to refuse to sell houses required for educational purposes[51] following the decision in *Hill v. Orkney Islands Council*.[52] However, the 1987 Act did not define "islands council" in this context. In *MacDonald v. Strathclyde Regional Council*[53] it was unsuccessfully argued that this special consideration should also be available to an authority which had an island in its area and thus could be regarded as an "islands council". The Local Government etc. (Scotland) Act 1994 altered the coverage of this section to mean the local authority for either Orkney Islands, Shetlands Islands or Western Isles.

In *De Fontenay v. Strathclyde Regional Council*[54] the same practical issue was dealt with in a slightly different way. Here the authority refused, using paragraph 1 suggesting that the property was required for the better performance

[45-46] *Barron v. Border R.C.*, 1987 S.L.T. (Lands Tr.) 36.
[47] Lands Tribunal for Scotland, Sept. 7, 1989.
[48] 1990 S.L.T. (Lands Tr.) 17.
[49] P. Watchman and E. Young, "The Meaning of Curtilage", 1990 S.L.T. 77; *Dyer v. Dorset C.C.* [1988] 3 W.L.R. 213.
[50] 1989 S.L.T. (Lands Tr.) 82. See also *Fisher v. Fife R.C.*, 1989 S.L.T. (Lands Tr.) 26.
[51] s. 70 (introduced by s. 4 of the Tenants' Rights Etc. (Scotland) Amendment Act 1984).
[52] 1983 S.L.T. (Lands Tr.) 2.
[53] 1990 S.L.T. (Lands Tr.) 10.
[54] Lands Tribunal for Scotland, July 24, 1989, unreported, and 1990 S.L.T. 605 on appeal.

of the teacher's duties. They were able to argue successfully that if the sale were allowed to go ahead it would prevent subsequent teachers from performing their duties at all, as there would be nowhere for them to live.

2. HOUSING ASSOCIATION TENANCIES

The Housing and Planning Act 1986 introduced the right to buy for housing   7–19 association tenancies. For tenancies entered into on or after January 2, 1989 in terms of the Housing (Scotland) Act 1988 these rights are abolished.[55] The right to buy of pre-1989 tenants continues to be exercisable.

Houses with special facilities or adaptations

There is no right to buy where a house is one of a group which has been   7–20 provided with facilities (including a call system and the services of a warden) specially designed or adapted for the needs of persons of pensionable age or disabled persons.[56-57] The meaning of "call system" and "warden" was discussed in *Crilly v. Motherwell District Council*.[58] The absence of a warden and call system was not fatal to the operation of the exclusion provision for a house adapted for a person with spina bifida.[59]

Over the years the approach to this by the Lands Tribunal has been quite restrictive. The matter has been examined by the Inner House in *City of Dundee District Council v. Anderson*.[60] Their Lordships indicated that a two-stage decision process was involved—were there facilities? was the house in a group? As to whether the call system and warden facilities mentioned should be treated as mandatory or simply as an example was not an issue the Inner House were prepared to give a view upon.

In order to be excluded from the right to buy, a house must be one of a   7–21 group of such houses in the geographical sense of a group of houses standing together or in close proximity. In *Martin v. Motherwell District Council*[61] the house in question was not excluded from the right to buy where it was one of a pair of semi-detached houses with facilities and there were some 36 such houses spread throughout a scheme. Similarly, in *Holloran v. Dumbarton District Council*[62] a house was not excluded from the right to buy in a block converted for the provision of facilities but where the house was not so converted. The Lands Tribunal in *Moonie v. City of Dundee District Council*[63] stressed that consideration had to be directed at the house rather than the individual tenant, in excluding from the right to buy a house which had facilities of which the tenant was unaware and where the facilities were not used by the tenant.

---

[55] s. 43(3).
[56-57] s. 61(4)(a).
[58] 1988 S.L.T. (Lands Tr.) 7.
[59] See also *Heenan v. Motherwell D.C.*, Lands Tr., Aug. 6, 1987, unreported.
[60] 1994 S.L.T. 46.
[61] 1991 S.L.T. (Lands Tr.) 4.
[62] 1992 S.L.T. (Lands Tr.) 73.
[63] 1992 S.L.T. (LandsTr.) 103.

Other housing association exemptions

7–22   Other exempt properties are specified in the 1987 Act—those of a registered housing association which has received no grants from public funds[64]; where a housing association has at no time let (or had available for letting) more than 100 dwellings,[65] where a housing association has charitable status[66]; where, within a neighbourhood, the house is one of a number (not exceeding 14) of houses with a common landlord which is a registered housing association, and where it is the practice of that landlord to let at least half of those houses for occupation by any or all of (i) persons who have suffered from or are suffering from mental disorder, physical handicap or addiction to alcohol or other drugs, (ii) persons who have been released from prison or other institutions, (iii) young persons who have left the care of a local authority or a social service, or special facilities are provided wholly or partly for the purpose of assisting those persons[67]; co-operative housing associations are also exempt since the Housing (Scotland) Act 1987 provides that such tenancies are not secure tenancies.[68]

3. Secretary of State's Power to Refuse

7–23   The 1987 Act also provides that the Secretary of State may authorise refusal to sell certain houses provided for persons of pensionable age. This provision applies to a house which has facilities which are substantially different from those of an ordinary house and which has been designed or adapted for occupation by a person of pensionable age whose special needs require accommodation of the kind provided.[69] There is guidance on how the Secretary of State would operate this exemption.[70] Where there is an application to purchase and the landlord is of the opinion that this section applies the matter must be referred to the Secretary of State within one month. The landlord must specify the facilities and features of design or adaptation which cause the house to come within the coverage of the section. The Secretary of State, if of the view that the section applies, must authorise the landlord to issue a notice of refusal to sell. Where the landlord's application for exempt status is refused then the landlord must make an offer to the tenant in accordance with the standard sale procedure. This exemption applies only to houses let before January 1, 1990.[71]

4. Price and Discount to be Applied to Sales

7–24   The legislation makes provision for both the sale price and a discount facility.[72] The legislation was introduced in order to encourage tenants to buy up public sector property.[73] The price was to be fixed at market price from which a discount

---

[64] s. 61(4)(b); as noted, the right to buy from housing associations ended for tenancies entered into after January 2, 1989.

[65] s. 61(4)(c).

[66] s. 61(4)(d) and (e).

[67] s. 61(4)(f).

[68] s. 45; as noted, the right to buy for tenants of housing associations does not apply to tenancies entered into after January 2, 1989.

[69] s. 69.

[70] Env. Circular 12/1992.

[71] s. 69(1A) (inserted by the Local Government and Housing Act 1989, s. 177(1)).

[72] s. 62.

reflecting the number of years spent by the buyer in public sector property but ignoring any work which would qualify for a reimbursement in terms of section 58.[74]

Price

The price is to be the market value of the house less any discount for years of   7–25
occupancy.[75] The calculation of the years of occupancy covers occupancy as an "appropriate person".[76] This includes occupation as the spouse of a tenant including a previous spouse.[77] It also includes years as a child when a person directly succeeds a tenant.[78] It does not, however, include years living as a child of a tenant where there was an indirect succession, as in *Hamilton*,[79] where a son succeeded as joint tenant of his mother after living with his parents when his father was tenant. Discount was only available for the years when he lived with his mother as tenant. The market value of the house is to be decided by the district valuer or a qualified valuer nominated by the landlord and accepted by the tenant. It is up to the landlord which of these individuals is selected.[80] In fixing the market value the assumption must be made that the house is available for sale on the open market with vacant possession at the date of service of the application to purchase.[81] In addition, there is provision for the tenant to enjoy a fixed-price option where the application to purchase has been met with an offer to sell.[82] Where tenants are unable to obtain loans, they may pay a deposit of £100 and defer purchase for up to two years at the price fixed in the offer to sell.[83] If the tenant is not able to take up the option the deposit is recoverable.[84]

Discount

The discount varies as between flats and houses and depends on the extent of   7–26
the occupation by the tenant. There are maximum discounts available which vary as between houses and flats. This reflects the lower levels of demand for flats. Lower discount levels are available for those purchasing houses covered by the Housing Defects Act 1984.[85]

Houses

The discount on houses is offered at 32 per cent of the market value together   7–27
with an additional 1 per cent of the market value for every year beyond two of continuous occupation by the appropriate person immediately preceding the date of service of the application to purchase the house.[86] The period for

---

[73] C.M.G. Himsworth, *Housing Law in Scotland* (1994).
[74] s. 62(2).
[75] s. 62(1).
[76] s. 62(4)(a).
[77] *McLean v. Cunninghame D.C.,*1996 S.L.T. (Lands Tr.) 2.
[78] s. 61(10)(a)(iv).
[79] *Hamilton v. City of Glasgow D.C.,*1996 S.L.T. (Lands Tr.) 14.
[80] s. 62(2).
[81] *ibid.*
[82] s. 67.
[83] *ibid.*
[84] s. 67(2).
[85] s. 62(3)(a)(ii)—basic 30% (house), 40% (flat), with yearly additions of 1% (house) and 2% (flat).
[86] s. 62(3).

continuous occupation includes a series of houses provided by any of the noted bodies,[87] as well as any armed services accommodation provided by the Crown. The maximum discount is 60 per cent[88]; this would be reached after 30 years.

Flats

7–28   The discount on flats is offered at 44 per cent of the market value together with an additional 2 per cent of the market value for every year beyond two of continuous occupation by the appropriate person immediately preceding the date of service of the application to purchase the flat.[89] Again, succession of occupation is permitted. The maximum discount for flats is 70 per cent of the market value[90]; this would be reached after 15 years. For discount purposes the tenant is the appropriate person unless there would be a higher discount by looking to the spouse—provided that the spouses are cohabiting at the time of date of service of the application to purchase.

Effect on the price of improvement work by public sector landlord

7–29   There is provision for the price to be adjusted where there is an outstanding debt on a property incurred by a local authority in making improvements. The Housing (Scotland) Act 1987 provides that the discount must not reduce the price below a specified amount which is to represent the costs incurred in respect of the house. This is determined by looking to the costs incurred beginning in the financial year for the period five years before the date when the application to purchase was served.[91] The relevant costs are the cost of erection or acquisition of the house, the acquisition of the site of the house, any works of improvement to the house (except repair and maintenance) and administrative costs.[92] There is no discount limitation where the costs are below £5,000.

Distinguishing between repair and improvement

7–30   In *Wingate v. Clydebank District Council*[93] the Wingates applied to purchase the local authority house which they had rented from Clydebank District Council for many years. They were entitled to the maximum discount of 70 per cent on the market value of £21,500, *i.e.* £6,450. The district council served an offer to sell at the price of £17,000. This made allowance for expenditure by the local authority on improvements to the property. The applicants took their claim to the Lands Tribunal.

The question was whether or not the expenditure was spent wholly on making improvements as opposed to repairs and maintenance work which did not make the property any better than it was before the deterioration which made such work necessary. The house in question was an Atholl steel house built about 40 years ago. These houses have a rust problem which affects the steel structure. In addition, the way of dealing with repair, maintenance and improvement by the district council had been to do work on housing as a group: "If it was decided

---

[87] s. 61(11).
[88] s. 62(3)(b).
[89] s. 62(3)(a)(i).
[90] s. 62 (3)(b).
[91] s. 62(6A).
[92] Housing (Scotland) Act 1987 (Right to Buy) (Cost Floor) Determination 1988—appended to SDD Circular No. 32/1988.
[93] 1990 S.L.T. (Lands Tr.) 71.

that most of the houses in such a group or scheme needed work to be done, it was done in all, whether they needed it or not." This meant that there were no available records of the work done on each house or of the extent to which the work done was either repair or maintenance. The records covered the total work. The Tribunal duly set about the task of distinguishing between debts incurred in making improvements and debts incurred by way of repair or maintenance. The latter did not count for the purposes of reducing the applicant's discount.

The Tribunal went through the various items assessing whether they seemed to amount to improvements or repairs and maintenance—builder work, roof tile work, installation of gas heating and a new system of water heating, refitting of the kitchen and bathroom, replacing existing wall linings with insulated plasterboard, plumber work, electrical work, external wall insulation and rendering, glazier work and painter work. Some items were clearly improvements, such as the refitting of the kitchen and bathroom units, while the external wall insulation and rendering was work of repair and maintenance since it stemmed from the underlying corrosion along the joints of the steel plates. In financial terms, the actual expenditure on improvements to the Wingates' house was a little under £8,000 rather than the £17,000 suggested originally. There are problems in disaggregating repair sums where these are done on a group basis, but the Lands Tribunal have made it clear that more care will need to be exercised in the future in this area of fixing financial liability.

Restriction on double discount

There is also a limitation on applicants receiving more than one discount. 7–31
Where a tenant has in the past received a discount from a public sector landlord in the United Kingdom[94] the Act provides for the deduction of an amount equal to any previous discount received. This restriction is effective from September 27, 1993.[95] It covers households and applies to the "appropriate person". This term is defined as covering the tenant or the tenant's spouse if living with the tenant at the date of service of the application to purchase or the deceased spouse if living with the tenant at the time of death or any joint tenant who is a joint purchaser of the house. Where there were joint purchasers who subsequently divorced the level of discount available to the remarried wife was disputed where a second right to buy was exercised. The Lands Tribunal determined that only that portion of the discount available to the applicant fell to be deducted rather than the full discount paid.[96] It is not clear from the language of the statute whether there is any statutory basis for this determination.

Repayment of discount

In the event of the tenant selling the property before the expiry of three years 7–32
from the date of service of a notice of acceptance by the tenant, landlords are authorised[97] to recover a proportion of the difference between the market value of the house and the discounted price at which the tenant purchased the property. This does not apply where part only of the property is sold and the remainder

---

[93a] 1990 S.L.T. (Lands Tr.) p. 72L.

[94] s. 62(3A).

[95] Inserted by the Leasehold Reform, Housing and Urban Development Act 1993, s. 157(4)—S.I. 1993 No. 2163.

[96] *Tennant v. East Kilbride D.C.,*1997 Hous.L.R. 44.

[97] s. 72.

continues to be the only or principal home of the purchasing tenant. It only applies on the first disposal during the period.

The proportion of the difference is:

(1)   100% where the disposal occurs in the first year,
(2)   66% during the second year,
(3)   33% during the third year.

There is no recovery of discount where the disposal is by the executor of the deceased owner [98] or as a result of a compulsory purchase order, or the disposal is to a member of the owner's family who has lived with him for a period of 12 months before the disposal and there is no payment involved.[99] However, if the disponee sells the house before the expiry of the three-year period from the service of the notice of acceptance, then the discount is recoverable in the same way as if it had been a disposal by the acquiring tenant.[1]

Entitlement to a loan

7–33   Where tenants are exercising the right to buy, they are entitled to a loan from the local authority[2] or, where appropriate, Scottish Homes.[3] Any applicant who receives an offer to sell from an authority is entitled to apply for a loan of an amount not exceeding the price fixed for the house.[4] There is a timetable laid down for the local application procedure.[5] The local authority must make an offer of a loan calculated in accordance with regulations laid down by the Secretary of State.[6] These lay down that the amount of the loan is normally two and a half times the annual net income of the applicant or the annual income of joint purchasers.[7] If the loan is refused on the grounds of incorrect information supplied, the disappointed applicant can apply to the sheriff for a declarator of entitlement to loan.[8] The loan is to be a variable interest home loan.[9]

5. RIGHT TO BUY PROCESS

7–34   A specific procedure is laid down for the purchase of public sector housing under the Housing (Scotland) Act 1987[10] with strict timetables and default procedures built in to prevent local authorities obstructing what was perceived as a sell-off of community assets. Further sanctions by way of complex financial penalties for failing to meet response times were added by the Leasehold Reform, Housing and Urban Development Act 1993.[11]

---

[98]   *Clydebank D.C. v. Keeper of the Registers of Scotland,* 1994 S.L.T. (Lands Tr.) 2.
[99]   s. 73.
[1]   *ibid.*
[2]   s. 216.
[3]   For sales by housing associations or Scottish Homes themselves—s. 216(1)(a),(b) and (b)(i).
[4]   s.216(1).
[5]   s. 216(1)(c).
[6]   s. 216(3).
[7]   Right of Purchase (Loans) (Scotland) Regulations 1980 (S.I. 1980 No. 1430).
[8]   s. 216(7).
[9]   s. 219(1).
[10]   s. 63.
[11]   Housing (Scotland) Act 1987, s. 66A.

Application to purchase

A tenant who seeks to exercise a right to purchase a public sector house must 7–35
serve on the landlord an "application to purchase" notice in proper form.[12] This
notice must contain a declaration that the tenant seeks to exercise the right to
purchase, a statement of any period of qualifying occupancy and the name of
any joint purchaser.[13]

Offer to sell

The landlord must, unless disputing the application, serve an "offer to sell"[14] 7–36
within two months of receipt of an application to purchase. This must contain
the market value of the house, the discount and the resulting price of the house,
along with any conditions the landlord intends to impose and an actual offer to
sell the house at the price and under the conditions mentioned. If the landlord
fails to do this timeously, the Lands Tribunal is obliged to issue an offer to sell[15]
where the tenant applies to the Tribunal.[16]

Notice of acceptance

Where an offer to sell is served on a tenant and he wishes to exercise his 7–37
right to purchase and does not dispute the terms of the offer, he must serve a
"notice of acceptance" on the landlord within two months of the offer to sell or
of any date resolving a dispute on any aspect of the sale.[17]

Conditions of sale

Reasonable conditions of sale may be included in the offer to sell[18] provided 7–38
that the conditions allow the tenant to have as full enjoyment and use of the house
as owner as he had as tenant.[19] Thus the Lands Tribunal have imposed a requirement
on a purchasing tenant to ensure the continued availability of an emergency exit
from adjoining premises owned by the local authority.[20] Also, the seller must
secure to the tenant such additional rights as are necessary for his reasonable
enjoyment and use of the house as owner as well as imposing on the tenant any
necessary duties relative to rights so secured. The conditions must include such
terms as are necessary to entitle the tenant to receive a good and marketable title
to the house. Where the authority is incapable of conveying the subjects let—for
example, the subjects have been destroyed or conveyed in error to another party—
the Inner House have suggested that the authority might append, in clear, explicit
and unambiguous terms, a condition that the subjects to be conveyed were the
subjects let less such part as it was not in their power to convey.[21]

---

[12] s. 63(1)—S.I. 1993 No. 2182—Himsworth points out that the consent of the spouse is omitted
in the form. This would appear to be a dealing within the terms of the Matrimonial Homes
(Family Protection)(Scotland) Act 1981, s. 8.
[13] s. 63(1).
[14] s. 63(2).
[15] *Livingstone v. East of Scotland Water Authority,* 1997 S.L.T. (Lands Tr.) 28.
[16] s. 71.
[17] s. 66.
[18] s. 64.
[19] *McLuskey v. Scottish Homes,* 1993 S.L.T. (Lands Tr.) 17—liability for maintenance of common
parts.
[20] *MacDonald v. Strathclyde R.C.,*1990 S.L.T. (Lands Tr.) 10.
[21] *City of Glasgow D.C. v. Doyle,* 1993 S.L.T. 604 at 610.

If there is a condition which imposes a new charge or an increase of an existing charge for the provision of a service in relation to the house, the landlord must provide for the charge to be in reasonable proportion to the cost of providing the service. No condition is to be imposed which has the effect of requiring the tenant to pay any expenses of the landlord. Option to purchase clauses in favour of the landlord are not permitted[22] unless they are in relation to a house which has facilities which are substantially different from those of an ordinary house and which has been designed or adapted for occupation by a person of pensionable age or a disabled person with a special needs requirement.[23] Where there is such a permitted option to purchase, the price is to be determined by the district valuer on a market value basis taking account of any early-sale discount recovered.[24]

Variation of conditions

7–39   Where the tenant wishes to exercise the right to buy, but considers that a condition in the offer to sell is unreasonable, or wishes to have a new condition included or has not previously indicated that it is to be a joint purchase or has decided against a previous joint purchase, the landlord may be requested to make the appropriate change in the offer to sell. If the landlord refuses the tenant may simply accept the matter and accept the unamended offer within the original two-month period. Alternatively, the tenant may, within one month of the refusal, refer the matter to the Lands Tribunal. The Lands Tribunal has the power to uphold the condition, strike it out, vary it or insert the new condition including joint purchase changes. Where its determination results in a variation of the terms of the offer to sell, the Tribunal will order the landlord to serve on the tenant an amended offer to sell within two months of its determination.[25]

The market value does not constitute a condition which can be challenged.[26] The Lands Tribunal has indicated in various cases that certain conditions are acceptable and others unacceptable. Thus, a requirement that a resale be to a person already resident in the area or to a person who required to reside in the area was rejected as too vague as well as going beyond what Parliament had intended.[27] The repayment of a sum to cover the cost of a grant for central heating which was available to council tenants was not accepted.[28] A condition requiring tenants to acknowledge the structural problems of the steel housing they were buying in any subsequent sale and agree to pay for structural work in the future has also been rejected by the Lands Tribunal.[29]

Refusal of applications

7–40   Where the landlord disputes the tenant's right to purchase it must serve a "a notice of refusal" to be served within one month of the service of the "application to purchase". A notice of refusal must specify the grounds on which the landlord disputes the tenant's right to purchase or the accuracy of the information upon

---

[22] *Ross and Cromarty D.C.v. Patience*, 1997 S.L.T. 463.
[23] s. 64(4).
[24] s 64(5).
[25] s. 65.
[26] *MacLeod v. Ross and Cromarty D.C.*, 1983 S.L.T. (Lands Tr.) 5.
[27] *Pollock v. Dumbarton D.C.*, 1983 S.L.T. (Lands Tr.) 17.
[28] *Brookbanks v. Motherwell D.C.*, 1988 S.L.T. (Lands Tr.) 72.
[29] *Forsyth v. Scottish Homes*, 1990 S.L.T. (Lands Tr.) 37.

which the purported right is founded. If a landlord serves a notice of refusal the tenant may, within one month of receipt of such a notice, apply to the Lands Tribunal for a finding that he has a right to purchase the house on such terms as it may determine.[30]

If the landlord has houses which have facilities substantially different from those of an ordinary house and which have been designed or adapted for occupation by a person of pensionable age whose special needs require accommodation of the kind provided by the house, then the landlord may apply to the Secretary of State for permission to serve a notice of refusal. If granted, the notice of refusal must be served as soon as is practicable and in any event within one month of authorisation; where it is not granted, then the tenant must be served an offer to sell.[31]

Similarly, as noted, it is provided that where the local authority for Orkney Islands, Shetland Isles or Western Isles[32] (formerly known as an islands council) is landlord of property held for the purposes of education and required for accommodation of a person who is or will be employed by the council for educational purposes, and other suitable accommodation cannot be provided by the council, the landlord may serve a notice of refusal within one month of the service of the application to purchase.[33]　7–41

Delays between date of entry and title transfer

A further problem emerged in a series of applications to the Local Ombudsman in late 1990. In applications relating to Motherwell District Council, Edinburgh District Council, Glasgow District Council and Renfrew District Council, the ombudsman was presented with a problem not covered in the legislation, *i.e.* what was the remedy for tenants whose date of entry was delayed after the conclusion of missives? These people had to carry on paying rent and could not start paying off their mortgages until the conveyancing was completed. In the various cases which came to light in September and October 1990 delays ranging from five months up to 30 months were encountered. It was pointed out that there was no statutory remedy and, while the ombudsman was aware that there had been problems both of obtaining personnel and of financial restraints, he considered such delays constituted maladministration and caused injustice. He was prepared to recommend the award of sums of between £100 and £400 to those affected.[34]　7–42

This issue was addressed in the financial penalty sanctions introduced by the Leasehold Reform, Housing and Urban Development Act 1993 covering the period after missives have been concluded.[35] If the landlord has failed to deliver a good and marketable title the tenant may at any time serve a notice of delay. This must set out the landlord's failure and indicate the last action taken by the landlord. It must also provide a minimum one-month period for the landlord to respond with a counter-notice. Where the landlord fails to respond in this one-month period to the initial notice of delay, the tenant may serve a further notice which has the effect of reducing the price payable by the rent paid during　7–43

---

[30] s. 68.
[31] s. 69.
[32] Local Government etc. (Scotland) Act 1994, Sched. 13, para. 152(4).
[33] s. 70.
[34] These decisions are reported in more detail in (1991) 14 S.H.L.N. 50–55.
[35] s. 70 (as amended).

the period starting with the service of this second delay notice (operative notice of delay). The price is reduced by the rent paid by the tenant between the service of this second notice of delay and either the service of a counter-notice or the delivery of a good and marketable title. The landlord may serve a counter-notice; this cancels the notice of delay. If the counter-notice is received within the response period of one month, the matter may be referred by the tenant to the Lands Tribunal.

The Tribunal must consider whether or not the landlord could have taken action which would have enabled a good and marketable title to be delivered to the tenant. If it makes such a finding this enables the tenant to serve the second notice of delay as if the counter-notice had not been served. For the purposes of the reduction, the second notice is taken to be the first date that it could have been served, *i.e.* one month after the service of the initial notice of delay.

There is provision for aggregation of more than one period of delay as could occur where there are delays both in agreeing an offer as well as carrying out the conveyancing tasks. Where the delay period amounts to more than 12 months, the amount of the reduction is increased to 50 per cent of the price. The Secretary of State has the power to increase this percentage by statutory instrument. There is also provision for shifting the date of the three-year period for the calculation of the discount repayment period.

Death of the tenant prior to title transfer

7–44   Where an offer to sell has been served on the tenant and a relative notice of acceptance has been served on the landlord, a contract of sale of the house shall be constituted between the landlord and the tenant on the terms contained in the offer to sell. The question has arisen as to what happens to this agreement if the tenant dies after the contract has been concluded, but before the conveyancing is completed. This issue has arisen in a Scottish case as well as under similar legislation covering England and Wales. The 1987 legislation provides for a series of steps up until the making of the contract, but is silent on the enforcement of that contract.

7–45   In *Cooper's Executors v. Edinburgh District Council*[36] the matter was decided in favour of the executrix of a deceased tenant and the decision was sustained on appeal to the House of Lords.[37] In January 1988 George Cooper, a 75-year-old widower who lived alone, applied to purchase his house in Edinburgh. He was a secure tenant in terms of the Housing (Scotland) Act 1987 and had the right to buy. The discounted price was £6,900. However, before the price was paid and title delivered, Mr Cooper died. The district council decided that this ended the matter, but his executors, his daughter and son-in-law, wished the contract to be enforced and title given in their favour. In August 1989 the matter came before Lord Sutherland who found in favour of the executors of the deceased tenant. The district council appealed.

The First Division were of the view that a contract of sale was established under the 1987 Act once a tenant's application to buy, the council's offer to sell and the tenant's notice of acceptance had all been served. There was nothing laid down by way of further statutory procedure which had to be done to give effect to the contract. Enforcement of the contract was to be left to the normal

[36] 1990 S.L.T. 621.
[37] 1991 S.L.T. 518.

principles of the common law. The Act did not state that the contract had to remain personal to the tenant and that his rights under it could not transfer to his next-of-kin. The council was, in the view of the Lord President and Lords Cowie and Grieve, obliged by the contract to sell the house to Mr Cooper or, after his death, his representatives.

The House of Lords decided that once a right to buy had been exercised it did not revive in favour of a person who might succeed to a tenancy on the death of the secure tenant prior to settlement of the transaction.[38]

Recoverability of discount

The discount recoverability provisions[39] do not apply to any representatives 7–46 seeking to dispose of the property in certain limited circumstances.[40] The situations covered are where the disposal is made to a member of the owner's family who lived with the owner for a period of 12 months before the disposal and that the disposal is for no consideration. The issue of disposal by executors was not within the scope of *Cooper's Executors*[41] but recovery of discount was discussed in *Jack's Executrix v. Falkirk District Council*.[42] The Court of Session decided that repayment of discount was required. In such cases executors might be advised to let the property on a short assured tenancy covering the remainder of the discount repayment period with an option to purchase at the end of this period. The position in England is somewhat different[43] but the courts have been somewhat reluctant to use interpretations based on the Housing Act 1985.

6. LANDLORDS' RIGHTS TO BUY RENTED PROPERTY

Introduction

Landlords in the private sector have no right to purchase any other landlords' 7–47 properties. They may negotiate such a purchase and, if they do so, tenants have no right to consultation. As far as the legal position of tenants is concerned, this remains unaffected by the transaction. In fact, landlords who purchase private sector properties with sitting tenants are not entitled to use the repossession case for landlords who reasonably require the property for themselves.[44]

In the public sector, however, there are two ways in which tenants can end up with new landlords. In both processes, however, there must be an element of tenant participation. In "voluntary" transfers there must be consultation of tenants, whereas approved landlords exercising their right to buy must obtain the permission of affected tenants. In this section we will look in detail at the legal effects of transfers of public sector tenancies—for simplicity, these have been termed estate transfers and the tenant's right to choose a landlord.

---

[38] 1991 S.L.T. 518.
[39] s. 72.
[40] s. 73.
[41] 1990 S.L.T. 621.
[42] 1992 S.L.T. 5.
[43] *McIntyre v. Merthyr Tydfil B.C.* [1990] 88 L.G.R. 1; see also *Harrow LBC v. Tonge* (1993) 25 H.L.R. 99.
[44] Rent (Scotland) Act 1984, Sched. 2, cord. 8; Housing (Scotland) Act 1988, Sched. 5, Pt IV, para. 9.

Estate transfers

Introduction

7–48   The policy of governments over the years has been to allow local authorities to determine their own local housing strategy. Part of this has been the need for any authority to obtain the permission of the Secretary of State for Scotland where sales of housing stock are planned. For most local authority stock sales the Secretary of State may have regard to certain specific matters such as the terms of the disposal in deciding whether to give consent and, if so, what conditions should be imposed. These matters include the extent to which the intending purchaser is or is likely to be dependent upon, controlled by, or subject to influence from the local authority making the disposal or any members or officers of that authority.[45] In addition, the Secretary of State may have regard to the extent to which the proposed disposal would result in the intending purchaser becoming the predominant or a substantial owner in any area of rented housing.[46] The Secretary of State has issued an "Information Paper" on the criteria to be satisfied if consent is to be granted.[47]

Consultation

7–49   Where an authority is seeking the consent of the Secretary of State for a disposal there must be consultation before there can be a disposal[48]; consultation must follow certain requirements.[49] A local authority must serve a notice in writing providing such details of its proposal as it considers appropriate: the information must, however, include the identity of the person to whom the disposal is to be made. An authority must inform its tenants of the likely consequences of the disposal for tenants and the effect of the preservation of the right to buy provisions. Tenants must be informed of their right to make representations within at least 28 days of the service of the notice of information. The local authority must consider any such representations made to it and must tell the tenants if there are any significant changes in its proposal, and of the tenant's right to communicate any objection to the Secretary of State, and the fact that consent must be withheld if a majority of tenants are opposed. The method of determining the views of tenants will normally be by ballot.[50]

The Secretary of State may require the local authority to carry out further consultation with its tenants and to provide to the Secretary of State the results of that additional consultation as directed.[51] If it appears to the Secretary of State that a majority of the tenants of the affected houses do not wish the disposal to proceed he must not give his consent. In addition, he may also refuse consent on other grounds. The Secretary of State may have regard to any information available to him and the local authority must give him information as to the representations made to it by tenants and others as well as other relevant matters.[52]

---

[45] s. 13(2)(a).
[46] s. 14(2)(b).
[47] Voluntary Transfers of Local Authority Housing to Private Bodies SDD (Sept. 27, 1988).
[48] Housing (Scotland) Act 1987, s. 81B and Sched. 6A (inserted by Sched. 16 to the Housing Act 1988).
[49] *ibid.* Sched. 6A, para. 3.
[50] SDD Information Paper (Sept. 27, 1988).
[51] Housing (Scotland) Act 1987, s. 81B and Sched. 6A, para. 4.
[52] *ibid.* Sched. 6A, para. 5.

The fact of the Secretary of State or the local authority failing to comply with the consultation requirements does not invalidate any such consent.[53]

Preservation of the right to buy

The preservation of the right to buy is an issue on which the Government 7–50 decided to provide certain guarantees. The right to buy provisions continue to apply where a person ceases to be a secure tenant by reason of the disposal by the landlord to a private sector landlord.[54] In certain circumstances as laid down by the Secretary of State, however, the right to buy provisions do not continue to apply.[55] The regulations state that the right to buy is not to apply where the disposal is in exercise of the tenant's right to choose a landlord,[56] or where the disposal is to a co-operative housing association.[57]

Where the right to buy continues to apply the private sector landlord must not dispose of less than the whole interest in the relevant house without the written consent of the Secretary of State unless that disposal is of a "qualifying house" to a "qualifying person". The regulations define a "qualifying house" as the house occupied by a "qualifying person".[58] "Qualifying person" is defined as the former secure tenant who occupied the house when the tenancy ceased to be a secure tenancy, the person entitled to succeed on the death of the former secure tenant in terms of section 31 of the Housing (Scotland) Act 1988, as well as the spouse of a former secure tenant who becomes tenant of the relevant house under a transfer of tenancy order under the Matrimonial Homes (Family Protection) (Scotland) Act 1981.[59]

Subsequent disposals

If there is a subsequent disposal the consent of the Secretary of State is 7–51 required.[60] Before giving any consent the Secretary of State must be satisfied that the person who is seeking the consent has taken appropriate steps to consult every tenant of any house proposed to be disposed of and must have regard to the responses of any such tenants.[61] No detailed criteria appear to have been laid down for such consultations. Consent can be made subject to conditions and may be in respect of a particular disposal or in respect of disposals of any class or description including disposals in particular areas.[62]

Houses sales requiring no Secretary of State consent

The Housing (Scotland) Act 1987 makes provision for certain houses to be 7–52 exempted from the requirement for permission where there is a house to which the Housing Revenue Account does not apply. Most local authority stock will be covered by the Housing Revenue Account.[63] Permission is not required where

---

[53] Housing (Scotland) Act 1987, Sched. 6A, para. 6.
[54] s. 81A (inserted by the Housing Act 1988, s.128).
[55] Housing (Preservation of Right to Buy) (Scotland) Regulations 1992 (S.I. 1992 No. 325).
[56] See para. 7–53 *et seq.*
[57] reg. 5.
[58] reg. 2.
[59] *ibid.*
[60] s. 12A (inserted by the Housing Act 1988, s. 134).
[61] s. 12A(3).
[62] s. 12A(2).
[63] C.M.G. Himsworth, *Housing Law in Scotland* (1994).

it is housing being bought under the tenant's right to buy, nor is it necessary where the house is unoccupied and surplus to requirements or difficult to let.[64] A house is deemed difficult to let if it has been continuously vacant for a period of not less than three months before the date and during that period it has been on unrestricted offer to any applicant on the local authority's housing list.

7. TENANTS' RIGHTS TO CHOOSE LANDLORD

Introduction

7–53   The Housing (Scotland) Act 1988 makes provision for certain approved landlords to purchase public sector housing.[65] The Scottish legislation is significantly different from that which was introduced by the Housing Act 1988 in England and Wales. Its central features are that the tenant has the right to reject any approach by a potential new landlord and that the local authority does not have the right to retain the housing in question. A detailed timetable is laid down akin to that found with the tenant's right to buy although this can be extended upon service of notice to the other party.[66]

Exempt property

7–54   This part of the legislation does not apply to a house which is one of a group of houses provided with facilities specially designed or adapted for the needs of persons of pensionable age or disabled persons.[67] Nor does it apply where the house has facilities which are substantially different from those of an ordinary house and has been designed or adapted for occupation by someone of pensionable age or a disabled person.[68] In addition, the Secretary of State has the power to designate a "rural area" where asked by the relevant islands council or council and a house in such an area is exempt.[69] The designation of a rural area may be made only if, within the area to be designated, more than one-third of all relevant houses have been acquired under the right to choose a landlord or right to buy provisions or in some other way and the Secretary of State is satisfied that an unreasonable proportion of the houses so acquired or purchased consists of houses which have been resold and are not being used by owner-occupiers as principal or only homes nor being rented out.[70] The category of exempt properties includes a house held by an islands council for the accommodation of a person who is or will be an employee involved in operating its educational functions.[71]

"Approved persons" who may exercise the right to buy

7–55   The new landlord must be approved by Scottish Homes, but may not include a public sector landlord. The only exception is Scottish Homes itself.[72] An

---

[64] s. 14(2)(b).
[65] Pt III. (The following references relate to the Housing (Scotland) Act 1988 unless stated otherwise).
[66] s. 64.
[67] s. 56(5)(a).
[68] s. 56(5)(b).
[69] s. 56(5)(c).
[70] s. 56(7).
[71] s. 56(6).
[72] s. 57(1).

approval can be revoked although (controversially) this does not affect any transactions already completed.[73]

Application and offer to sell

In order to exercise the right to buy the approved person must serve a notice on the existing landlord indicating that the applicant wishes to purchase the property and has the written consent of the tenant that an approach be made to the existing landlord.[74] This notice must be served on the tenant and Scottish Homes.[75] The existing landlord must serve a notice offering to sell the property indicating the price and any conditions attached to the sale.[76] The price is to be the market value and is to be decided by either a qualified valuer nominated by the landlord and accepted by the applicant or the district valuer.[77] The market value is that which the house would realise if sold on the open market by a willing seller making certain assumptions.[78] The valuer must assume that there is vacant possession subject only to the secure tenant's tenancy. He must also assume that the rights and obligations of Part III of the Housing (Scotland) Act apply and that the only prospective purchasers are Scottish Homes or one of the approved persons. Finally, it is assumed that the new landlord would, within a reasonable period, carry out such works of repair as are necessary to put the house into the state of repair required by the landlord's repairing obligations.[79]

Conditions which may be imposed

Reasonable conditions may be included in the offer to sell which do not 7–56 reduce the tenant's enjoyment and use of the house as previously enjoyed.[80] If conditions are included which impose a new charge or increase an existing charge for the provision of a service in relation to the house this charge must be in reasonable proportion to the cost to the landlord of providing the service.[81] New services are not covered by this provision. It is not permitted to impose a condition requiring the applicant or the tenant to pay any expenses of the landlord.[82] Nor are pre-emption clauses permitted as these are in conflict with section 63 which requires the approval of Scottish Homes for the disposal of homes.[83]

Where conditions are imposed in the offer to sell, it is possible for acquirers to challenge those considered to be unreasonable.[84] If the landlord does not respond to a request to strike out or vary the condition and amend the offer to sell accordingly, the potential new landlord may refer the matter to the Lands

---

[73] s. 57(3).
[74] s. 58(1).
[75] s. 58(3).
[76] s. 58(5).
[77] s. 58(6).
[78] s. 58(7).
[79] See para. 3–22 *et seq.*
[80] s. 58(10).
[81] s. 58(11).
[82] s. 58(12).
[83] *Waverley Housing Trust Ltd v. Roxburgh D.C.,* 1995 S.L.T. (Lands Tr.) 2.
[84] s. 59(1)(a).

Tribunal.[85] The Lands Tribunal may uphold the condition or strike it out or vary it, and where its decision results in a variation of the offer to sell must order the landlord to serve an amended offer to sell.[86] The same provisions are available where the applicant seeks to have a new condition included in the offer to sell.

Notice of acceptance

7–57   If the offer to sell is served on the potential new landlord and is acceptable, then there needs to be a notice of acceptance from the applicant.[87] This must be served within two months of the original or amended offer to sell or of any Lands Tribunal determination.[88] The effect of the notice lapses if the new landlord and tenant do not conclude a lease.[89] This is aimed at preventing landlords buying up rented property for immediate sale.

Refusal of applications

7–58   As indicated above, landlords may refuse an application by serving a notice of refusal within one month of being served with the application where the point at issue is the right of the applicant to purchase the property.[90] In addition, where the landlord considers the information contained in the application is incorrect on a material point, the legislation allows the landlord two months to refuse such an application.[91] The notice of refusal must specify the basis for it being made.[92] The applicant in turn has one month from receiving the notice of refusal to apply to the Lands Tribunal for a finding that the applicant is entitled to exercise the Part III right to change landlord.[93]

Reference to Lands Tribunal

7–59   In a number of situations the Lands Tribunal may be called upon to act in relation to a change of landlord under Part III. The applicant may refer the matter to the Lands Tribunal where the landlord has failed to respond in time to an application with an offer to sell or a notice of refusal.[94] The applicant may also refer where the landlord has failed to amend the offer to sell after the Lands Tribunal has made a finding that this should be done.[95] There is provision for dealing with the situation where the tribunal has indicated that the landlord may not issue a notice of refusal and the landlord has not gone on to progress the application within two months.[96] Finally, where the landlord has served a defective offer to sell this may be brought to the attention of the Lands Tribunal. In such instances the Lands Tribunal, where it finds that the landlord has failed

---

[85] s. 59(2).
[86] s. 59(3).
[87] s. 60.
[88] s. 60(1)(b).
[89] s. 60(2).
[90] s. 60(1)(a).
[91] s. 60(1)(b).
[92] s. 61(2).
[93] s. 61(3).
[94] s. 62(1)(a).
[95] s. 62(1)(b).
[96] s. 62(1)(c).

to meet the statutory requirements, may do what the landlord should have done and anything done by it shall have the same effect as if done by the landlord.[97] This does not displace any other remedies that exist.[98]

Consent for subsequent disposals

Any new landlord who acquires local authority property under Part III must obtain the written consent of Scottish Homes for a subsequent disposal.[99] Scottish Homes, of course, are exempt from this procedure when they are selling on acquisitions. The consent may be given for individual disposals or for disposals of any class or description including disposals in particular areas.[1] This covers sales or contracts to sell including options to buy.[2] The consent requirement has the effect of preventing the operation of pre-emption rights.[3]   7–60

8. RENT TO LOAN

The Government's rent-to-loan scheme introduced in 1993 involves tenants moving into partial home ownership through making an initial capital payment, with the remaining outstanding sum being deferred. The standard offer to sell includes a clause to the effect that, in exchange for the initial capital payment, the tenant will be entitled to ownership of the house. The outstanding amount is secured by a standard security over the house.   7–61

Fixing the price

The price is to be fixed through the section 62 mechanism although the discount levels are 15 per cent less than those available under that section. This means that anyone living in a house is able to buy at market value less a discount of 17 per cent after two years going up by 1 per cent a year to a maximum after 30 years' tenancy. For flats the discount starts at 20 per cent and goes up by 2 per cent to a maximum of 55 per cent after 15 years' tenancy.   7–62

Initial capital payment

The rent-to-loan scheme requires those taking advantage of it to make an initial capital payment to be determined by themselves. They must, however, pay a minimum amount. This is determined by calculating what 90 per cent of the weekly rent payable at the time of application would capitalise at if repaying on a loan at the statutory rate of interest. The loan period must be the lesser of two alternatives (subject to a 10-year minimum): (i) when the applicant would reach pensionable age, (ii) 25 years. Pensionable age is defined in terms of the Social Security Act 1975 as 65 for men and 60 for women. The current authority is the Social Security Contributions and Benefits Act 1992, s. 122(1). Pensionable age for women will be increased from 60 to 65 between   7–63

---

[97] s. 62(2).
[98] s. 62(3); Court of Session Act 1988, s. 45; Local Government (Scotland) Act 1973, s. 211 (as amended by the Local Government etc. (Scotland) Act 1994, Sched. 14).
[99] s. 63.
[1] s. 63(2).
[2] s. 63(4).
[3] *Waverley Housing Trust Ltd v. Roxburgh D.C.*, 1995 S.L.T. (Lands Tr.) 2.

2010 and 2020. There are sliding provisions for women born between April 6, 1950 and April 5, 1955.[4]

Deferred financial commitment

7–64   The deferred financial commitment is the difference between the price fixed by the district valuer and the initial capital payment. This is expressed as a percentage of the market value of the house at the time. That percentage figure is then reduced by a figure to be prescribed (currently 7). There is also a reduction where an additional payment has been made to reduce the ultimate outstanding amount although there are limitations designed to ensure that minimum sums are paid. The current minimum figure is £1,500.[5] Only one payment can be made per year. The maximum additional instalment which can be paid is the difference between the initial capital payment and 7.5 per cent of the property value.

There is no interest on the deferred financial commitment. Payment of the whole of this sum may be made in whole at any time. It must, however, be made on the sale or disposal of the house by the purchaser or on that person's death. It must also be repaid as soon as may be where there is destruction of or damage to the house through fire, tempest, flood or any other normal insurance risk, unless the property is rebuilt or reinstated.

Standard securities granted to cover the deferred financial commitment have priority before any standard security securing repayment of the discount where there is an early sale. They do not, however, outrank a standard security from a recognised lending institution made to enable satisfaction of the initial capital payment or deferred commitment instalments. Section 222 of the Act defines a recognised lending institution as one which is recognised by the Secretary of State as providing assistance to first-time purchasers of house property in Great Britain.

7–65   Where there is destruction or damage of the house and there is payment of the deferred financial commitment, the resale value of the property is the price at which it is being sold with vacant possession and a good marketable title on the open market. If the rent-to-loan purchaser has died the value is that in the confirmation. In any other case the amount is that agreed by the rent-to-loan purchaser and the original seller. Where they cannot agree on a value an independent valuation is provided for and must assume that a sale on the open market is imminent. In the calculation of the resale value of the house no account is to be taken of anything done such as improvements to the house by the ex-tenant which have added value to the property or any failure to keep the house in good repair.

The deferred financial commitment is not payable where there is a sale or disposal to a partner and certain other events occur—for example, where a rent-to-loan purchaser sells or otherwise disposes of the property to her spouse or cohabitee and the house is that partner's only or principal home and where the partner dies and a person succeeds to the house whose only or principal home during the 12 months prior to the second purchaser's death was the house purchased. Nor is the deferred financial commitment payable where the house was purchased jointly and one of the joint purchasers dies.

---

[4]   Pensions Act 1995, s. 126 and Sched. 4.
[5]   s. 73D(3).

CHAPTER 8

OCCUPANCY RIGHTS, TENANTS AND LANDLORDS

When legislation dealing with violence in the home was brought into effect in   8–01
September 1982 it provided both property rights as well as protection against
violence. These property rights come in the form of occupancy rights and they
are buttressed by exclusion orders, matrimonial interdicts and powers of arrest.
In addition to these rights which applied equally to those renting property and
those owning it the legislation introduced a new procedure for the transfer of
most tenancies.

1. OCCUPANCY RIGHTS

Background

   Prior to the introduction of the Matrimonial Homes (Family Protection) (Scotland)   8–02
Act 1981 there was no legal right of property in the matrimonial home for any
spouse or cohabitee who was neither owner (including joint owner) nor tenant
(including joint tenant) of the matrimonial home. Much local authority and private
rented housing had until the end of the 1970s been put in the name of the husband.[1]
It was not at all unusual for husbands to throw their wives out of the house during
marital disputes and the courts sanctioned such eviction.[2] The plight of battered
wives brought this issue to the attention of Government in the 1970s and, as part of
its remit, the Scottish Law Commission was instructed to examine ways in which
women could be protected from arbitrary eviction by their husbands.[3] Their solution
was that on marriage occupancy rights would be conferred automatically on any
spouse who had no formal legal rights to stay in the matrimonial home. There is no
need for such rights to be registered or formally claimed.

The meaning of "occupancy rights"

   The notion of occupancy rights for spouses despite the absence of property   8–03
rights was a novel concept in Scots law when it was introduced in the Matrimonial
Homes (Family Protection) (Scotland) Act 1981. It provided that where one
spouse had a title to stay in a house, either as owner or tenant then the other
spouse, who was neither tenant nor owner, was given the following rights—
(1) if in occupation, a right to continue to occupy the matrimonial home; (2) if
not in occupation, a right to enter and occupy the matrimonial home.[4]

---

[1]   Scottish Housing Advisory Committee, *Allocation and Transfer of Council Houses* (HMSO, 1980).
[2]   Alice A. Jackson, Marie Robertson and Peter Robson, *The Operation of the Matrimonial Homes (Family Protection) (Scotland) Act 1981* (Scottish Office, 1988), Chap. 1.
[3]   Scottish Law Commission Memorandum No. 41, Vol. 2.
[4]   s. 1(1).

This provision includes the right to ccupy with any child of the family.[5] Where the spouse who is owner or tenant refuses to allow the other partner the right to enter and occupy, this right may only be exercised with the leave of either the Sheriff Court or Court of Session, *i.e.* there should be no "self-help".[6]

Property covered by occupancy rights

8–04   Occupancy rights can be exercised over the matrimonial home. This is defined as "any house, caravan, houseboat or other structure which has been provided or has been made available by one or both of the spouses, or has become a family residence."[7] Any garden or other ground or building attached and usually occupied with or required for the amenity and convenience of the dwelling in question is also included.

In general terms, where a property is tenanted by one of the partners prior to marriage/cohabitation then this would become the matrimonial home upon marriage or when the couple can be said to be a cohabiting couple. The term "matrimonial home" does not, however, include a residence provided or made available by one spouse for herself to reside in separately from the other spouse. Nor in such a situation would the fact that any child of the family was living in such a house alter its status to be a matrimonial home.[8] By the same token there is authority which indicates that where a property is provided for the other spouse to live in this is not a matrimonial home either. This interpretation of the 1981 Act was given by Lord Mayfield in the Outer House in *McRobbie v. McRobbie*.[9] Here a husband had purchased a house for his wife and child to live in after separation and did not ever live in the property himself. In due course divorce proceedings were started and the wife attempted to obtain an order for occupancy rights. His Lordship was not satisfied that this was a matrimonial home in terms of the Act.

8–05   As far as tenancies are concerned the 1981 Act confirms that possession by the non-entitled spouse allows continuation of the tenancy where the entitled spouse has abandoned possession.[10] However, this only applies if the property has been a matrimonial home. The consequences may be particularly unfortunate as seen in a case involving the parallel legislation on this issue in England and Wales.[11] In *Hall v. King*[12] the husband took the tenancy of a cottage for the wife after the breakdown of their marriage and the wife's illness. The property was provided for the wife to live in with their young son. The husband was living elsewhere with another woman and there was no prospect of a marital reconciliation. In due course the landlord terminated the husband's tenancy and sought repossession on the grounds that the husband did not occupy the dwelling-house as his residence.[13] The Court of Appeal was not prepared to accept that

---

[5] s. 1(1A).
[6] *Nimmo v. Nimmo*, Glasgow Sh. Ct., Aug. 12, 1983, discussed in *The Operation of the Matrimonial Homes (Family Protection) (Scotland) Act 1981, op. cit.*, p. 40.
[7] s. 22.
[8] s. 22 (as amended by the Law Reform (Miscellaneous Provisions) (Scotland) Act 1985, s. 13(10)).
[9] (1984) 29 J.L.S.S. 5.
[10] s. 2(8).
[11] Matrimonial Homes Act 1983, s. 1(10): "This Act shall not apply to a dwelling-house which has at no time been a matrimonial home of the spouses in question."
[12] [1987] 2 E.G.L.R. 121.
[13] See paras 2–30 and 2–31.

this had ever been the spouses' matrimonial home and so the wife was not entitled to any security of tenure.

The regulation of occupancy rights

Consequent to the provision of the basic occupancy rights there are provisions 8–06 for the courts to declare, enforce, restrict, regulate and protect these rights.[14] The courts must grant an application for a declarator where it appears to the court that the application relates to a matrimonial home. The criterion for the enforcement, restriction, regulation and protection of occupancy rights is whether it is:

> "just and reasonable having regard to all the circumstances of the case including—
> (a) the conduct of the spouses in relation to each other and otherwise;
> (b) the respective needs and financial resources of the spouses;
> (c) the needs of any child of the family;
> (d) the extent to which the matrimonial home is used in connection with a trade, business or profession;
> (e) whether there has been an offer of suitable alternative accommodation to the non-entitled spouse."[15]

It was opined in *Welsh v. Welsh*[16] that an applicant must seek a declarator of occupancy rights before she can competently seek an order for their enforcement, restriction, regulation or protection. Where occupancy rights exist, a spouse may also apply to the court for an order granting the possession or use of furniture in the matrimonial home which is owned or hired by the other spouse.[17]

As well as the above main orders there are also available interim orders 8–07 which can be applied for pending the making of a main order. These interim orders are to be made in relation to:

(a) the residence of either spouse in the matrimonial home;
(b) the personal effects of any child of the family;
(c) the furniture and plenishings.

The non-applicant spouse must, however, be afforded the opportunity of being heard before an interim order can be given and the court may grant an interim order "as it may consider necessary or expedient".[18]

Subsidiary and consequential rights

The 1981 Act also created a number of subsidiary rights designed to facilitate 8–08 the continued and reasonable occupation of the matrimonial home. The following rights may be exercised by the non-entitled spouse without the consent of the entitled spouse:

(a) to make any rent/mortgage payments due by the entitled spouse (and request an order for the apportionment of expense between the spouses);

---

[14] s. 3.
[15] s. 3(3).
[16] 1987 S.L.T. (Sh.Ct.) 30.
[17] s. 3(2).
[18] s. 3(4).

(b)   to perform any obligation incumbent on the entitled spouse (not being non-essential repairs);

(c)   to enforce performance of obligations owed by third parties to the entitled spouse, in so far as the entitled spouse could have enforced them;

(d)   to carry out essential repairs;

(e)   to carry out non-essential repairs which have been authorised by the court.[19]

A spouse may also, without the consent of the other spouse, make payments in relation to furniture in the matrimonial home and carry out essential repairs to such furniture.[20] The court may apportion expenditure incurred in exercising all of the above rights.[21] An application to the court for such an apportionment of expense must be made within five years of the payment having been made.[22]

The termination of occupancy rights

8–09   Occupancy rights come to an end in a variety of circumstances. The most common which should be noted are when:

(a) the marriage ends;

(b) the owner/tenant loses those ownership/tenancy rights;

(c) the matrimonial home ceases to exist;

(d) the rights are renounced in the form prescribed by the 1981 Act.

No cases from the Court of Session are known to the authors on the interpretation of these matters. The relationship between termination of a tenancy and occupancy rights has been discussed in three sheriff court cases where spouses argued that the tenancy should not be ended as they were seeking to have their occupancy rights declared and a transfer of tenancy effected. In both *Stables v. Stables*[23] and *Morgan v. Morgan and Kyle and Carrick District Council*[24] it was decided that that occupancy rights cease when the tenancy is ended. Commencing an action for transfer of tenancy after eviction proceedings had started did not avail the wives in these cases. In *Stables* the sheriff explained:

"Nowhere in the Act is there any indication that the right of occupancy in the matrimonial home of the non-entitled spouse is a vested one, or is secured ... that right is dependent on the right of the entitled spouse, and once that right ceases for any reason ... so does the right of the non-entitled spouse."

There is some conflict over what the date of termination of a tenancy is, however. Sheriff Principal Gillies was of the view in *Morgan* that the date of termination was the appointed day for eviction rather than the date of decree which was the view taken in the *Stables* case.

---

[19] s. 2(1).

[20] s. 2(5).

[21] s. 2(3),(4)(b) and (5)(b).

[22] s. 2(7).

[23] Edinburgh Dist. Ct., July 26, 1983, unreported.

[24] Ayr Sh. Ct., June 12, 1984, unreported, approved in *City of Glasgow District Council v. Murray*, 1998 Hous.L.R. 27, *per* Sheriff Principal Bowen.

Joint tenancies, sole tenancies and the protection of occupancy rights against dealings

Occupancy rights conferred by the 1981 Act are protected against the dealings 8–10
of an entitled spouse with a third party.[25] These sections of the Act are most
easily understood in relation to the sale of a house by the entitled spouse.
However, they have application in relation to the positions of tenants.

In relation to local authority tenancies, the general trend since the mid-1970s
has been to offer joint tenancies. Although such arrangements are normally
referred to as "joint tenancies", it should be noted that, strictly speaking, they
are tenants in common. At common law joint tenants have distinct rights to the
subjects *pro indiviso* which can be separately transmitted or assigned without
affecting the entitlements of the other tenant.[26] This does not mean, however,
that one joint tenant can renounce his entitlement to the joint tenancy and thereby
leave the remaining tenant as a sole tenant. Renunciation requires the agreement
of the landlord and tenant. It would not be possible for a contract of lease
involving joint tenants to be converted to a different contract involving a sole
tenant by the actions of a single tenant and the landlord.[27] Nevertheless, tacit
relocation will be prevented from occurring where one joint tenant serves a
notice to quit on a landlord.[28] The doctrine of tacit relocation is premised upon
the implied agreement of all the parties to a lease, through their silence, to
prolong the terms of the lease for a maximum of a further year. If one joint
tenant serves notice on a landlord this signifies the lack of agreement on his
part.

The question of dealings with third parties where both spouses are entitled is 8–11
specifically dealt with in the 1981 Act.[29] The assignation by one spouse of his
rights in the joint tenancy constitutes a dealing with a third party. The frustration
of tacit relocation by one joint tenant would only be afforded protection by the
1981 Act where it prejudiced the occupancy rights of the other spouse. This
would not be the case where the tenancy was statutorily protected. In this situation
the contractual tenancy would be brought to end and the joint tenancy would
become a statutory joint tenancy.

As regards sole tenancies, non-entitled spouses are similarly protected against
renunciation or assignation. The granting of a sub-tenancy would also constitute
a dealing against which the non-entitled spouse is protected. Where a tenant
spouse abandons possession of the matrimonial home, the tenancy will continue
by the possession of the non-entitled spouse.[30] The practice of local authorities
in relation to sole tenants giving up tenancies has been highly variable. Many
did not appreciate that renunciations and assignations of tenancies constitute
dealings under the 1981 Act.[31] Practices[32] have ranged from those who went

---

[25] ss. 6–12.
[26] *Coats v. Logan,* 1985 S.L.T. 221 at 225; G. Paton and J. Cameron, *Landlord and Tenant* (1967), p. 60.
[27] See the opinion of Lord Skerrington in *Graham v. Skerrington,* 1922 S.C. 90 at 107. A similar point was also made in *Smith v. Grayston Estates Ltd,* 1961 S.L.T. 38 in relation to the question of whether a timeous notice to quit of one joint tenant could have the effect of ending the tenancy of the tenant who gave notice thus leaving the other as sole tenant.
[28] *Smith v. Grayton Estates Ltd,* 1961 S.L.T. 38.
[29] s. 9.
[30] s. 2(8).
[31] Institute of Housing/Scottish Homeless Group, *Housing and Marital Breakdown*, Feb. 1985, para. 7.1–7.9.
[32] (1983) 4 S.H.L.N. 2.

through the full section 13 transfer procedure in court to those who advised wives to allow rent arrears to build up and then evicted the disappeared husband for rent arrears and rehoused the wife in the former matrimonial home. The third kind of approach that was reported was those who treated the tenancy as abandoned and went through the abandonment procedure and then reallocated it to the wife. One leading authority has opined that the onus would be on the non-entitled spouse to establish rights and that there really is no practical problem since local authorities can always offer suitable alternative accommodation. There must be doubts as to whether the courts would take such a cavalier approach to the protections provided for spouses by Parliament.

Domestic violence and secure tenancies: contrast between Scotland and England and Wales

8–12   In England and Wales it has been held that a notice to quit from one joint tenant will have the effect of determining a "periodic" secure tenancy, thereby leaving the remaining tenant without security of tenure.[33] It has been common practice in England and Wales for local authorities to advise a spouse who is a joint secure tenant and has to leave the home because of violence to serve on them a notice to quit. This means that when the wife and the children are rehoused under homelessness legislation, the council can claim back the other "family sized" home where the husband remains. This option is not open to Scottish local authorities. The consent of all joint tenants is required to terminate a tenancy, either by the written agreement between the landlord and tenant,[34] or by four weeks' notice given by the tenant to the landlord.[35] "Tenant" is later defined for the purposes of this Part of the Act as meaning "in the case of joint tenants … all the tenants."[36]

Exemptions to protection against dealings with third parties

8–13   Protection against third party dealings does not apply where the spouse has consented to the dealing in writing and in the prescribed form,[37] or has renounced her occupancy rights in the stipulated fashion.[38] Protection will similarly not exist where the dealing consists of a binding obligation entered into prior to the marriage or before September 1, 1982. An entitled spouse may apply to the court to dispense with the need for consent.[39] It must be established either that consent is unreasonably withheld, consent is not possible by reason of physical or mental disability or the other spouse cannot be found after reasonable steps have been taken to trace him. The criteria for deciding on such a request are the same set of criteria provided for the regulation of occupancy rights and for the granting of actions of division and sale by common owners of matrimonial homes.[40] The question of the unreasonable withholding of consent and the dispensation of consent to a sale has been dealt with in various cases[41] as has

---

[33] *London Borough of Greenwhich v. McGrady* (1984) 16 H.L.R. 36 at 40.
[34] Housing (Scotland) Act 1987, s. 46(1)(c).
[35] *ibid.* s. 46(1)(f).
[36] *ibid.* s. 82.
[37] Matrimonial Homes (Forms of Consent) (Scotland) Regulations 1982 (S.I. 1982 No. 971).
[38] s. 1(6).
[39] s. 7.
[40] s. 3(3), noted at para. 8–06.
[41] *Hall v. Hall,* 1987 S.L.T. (Sh.Ct.) 15; *O'Neill v. O'Neill,* 1987 S.L.T. (Sh.Ct.) 26; *Milne v. Milne* 1994 S.C.L.R. 437.

the question of what amounts to a proposed sale ("dealing") to which the non-owner may be asked to consent.[42]

2. TRANSFER OF TENANCY

Introduction

Until relatively recently, transfer of tenancy within the same household had   8–14
normally been considered the concern of the landlord. The Matrimonial Homes (Family Protection) (Scotland) Act 1981 changed that by making it also the concern of the courts. Prior to the introduction of security of tenure in public sector tenancies[43] local authorities could transfer a tenancy from the tenant to the other spouse in cases of marital breakdown. Provision was made from 1980 to enable local authorities to apply to the court for possession, on the ground that they were going to transfer the tenancy from the tenant to his partner because either party no longer "wished to live with the other".[44] This temporary measure was replaced by the transfer of tenancy provisions of the 1981 Act. There was no equivalent ground for possession for landlords in the private sector where the ability of landlords to recover possession was restricted to various conduct grounds.[45]

Transfer of tenancy order

The courts are required to operate section 13 of the 1981 Act concerning the   8–15
transfer of tenancy. They must be satisfied that the formalities of notice to the other party and the landlord have been complied with. The non-entitled spouse must serve a copy of the application for transfer on the landlord and before making the order the court must give the landlord an opportunity of being heard by it.[46]

On the application of a non-entitled spouse the court can make an order transferring the tenancy of a matrimonial home to that spouse. In determining whether to grant such an application above the court must have regard to all the circumstances of the case including the matters specified in (a)–(e) of section 3(3) of the 1981 Act—the conduct of the spouses in relation to each other; the respective needs and financial resources of the spouses; the needs of any child of the family; the extent (if any) to which the matrimonial home is used in connection with a trade, business or profession of either spouse; and whether the entitled spouse offers or has offered to make available to the non-entitled spouse any suitable alternative accommodation. They must also consider the suitability of the applicant to become the tenant and the applicant's capacity to perform the obligations under the lease of the matrimonial home.[47] Where joint tenancies exist the court also has the power to vest the sole tenancy with one of the tenants.[48]

---

[42] *Dunsmore v. Dunsmore,* 1986 S.L.T. (Sh.Ct.) 9; *Fyfe v. Fyfe,* 1987 S.L.T. (Sh.Ct.) 38; *Berry v. Berry* (No. 2), 1989 S.L.T. 292.
[43] Tenants' Rights, Etc. (Scotland) Act 1980, s. 12.
[44] *ibid.* Sched. 2, para. 6.
[45] Rent (Scotland) Act 1971, Sched. 3, Pt I.
[46] s. 13(4).
[47] s. 13.
[48] *ibid.*

Exemptions

8–16   Certain tenancies cannot be transferred by the court. These include property
let to the entitled spouse by his or her employer as an incident of employment
where the lease is subject to the requirement that the entitled spouse must reside
there.[49] Also exempted are the situations where the matrimonial home is, or is
part of, an agricultural holding,[50] is on, or pertains to, a croft or the subject of a
cottar or the holding of landholder or statutory small tenant.[51] The exclusion
also applies to those matrimonial homes let on long leases[52] or where they are
part of the tenancy land of a tenant-at-will.[53] These excluded tenancies can,
however, be transferred by the court on divorce or annulment.[54]

Criteria for transfer

8–17   The criteria which have guided the courts in deciding on transfers of tenancy
have demonstrated a pragmatic approach concentrating on comparing the claim
of the would-be tenant with the needs of the current tenant.[55] Crucial factors in
court transfer decisions have been to the relative responsibility of the parties
for the breakdown of the relationship,[56] the availability of alternative
accommodation elsewhere,[57] the disruption of schooling of children[58] and the
operation of a small business.[59]

8–18   In deciding to grant a transfer of tenancy in *McGowan v. McGowan*,[60] Lord
Kincraig looked at the reasons for the breakdown of the marriage and concluded
that it was the defender's conduct which was "solely responsible" and was of
an "extremely unreasonable nature". He recognised the pursuer as being a
suitable person to become the tenant who would meet the obligations of the
lease. While accepting that the financial resources of both parties were equal,
he took the view that the pursuer had proved her need for the accommodation
because of the overcrowded conditions she was now living in with her daughter
and the strain that was having on her daughter's marriage. Her need for
accommodation was greater than that of the defender's even though he claimed
that he would be homeless if the transfer application was granted. Lord Kincraig
was not satisfied that homelessness would result and stated that, "even if it
were I would have been inclined, nevertheless, to grant the transfer."[61]

In *Wilson v. Wilson*,[62] Lord Wylie was faced with parties who had no income
or capital resources as both were dependent on public funds and had been living

---

[49] s.13(7)(a).
[50] s.13(7)(b).
[51] s.13(7)(c).
[52] As defined in s. 28(1) of the Land Registration (Scotland) Act 1979 and discussed in
W. M. Gordon, *Scottish Land Law* (1989), paras 19-126 *et seq.*
[53] As defined in s. 20(8) of the Land Registration (Scotland) Act 1979 and discussed in
W. M. Gordon, op cit., para. 19-104.
[54] Family Law (Scotland) Act 1985, ss. 8(1)(a) and 27(1).
[55] The Strathclyde Report indicates at pp 58–60 a number of early sheriff court decisions in this
area. These appear to have been decided wrongly on considerations outwith the criteria in s. 13.
[56] *McGowan v. McGowan*, 1986 S.L.T. 122.
[57] *McGowan v. McGowan*, above; *Wilson v. Wilson*, Jan. 10, 1986, OH; unreported but noted in
(1987) 5 S.H.L.N.
[58] *Russell v. Russell*, Feb. 18, 1986, OH, unreported but noted in (1987) 5 S.H.L.N.
[59] *ibid.*
[60] 1986 S.L.T. 122.
[61] *ibid.* at 124.
[62] cited above.

in the matrimonial home for some five years. There were no dependent children. The desire of the applicant wife to have access to the garden of the matrimonial home for her hobby as opposed to living in a flat, together with the possibility of her living with a female relative, was not considered enough to outweigh the lack of alternative accommodation available to her husband.

By contrast, in *Russell v. Russell*[63] the matter was complicated by a custody dispute between the parties involving their three children. One of the children wished to stay with the father who was tenant of the matrimonial home. The wife had been living in a nearby local authority house since the marital separation. She had custody of the two younger children. Lord Weir, looking to the preference of the son to remain with his father and the fact that refusing the order would mean no interruption of the schooling of the children, opted for this course of action. He also noted that moving would affect the car repair business carried on by the husband from the house in question.

The existence of a transfer of tenancy does not affect the occupancy rights of 8–19 the partner. Accordingly, where the parties do not wish to live together a transfer of tenancy order is only of value where combined with a divorce or an exclusion order. The reported low level of granting of section 13 orders stems from the fact that local authority policies on rehousing and voluntary transfers are frequently a much swifter route than a court transfer. There is no provision for interim orders where tenancy transfer is concerned so that by the time the divorce or separation reaches its final order stage the question of tenancy has been resolved between the parties and the local authority.[64] Often voluntary transfers are negotiated after legal action for transfer has been initiated. The husband agrees that if the wife will drop the court action, he will "sign over" the house.

Transfers and arrears of rent

It was a common practice of local authorities, prior to the Tenants' Rights 8–20 Etc. (Scotland) Act 1980 to hold a spouse who was not the tenant liable for rent arrears accrued by the tenant, when a transfer of tenancy between spouses took place. This practice had always been regarded as legally dubious and was clearly made unlawful by the 1980 Act. The 1981 Act was also explicit in determining that a non-entitled spouse who becomes the tenant after a section 13 transfer of tenancy order shall not be liable for any rent arrears during the period prior to the transfer.[65] In the case of joint tenants they remain jointly and severally liable for arrears. In considering an application for admission to a housing list and in the allocation of local authority housing a council must take no account of any outstanding liability (for payment of rent or otherwise) attributable to the tenancy of any dwelling-house of which the applicant is not, and was not when the liability accrued, the tenant.[66] The unwillingness of some local authorities to deal with requests for transfer of tenancies where there are outstanding arrears appears to be contrary to the intentions behind the 1981 Act, and the express terms of section 13(5).

---

[63] Feb. 18, 1986, OH, unreported.
[64] Institute of Housing and Scottish Homeless Group, *Report on Housing and Marital Breakdown* (1985).
[65] s. 13(5).
[66] Housing (Scotland) Act 1987, ss. 19(1)(d) and 20(2)(a)(ii).

Administrative transfers

8–21   Public sector landlords have the opportunity to seek a transfer of tenancy order where the spouse, former spouse, cohabitee or former cohabitee wishes a transfer of tenancy and no longer wishes to live with the other party.[67] The courts have to decide whether it is "reasonable" to grant possession orders in such cases but they must also be satisfied that "other suitable accommodation will be available". The new entitled spouse could then debar the evicted spouse's entry to his former home and he could only obtain re-entry by going to court and seeking to have his occupancy rights enforced.[68]

3. Interdicts, Matrimonial Interdicts and Powers of Arrest

Common law interdict

8–22   By way of brief introduction it is necessary to explain the relationship between interdicts in Scots law and the specific forms of interdicts which involve an element of police enforcement- matrimonial interdicts.

Prior to the introduction of the Matrimonial Homes (Family Protection) (Scotland) Act in September 1982 any spouse seeking protection from her partner was in the same position as any other citizen. She could ask the court for an order prohibiting actions which infringed her rights, known in Scotland as an "interdict". Interdicts are available to any person against anyone or any body which threatens any legal rights the applicant may have. They range from the protection of business rights like trade marks, to preventing people coming on to one's land as well as covering molestation or annoyance in the home or in the street. The activities complained of must involve some form of wrongdoing. The precise boundaries may not always be clear as the writer of the classic work on the subject of interdict remarked:

> "Great personal annoyance might no doubt be caused without the commission of definable wrongs (such as trespass or nuisance) as, for example, by persistently following another person in the streets. How far such conduct is legally wrongful and restrainable by interdict may present questions of difficulty."[69]

Traditionally there has been no problem in obtaining interdicts in the sheriff court or Court of Session against either personal violence or annoying activities. These have been successfully sought against both current husbands or partners as well as against former spouses or friends. They continue to be sought in the courts.

8–23   The fact that the courts require that there be a definable wrong, which the interdict is designed to prevent, led one man to argue that he should not be interdicted from removing any furniture or plenishings from the matrimonial home. In *Welsh v. Welsh*[70] it was argued that a common law interdict could not be used to prevent a man from exercising his lawful right to deal with his own

---

[67] Housing (Scotland) Act 1987, Sched. 3, para. 16.
[68] See paras 8–06 and 8–07.
[69] Burn Murdoch, *Interdict* (1933), p. 378.
[70] 1987 S.L.T. (Sh.Ct.) 30.

property as he wished. This contention was rejected by Sheriff Principal Gillies, who explained that:

> "It would be, at least, unfortunate if an angry spouse were to be afforded the opportunity to put such threats [to remove the property] into operation by being given some days' warning that the court was to be asked to prevent him from doing this."[71]

He also relied on Burn Murdoch where it was stated, "A party may be restrained by interdict from destroying or parting with, or from selling or removing moveable property that is the subject of litigation."[72] Since the furniture was part of such litigation then restraint by interdict was not unreasonable. This did not prevent the parties reaching an agreement about disposal of the property and, failing agreement, coming to court about the matter. Essentially the husband would not be prejudiced. It is worth pointing out that the fear that husbands would dispose of property before an action reached court has been a reality in the past. This is an interesting reminder that the practice of seeking interdicts at the earliest stages in a matrimonial dispute is not only often a useful tactic but also entirely competent. The concern expressed by the wife in this case has indeed occurred in situations where the recipient of an initial writ has cleared out the house before the matter came to court. *Welsh* makes it clear that it is possible to guard against this.

The advantage of the common law interdicts is that they can be obtained *ex parte* at the stage of warranting the action, *i.e.* without the other party having the opportunity of being heard. Thus they can forestall counteraction.

Another kind of problem which women experience is where men continue 8–24 to hang around near the old home after separation or divorce or follow women in the street. Exactly what form the interdict takes depends on what kind of activity is being complained of. However, the Court of Session has made it plain that it must be clear to the person who is subject to the order what exactly they are prohibited from doing. Since fine or imprisonment may follow breach of a court order, it has been stated:

> "[W]here interdict is granted by the court the terms of the interdict must be no wider than are necessary to curb the illegal actings complained of, and so precise and clear that the person interdicted is left in no doubt what he is forbidden to do."[73]

In the event of a breach of the order, the procedure for a traditional (it is sometimes referred to as a molestation or "Murdoch") interdict is in the hands of the individual who obtained the order in the first place. This involved a further appearance in court. The court will then require the party allegedly in breach to appear before it. Such an order will be presented by the officers of the court— either a sheriff officer for the sheriff court or the messenger-at-arms for the Court of Session. In the event of failure to comply the powers of the judge are unlimited as regards fine and/or imprisonment.

---

[71] 1987 S.L.T. (Sh.Ct.) 30 at 32.
[72] Burn Murdoch, *loc. cit.,* p. 391.
[73] *Murdoch v. Murdoch,* 1973 S.L.T. (Notes) 3.

Matrimonial interdict

8–25   A matrimonial interdict is the term given to those interdicts to which a power of arrest can be attached in terms of the Matrimonial Homes (Family Protection) (Scotland) Act 1981.[74] The definition covers any interdict which:

(a)   restrains or prohibits any conduct of one spouse towards the other spouse or a child of the family, or

(b)   prohibits a spouse from entering or remaining in a matrimonial home or in a specified area in the vicinity of the matrimonial home.[75]

Matrimonial interdicts are also available to parties who are living together as if they were man and wife (a "cohabiting couple").[76]

Since they are interdicts, matrimonial interdicts can only prevent a purported wrong and may not be used to take away rights such as occupancy rights. They have, however, been approved in one particular form which appears to have this effect. In *Tattersall v. Tattersall*[77] the First Division approved the granting of an interdict which had the effect of excluding a non-entitled spouse who was out of the matrimonial home. In such cases the non-applicant spouse could go to court to seek a declaration of occupancy rights. It would then be up to the court to decide whether or not it considered it to be just and reasonable having regard to all the circumstances. Matrimonial interdicts are, of course, available to those who are tenants or occupiers of rented accommodation.

4. POWERS OF ARREST

Granting powers of arrest

8–26   Powers of arrest are available to successful applicants for exclusion orders under the Matrimonial Homes (Family Protection) (Scotland) Act 1981 and to matrimonial interdicts which are not granted *ex parte*. At least seven days' notice is required of an application for attachment in the Court of Session.[78] No such time period is required in actions in the sheriff court.[79] Where an interdict with a power of arrest attached is varied or recalled, the spouse who applied for such must send a copy of the application for variation or recall and a copy of the interlocutor granting variation or recall to the chief constable of the area in which the matrimonial home is situated. If the applicant spouse lives in another area, he must also send the above documents to the chief constable of that area.[80] Similarly, should the parties get divorced, the interdict will cease to have effect. In this situation, the pursuer in the divorce action must send a copy of the interlocutor granting decree to the chief constable of the area in which the matrimonial home is situated, and, where the applicant spouse resides in another area, to the area of the applicant spouse's residence.[81]

---

[74]   s. 15.

[75]   s. 14.

[76]   s. 14(1).

[77]   1983 S.L.T. 503.

[78]   Rules of the Court of Session 1994, r. 49.67(2).

[79]   Ordinary Cause Rules 1993, r. 33.69(2).

[80]   s.15(5).

[81]   Ordinary Cause Rules 1993, r. 33.72(2); Rules of the Court of Session 1994, r. 49.70(2).

Exclusion orders and powers of arrest

Where there is a matrimonial interdict which is ancillary to an exclusion 8–27
order and the applicant requests the court for attachment of a power of arrest
then the court must make such an order.[82] One of the problems that was identified
shortly after the introduction of the legislation was that powers of arrest were
sometimes not sought.[83] There was evidence that the judiciary was either
unwilling to operate the clear directive nature of the section[84] or did not appreciate
that this was the case.[85] The language of the section is clear that refusal to attach
a power of arrest, where one is requested, is not an option.

Non-exclusion-related matrimonial interdicts and powers of arrest

Where there is any other matrimonial interdict and the applicant requests 8–28
attachment of a power of arrest the position is slightly different. If the court is
satisfied that the other party has had the opportunity to be heard or represented
before the court, then the court must make such an order unless it appears to the
court that in all the circumstances of the case such a power is unnecessary.[86]
The onus is on the defender to establish that the power of arrest should not be
attached rather than on the applicant to establish that it should.[87]

Operation of the power of arrest

Effecting a power of arrest

As indicated, a power of arrest cannot be attached in Scotland without the defender 8–29
knowing that it is being sought. In addition, any power of arrest attached must be
served on the defender.[88] In order to become operational the applicant must serve on
the police a copy of the order sought and the proof of the granting of the order by the
judge—the interlocutor.[89] These must be served on the chief constable in the area of
the matrimonial home and the chief constable where the applicant lives if this is in
a different police area. Both the interdict and power of arrest must be included.[90]

Using the power of arrest for breach

Once granted and duly served, the power of arrest becomes operational. It is 8–30
common practice to provide a copy to the local police where the applicant stays

---

[82] 1981 Act, s. 15(1)(a).
[83] Marie Robertson and Peter Robson, *Operating the Matrimonial Homes Act—the first six months* (1983).
[84] Alice Ann Jackson, Marie Robertson and Peter Robson, *The Operation of the Matrimonial Homes (Family Protection) (Scotland) Act 1981*, (1988).
[85] *Raeburn v. Raeburn,* Dec. 21, 1989; "It appears to me that at this stage the pursuer has made out a case of necessity under section 4 of the Act … It also follows that the interdict finally sought in relation to molestation is one that I should grant but I am not persuaded that I need to attach thereto a power of arrest; that appears to me to be an extreme measure which the present circumstances do not warrant" (*per* Lord McCluskey).
[86] 1981 Act, s. 15(1)(b).
[87] David Nichols and Michael Meston, *The Matrimonial Homes (Family Protection) (Scotland) Act 1981* (2nd ed., 1986) suggest at p. 39 that the court considers that in all the circumstances a power of arrest is necessary. The legislation states that the power must be attached "unless it appears to the court that such a power is unnecessary". This makes it clear that it is up to the non-applicant to show why a power of arrest should not be attached.
[88] 1981 Act, s. 15(2).
[89] *ibid.* s. 15(4).
[90] Law Reform (Miscellaneous Provisions) (Scotland) Act 1990, s. 64.

as well as to headquarters. A constable may arrest without warrant the non-applicant spouse if he has reasonable cause for suspecting that spouse of being in breach of the interdict.[91] This element of discretion has been discussed in the Lord Advocate's Guidelines[92] and these indicate that arrest should take place in all but the most "trivial cases".

Post arrest procedure

8–31   The police have two initial options. They may, if they consider that there is no likelihood of violence to the applicant spouse or any child of the family, liberate the person who has breached the interdict unconditionally.[93] Alternatively they may hold an arrested man until his appearance in court on criminal charges or to allow arrangements for a civil hearing for breach of interdict.[94] In either case a report will go to the public prosecutor, the procurator fiscal who decides whether or not to bring criminal charges.[95] If there are criminal charges then these proceed normally. However, if no charges are brought then the fiscal must tell the spouse who holds the interdict and her solicitor so that civil proceedings can be brought for breach of the interdict.[96] Where the person has been freed then there will be service on that party requiring him to appear in court at some specified date to answer the question of whether there has been a breach or not. If the spouse has been detained, then there is a court appearance where the fiscal presents a petition indicating what has happened and requesting detention for a further period not exceeding two days so that civil proceedings may be brought.[97] At this stage the sheriff must decide whether there is substantial risk of violence. If it seems to the sheriff that civil proceedings will be brought and that there is a substantial risk of violence to the applicant or any child of the family, detention may be ordered for up to two further days.[98] Otherwise the party who has been detained must be released from custody.[99] This procedure was not invoked a great deal during the first five years of the Matrimonial Homes Act and no decided cases on the issue have been brought to the authors' attention.[1–2]

5. Exclusion Orders

Introduction

8–32   The Matrimonial Homes (Family Protection) (Scotland) Act 1981 made provision not only for the introduction of occupancy rights and their regulation but also, equally importantly, for their suspension. In certain circumstances it is possible that a spouse or cohabitee can lose the occupancy rights in the rented property he occupies.

---

[91] 1981 Act, s. 15(3).
[92] (1987) 2 S.H.L.N. 50.
[93] 1981 Act, s. 16(1)(a).
[94] *ibid.* s. 16(1)(b).
[95] *ibid.* s. 16(2).
[96] *ibid.* s. 17(4).
[97] *ibid.* s. 17(5)(a).
[98] *ibid.* s. 17(5)(b).
[99] *ibid.* s. 17(5)(c).
[1–2] *The Operation of the Matrimonial Homes (Family Protection) (Scotland) Act 1981, op. cit.*

The courts, if they are suspending occupancy rights, are required under the 1981 Act to grant a court order prohibiting the other party from entering the matrimonial home without the express permission of the applicant. To make this exclusion effective the court must also grant two other related orders— unless the other spouse can show the court that it is unnecessary to do so.[3] These involve the granting of an order for summary ejection of the other party from the matrimonial home and an order prohibiting the removal by the other party of any furniture from the matrimonial home. The court may add such terms and conditions as it chooses to such orders.[4] Interim orders are also available pending the making of exclusion orders.[5]

In addition the court may make an order prohibiting the other party from   8–33 entering or remaining in the vicinity of the matrimonial home, adding such terms and conditions as it considers appropriate.[6] There is also a discretion to give directions about the preservation of the other party's goods and effects remaining in the matrimonial home where an order has been granted for the summary ejection in the absence of the other party.[7]

Exemptions from exclusion orders

The Act specifies certain circumstances in which the court cannot make an   8–34 exclusion order, even where the primary test of necessity may be met.[8] This exemption applies to tied dwellings let by an employer on the condition that the non-applicant spouse or both spouses must live there. The rationale behind this exemption is that granting an exclusion order in such cases would lead to the end of the tenancy itself, thus terminating the occupancy rights of the family as well as the employment of the entitled spouse.

Duration and expiry

Any exclusion order or interim exclusion order, or any of the ancillary orders,   8–35 is subject to recall or variation by the court on application of either party. The rights of third parties owning or having disposal of the matrimonial home or furnishings therein are not restricted by the Act and any order relating to furniture and plenishings will cease to have effect if these are removed by the third party. Similarly, if the permission to occupy the home is withdrawn by a third party, the exclusion order ceases to have effect. Finally, the termination of marriage whether due to death, divorce or annulment has the effect of terminating any order made under the 1981 Act. In the interval between granting an interim and full order, an application for recall of the interim order by the non-applicant is competent.

General principles for suspension of occupancy rights

Most of the legal controversy to date in this area centres around the swift   8–36 procedure provided for interim suspension of occupancy rights. Provision is made for a very early hearing on the question of exclusion usually within a

---

[3] 1981 Act, s. 4(4).
[4] *ibid.* s. 4(5)(c).
[5] *ibid.* s. 4(6).
[6] *ibid.* s. 4(5)(a).
[7] *ibid.* s. 4(5)(b).
[8] *ibid.* s. 4.

week of starting court proceedings.[9] In legal terms this is extremely swift since it is only a little longer than the time it takes to serve the legal documents on the other party. Any decision to grant an exclusion order at this time has the same effect as a full hearing after all the legal procedures of a normal ordinary civil action have been completed. The area of interim exclusion orders is the one most often dealt with in applications under the 1981 Act as these are usually part of an action for divorce. Since orders such as exclusion orders end on divorce, there is little incentive to obtain a final order prior to the dissolution of the relationship. The legal tests are the same in any event for interim and final orders.

The exclusion order tests in practice

Primary test: necessity

8–37 Since the Matrimonial Homes (Family Protection) (Scotland) Act 1981 came into force in September 1982 the Court of Session's major concern under this legislation has been in relation to the granting of exclusion orders, specifically on applications for interim orders. The primary test which the courts must employ is contained in section 4(2). Exclusion orders are to be granted:

> "[W]here it appears to the court that the making of the order is necessary for the protection of the applicant or any child of the family from any conduct or threatened or reasonably apprehended conduct of the non-applicant spouse which is or would be injurious to the physical or mental health of the applicant or child."

Despite this, the early liberal interpretation of the legislation was typified by the tendency to grant orders on what appeared to be the balance of convenience.[10] This pattern changed as a result of the first decisions on appeals to the Second Division of the Court of Session in *Bell*[11] and *Smith*.[12] In these cases the court laid down the importance of the necessity test. However, additional remarks were made which indicated that exclusion orders were likely to be difficult to obtain. The precise details of these glosses on the wording of the statute were dealt with extensively in the literature of the day.[13] In subsequent decisions both Divisions of the Court of Session retreated from all the distinct aspects of this restrictive position. The culmination of these developments occurred in the *McCafferty* case.[14] In this case the Court of Session confirmed the central role of the necessity test. Bearing in mind the fact of the centrality of necessity as the key to obtaining an exclusion order, a number of pointers can be gleaned from the various cases which have come before the Inner House:

    (a)   the test of balance of convenience is inappropriate[15];

---

[9] 1981 Act, s. 4(6).

[10] Marie Robertson and Peter Robson, "Exclusion Orders—the Emerging Criteria", Marie Robertson and Peter Robson (1983) 28 J.L.S.S. 396 and *The Operation of the Matrimonial Homes (Family Protection) (Scotland) Act 1981*, (University of Strathclyde, 1983).

[11] 1983 S.L.T. 224.

[12] 1983 S.L.T. 275.

[13] "First Cases under the Matrimonial Homes Act", 1982 S.L.T. (News) 113; (1983) 28 J.L.S.S. 396 ; (1985) 30 J.L.S.S. 299; (1986) 31 J.L.S.S. 365.

[14] *McCafferty v. McCafferty,* 1986 S.L.T. 650.

[15] *Smith v. Smith,* 1983 S.L.T. 275.

(b) the decision is a discretionary one of the judge of first instance and will be interfered with only where the wrong test is applied,[16] or an absurd conclusion reached on the facts[17];

(c) if there is additional material available at the time of an appeal this may be taken into account in deciding whether or not an order should have been granted[18];

(d) there must be harm or likely injury to the health of the applicant or child of the family rather than mere distress[19];

(e) the injury may be to either the physical[20] or the mental[21] health of the applicant or child of the family;

(f) there does not need to be an intention to cause harm or injury on the part of the non-applicant.[22]

In subsequent cases Outer House judges and sheriffs have appeared to adopt the sequential approach outlined in *McCafferty* by Lord Dunpark of looking at the nature and quality of the alleged conduct, the likelihood of it continuing, and its potential to injure the health of the applicant or child of the family.[23] From these applications of the test, a number of factors which have been central to the decision can be identified:

(a) threats made in anger may be taken at less than face value[24];

(b) evidence of harm to mental health must be clearly linked to the conduct of the other party[25];

(c) the needs of the children are part of the equation in determining whether a case of necessity is made out[26] but cannot be the only matter considered[27];

(d) evidence of children of the marriage as to allegations and counter-allegations will be given a good deal of weight[28];

(e) it may be that the necessity for protection from harm can be modified by the presence of another adult in the household acting as a restraint on harmful conduct[29];

(f) a delay between an act of violence and a hearing on an exclusion order does not of itself preclude the success of the application[30];

---

[16] *Gillespie v. Gillespie*, IH. May 11, 1984, unreported.

[17] *McCafferty v. McCafferty*, 1986 S.L.T. 650 at 655, *per* Lord Robertson; see also *Coster v. Coster*, 1992 S.C.L.R. 210 on new material.

[18] *Ward v. Ward*, 1983 S.L.T. 472.

[19] *McCafferty v. McCafferty*, 1986 S.L.T. 650 at 655, *per* Lord Robertson.

[20] *Brown v. Brown*, 1985 S.L.T. 376.

[21] *McCafferty v. McCafferty*, 1986 S.L.T. 650.

[22] *ibid.* at 656, *per* Lord Dunpark.

[23] *ibid.*

[24] *Barbour v. Barbour*, Court of Session (OH) Nov. 24, 1989, unreported—threat to "crucify" wife.

[25] *Davidson v. Davidson*, Court of Session (OH) Oct. 9, 1991, unreported.

[26] *Raeburn v. Raeburn*, Court of Session (OH) Dec. 21, 1989, unreported; *Cowie v. Cowie*, Court of Session Nov. 4, 1986 unreported.

[27] *Hampsey v. Hampsey*, 1988 G.W.D. 24–1035 (Sh. Pr. Caplan).

[28] *Sellars v. Sellars*, Court of Session (OH) June 6, 1986, unreported; *Barbour v. Barbour*, Court of Session (OH) Nov. 24, 1989, unreported.

[29] *Mather v. Mather*, 1987 S.L.T. 565 (OH)—suspension of exclusion order while adult son living in matrimonial home.

[30] *Millar v. Millar*, 1991 S.C.L.R. 649.

(g) if there is additional material available at the time of an appeal this may be taken into account in deciding whether or not an order should have been granted[31];

(h) conduct means more than the mere presence of the other party[32];

(i) in appeals against interim exclusion orders a failure to lodge a notice of intention to defend did not prevent an appeal.[33]

Secondary test: unjustified or unreasonable

8–38   Supplementary to the necessity test is the requirement on the court to assess whether an order would be "unjustified or unreasonable"[34] having regard to "all the circumstances of the case", including the matters specified in paragraphs (a)-(e) of section 3(3) of the Act.

Originally, the Scottish Law Commission had proposed that the court should have regard to the "balance of hardship" between the spouses including the availability and suitability of any alternative accommodation for the spouse whose occupancy rights are sought to be suspended. However, after a critical reception of this proposal in some quarters, the Commission's final recommendations withdrew from this position as it might inhibit the making of many justifiable exclusion orders. The primacy of the need for protection was thus firmly established, as was the onus for demonstrating that the order is unjustified or unreasonable having regard to certain important factors. Such onus rests with the non-applicant spouse. The relevant factors[35] are the conduct of the spouses in relation to each other and otherwise; the respective needs and financial resources of the spouse; the needs of any child of the family; the extent (if any) to which the matrimonial home and any relevant item of furniture and plenishings is used in connection with a trade, business or profession of either spouse; and whether the entitled spouse offers or has offered to make available to the non-entitled spouse any suitable alternative accommodation.

The purpose of including a requirement concerning justifiability and reasonableness as well as the test of necessity was to ensure that the court recognised in certain circumstances that exclusion would be an inappropriate remedy as it might have serious economic consequences for the whole family. Despite the doubts of the senior Scottish judiciary as to the specific circumstances when this test could override necessity[36] and the recommendation that it should be abolished,[37] the Scottish Law Commission remain convinced of its potential practical value.[38]

Evidence

8–39   Establishing the need for the protection of an exclusion order was a practical problem which was also looked at in the cases of *Bell* and *Smith*. Whilst it might be reasonably simple to obtain evidence in an ordinary action, the speed with which interim hearings reached court meant that problems could arise in getting satisfactory evidence to back up claims or harm or threats. The Court of Session made it clear that they were unhappy about sheriffs simply accepting the *ex parte* statements of the applicant as opposed to their denial by the other

---

[31] *Coster v. Coster,* 1992 S.C.L.R. 210 at 211.
[32] *Matheson v. Matheson,* 1986 S.L.T. (Sh.Ct.) 2 at 5.
[33] *Nelson v. Nelson,* 1988 S.L.T. (Sh.Ct.) 26.
[34] s. 4(3).
[35] s. 3(3).
[36] *The Operation of the Matrimonial Homes (Family Protection) (Scotland) Act 1981,* p. 98.
[37] *ibid.* p. 101.
[38] *Report on Family Law* (Scot. Law Com. No. 135) (1992) at para. 11.29.

party. Where possible some external evidence was to be provided such as convictions, medical certificates or an independent report, usually by an advocate or solicitor.

Subsequently, affidavits have been approved as a more reliable source than mere statements by the parties since, as Lord Wheatley pointed out hearing the *Brown* appeal, they are made under oath. They are now frequently used and accepted as satisfactory evidence in applications at interim exclusion order hearings. Provision is made for them by the Rules of the Court of Session[39] and the Ordinary Cause Rules.[40]

6. Cohabitation and the Matrimonial Homes Legislation

Introduction

Section 18 of the 1981 Act deals with the position of cohabitees. Much of the Act applies to cohabitees as it does to spouses. Significantly, however, where only one of a couple is entitled to occupy the home, the non-entitled cohabitee must apply to the court for a grant of occupancy rights. Such rights can initially be granted for a maximum of six months.[41] Originally this was limited to three months. There is provision for extensions beyond the initial period although these may not exceed six months at a time.[42] Where both cohabitees are entitled, no such application is necessary.   8–40

The parts of the Act which apply to cohabiting couples where both are entitled or occupancy rights have been granted are those relating to subsidiary and consequential rights; the regulation of occupancy rights; exclusion orders; matrimonial interdicts and powers of arrest; and transfer of tenancies. The sections of the 1981 Act relating to protection against dealings do not apply to cohabitees and so the protection to tenants afforded by these sections, discussed above, will not apply. Section 2(8), which provides that a tenancy will be continued by the possession of a non-entitled party where the entitled party has abandoned possession, does apply to cohabitees. However, it is suggested that this would not afford any substantive protection for non-entitled cohabitees in this position in that she would be obliged to apply for a grant of occupancy rights and would face difficulties in persuading the court that she was still part of a cohabiting couple.

Criteria for determining whether a couple is cohabiting

The relevant factors in deciding when a couple are cohabiting in terms of the 1981 Act specifically include the length of time for which it appears they have been living together and whether there are any children of the relationship.[43] There are no reported cases on the interpretation of this point, although one judge indicated to the Scottish Office Project carried out by Strathclyde University into the operation of the Matrimonial Homes Act that "around six months might be about right" and the police in one Scottish Division have maintained to officers in their area that "after 9 months a couple are cohabitees"   8–41

---

[39] RCS 1994, r. 49.71(1).
[40] OCR 1993, r. 33.27.
[41] s. 18 (as amended by s. 13(9) of the Law Reform (Miscellaneous Provisions) (Scotland) Act 1985).
[42] s. 18(1).
[43] s. 18(2).

and after this a woman could not be turned out into the street by her partner.[44] A period of cohabitation of 18 months where there were no children of the relationship was accepted in a Rent Act succession case.[45] This was in the context of the test which has developed as to whether a sufficient state of permanence and stability had been reached for it to be said that the occupant was a member of the family of the deceased.[46]

At the present time only heterosexual relationships are likely to be recognised by the law in this area. This was the rationale in a case involving an attempt to succeed to a local authority tenancy by the lesbian partner of a deceased tenant in *Harrogate Borough Council v. Simpson,*[47] and more recently in relation to a protected tenancy in *Fitzpatrick v. Sterling Housing Association Ltd.*[48] However, the law this century has changed its attitude to non-married heterosexual couples so that they are accorded similar status to married couples.[49] A similar change may occur in relation to homosexual relationships.[50]

Exclusion orders and cohabitees

8–42   There has now been a fair amount of litigation which has explored the tension between the concept of cohabitation and the aims of an Act designed to facilitate the needs of people to live separately from partners who pose a risk to safety. This has particularly been so in relation to applications for exclusion orders. The courts had initially adopted a literal approach to the construction of the 1981 Act, resolving that a couple ceased to cohabit when one partner left the other for reasons of safety.[51] A more purposive approach to this problem has now been authoritatively established by the Inner House in *Armour v. Anderson.*[52] Armour and Anderson were joint tenants. Armour had left the home following violent behaviour by her partner. Ten months later she successfully applied for an interim exclusion order. Anderson appealed to the sheriff principal, who recalled the sheriff's interlocutor, holding that Armour and Anderson had ceased to be a cohabiting couple. On appeal to the Inner House it was established that in considering the question of whether or not a couple had ceased to cohabit, the courts should focus on the point in time immediately prior to the conduct which gave rise to the application. It would be absurd, the Court noted, to construe the 1981 Act in such a way that it would be impossible for a former cohabitee to benefit from the Act without exposing her to further risk of violence.

Nevertheless, despite the judgment in *Armour*, problems remain which call for attention. In *Clarke v. Hatten*[53] it was established that a cohabitee who was

[44] *The Operation of the Matrimonial Homes (Family Protection) (Scotland) Act (1981),* pp. 52 *et seq.*
[45] *Chios Property Investment Co Ltd v. Lopez* [1988] 1 E.G.L.R. 98—although Sir George Waller did suggest that this was a most exceptional case and should not be regarded as a precedent.
[46] *Dyson Holdings v. Fox* [1976] Q.B. 503; *Helby v. Rafferty* [1979] 1 W.L.R. 13; *Watson v. Lucas* [1980] 1 W.L.R. 1493.
[47] (1984) 17 H.L.R. 205.
[48] [1998] 2 W.L.R. 225.
[49] *Upfill v. Wright* [1911] 1 K.B. 506, on the issue of arrears of rent in a lease due to it being unenforceable as being immoral, on which serious doubt is cast in *Heglibiston Establishment v. Heyman* (1977) 36 P. & C.R. 351.
[50] A more progressive approach has been signalled recently in the Inner House in the decision of *T, Petr,* 1997 S.L.T. 724.
[51] *Verity v. Fenner,* 1993 S.C.L.R. 223.
[52] 1994 S.C.L.R. 645.
[53] 1987 S.C.L.R. 521.

the tenant and had left the home due to violence could not apply for an exclusion order where the other party did not seem to have had his occupancy rights declared. Where only one cohabitee is entitled, occupancy rights must be granted by the court before the other provisions of the Act can come into play.[54] Accordingly, Clarke was left without a remedy under the 1981 Act, although she did have a remedy in a common law action of ejection or interdict. The disadvantage is that this remedy does not carry with it the power of arrest.

Another disadvantage suffered by cohabitees is that non-entitled cohabitees 8–43 may be refused the emergency relief which is afforded to spouses. In *Smith-Milne v. Gammack*[55] the non-entitled pursuer was ejected from the home. She sought an interim order granting leave to enter and occupy the home. The sheriff was prepared to regard this crave as an application for the grant of occupancy rights, but held that it was incompetent. There is no provision in the Act for the interim grant of occupancy rights to cohabitees. Instead the matter had to proceed to proof in order to establish the question of whether the couple was a cohabiting one.

---

[54] s. 18(3).
[55] 1995 S.C.L.R 1058.

Chapter 9

SUCCESSION TO A TENANCY

1. General Law of Succession as it Relates to Leases

9–01   Particular rules exist in the Rent (Scotland) Act 1984 and the Housing (Scotland) Acts 1987 and 1988 concerning rights of succession to leases governed by the legislation. These rules cover most residential tenancy situations. However, before looking at them in detail, it is necessary to consider the general law of succession[1] in relation to leases. Contractual rights of succession may also be conferred in addition to statutory rights.[1a]

Tenants with the power to assign their lease

9–02   Where tenants have the power to assign their lease, they may make a valid bequest of the lease by will or other testamentary writing. Tenants may have a right to assign their lease under contract. In the absence of express contractual terms the common law provides that tenants of unfurnished urban lets have the right to assign, but that tenants of furnished leases do not.[2]

Tenancies with implied prohibition on assignation

9–03   Where a tenant has, in theory, the ability to assign his lease but the lease contains an implied prohibition against assignation, the Succession (Scotland) Act 1964[3] nevertheless allows him to bequeath the lease. This is not, however, permissible where the contractual prohibition is express. Permitted legatees under this provision are persons who, had the tenant died intestate, would have been those entitled to share in the estate of the deceased. Where tenants have not exercised this right, or have not made a valid bequest of the lease, additional powers exist for the executor of the deceased's estate to transfer the lease to another. These powers are discussed in the following section.

Tenancies with express prohibition on assignation

9–04   Where a lease expressly prohibits assignation, the interest in the lease may not be bequeathed. However, powers exist under section 16 of the Succession (Scotland) Act 1964 for the executor to transfer the lease, subject to the landlord's permission, to any person entitled to succeed to the intestate estate, or to claim

---

[1]   See, in general, D. R. Macdonald, *Succession* (2nd ed., 1994); M.C. Meston, *The Succession (Scotland) Act 1964* (4th ed., 1993).
[1a]   For a discussion of the complexities which may arise in this situation see City of Glasgow District Council v. Mullen, 1998 Hous.L.R. 89.
[2]   See para. 1–56 *et seq.*
[3]   s. 29.

legal rights or the prior rights of a surviving spouse. This power also relates to the situation where tenants could have bequeathed their interest in a lease under the power granted by section 29 of the 1964 Act but failed to do so, and to situations where a valid bequest has not been made or where a bequest is not accepted by the legatee.

Either executor or landlord may terminate the lease irrespective of other conditions—if the executor is satisfied that the lease cannot be disposed of according to law and informs the landlord; if the lease is not disposed of within either one year or such longer period as may be fixed by agreement (or by the sheriff on the application of the executor, failing such agreement).[4] Six months' notice of such termination must be given, subject to any statutory provision prescribing a shorter period for the lease in question.[5] No rights of compensation or damage are to be prejudiced by statutory termination. As far as the tenant is concerned, they fall on the executory estate, not the executor personally.[6]

Prior right of surviving spouse

Where a tenant dies intestate and leaves a surviving spouse, the executor of the   9–05
deceased's estate, as noted above, is empowered to transfer a lease to the surviving spouse. Such may occur in fulfilment of the surviving spouse's prior rights in the intestate estate. The surviving spouse has a prior right to any single property including leasehold up to a certain value.[7] If there is more than one property in which the surviving spouse was ordinarily resident then the surviving spouse has six months to select which property to take. Where a lease is worth more than the designated value, the surviving spouse, instead of receiving occupation under the lease, receives the equivalent in cash. Also, where the lease is part of larger subjects or where the separate disposal of the dwelling-house would lessen the value of the estate as a whole (as where there is a house attached to a doctor's surgery or it is a farm house or an integral house/shop), the cash value of the lease will be given to the surviving spouse subject to the relevant maximum.[8]

Excluded from prior rights are dwelling-houses covered by the Rent Acts.[9] Nonetheless, the surviving spouse may succeed to a regulated, assured or secure tenancy. Where either the surviving spouse does not take advantage of this prior right or where there is more than one tenancy, the lease not taken vests in the executor who may assign it to any one of the persons entitled to succeed to the tenant's estate including prior and legal rights claimants, irrespective of prohibitions on assignation, express or implied. There is nothing to stop assignation to anyone where there is no prohibition or with the landlord's consent.

2. SUCCESSION TO REGULATED TENANCIES

Introduction

The Rent (Scotland) Act 1984 provides that certain members of the family   9–06
of the tenant may succeed to the tenancy. This right to succeed is not unrestricted,

---

[4] s. 16(3).
[5] s. 16(4)(b).
[6] s. 16(5).
[7] 1964 Act s. 8(1); currently set at £110,000 by S.I. 1993 No. 2690.
[8] *ibid.* s. 8(1)(a)(ii) and (2).
[9] *ibid.* s. 8(6)(d).

and certain criteria must be satisfied. The Housing (Scotland) Act 1988 places further limitations upon who qualifies to succeed to a protected tenancy as well as limiting the rights to which they succeed. It is possible for succession in relation to regulated tenancies to occur twice in relation to a single tenancy. The 1984 Act uses the terms "original tenant" and "first successor" to denote these different stages of succession.[10-11]

Succession to original tenant

9–07	The rules of succession concerning tenants who died on or after January 2, 1989[12] are laid out in Schedules 1A and 1B to the Rent (Scotland) Act 1984 (as amended[13]) and apply where the dwelling-house was the only or principal home of the tenant.[14] Where there is to be a succession after the death of the person who was a regulated or statutory tenant of the dwelling-house, there is an order of entitlement to succeed.

Surviving spouse succession

9–08	The tenant's surviving spouse may take on the tenancy, provided that she retains possession of the dwelling-house. This implies that she must have been residing with the tenant at the time of the death. However, there is no specific qualifying time laid down. The surviving spouse takes as a statutory tenant.[15] This means that she retains the right to have a fair rent fixed and that the repossession provisions of the Rent (Scotland) Act 1984 apply.[16] Surviving spouse rights are available to the surviving spouse of the deceased as well as to anyone who was living with the tenant as his or her wife or husband.[17]

Member of the tenant's family

9–09	If there was no surviving spouse then such member of the tenant's family who was residing with the tenant at the time of death and for two years beforehand is entitled to succeed. The member of the family succeeds to a statutory assured tenancy.[18] If there is more than one person entitled to succeed in this way and the members of the family are unable to reach agreement, the succession is to be decided by the sheriff.[19] Remarriage does not bar the continuation in the tenancy.

Succession to first successor

9–10	Where a first successor dies there may be a further succession. However, this may only occur if there is a person who was a member both of the original tenant's and the first successor's family. Additionally, such a person must have

---

[10-11]	Sched. 1A, paras 1 and 4.

[12]	The rules as to qualifying period prior to this date were less onerous. The extension of the qualifying period of residence under the Housing (Scotland) Act 1988 from six months to two years meant that there were transitional arrangements to ensure that the legislation did not take away rights retroactively, see P. Robson, *Succession to Protected Tenancies* (LSA 1989).

[13]	Amended by s. 46 of and Sched. 6, Pt 1 to the Housing (Scotland) Act 1988.

[14]	Sched. 1A, para. 2(1).

[15]	Sched. 1A, para. 2(1) (inserted by Sched. 6 to the Housing (Scotland) Act 1988).

[16]	See Chapter 5.

[17]	Sched. 1A, para. 2(2).

[18]	Sched. 1A, para 3.

[19]	*ibid.*

been residing with the first successor at the time of that person's death and for two years immediately prior to the first successor's death.[20] The "second successor" succeeds to a statutory assured tenancy. Again, if there are rival claims and the members of the family are unable to reach agreement, the succession is to be decided by the sheriff.[21]

New tenancy to successor

If there is a grant to a successor of a new tenancy this does not have the effect of creating a new chain of first succession. The individuals who were first successor and original tenant at the time of the succession remain so.[22] 9–11

3. Assured Tenancies

Introduction

The question of succession was initially not mentioned in the Bill introducing assured tenancies. However, at the Report stage in the House of Lords a truncated order of succession was introduced for spouses[23] and those living together as husband and wife.[24] They are protected from the rights of repossession which the legislation gives landlords.[25] However, the rights of succession enjoyed by members of the deceased's family under the Rent (Scotland) Act 1984 were not duplicated under the assured tenancy regime. Assured tenancies may only be succeeded to once.[26] 9–12

Succession to original tenant

Where the original tenant was sole tenant under an assured tenancy,[27] the surviving spouse is entitled to a statutory assured tenancy where the survivor was occupying the house as his or her only or principal home immediately prior to the death.[28] The survivor must retain possession of the house to enjoy the right of succession. 9–13

Succession to first successor not permitted

The 1988 Act prohibits the succession to an assured tenancy where the deceased tenant had himself already succeeded to the tenancy.[29] There are a number of ways whereby a tenant may be regarded as already having succeeded to a tenancy. The tenancy may have vested in him under a will or intestacy, by operation of section 3A of the Rent (Scotland) Act 1984 (succession following the death of a regulated tenant) or by operation of this part of the legislation, or by surviving the death of a joint tenant.[30] Also, where a new tenancy of 9–14

---

[20] Sched. 1A, para 6; Sched. 1B, para 3.
[21] *ibid.*
[22] Sched. 1A, para. 7; Sched. 1B, para 4.
[23] 1988 Act, s. 31(1).
[24] *ibid.* s. 31(4).
[25] *ibid.* s. 31(3).
[26] *ibid.* s. 31(1)(c).
[27] *ibid.* s. 31(1)(a).
[28] *ibid.* s. 31(1)(b).
[29] *ibid.* s. 31(1)(c).
[30] *ibid.* s. 31(2)(a)–(c).

substantially the same house as he or she was a successor to is granted, this too will be regarded as succession.[31] Where the deceased spouse was a successor, the legislation provides for the landlord to be able to regain possession provided that possession proceedings are commenced within a year of the death.[32]

4. SECURE TENANCIES

Introduction

9–15   The Housing (Scotland) Act 1987 makes a similar kind of provision for relatives to succeed to secure tenancies as occurs in the private rented sector. As housing associations' practice makes clear, landlords may choose to grant more extensive succession rights to their tenancies than those indicated in the legislation. The 1987 Act lays down an order of succession, as well as indicating what is to happen if the person with the right to succeed chooses not to take up this option. As with assured tenancies succession to secure tenancies can occur only once.

Succcession by qualified person

9–16   On the death of the tenant the tenancy normally passes by operation of law to a qualified person.[33] This does not occur where there is no qualified person[34] or the qualified person declines the tenancy or if the tenancy is terminated because it has already been passed.[35]

Qualified person: spouse, cohabitee and surviving joint tenant

9–17   A qualified person is the person whose only or principal home at the time of the tenant's death was that house and who was at that time either the spouse of the tenant or living with the tenant as husband and wife.[36] This applies to a joint tenancy where the jointly tenanted house was the only or principal home of the surviving spouse at the time of the tenant's death.[37]

Qualified person: member of deceased tenant's family

9–18   Where there is no surviving spouse the next qualified person is any member of the tenant's family who has attained the age of 16 provided that the house was his or her only or principal home throughout the 12 months preceding the tenant's death.[38] In the event of more than one person qualifying by this route, then the qualified persons may agree to whom the tenancy should be passed. Failing agreement within four weeks of the death, the landlord decides which of the qualified persons shall succeed.[39]

---

[31] 1988 Act, s. 31(2)(d).
[32] *ibid.* Sched. 5, ground 7.
[33] 1987 Act, s. 52(1).
[34] *ibid.* s. 52(1)(a).
[35] *ibid.* s. 52(5).
[36] *ibid.* s. 52(2).
[37] *ibid.* s. 52(2)(b).
[38] *ibid.* s. 52(2)(c).
[39] *ibid.* s. 52(3).

"Family" is defined in the 1987 Act. Section 83 states that a person is a   9–19
member of another's family if that person is the spouse (or person living with
another as husband or wife) or the parent, grandparent, child, grandchild, brother,
sister, uncle, aunt, nephew or niece. It indicates that relationships by marriage
are to be treated as a relationship by blood and one of the half-blood as of the
whole blood. Finally, stepchildren and the children of unmarried parents are to
be treated as the children of those parents.

Rights of qualified person after death of first successor

If there has already been a succession then a qualified person, although not   9–20
being entitled to succeed, is entitled to continue as tenant for a period not
exceeding six months. Such occupation shall not be as a secure tenant.[40] This
means that the occupying tenant has no statutory security of tenure nor the right
to buy.

Declining succession

Any qualified person who is entitled to succeed, but who wishes to decline   9–21
the tenancy may do so by giving written notice within four weeks of the death
of the tenant. The house must be vacated within three months thereafter and
the rental due shall cover only the period of occupation after the death of the
tenant.[41]

Effect on succession rights of moving from one secure tenancy to another

Where a tenant gives up a secure tenancy in order to occupy another house   9–22
subject to a secure tenancy, whether by agreement or because of a management
possession order, these tenancies are to be treated as a single secure tenancy.[42]
One of the problems which section 52 addresses is the situation where tenants
have given up tenancies to go and look after ageing relatives. Litigation has
stemmed from a tenant doing just this. In *Hamilton District Council v. Lennon*,[43]
Dominic Lennon gave up a joint tenancy with his brother to go and look after
his aunt who was herself a secure tenant. The Inner House held that this
provision only relates to the situation where the person(s) relinquishing the
secure tenancy is the same person who then occupies another house subject to
a secure tenancy.[44] The relinquished secure tenancy in question was a joint
tenancy of Mr Lennon and his brother. However, it was Mr Lennon alone
who then occupied his aunt's house. Accordingly, he could not rely on the
provisions of this subsection. Further, it could not be inferred that Mr Lennon
had become a joint secure tenant with his aunt. Mr Lennon nevertheless
successfully challenged the district council by judicial review on their failure
to follow their own allocation policy.[45]

---

[40] 1987 Act, s. 52(6).
[41] *ibid.* s. 52(4).
[42] *ibid.* s. 52(7).
[43] 1990 S.C.L.R. 297, 1990 S.L.T. 533.
[44] *ibid.*
[45] 1990 S.C.L.R. 514.

"Family"

9–23   Succession to family members is not an issue with assured tenancies, where succession is permissible only to spouses and cohabitees. However, succession to family members is possible under the regulated and secure tenancy regimes. "Family" is not defined in the Rent (Scotland) Act 1984 but is defined for the purposes of the Housing (Scotland) Act 1987.[46] However, this definition does not cover the whole range of problems that have come before the courts and should therefore be read along with the case law which has developed on the meaning of "family", most of which is English but relates to comparable legislation.

"Family" has been broadly construed in the courts. Whether or not a person is a member of another's family is a question of law.[47] In each case the question is whether the person would, in ordinary language, be said to be a member of the family. In addition to the relationship, the way the parties have acted is also taken into account. Thus, as well as married sons and their wives, brothers and sisters and adopted children, and cohabitees have all been held to be "family". The Court of Appeal indicated in *Dyson Holdings Ltd v. Fox*[48] that the meaning of "family" is not fixed but will evolve as societal attitudes develop. It is not limited to a strict legal familial nexus, but requires at least "a broadly recognisable *de facto* familial nexus".[49]

9–24   Nevertheless, the courts have shown some reluctance in recognising certain relationships as falling within the meaning of "family". *Sefton Holdings Ltd. v. Cairns*[50] involved a young woman taken in during the Second World War by a family with whom she had no blood relationship. She lived with them after the death of her parents and boyfriend for 45 years. She called the parents "Mom and Pop" and was treated as a daughter. The Court of Appeal were of the view that there was a difference between "living as a member of a family" and "being a member of the family" and that she did not cross this threshold through her informal adoption.

In *Joram Developments Ltd v. Sharratt*[51] the House of Lords dealt with the claim of a middle-aged man to succeed to the tenancy of a lady who died aged 94. The man, who was more than 50 years her younger, had lived with the tenant for over 20 years and cared for her in the final years before her death. He claimed that he should be regarded as part of her family. He was not actually related to the tenant, but she had always called him her "nephew" to outsiders. The House of Lords distinguished between the concepts of "household" and that of "family". In the Court of Appeal, Browne, L.J. had explained the difficulty:

> "the line must be drawn somewhere, and if he could be included among those who can be members of the tenant's family it would be difficult, if not impossible to exclude two old cronies sharing a house, and perhaps, calling themselves and each other brothers or sisters."[52]

---

[46] s. 83.
[47] *Joram Developments v. Sharratt* [1979] 1 W.L.R. 928.
[48] [1976] 1 Q.B. 503.
[49] *Ross v. Collins* [1964] 1 W.L.R. 425.
[50] [1988] 1 E.G.L.R. 99.
[51] [1979] 1 W.L.R. 3.
[52] *ibid.*

The House of Lords supported this decision and took the view that a relationship which had been platonic and filial did not amount to a family relationship.[53]

It has also been argued before the courts that having lived with a deceased tenant as husband and wife amounts to a relationship of "family", and the courts, in general, have found it easier to recognise such relationships as being "family" ones. Such an argument is only now pertinent to regulated tenancies (as the Housing Acts of 1987 and 1988 expressly provide that persons living together as husband and wife will be deemed to be spouses for succession purposes) and to homosexual relationships.

The crucial factors in a relationship which the courts wish to find before regarding cohabitation as amounting to "family" relations are permanence and stability. In *Dyson Holdings Ltd v. Fox*[54] an unmarried woman and an unmarried man lived together for 21 years. There were no children to the relationship. She had taken his name. The Court of Appeal held that their union was permanent and stable enough to make her a member of his family. Similarly, in *Watson v. Lucas*[55] a married man lived with another woman for 19 years until her death. There was no pretence of being married. They kept their own names. Mr Watson was a Catholic and had refused to grant his wife a divorce. The judge at first instance held that his married status acted as a bar to Mr Watson being a member of his cohabitee's family. The Court of Appeal, however, held that, given the facts of the case, his marital status and the fact that his partner retained her own name were not indications of independence and instability and regarded Mr Watson as having been a member of his partner's family. 9–25

However, it has been held that making no pretence of marriage and the retention of names is an indication of instability and impermanence. In *Helby v. Rafferty*,[56] Mr Rafferty lived with his partner for 5 years. He nursed her during the last three years of their cohabitation until her death. There was, however, no attempt to call themselves husband and wife to the community at large, and they had attempted at times to conceal the depth of their attachment. This continued independence of Miss Taylor seemed to lead the Court of Appeal to take the view that no family unit existed in this instance. It is suggested, however, that developing social attitudes towards cohabitation render it increasingly difficult for the court to place weight on such factors as indicators of permanence and stability.

Although the Court of Appeal stressed that it was a most unusual case and should not be regarded as a precedent from which it would be possible to draw a similar conclusion, a period of cohabitation of less than two years by a couple who were engaged to be married was accepted in *Chios Property Investment Co. Ltd v. Lopez*.[57] The blessing of both families to the cohabitation while the couple saved to get married was significant to the decision in this case. In fact, the length of time is considerably more than has been discussed in terms of cohabitation under the Matrimonial Homes (Family Protection) (Scotland) Act 1981.[58] 9–26

A recent attempt has been made to argue that a gay partner of a deceased tenant had been a member of the tenant's family. It was argued that changing social attitudes towards homosexuality permitted such a decision. However,

---

[53] *sub nom. Carega Properties SA v. Sharratt* [1979] 1 W.L.R. 928 at 930.
[54] [1976] 1 Q.B. 503.
[55] [1980] 1 W.L.R. 1493.
[56] [1979] 1 W.L.R. 13.
[57] [1988] 1 E.G.L.R. 98.
[58] Jackson *et al.*, *The Operation of the Matrimonial Homes (Family Protection) (Scotland) Act 1981* (1988), p. 52; see para. 8–40 *et seq.*

the Court of Appeal, with some reluctance, (Ward L.J. dissenting) held that until Parliament expressly provides for it, homosexual relationships will not amount to "family" ones. Waite, L.J. said:

> "[T]he law in England regarding succession to statutory tenancies is firmly rooted in the concept of the family as an entity bound together by ties of kinship (including adoptive status) of marriage. The only relaxation … has been a willingness to treat heterosexual cohabitants as if they were husband and wife. That was a restrictive extension, offensive to social justice and tolerance because it excludes lesbians and gays."[59]

9–27   It is unclear whether the Scottish courts would follow suit. The decision in *Dyson*[60] paves the way for a more progressive interpretation which has not yet been realised in the English courts.[61] However, the decision has been much criticised[62] and may not be followed in Scotland. Nevertheless, the decision of the Inner House in *T, Petitioner*[63] may signal a more enlightened approach in general towards homosexuality.

"Living together as husband and wife"

9–28   The question of whether this phrase is broad enough to encompass gay and lesbian relationships has been considered by the English courts.[64] Most recently, in *Fitzpatrick v. Sterling Housing Association*, the Court of Appeal decided that this phrase could only refer to heterosexual relationships but did state that it was "out of tune with modern acceptance of the need to avoid any discrimination on the ground of sexual orientation" and was for Parliament to reform the law accordingly.[65]

"Only or principal home"

9–29   The legislation requires that the property to which one succeeds must have been the "only or principal home" of the successor. As noted by Sheriff Principal Nicholson in *Roxburgh District Council v. Collins*,[66] this is to be contrasted with the position of secure tenants in England and Wales where there is the separate requirement that the potential successor *occupied* the home and *resided with* the deceased tenant. Caution must be exercised in relying on English authority for this question, although case law from south of the border is helpful in considering the meaning of "occupation" and "residence" which are pertinent to succession under the regulated and assured regimes.[67] Different tests are to be applied when considering these different statutory requirements, although it is suggested in practice that the applications of the different tests may often produce the same conclusion.

Sheriff Principal Nicholson noted that periods of absence from a home do not, by themselves, preclude the home from being an only or principal home. He continued:

---

[59] Fitzpatrick v. Sterling Housing Association [1998] 1 W.L.R. 225.
[60] [1976] 1 Q.B. 503.
[61] See the dissenting judgment of Ward, L.J. in *Fitzpatrick v. Sterling Housing Association Ltd* [1998] 1 W.L.R. 225 at 244.
[62] *Helby v. Rafferty* [1979] 1 W.L.R. 13; *Watson v. Lucas* [1980] 1 W.L.R. 1493.
[63] 1997 S.L.T. 724—case concerning adoption of a child by a homosexual.
[64] *Harrogate Borough Council v. Simpson* (1984) 17 H.L.R. 205; *Fitzpatrick v. Sterling Housing Association Ltd* [1998] 2 W.L.R. 225.
[65] [1998] 1 W.L.R. 225 at 238.
[66] 1991 S.C.L.R. 575.
[67] See paras 9–06 to 9–11 and 9–12 to 9–14.

"[E]very case will turn on its own facts and, given my view that regular or habitual residence is not a prerequisite, it seems to me that the questions which must be asked in cases where such residence is lacking is: On the facts of the case, did the person concerned have such a real, tangible and substantial connection with the house in question that it, rather than any other place of residence, can properly be described as having been his only or principal home during the relevant period?"[68]

In *Roxburgh* the defender, having previously lived with his mother, moved to London to find work. He found accommodation there in a lodging house. However, his bedroom in his mother's house was kept for his exclusive use. He kept his possessions there and returned during Christmas, Easter and summer holidays. He retained a bank account in the town of his mother's home. He continued to be registered with his childhood GP despite his period of residence in London. This arrangement continued for six years until his mother's death. It was held that the defender's only or principal home was with his mother.

"Occupation" and "residing with"

As noted above, there is a requirement in the Housing (Scotland) Act 1988 that the succeeding spouse was occupying the house in question as his or her only or principal home and had resided with the deceased tenant.[69] In the Rent (Scotland) Act 1984 the concept of "residing with" pertains to succession by family members.[70] A common test for assessing the meaning of "occupation" in Scotland and "residence" in England has emerged.

9–30

In Scotland the meaning of "occupation" has been discussed in relation to the right to buy. In *Beggs v. Kilmarnock and Loudon District Council*[71] the Inner House came to a view on the meaning of "occupation" which is in keeping with established English authority on the meaning of "residence". It held that it is possible to be temporarily absent from a house and still to be in occupation of it. What mattered was that there were physical signs that the person remained in occupation and that there was an intention to return.

This has been the position under English law, as evidenced by a long line of authority and ending, most recently, with *Camden London Borough Council v. Goldenberg*.[72] In *Camden* the appellant had been living with his grandmother, but left when he got married. For two months he "house sat" with his wife for a friend. When the friend returned, he and his wife returned to their respective former homes as they could not afford to live together. While the appellant was absent his brother had lived in his room. He had left most of his possessions behind. The grandmother moved into a nursing home six months after the appellant moved back in. She signed a deed assigning the tenancy to the appellant. In evidence the appellant confirmed that if somewhere else had become available where he and his wife could live together, he would have taken it as opposed to returning to his grandmother's home. The issue for the Court of Appeal was whether the appellant had resided with his grandmother throughout the period of 12 months before she went into a nursing home. It confirmed that residence

---

[68] 1991 S.C.L.R. 575 at 578 D–E.
[69] s. 31(1).
[70] Sched. 1, para. 3.
[71] 1995 S.C.L.R. 435.
[72] [1997] 1 F.L.R. 556; [1997] Fam. Law 90; 95 L.G.R. 693.

was a question of fact and degree and quoted with approval the test to be applied as espoused by Parker, L.J. in *Crawley Borough Council v. Sawyer*:[73]

> "Going through the whole thread of these matters is the common principle that in order to occupy premises as a home, first, there must be signs of occupation—that is to say, there must be furniture and so forth so that the house can be occupied as a home—and secondly, there must be an intention, if not physically present, to return to it."[74]

It was held in *Camden* (McGowan, L.J. dissenting) that the intention to return unless alternative unexpected accommodation came up was of a sufficient quality to justify the finding that he had resided with his grandmother for the required period.

Relationship between "only or principal home" and "occupation and residence"

9–31   Although separate tests have emerged for the application of these different statutory requirements, it is suggested that in practice they will often produce the same result. If a person passes the test of having a "real, tangible and substantial connection" with a house, he often will also be able to pass the two-stage test of (1) there being physical signs of remaining in occupation, and (2) an intention to return. The facts of the *Roxburgh* case support this view. In particular, when determining whether someone has occupied a property as his only or principal home, it should not be considered that there are two tests to apply consecutively; that is, to ask if there was a real, tangible and substantial connection with the house, and then to ask if there are physical signs of remaining in occupation and an intention to return. The conept of "occupying as an only or principal home", it is suggested, is a singular unified concept, and should not be broken down into constituent parts.

---

[73] (1988) 20 H.L.R. 98.
[74] (1988) 20 H.L.R. 98.

CHAPTER 10

MISCELLANEOUS

1. PREMIUMS

Introduction

The Rent Acts always prohibited premiums in order to avoid tenancies having their rents restricted and these rents then being inflated by hidden charges. The interpretation of when a payment is a premium has been the scene of quite extensive litigation, mainly in England and Wales. The statutory control is found in Part VIII of the Rent (Scotland) Act 1984. Most of the provisions of Part VIII were incorporated into the Housing (Scotland) Act 1988[1] and references to "tenancies" in this section should be read as meaning protected and assured tenancies. A premium includes any fine or similar penalty and any other pecuniary consideration paid in addition to rent.[2] Certain specific offences are created in Part VIII and the penalty is a fine on level 3 of the standard scale.[3]

10–01

Protected tenancies—prohibition of premiums and loans

The 1984 Act makes it unlawful for any person to require payment as a condition of the renewal or continuance of a protected tenancy whether by way of a loan or a premium.[4] It also makes payment unlawful in relation to grants of tenancies. The prohibition applies not only to landlords, but also to tenants, agents and others.[5] The payment must be pecuniary.[6]

10–02

Assignation of tenancies—prohibition of premiums and loans

The prohibition also applies to payment for the assignation of a tenancy.[7] Again, the party requiring payment, as well as any other party receiving the money, is covered.[8] Excepted from the prohibition are payments such as for the alteration or improvement of any fixtures or goodwill payments.[9] Where unreasonable sums are required for improvements or goodwill, then these are recoverable[10] and the convicting court may order such repayment.[11]

10–03

---

[1] Housing (Scotland) Act 1988, s. 27.
[2] s. 90(1).
[3] For scale, see the Criminal Procedure (Scotland) Act 1995, s. 225(2).
[4] 1984 Act, s. 82.
[5] *Farrell v. Alexander* [1977] A.C. 59.
[6] *Elmderle Estates Ltd v. White* [1960] A.C. 528.
[7] Rent (Scotland) Act 1984, s. 83.
[8] *ibid.* s. 83(1) and (2).
[9] *ibid.* s. 83(4).
[10] *ibid.* s. 88(1).
[11] *ibid.* s. 83(7).

Excessive price for furniture

10–04   Where the purchase of any furniture has been required as a condition of the grant, renewal, continuance or assignation of a tenancy, then this may be treated as a premium. This will occur where the sum charged for the furniture exceeds the reasonable price of the furniture.[12] This is determined by looking at whether the furniture is offered at a price which the offeror knows or ought to know is unreasonably high or otherwise seeks to obtain such a price for the furniture or fails to provide a written inventory of the furniture specifying the price sought for each item.[13]

Local authorities in situations where they have reasonable grounds for suspecting that an offence has been committed in connection with excessive prices for furniture may, on notice, obtain entry to the house and inspect the furniture.[14] Failure to allow access is a separate offence.[15]

2. DEPOSITS

10–05   For the avoidance of doubt, following decisions in the courts in England,[16] the legislation specifies that any deposit returnable at the termination of the agreement and given as security for the tenant's obligations for accounts for supplies of gas, electricity, telephone or other domestic supplies and for damage to the house or its contents is not a premium provided that it does not exceed two months' rent.[17]

3. RENT BOOKS

10–06   Under a protected or statutory tenancy, where rent is payable weekly the landlord must provide a rent book or other similar document for use in respect of the dwelling-house.[18] If the landlord fails to comply there is provision for a fine not exceeding level 4 on the standard scale.[19] The rent book must comply with the prescribed requirements.[20] The same requirement applies to assured tenancies.[21] There must be rent books for those paying rent weekly and certain information is prescribed by regulation.[22] This includes the address of the house, name, address and telephone number of the landlord (and agent if any), rent, type of assured tenancy, rent adjustment, determination by a rent assessment committee, security of tenure and housing benefit. Again, failure to provide a rent book is

---

[12] Rent (Scotland) Act 1984, s. 86.
[13] *ibid.* s. 87.
[14] *ibid.* s. 87(2)–(5).
[15] *ibid.* s. 87(7).
[16] See *R. v. Ewing* (1977) 65 Cr.App.R. 4 and cases cited in Megarry (11th ed., 1988), Vol. 1, p. 687.
[17] 1984 Act, s. 90(3).
[18] *ibid.* s. 113(1).
[19] *ibid.* s. 113(2). For scale, see the Criminal Procedure (Scotland) Act 1995, s. 225(2).
[20] Rent Regulation (Forms and Information Etc.) (Scotland) Regulations 1991 (S.I. 1991 No. 1521) as amended by S.I. 1993 No. 647.
[21] Housing (Scotland) Act 1988, s. 30(4).
[22] Assured Tenancies (Rent Book) (Scotland) Regulations 1988 (S.I. 1988 No. 2085) as amended by S.I. 1993 No. 649.

an offence punishable with a level 4 fine.[23] In the assured tenancy legislation, it is also provided that where a rent book offence is committed by a body corporate and it is proved to have been committed with the consent or connivance of or to be attributable to any neglect on the part of a director, manager, secretary or other similar officer of the body corporate, or a person purporting to act in any such capacity, that person as well as the body corporate is guilty of an offence.[24]

4. ACCOMMODATION AGENCIES

The Accommodation Agencies Act 1953 was made permanent by the Expiring Laws Act 1969 and has not been effective in dealing with the problem it addresses. It makes it a criminal offence to demand or accept payment for registering or undertaking to register the name or requirements of any person seeking the tenancy of a house.[25] It is also illegal to demand or accept payment for supplying or undertaking to supply to any person the addresses or other particulars of houses to let.[26] Finally, the legislation makes it an offence to issue an advertisement, list or other document describing any house as being to let without the authority of the owner or agent.[27] The statute does not apply to sums paid by potential landlords,[28] nor does it cover solicitors' legal work,[29] nor shop or newspaper adverts.[30] Its provisions "are not nearly as well-known as they ought to be".[31]

10–07

5. OVERCROWDING

Introduction

In the past the extent of overcrowding has been taken as a valuable indicator of housing need and its elimination is one of the goals of housing policy. Overcrowding is an offence punishable by a fine. However, from the nineteenth century on there has always been a limitation, in practice, in that authorities have been loath to operate the overcrowding legislation if this moves people from overcrowded accommodation into a situation of no accommodation at all. Where tenants are overcrowded a landlord is allowed to recover possession under the Rent (Scotland) Act 1984.[32] In practice this did not seem to occur frequently.[33]

10–08

Since the introduction of the Housing (Homeless Persons) Act 1977 certain obligations towards homeless people have rested on local authorities. This should allow a co-ordinated policy in this respect. In fact, since the amendments to the

---

[23] 1984 Act, s. 30(6).
[24] *ibid.* s. 30(7).
[25] s. 1(1)(a).
[26] s. 1(1)(b).
[27] s. 1(1)(c).
[28] s. 1(2).
[29] s. 1(3).
[30] s. 1(4).
[31] *Crouch and Lees v. Haridas* [1972] 1 Q.B. 158 at 166.
[32] See para. 5–86.
[33] However, see *Trustees of Henry Smith's Charity v. Bartosiak-Jentys* (1992) 24 H.L.R. 627 where this was successfully done.

homelessness legislation following the *Puhlhofer* case,[34] and now contained in Part II of the Housing (Scotland) Act 1987, one of the definitions of homelessness specifically includes those whose accommodation is overcrowded and may endanger the health of the occupants.[35] In addition, an authority does not fulfil its obligations towards homeless people if it offers accommodation which is overcrowded.[36]

Local authority powers to deal with overcrowded rented housing

10–09   A local authority must carry out an inspection of its district to identify houses that are overcrowded and report the results of that inspection to the Secretary of State.[37] The report must indicate the additional accommodation required to put an end to the overcrowding and make proposals to make this available. The inspection must be carried out at such times as it appears to the local authority that there is occasion to do so or as the Secretary of State directs. Subject to the various exemptions and exceptions noted below, local authorities must enforce the overcrowding provisions of the legislation and do not have a discretion to ignore overcrowding in their districts.

Local authorities must inform landlords and the occupiers of a house, in writing, of the permitted numbers of persons in relation to the house as soon as they have ascertained the floor area of the rooms.[38] They also have the power to require occupiers to give them a written statement within 14 days of the number, ages and sexes of persons sleeping in the house.[39] Failure to respond or making a false statement is an offence punishable by a level 1 fine.[40]

It is an offence punishable by a level 1 fine to let property without telling the prospective tenant the permitted number of persons allowed in the property.[41]

Definition of "overcrowding"

10–10   Originally the overcrowding provisions applied only to houses below a certain rateable value. However, following the changes to the homelessness legislation after *Puhlhofer* noted above, it was realised that many houses were above the level set in 1935. This was amended in the Housing (Scotland) Act 1988 where Schedule 8, paragraph 3 provides that the overcrowding provisions apply to all houses. "House" is defined as meaning "any premises used or intended to be used as a separate dwelling".[42] It has been held that this does not include caravans on a local authority travellers' site, but may include a static mobile home on a permanent site.[43]

The Housing (Scotland) Act 1987, Pt VII defines overcrowding in two alternative ways. A property is overcrowded if it contravenes either the room standard or the space standard.

---

[34] *Puhlhofer v. Hillingdon LBC* [1986] 1 All E.R. 467.
[35] Housing (Scotland) Act 1987, s. 24(3)(d).
[36] *ibid.* s. 32(5).
[37] *ibid.* s. 146.
[38] *ibid.* s. 148.
[39] *ibid.* s. 147.
[40] For scale, see the Criminal Procedure (Scotland) Act 1995, s. 225(2).
[41] See below concerning the delayed implementation of this provision.
[42] 1987 Act, s. 151.
[43] *Stewart v. Inverness D.C.*, 1992 S.L.T. 690.

The room standard

The room standard is contravened when the number of persons sleeping in a 10–11
house and the number of rooms available as sleeping accommodation is such
that two persons of opposite sexes who are not living together as husband and
wife must sleep in the same room.

Children below the age of 10 are not counted in this calculation. A room is
available as sleeping accommodation not only if it is normally a bedroom, but
also if it is used as a living room.

The space standard

The space standard is contravened when the number of persons sleeping in 10–12
the rooms available as sleeping accommodation exceeds the permitted number.
Sleeping accommodation includes bedrooms and living rooms. No account is
taken of rooms having a floor area of less than 50 square feet. This means that
in looking to either the number of rooms or their size, accommodation such as,
for example, an 8 by 6 feet boxroom is assumed not to exist.

In making the space standard calculations children are treated as follows:

children 10 plus	1 full unit (*i.e.* adult)
children between 1 and under 10	0.5 of a unit
children below 1	0

In deciding how many people can be accommodated there are two alternative
methods of calculation. The lesser number is allowed, looking at either room
numbers or room size.

Number of rooms. The following numbers are permitted[44]:   10–13

Number of rooms	Number of persons
1	2
2	3
3	5
4	7.5
5 or more	2 per room

(As indicated, the total only includes rooms with a square footage in excess of 50.)

Room size. In calculating how many people are permitted in a house, it is 10–14
necessary to carry out a calculation depending on the size of the individual
rooms using the following statutory criteria:

Floor area of room	Number of persons
110 sq ft or more	2
90 sq ft plus (below 110)	1.5
70 sq ft plus (below 90)	1
50 sq ft plus (below 70)	0.5
below 50 sq ft	0

There is provision for the Secretary of State to make regulations as to how these
square-footage calculations are to be made, what is to be excluded and how
rooms below a certain height should be treated.

---

[44] Housing (Scotland) Act 1987, s. 137.

Increases and exemptions

10–15   There are provisions for temporary area increases,[45] exceptions for children reaching the age of one or 10, exceptions for temporary visitors, licensed increases and exceptions for holiday visitors.

The Secretary of State may authorise increases in the number of persons permitted. He may do this when a local authority satisfies him that such houses constitute so large a proportion of its housing accommodation in its district or part of it that it would be impracticable to use the statutory space/room standards. Modifications are permitted for a period not exceeding three years. There may be different modifications for different classes of houses. After consultations with the local authority there may be variation or revocation of such an order by the Secretary of State.

In addition, where a child attains the age of either one or 10 (and would normally be counted as a half or go up to a full unit value), no offence is committed if the house would become statutorily overcrowded provided certain conditions are met:

(1)   the persons sleeping in the house continue to be those who were there at the time the child became one or 10;
(2)   the occupier does not refuse an offer of suitable alternative accommodation;
(3)   the occupier secures the removal of any person living in the house who is not a member of his family and whose removal is reasonably practicable.[46]

10–16   The occupier of a house is not guilty of an offence if the overcrowding is caused by a temporary resident whose stay does not exceed 16 days and to whom lodging is given otherwise than for gain. This covers short visits from both relatives and friends.[47] The occupier or intending occupier of premises may apply to the local authority for a licence increasing the number of occupants in excess of the permitted number. The authority may grant the licence if it appears that there are exceptional circumstances and that it is expedient to do so. It must specify the number permitted. The licence can be revoked by giving at least one month's notice to the occupier that the licence will cease to be in force; unless revoked, such a licence continues in force for such period not exceeding 12 months as is specified in the licence.[48] Local authorities have the power to make arrangements to increase permitted numbers to deal with any seasonal increase of holiday visitors in their area. This may be done generally for all houses or houses of a specified class. Any schemes must be approved by the Secretary of State, but may not operate for more than 16 weeks in the year.[49]

Delayed implementation of certain provisions

10–17   The provisions relating to the power of the Secretary of State to increase the permitted number of persons temporarily (section 138), the offence of an occupier allowing overcrowding to occur (section 139), the exemption from this offence for overcrowding by virtue of children attaining the ages of one and ten (section 140),

---

[45] ss. 138, 151.
[46] s. 140.
[47] s. 141.
[48] s. 142.
[49] s. 143.

and the offence of landlords not informing occupiers of the permitted number of persons (section 144) have been delayed until such time as an appointed day has been given by the Secretary of State for the provisions to come into effect.[50] Only two localities were given such appointed days—the Dysart ward of the Burgh of Kirkcaldy and the Burgh of Queensferry.

6. HOUSES IN MULTIPLE OCCUPATION

There are special provisions for the supervision and control of properties where   10–18 facilities are shared, such as bedsits. This has been a growing problem with the growth of new household formation and the lack of availability of self-contained rented accommodation. The law on this topic is to be found in Part VIII of the Housing (Scotland) Act 1987.

Definition of houses in multiple occupation

Houses in multiple occupation are defined as[51]:   10–19

  (a)   houses which are let in lodgings, in whole or in part;
  (b)   houses which are occupied by members of more than one family;
  (c)   buildings which comprise separate dwellings, two or more of which lack either or both of the following:
    (i) sanitary convenience accessible only to those living in the dwelling;
    (ii) personal washing facilities accessible only to those living in the dwelling.

This means that there may be more than one household in the dwelling or that there are shared toilet and washing facilities. If the living accommodation is self-contained, but there is a shared bathroom this would come within the definition of a house in multiple occupation. However, a situation in which there are two or more completely self-contained flats in a house would not result in it being a house in multiple occupation.

There has been a limited amount of litigation on aspects of the equivalent   10–20 English provisions—found in the Housing Act 1961 and now the Housing Act 1985, Part XI, as amended by Part II of the Housing Act 1996. The case *Silbers v. Southwark London Borough Council*[52] concerned a lodging house for women. The question arose as to whether this was "occupied" in terms of the multiple-occupancy legislation. The accommodation was of a dormitory kind available from 4p.m. to 10 a.m. Personal belongings were stored in lockers. The number of times women stayed there varied from a night to a few weeks and, in some cases, for years. There were no cooking facilities and no food was provided. Cold water was available and could be heated over the fire. The Court of Appeal accepted that "occupied" did not require individuals to have exclusive occupation and was broadly synonymous with "lived in".

Simmons v. Pizzey[53] dealt with a slightly different set of circumstances in that the case centred on occupation of a house in Chiswick as a battered women's refuge. The house, on occasions, was inhabited by up to 75 women and children.

---

[50] s. 151 (as amended by the Housing (Scotland) Act 1988, Sched. 7, para. 6).
[51] s. 152.
[52] (1978) 76 L.G.R. 421.
[53] [1979] A.C. 37.

Here the local authority tried to take action to control the numbers living in the refuge to a maximum of 36. It was claimed that the legislation did not apply because the residents formed a single household and that there was no evidence otherwise. The House of Lords was of the view that whether a group of people formed a single household was a matter of fact and degree, and that no one properly directing themselves could conclude that 75 people constituted a single household. Most recently, in *R. v. Hackney London Borough Council, ex parte Thrasyvoulou*,[54] the question was raised whether a hotel used as interim accommodation for homeless families under the homelessness legislation could be said to be occupied by the homeless families who passed through it. The local authority attempted to serve notices in terms of the overcrowding legislation on the owners of the premises. Although the premises were referred to as "hotels" and this indicated that they were lived in by people in transit, without any degree of permanence, this was not accepted as depriving the occupants of protection through the multiple occupancy provisions. The Court of Appeal explained their thinking:

> "where one has, as here, persons who are homeless, and whose only residence (even though for the time being until they are found a permanent home) is the premises in question, it would be a misuse of language to say that they were not occupying those premises or living at the premises."[55]

Some doubt has been cast on how the legislation can be effectively used by the subsequent Divisional Court decision in *R. v. Hackney London Borough Councils, ex parte Evenbray*,[56] where there was an attempt to use the multiple-occupancy provisions to control the standards in a hotel annexe used to accommodate homeless families. The *Thrasyvoulou* case was not cited in *Evenbray* although the judge did accept that a hotel was a "house" and, therefore, technically covered by the multiple occupancy rules. He seemed concerned at the use of a section which indicated that the authority regarded the property as being defective in relation to storage, preparation and the cooking of food when these facilities were entirely absent from the hotel (and justifiably in the view of Mr Justice Kennedy).

Dealing with multiple-occupancy housing

10–21   Part VIII of the 1987 Act provides for registration schemes, management codes, special overcrowding regulations and control orders in relation to multiple-occupancy housing. To this list must be added licensing, under the Civil Government (Scotland) Act 1982.

Registration schemes

10–22   Local authorities have the power to make a register for their district of houses in multiple occupation (HMOs).[57] Their proposals must be confirmed by the Secretary of State, with or without modification. The local authority must publish notice of its intention to submit a registration scheme to the Secretary of State in newspapers. If the scheme is confirmed, the authority must give it further

---

[54] (1986) 84 L.G.R. 823.
[55] *ibid.* at 828.
[56] (1988) 86 L.G.R. 210.
[57] Housing (Scotland) Act 1987, s. 152.

publicity, indicating where the details of the scheme can be examined at all reasonable hours. The register may cover the whole district or part of it, and can be for only some of the kinds of property specified above in the definition of houses in multiple occupation. A registration scheme may vary or revoke a previous scheme; revocation of a registration scheme requires the Secretary of State's consent. There is no obligation on local authorities to institute registration schemes. The registration scheme may require the owners of the houses covered by the scheme to notify the local authority of registrable houses. Failure to comply is an offence punishable by a level 2 fine.

A registration scheme is limited in that it merely provides information about certain HMOs. It is not a licence or guarantee of quality. To be entered on the register, HMOs do not need to meet minimum standards. Local authorities, according to SHELTER, may be able to gather such information from other sources and may, therefore save considerable time and administrative work by not having a registration scheme.[58]

Management codes

The Secretary of State has the power to make regulations to provide a code   10–23 for the management of houses let in lodgings or occupied by members of more than one family.[59] The regulations in the code are designed to ensure that the person managing the house let in lodgings or occupied by members of more than one family observes proper standards of management. Subject to the general management test, the specific issues mentioned in the statute, as covered by the regulations, are to ensure the repair, maintenance, cleansing and good order of:

    (a)   all means of water supply and drainage in the house;
    (b)   kitchens, bathrooms and water closets used in common by persons living in the house;
    (c)   sinks and wash-basins used in common by persons living in the house;
    (d)   the roof and windows forming part of the house;
    (e)   common staircases, corridors and passage ways;
    (f)   outbuildings, yards and gardens used in common by persons living in the house;

and to make satisfactory arrangements for the disposal of refuse and litter from the house.

The management regulations may make different provision for different types   10–24 of houses and may provide for keeping a register of those who are managers of houses. Owners may be required to give information to the local authority and, particularly, details of acquisition or disposal. There may be obligations on occupiers to allow the manager to carry out effectively the duties imposed on him. The manager may be required to display the regulations in a suitable position in the house. Failure to comply with the regulations is an offence punishable by a level 3 fine.[60]

The code is to be applied when the house is in an unsatisfactory state in consequence of failure to maintain proper standards of management. The local

[58] Shelter (Scotland), "Houses in Multiple Occupation: Possible Changes in the Law" (Oct. 1988).
[59] s. 156.
[60] For scale, see the Criminal Procedure (Scotland) Act 1995, s. 225(2).

authority must serve a notice on the owner and such tenants as it knows of, not less than 21 days before making an order to apply the management code to a property.[61] It must also post such a notice in the house (and in a part of the house accessible to all the residents). The authority must give those persons on whom the notice is served an opportunity to make representations about the proposal to make a management order. When an order is made, it comes into effect on the date it is made and must be served within seven days on the owners and known tenants and, again, a copy must be posted in the house in a position accessible to those living in it. The local authority may, at any time, revoke the order on application by a person having an estate or interest in the house.

10–25   An order in force must be registered in the Land Register/General Register of Sasines as soon as practicable and any notice of revocation must also be recorded.[62] The owner or tenant may, within 14 days from the latest date of service, appeal to the sheriff on the ground that the making of the order was unnecessary.[63] The sheriff must take into account the state of the house at the time when the local authority served its notice of intention to make the order. The sheriff must disregard any improvement in the state of the house between the times of serving the notice and his decision, unless he is satisfied that effective steps have been taken to ensure that the house will in future be kept in a satisfactory state. This means he must ignore mere window-dressing.

Action by local authorities to ensure better conditions in multiple occupancy property

10–26   There are three kinds of notice which may be served in connection with the operation of good standards of management in houses in multiple occupation.

10–27   **Notice requiring compliance with the management code.**[64] Works to ensure compliance with the management code can be required by a local authority where, in its opinion, the condition of the house is defective in consequence of neglect. In such circumstances the authority can serve on the persons managing the house a notice specifying the works to be done to make good the neglect. These works must be executed within the time specified in the notice, but at least 21 days must be given. The period may be extended by written permission of the local authority. If there are difficulties in ascertaining who is manager of the property, then the notice may be served by delivery on some person on the premises and addressed to the "manager of the house".

10–28   **Notice requiring compliance with standards.**[65] The local authority may serve a notice in relation to housing let in lodgings or occupied by more than one family which is so defective as not to be reasonably suitable for occupation by those individuals or households or both, who are accommodated for the time being on the premises. The notice must be served on either the person having control of the house or the factor/agent or any tenant. In addition, the authority must notify any mortgage holder. The test of whether the property is defective depends on the following matters:

---

[61] s. 157.
[62] s. 159.
[63] s. 158.
[64] s. 160.
[65] s. 161.

(a) natural and artificial lighting,
(b) ventilation,
(c) water supply,
(d) personal washing facilities,
(e) drainage and sanitary conveniences,
(f) facilities for the storage, preparation and cooking of food, and for the disposal of waste water,
(g) installations for space heating or for the use of space-heating appliances.

The notice must give a specified time, with a minimum of 21 days, to carry out the specified works. If the local authority is satisfied that there has been a reduction in the number of occupants thereby rendering the work unnecessary and that this level of occupancy will either be maintained or further reduced, then it may give a written notice of withdrawal.

It should be noted, however, that the legislation gives no guidance to local 10–29 authorities on how to assess adequate facilities or amenities for the number of residents. There is no guidance either in the form of statute, regulations or circular. Some local authorities (including Edinburgh) passed a policy that fixed a ratio of five users to one bathroom, whilst others (including Glasgow) set the ratio for the same amenity at seven to one.[66]

Notice requiring provision of means of escape from fire.[67] If it appears to the 10–30 local authority that a house let either in lodgings or occupied by members of more than one family is not provided with such means of escape from fire as the authority consider necessary, it may serve a notice specifying the works needed to provide such means of escape. Again, notice may be served on the person having control, or the tenant or the factor/agent and such notice must stipulate a minimum of 21 days to do the work. Mortgage holders must also be informed. In *Pearson v. City of Glasgow District Council*[68] an owner of a house in multiple occupancy appealed against a section 162 notice, arguing that the requirement of providing means of escape from fire was unreasonable. He had had difficulties in obtaining permission from his neighbours to carry out the work, although he had not applied to the sheriff for consent[69] in light of this. He also could not afford to carry out the works on the "B" listed property. Glasgow District Council conceded that it was unlikely that Mr Pearson would obtain planning permission to do so. The sheriff held that it was competent to consider the issue of the costs of carrying out such works. Nevertheless, he held that when the safety of occupants was weighed up against the problems of costs and planning permission, it was reasonable to enforce the section162 notice, even if that meant that the owner was no longer able to rent the property out.

A person who has received either a notice relating to the management code or compliance with standards or a fire escape has 21 days from service of the relevant notice to lodge a written appeal to the sheriff on any of the specified seven grounds.[70] The appellant must serve notices on the other affected parties including any tenants. The sheriff has the power to make an order regarding

[66] H. Currie, "Multiple Occupancy—The Need for Change" (1987) 4 S.H.L.N. 22.
[67] s. 162.
[68] 1994 S.C.L.R. 447.
[69] s. 174.
[70] s. 163.

payment for the work required by any person who has had proper notice of the appeal. If, in an appeal against a compliance with standards notice, the sheriff is satisfied that the number of persons living in the house has been reduced and that adequate steps have been taken to prevent that number being increased again, the sheriff may revoke the order or vary the works required.

10–31   If any one of these three kinds of notice is not complied with, then the authority may itself carry out the work specified in the notice. A notice is not complied with if no appeal is lodged and the period specified elapses, or 28 days passes from the determination of any unsuccessful appeal which is brought. This period may be shortened if, before the expiry of the period of compliance, the person on whom the notice is served informs the authority in writing that they are not able to do the work in question. The local authority may recover expenses for any work it carries out.[71]

It is an offence to fail to comply with any of these notices, punishable by a level 3 fine for an offence concerning management orders and compliance with standards notices, and a level 4 fine for fire escape notices. If there is a subsequent offence in relation to such a notice, this is punishable by a level 4 fine.[72]

Overcrowding in multiple occupation[73]

10–32   In order to remedy or prevent a situation requiring a compliance with standards order a local authority has the power to fix a limit to the number of people who can live in a house in its present condition.[74] This goes back to the powers taken under local legislation by authorities such as Glasgow and Paisley in the middle of the nineteenth century to "ticket" houses. This used to involve affixing a brass plate outside houses indicating the number of persons permitted to live there.[75]

Prior to making a direction, the local authority must give at least seven days' warning to the owner and tenants as well as posting the intended notice in some accessible part of the house. This is to allow representations to be made to them on the making of a direction. Any direction which is then made must be served on the owners and tenants within seven days, and be posted in some place in the house accessible to those living there.[76]

When a notice is in force the local authority has power to require the following information from the occupier concerning the number of individuals staying in the house: the number of families or households these individuals belong to and the names, ages and sex of those individuals, plus the names of the heads of each family or household, as well as the rooms used by the individuals and families/households. Failure to provide the required information or knowingly providing false information is an offence subject to a level 2 fine.[77]

10–33   The making of a direction does not force the owner to lower the numbers directly. Its effect is to make it the duty of the occupier of the house not to permit any individual to take up residence in it so as to increase the number of individuals living in the house above the specified limit and, where the number residing exceeds the permitted number, not to fill any vacancy which arises.

---

[71] s. 164.

[72] For scale, see the Criminal Procedure (Scotland) Act 1995, s. 225(2).

[73] s. 166.

[74] s. 166.

[75] The Glasgow People's Palace exhibition of a tenement "single end" shows one of these from Glasgow.

[76] s. 167.

[77] s. 168. For scale, see the Criminal Procedure (Scotland) Act 1995, s. 225(2).

The occupier is the person who is entitled to permit individuals to take up residence in the house—this could cover an owner, agent or tenant.

The local authority may, on application, revoke any direction or vary it to allow more people to be accommodated, having regard to any works executed in the house or any other change in circumstances.[78] If the local authority refuses to revoke or vary a direction or fails to respond within 42 days from the making of such an application, there is an appeal to the sheriff. The sheriff has the power to revoke or vary a direction in the same way as was available to the authority.[79]

It should be noted that the legislation gives no guidance to local authorities on how to assess an adequate occupancy limit. The standard overcrowding criteria in Part VII do not apply and this has led authorities to devise their own standards, usually on a square metres per person basis. This has no statutory basis and may be challenged in the courts on the grounds of reasonableness. Writing in *Scottish Housing Law News*, Hector Currie took the view that "if different local authorities devised different measures the grounds for a successful appeal by an HMO owner could be compelling."[80]

The question of how this control on numbers is to be operated was discussed   10–34 in *R. v. Hackney London Borough Council, ex parte Evenbray.*[81] Hackney Council attempted to use its powers to control multiple occupancy to deal with a bed and breakfast "hotel" being used for interim accommodation for homeless people. There were 14 bedrooms with six bathrooms, but no kitchen facilities. Occupants were charged for room and breakfast. The local authority decided that the premises should be subject to multiple occupancy standards and went ahead and did this in relation to the number of kitchen facilities available. It fixed the numbers permitted at nil, which meant (as noted above) that the current occupants were not to be evicted, but simply not replaced. While accepting that the word "house" was to be widely construed, the court rejected the multiple occupancy approach to a "genuine hotel"; Mr Justice Kennedy regarded this as "patently unreasonable":

> "Of course it is right for a local authority to be anxious to ensure those (homeless) families were properly housed, and it is right that they should have standards, but if as an interim measure they choose to accommodate homeless families in an hotel, they should not then complain, or seek to invoke statutory powers, because the hotel lacks the facilities of a flat or house. If the local authority believes that the homeless families must have those facilities, then it should move the families elsewhere, but it cannot describe the hotel as defective because it lacks the facilities it never offered, and which no normal hotel user would expect to find."[82]

Control orders

In certain circumstances it is possible for a local authority to make a control   10–35 order in respect of any house in its area which is let in lodgings or occupied by members of more than one family.[83] This can occur where either: (a) one of three notices noted above has been served (requiring execution of works; limiting

---

[78] s. 169.
[79] s. 170.
[80] See n. 66.
[81] (1988) 86 L.G.R. 210.
[82] *ibid.* at 220.
[83] s. 178.

number of occupants; applying management code), or (b) it appears to the local authority that the state or condition of the house is such as to call for the taking of action by serving one of those notices, and it appears to the local authority that the living conditions in the house are such that it is necessary to make the control order in order to protect the safety, welfare or health of persons living in the house.

The control order comes into force when it is made and, as soon as practicable after making the order, the local authority must enter the premises and take all such immediate steps as appear to be required to protect the safety, welfare or health of persons living in the house. A copy of the control order must be posted as soon as is practicable in some position where it is accessible to those living in the house. A notice must be served on the owner, tenant, manager and any mortgage holder setting out the effects of the order, the rights of appeal and stating the principal grounds why the local authority has considered it necessary to make the control order. The control order must be recorded in the Land Register/General Register of Sasines as soon as possible. The local authority can exclude part of the house where one of the occupiers is the owner.

10–36   While a control order is in force the local authority has the right to possession of the premises and the right to do what the owner/tenant would be entitled to do, but for the making of the order.[84] If renting out the property the local authority shall not exceed periods of one month or periods requiring more than four weeks' notice. The normal rules relating to local authority tenancies do not apply where property subject to a control order is concerned.

Any tenant who is occupying a property affected by a control order continues with the same rights and obligations as existed prior to the order. The exemption from the coverage of protected and assured tenancies where the local authority is the landlord does not apply where there is a control order in force.[85] The sheriff has the power to modify a lease on the application of the landlord or tenant of any property affected by a control order, including terminating it, if he believes that the necessary work will be done by the owner and the local authority will revoke the order with the tenant gone.[86]

10–37   The local authority must exercise the powers conferred on it to maintain proper standards of management in the house and take such action as is needed to remedy all the matters it would have considered it necessary to remedy if it had not made a control order. This may include furnishing and fitting out the property with such furnishings, fittings and conveniences as appear to it to be required. It must make reasonable provision to insure the property; full accounts must be kept of its expenditure and income from the house, and it must afford to the dispossessed proprietor all reasonable facilities to inspect and take copies of same. Similarly, it must afford the dispossessed proprietor any reasonable facilities requested by him to inspect and examine the house.[87]

After a control order has been made, the local authority must prepare a management scheme and, not later than eight weeks after the date on which the control order comes into force, shall serve a copy of the scheme on the dispossessed proprietor, owner, tenant and mortgage holder or any other recipient of the control order.[88] Any person on whom the control order is served has six

---

[84] s. 179.
[85] s. 180.
[86] s. 185.
[87] s. 182.
[88] s. 184.

weeks from the date of service to appeal to the sheriff against the control order. The sheriff may, before hearing an appeal by a person not having an estate or interest in the property, require him to show that he may be prejudiced by the making of the control order. The grounds of appeal are:

(a) the state or condition of the house was not such as to call for the taking of action;

(b) that it was not necessary to make the control order in order to protect the safety, welfare or health of persons living in the house;

(c) where part of the property was occupied by the dispossessed proprietor, that it was practicable and reasonable for the local authority to exclude part of the property or a greater part than was excluded;

(d) the order is invalid due to some informality, defect or error in or in connection with the control order which has caused the interests of the appellant to be substantially prejudiced.

If a control order is revoked, then a notice must be put in the Land Register/ General Register of Sasines as soon as practicable.

A control order ceases to have effect on the expiry of five years from the date 10–38 it came into force. It can be revoked earlier either on application or on the local authority's initiative. Not less than 21 days before an order is revoked the local authority must serve notice of its intention on the persons occupying the house as well as any owner, tenant or mortgage holder. Where any person applies to the local authority for revocation and this is rejected, he must be informed of the reason for rejection. Where the local authority proposes to revoke a control order on its own initiative it must apply to the sheriff, who may approve one or more of the following:

(a) making of a management code order, or

(b) notice requiring compliance with management code, or

(c) notice relating to compliance with standards, or

(d) notice requiring provision of means of fire escape.

No appeal lies against any order or notice approved by the sheriff at this stage.[89]

Licensing

The Government's intentions to deal more effectively with multiple occupancy 10–39 were outlined by Lord James Douglas-Hamilton at the Institute of Housing Conference in March 1990. The Minister looked forward to HMOs in the 1990s meeting the undoubted demand for shared accommodation in a much more satisfactory way than had often been the case in the past. Licensing was chosen as the appropriate vehicle. A scheme was prepared using the Civic Government (Scotland) Act 1982. Section 44 of this legislation allows the Secretary of State to designate any activity as an activity for which a licence is required. This is done by means of a statutory instrument. Accordingly, in October 1990 a draft order was sent out for consultation. The final version was made on May 22, 1991 and came into force on June 3, 1991.

The Civic Government (Scotland) Act 1982 (Licensing of Houses in Multiple Occupation) Order 1991 designates the use of premises as a house in multiple occupation as an activity for which a licence is required. A house

---

[89] s. 188.

in multiple occupation is defined as the only or principal residence of more than four persons where the people are not all members either of the same family or of one or other of two families.

7. ELECTRICITY AND GAS RESALE PRICE RESTRICTIONS

10–40   There are restrictions on what price can be charged by landlords to their tenants in the resale of electricity and gas.[90] The Director General of Gas Supply must fix maximum prices at which gas may be resold and must publish the prices fixed in such a way as will secure adequate publicity for them.[91] If any landlord resells gas at a price exceeding the maximum price fixed, the amount of the excess (and if the direction provides for it, the interest on that amount) is recoverable by the tenant.[92] The Director General of Electricity Supply has a power to fix maximum prices, but no duty to do so.[93–95] If the landlord supplies at a higher price than that laid down it does not constitute a criminal offence.

8. AGRICULTURAL EMPLOYEES

10–41   As has been noted above there are a number of instances where the rules of Scots landlord and tenant law apply differently to agricultural property and provide less security of tenure rights to those occupying such property. There are special rules laid down in the Rent (Scotland) Act 1984[96] where the tenant[97] occupied premises under the terms of his employment as a person employed in agriculture.[98] The tenant is covered as well as the widow (or widower) of the tenant residing with him at his death or if there is no widow (or widower) any member of the tenant's family residing with him at his death.[99]

Where the order for possession is made within six months beginning with the date when the former tenancy came to an end, then in addition to the discretionary power of postponement noted below the court must suspend the order for possession for the remainder of six months[1] unless satisfied that one of four matters is applicable:

  (a)   that other suitable accommodation is or will be made available to the occupier, or
  (b)   that the efficient management of any agricultural land or the efficient carrying on of any agricultural operations would be seriously prejudiced, or

---

[90] The rights of consumers to supply of gas and electricity are outlined in Gray, Benison and Gallacher, *A Guide to Money Advice* (1997), Chap. 14.
[91] Gas Act 1986, s. 37(1) (substituted by the Gas Act 1995, Sched. 3, para. 45).
[92] *ibid.* s. 37(4).
[93–95] Electricity Act 1989, s. 44.
[96] s. 24.
[97] Including a person having a right to occupy premises as a dwelling otherwise than under a tenancy: s. 24(2A).
[98] As defined by the Agricultural Wages (Scotland) Act 1949, s. 17.
[99] Rent (Scotland) Act 1984, s. 24(2).
[1] *ibid.* s. 24(4).

    (c)   greater hardship would be caused by the suspension of the order or the occupier, or

    (d)   any person residing or lodging with him/her has been guilty of conduct which is a nuisance or annoyance to persons occupying other premises.[2]

In addition the sheriff must be satisfied on the general grounds of reasonableness.[3] Where the court does suspend the order for possession it may from time to time vary the period of suspension or terminate it and may vary the terms or conditions imposed.[4]

    The court also has the power to suspend the execution of any order for 10–42 possession of the premises on such terms and conditions as it thinks reasonable. This can mean postponing possession beyond the mandatory six-month period. The terms and conditions which may be imposed include conditions as to payment by the occupier of arrears of rent and compensation to the owner for loss of possession.[5] The criteria for deciding whether to suspend an order for possession using the discretionary powers are whether:

    (a)   other suitable accommodation is or can be made available to the occupier, or

    (b)   the efficient management of any agricultural land or the efficient carrying on of any agricultural operations would be seriously prejudiced, or

    (c)   greater hardship would be caused by the suspension of the execution of the order than by its execution without suspension.[6]

Where there is an order for suspension of a possession order there must be no order for expenses unless it appears to the court that, having regard to the conduct of the owner or the occupier, there are special reasons for making such an expenses order.[7] There is also provision for a payment by way of compensation for damage or loss sustained by the occupier where there is no suspension of the possession order because of misrepresentation or concealment of material facts by the owner where the defence of efficient management or efficient carrying out of operations is put forward.[8]

9. MOBILE HOMES

Security of tenure for tenants of mobile homes is dealt with in the Caravan Sites 10–43 Act 1968.[9] This provides that a person is guilty of an offence if, during the subsistence of a residential contract, he unlawfully deprives the occupier of his occupation on the protected site of any caravan which the occupier is

---

[2] Rent (Scotland) Act 1984, s. 24(4)(a).
[3] *ibid.* s. 24(4)(b).
[4] *ibid.* s. 24(5).
[5] *ibid.* s. 24(3).
[6] *ibid.* s. 24(6).
[7] *ibid.* s. 24(7).
[8] *ibid.* s. 24(8).
[9] Parts I and III were applied to Scotland by the Mobile Homes Act 1975, s. 8.

contractually entitled to occupy as his residence.[10] Eviction of an occupier at the end of a contract can only be done with a court order.[11] It is also a criminal offence to harass the occupier into abandoning occupation of the caravan or into refraining from exercising any rights in respect of the occupation.[12] This covers any acts calculated to interfere with the peace or comfort of the occupier or persons residing with him. It includes persistent withdrawing or withholding of services or facilities reasonably required for the occupation of the caravan as a residence on the site.[13] The legislation provides for the suspension of eviction orders for a period not exceeding 12 months and subject to such terms and conditions as the court thinks reasonable.[14]

The Mobile Homes Act 1983 further adds to the security of tenure of mobile home occupiers. It imposes a number of requirements on the owners of mobile home sites. Like the 1968 Act, the 1983 Act only applies to situations where a person occupies a mobile home as his only or principal home on a "protected site".[15] "Protected sites" are those which have been granted licences for permanent and not holiday or otherwise temporary residence.[16] The owners of protected sites are required to provide mobile home occupiers with a written statement setting out the particulars of the agreement concerning the occupancy of the site. This must be done within three months of the agreement having been made.[17] It will be an implied term of such a agreements that the right to remain on site will subsist until either the occupier gives four weeks notice in writing, planning permission for use of the site as a mobile home site expires (or the owner's interest in the land expires), or the owner obtains a court order. The court will grant permission for the termination of an agreement where it is satisfied that the occupier is in breach of one of the terms of the agreement and has not complied, within a reasonable period, with a notice requiring the remedy of the breach. There is an additional reasonableness requirement.[18] The court will also grant decree where it is satisfied that the occupier is no longer occupying the mobile home as his only or main residence.[19] Further, an agreement may be terminated at the end of five-yearly periods where the court is satisfied that the mobile home is having a detrimental effect on the amenity of the site, or is likely to have such an effect before the end of the next five year period.[20]

Occupiers may lawfully sell the mobile home and assign their rights in the agreement, and the consent of the site owner may not be unreasonably withheld.[21] The mobile home may also be gifted to a member of the occupier's family with the consent of the owner. Such consent may not be unreasonably withheld.

---

[10] Caravan Sites Act 1968, s. 3(1)(a).
[11] *ibid.* s. 3(1)(b).
[12] *ibid.* s. 3(1)(c).
[13] *ibid.*
[14] 1968 Act, s. 4.
[15] Mobile Homes Act 1983, s. 1.
[16] *ibid.* s. 5(1).
[17] *ibid.* s. 1.
[18] *ibid.* Sched. 1, para. 4.
[19] *ibid.* Sched. 1, para. 5.
[20] *ibid.* Sched. 1, para. 6.
[21] *ibid.* Sched. 1, para. 8.

The Act also includes succession provisions.[22] Agreements are enforceable 10–44
against the singular successors of the site owner. Certain persons may enjoy
succession rights to the occupiers. Where the widow or widower of the occupier
was residing with the deceased occupier at the time of death he or she may
succeed. Where there was no such person residing, a member of the deceased's
family may succeed if he was residing with the deceased at the time of death.
"Family" is defined[23] as including spouses, parents, grandparents, children,
grandchildren, siblings, uncles, aunts, nephews and nieces. Relationship by
marriage, half blood and step relationships will be treated as full blood
relationships. Illegitimate children will be treated as the legitimate children of
the mother and reputed father. "Family" also includes those who live together
as husband and wife. The Act unfortunately does not provide any mechanism
whereby a dispute can be resolved between more than one individual who is
entitled to succeed.

---

[22] Mobile Homes Act 1983, s. 3.
[23] *ibid.* s. 5.

APPENDIX

STATUTORY INSTRUMENTS

Appendix

Protected Tenancies (Exceptions) (Scotland) Regulations 1974

(S.I. 1974 No. 1374)

[14th August 1974]

In exercise of the powers conferred on me by section 2(4) of the Rent (Scotland) Act 1971 as added by section 2(2) of the Rent Act 1974 and of all other powers enabling me in that behalf, I hereby make the following regulations:—

Citation, commencement and interpretation
   1.—(1) These regulations may be cited as The Protected Tenancies (Exceptions) (Scotland) Regulations 1974 and shall come into operation on 14th August 1974.
   (2) The Interpretation Act 1889 shall apply for the interpretation of these regulations as it applies for the interpretation of an Act of Parliament.

Specified institutions
   2. There are hereby specified for the purposes of section 2(1)(bb) of the Rent (Scotland) Act 1971 as inserted by section 2(1) of the Rent Act 1974 (tenancies excepted from definition of "protected tenancy") the educational institutions set out in the Schedule annexed hereto and any other institution or body of persons by which any of the said educational institutions is provided.

Secure Tenancies (Proceedings for Possession) (Scotland) Order 1980

(S.I. 1980 No. 1389)

[12th September 1980]

In exercise of the powers conferred upon me by section 14(3) of the Tenants' Rights, Etc. (Scotland) Act 1980 and of all other powers enabling me in that behalf, I hereby make the following order:—

   1. This order shall be cited as the Secure Tenancies (Proceedings for Possession) (Scotland) Order 1980, and shall come into operation on 3rd October 1980.

   2. Any notice served under section 14 of the Tenants' Rights, Etc. (Scotland) Act 1980 on a tenant under a secure tenancy, within the meaning of Part II of that Act, shall be in the form set out in the Schedule to this order.

SCHEDULE

NOTICE OF PROCEEDINGS FOR RECOVERY OF POSSESSION

This notice is to inform you,   (name(s) of secure
tenant(s)) that   , being the landlord of the
dwelling-house at
may, at any time during the period of six months beginning on

(see Note 2), raise proceedings for possession of that dwelling-house on the following grounds:

which is/are deemed to fall within the terms of paragraph(s)   (see Note 3) of Part I of Schedule 2 to the Tenants' Rights, Etc. (Scotland) Act 1980.

Signed
Date

Notes for guidance of tenants

1. This notice is a warning that your landlord may be going to raise proceedings against you in the sheriff court to gain possession of your house. It is not a notice to quit and it does not affect your right to continue living in the house or your obligation to pay rent. You cannot be evicted from your house unless the sheriff court grants your landlord a possession order. You should read the rest of the notes carefully to find out what might happen if your landlord does start possession proceedings against you.

2. Now that this notice has been served on you there is no other preliminary step which your landlord need take before starting court action against you for possession of the house referred to in the notice. The date given in the notice is the earliest date on which your landlord can take court action. After that date the landlord is allowed to start possession proceedings against you at any time during the following six months. If that six month period passes without possession proceedings being started, your landlord would have to serve another one of these notices on you before it could start court action for possession and that notice would, like this one, have to give you at least four weeks' warning before court action could be started.

3. Your landlord has explained in the notice the reason or reasons why it is considering taking possession proceedings against you. In order to help you understand your legal position if proceedings are taken, the paragraph number (referring to Part I of Schedule 2 of the Tenants' Rights, Etc. (Scotland) Act 1980) which applies to your landlord's reason for considering possession proceedings is given near the end of the notice. (If, for example, your landlord's reason for considering possession proceedings is rent arrears, the paragraph number given will be 1.) If the number is between 1 and 7, read note 4 below; if the number is between 8 and 14, read note 5 below. If the number is 10, read paragraph 6 below as well as paragraph 5.

4. If the paragraph number given near the end of the notice is between 1 and 7, and your landlord does take court action for possession against you, the sheriff court will be concerned with whether the facts on which your landlord is founding are correct (for example, where you are in rent arrears if that is the reason which your landlord has given) and, if it decides that the facts are correct, whether it is reasonable that you should be evicted, which will depend on the circumstances of your case. The court can postpone a decision on the case and impose conditions on you, for example about paying off rent arrears, if it wishes; if you obey the conditions the court would not normally grant your landlord a possession order afterwards. If a possession order is granted against you your landlord will have to evict you once the date given in the order is passed, unless it decides to grant you a new tenancy of your house. If it evicts you it will not be under any obligation to rehouse you. Any action which might be taken by a local authority under its powers and duties in relation to some categories of homeless people is a separate matter and you should not assume that you will be entitled to rehousing.

5. If the paragraph number given near the end of the notice is between 8 and 14, the court must grant a possession order against you provided the landlord can show that it (the landlord) has arranged for suitable alternative accommodation to be available to you. In considering whether alternative accommodation offered to you is suitable the court has to take account of the following points:—

(*a*) how near it is to the place where you or any of your family work or go to school, college, etc., compared to the house which you live in now;

(*b*) how *large* a house you and your family need;

(*c*) its *character* compared to the house which you live in now;

(*d*) the *terms* on which it is offered to you compared to the terms of the tenancy of the house which you live in now;

(*e*) if the landlord provides any furniture in the house you live in now, whether the house offered will be provided with furniture which is as useful to you;

(*g*) any special needs of you and your family.

Your landlord must make you an offer of alternative accommodation in writing, and must give you at least fourteen days to make up your mind about the offer. Until your landlord has done this the court will not grant a possession order. Once it has been done the court will grant a possession order unless you tell the court that you do not consider the offer suitable and explain why.

6. If the paragraph number given near the end of the notice is 10, and your landlord only wants to move you out of your house temporarily while works are carried out, the court will make an order entitling you to return to your house once the works are completed. This will not affect your right to suitable alternative accommodation but you will not become the secure tenant of the house that you are moved to, so that you will have no right to stay there once the house which you live in now is ready for you to move back to.

7. If you are at all uncertain about what this notice means of your rights you should obtain advice as quickly as possible. You may be able to get this from your landlord, from a number of sources of free and independent advice such as your local Citizens' Advice Bureau or Housing Advice Centre or from a solicitor. If you need to employ a solicitor, legal aid may be available, depending on your income.

8. These Notes are intended for the guidance of tenants and are not to be regarded as an authoritative interpretation of the law.

Short Tenancies (Prescribed Information) (Scotland) Order 1980

(S.I. 1980 No. 1666)

[30th October 1980]

In exercise of the powers conferred upon me by section 34(4) of the Tenants' Rights, Etc. (Scotland) Act 1980, and of all other powers enabling me in that behalf, I hereby make the following order:—

Citation and commencement

1. This order may be cited as the Short Tenancies (Prescribed Information) (Scotland) Order 1980 and shall come into operation on 1st December 1980.

Prescription of notice

2. Where a landlord intends to grant a short tenancy within the meaning of section 34(1) of the Tenants' Rights, Etc. (Scotland) Act 1980 he shall, before the tenancy is created, serve on the person to whom the tenancy is to be granted a notice in writing in the form, or in a form substantially to the like effect, prescribed in the Schedule to this order.

SCHEDULE

Specimen of the form of notice that a person proposing to accept a short tenancy must receive from the landlord before the tenancy is created.

To...

(Names of proposed tenant)

IMPORTANT — PLEASE READ THIS NOTICE CAREFULLY.
IF THERE IS ANYTHING YOU DO NOT UNDERSTAND YOU
SHOULD GET ADVICE (FOR EXAMPLE, FROM A
SOLICITOR OR A CITIZENS' ADVICE BUREAU) BEFORE
YOU AGREE TO TAKE A SHORT TENANCY.

N.B. This document is important; keep it in a safe place.

1. You are proposing to take a tenancy of the dwelling-house at

....

from .... 19 .... to .... 19 ....
     (day)   (month)   (year)   (day)   (month)   (year)

2. Before you take the tenancy I am required by law to tell you that your tenancy is to be a *protected short tenancy*. Under a short tenancy provided you adhere to the conditions of the tenancy, you are entitled to remain in the dwelling-house for the period specified in paragraph 1. At the end of this period, however, unlike normal Rent Act tenancies, the landlord has an absolute right to repossession if he wants. Full details about short tenancies are given in the Scottish Development Department booklet "Short Tenancies" obtainable free from rent offices, council offices, housing aid centres and citizens' advice bureaux. You are strongly advised to read this booklet before you agree to take a short tenancy.

3. A fair rent of   per   is already registered for the dwelling-house under the Rent (Scotland) Act 1971.

This is the most you can be required to pay as rent until such time as a higher rent is registered. If I apply for a higher rent to be registered you will be told about my application and you will have the opportunity of a consultation with the rent officer if you disagree with the rent I propose. Unless there has been a change of circumstances I cannot apply until three years after the effective date of the existing registration.

3. A fair rent has not yet been registered for the dwelling under the Rent (Scotland) Act 1971. However, a certificate of fair rent under the Rent (Scotland) Act 1971 has been issued in respect of the dwelling-house. The rent specified in the Certificate is   per   and I am required by law to apply for this rent to be registered within 14 days of the start of the tenancy.

This is the most you can be required to pay as rent until such time as a higher rent is registered. If I apply for a higher rent to be registered you will be told about my application and you will have the opportunity of a consultation with the rent officer if you disagree with the rent I propose. Unless there has been a change of circumstances I cannot apply until three years after the effective date of the existing registration.

4. This notice (which does not commit you to taking the tenancy) is given to you on ....19..........

Signed ....

(on behalf of) ....

....

....
(Name and address of landlord)

SPECIAL NOTE FOR EXISTING TENANTS.
IF YOU ARE ALREADY A PROTECTED OR STATUTORY
TENANT UNDER THE RENT (SCOTLAND) ACT 1971
YOUR PRESENT TENANCY CANNOT BY LAW BE
CONVERTED INTO A SHORT TENANCY BUT IF YOU GIVE
IT UP AND TAKE A SHORT TENANCY IN SOME OTHER
ACCOMMODATION YOU WILL ALMOST CERTAINLY HAVE
LESS SECURITY THAN UNDER YOUR EXISTING TENANCY
WHEN THE SHORT TENANCY COMES TO AN END.

The landlord must delete whichever does not apply.

**Cancellation of Registration (Procedure) (Scotland)
Regulations 1980**

(S.I. 1980 No. 1670)

[30th October 1980]

In exercise of the powers conferred upon me by section 46 of the Rent (Scotland) Act 1971, as read with section 44A (4) of that Act as inserted by section 39 of the Housing (Financial Provisions) (Scotland) Act 1972, and as read with section 44B of that Act as inserted by section 50 of the Tenants' Rights, Etc. (Scotland) Act 1980, and of all other powers enabling me in that behalf, I hereby make the following regulations:—

1. These regulations may be cited as the Cancellation of Registration (Procedure) (Scotland) Regulations 1980 and shall come into operation on 1st December 1980.

2. In these regulations—
"the Act" means the Rent (Scotland) Act 1971;
"application" means an application for the cancellation of a registration which is made to the rent officer under section 44A or, as the case may require, under section 44B of the Act;

"rent agreement" means a rent agreement within the meaning of section 44A of the Act, of which a copy accompanies an application made under that section; and

"registration" means the rent registered for the dwelling-house under Part IV of the Act which it is sought to cancel by the application.

3. On receiving an application made under either section 44A or section 44B of the Act, the rent officer may, as the case may require, by notice in writing served on the landlord or the tenant or on both the landlord and the tenant require him or them to give to the rent officer, within such period of not less than 14 days from the service of the notice as may be specified in the notice, such information as he may reasonably require regarding such of the particulars contained in the application or such of the terms of the rent agreement as may be specified in the notice.

4. Where it appears to the rent officer, after making such inquiry, if any, as he thinks fit, and considering any information supplied to him in pursuance of regulation 3 above that in the case of an application made under section 44A of the Act the rent payable under the rent agreement does not exceed a fair rent for the dwelling-house, or that, in the case of an application made under section 44B of the Act, the dwelling-house is not let on or subject to a regulated tenancy, he shall, subject in the case of an application made under section 44A of the Act, to subsection (6) of that section, cancel the registration without further proceedings.

5. Where the rent officer, in carrying out his functions under these regulations in respect of an application made under section 44A of the Act, inspects a dwelling-house, he shall explain to the tenant or to his spouse, if either is present at the inspection, the procedure governing an application.

6.—(1) Where a rent officer does not cancel the registration in pursuance of regulation 4 above, he shall serve a notice under this regulation.

(2) Where the application was made under section 44A of the Act, a notice under this regulation shall be served on the landlord and the tenant informing them that the rent officer proposes, at a time (which shall be not earlier than seven days after the service of the notice) and place specified in the notice to consider, in consultation with the landlord and tenant, or such of them as may appear at that time and place, whether the registration ought to be cancelled.

(3) At any such consultation, the landlord and the tenant may each be represented by a person authorised by him in that behalf, whether or not that person is an advocate or solicitor.

(4) Where the application was made under section 44B of the Act, a notice under this regulation shall be served on the landlord informing him of the reasons why the rent officer cannot cancel the registration.

7. Any notice to be served under these regulations and any notification required to be given under section 44A (i) of the Act (notification of rent officer's decision) may be sent by post or delivered—

    (*a*)   to the landlord and, where there is one, to the tenant at their respective addresses given in the application; or

    (*b*)   where the application is made by an agent on behalf of the landlord or, where there is one, the tenant to that agent at the address of the agent given in the application.

8. The Cancellation of Registration (Procedure) (Scotland) Regulations 1972 are hereby revoked but the revocation shall not affect the validity of any application made or notice given under these regulations before the commencement of these regulations.

Protected Tenancies (Further Exception) (Scotland) Regulations 1982

(S.I. 1982 No. 702)

[21st June 1982]

In exercise of the powers conferred on me by section 2(4) of the Rent (Scotland) Act 1971 and of all other powers enabling me in that behalf, I hereby make the following regulations:—

Citation, commencement and interpretation
    1. These regulations may be cited as The Protected Tenancies (Further Exception) (Scotland) Regulations 1982 and shall come into operation on 21st June 1982.

Specified body
    2. The Royal College of Surgeons of Edinburgh is specified for the purposes of paragraph (bb) of section 2(1) of the said Act of 1971 (tenancies excepted from definition of "protected tenancy").

SCHEDULE

Educational institutions specified for the purposes of section 2(1)(bb) of the Rent (Scotland) Act 1971

    (*a*) Any university, university college and any constituent college, school or hall of a university.
    (*b*) Any Central Institution within the meaning of section 145(10) of the Education (Scotland) Act 1962 and recognised by the Central Institutions (Recognition) (Scotland) Regulations 1973.
    (*c*) Any College of Education within the meaning of section 145(14) of the Education (Scotland) Act 1962 as amended.
    (*d*) Any establishment of Further Education financed and controlled by an Education Authority within the meaning of sections 4 and 145(21) of the Education (Scotland) Act 1962 as amended.
    (*e*) Any approved Association approved by the Secretary of State under Regulation 8 of the Further Education (Scotland) Regulations 1959.

Matrimonial Homes (Form of Consent) (Scotland) Regulations 1982

(S.I. 1982 No. 971)

[1st September 1982]

In exercise of the powers conferred upon me by section 6(3)(*a*)(i), and by that section as applied by section 9(2), of the Matrimonial Homes (Family Protection)

(Scotland) Act 1981, and of all other powers enabling me in that behalf, I hereby make the following regulations:

1.—(1) These regulations may be cited as the Matrimonial Homes (Form of Consent) (Scotland) Regulations 1982 and shall come into operation on 1st September 1982.

(2) In these regulations—

"the Act" means the Matrimonial Homes (Family Protection) (Scotland) Act 1981,

and, in a case where section 9(1) of the Act applies, any reference in these regulations to the entitled spouse and to the non-entitled spouse shall be construed in accordance with section 9(2)(*a*) of the Act.

2. The consent of the non-entitled spouse to any dealing of the entitled spouse relating to a matrimonial home shall be—

    (*a*) where the consent is given in a deed effecting the dealing, in or as nearly as may be in the form set out in Schedule 1 to these regulations; or

    (*b*) where the consent is given in a separate document, in or as nearly as may be in the form set out in Schedule 2 to these regulations.

SCHEDULE 1

CONSENT TO BE INSERTED IN THE DEED EFFECTING THE DEALING

(The following words should be inserted where appropriate in the deed. The consenter should sign as a party to the deed.)

... with the consent of A.B. (*designation*), the spouse of the said C.D., for the purposes of the Matrimonial Homes (Family Protection) (Scotland) Act 1981 ... [To be attested]

SCHEDULE 2

CONSENT IN A SEPARATE DOCUMENT

I, A.B. (*designation*), spouse of C.D. (*designation*), hereby consent, for the purposes of the Matrimonial Homes (Family Protection) Act 1981, to the undernoted dealing of the said C.D. relating to (*here describe the matrimonial home or the part of it to which the dealing relates: see Note 1*).

Dealing referred to:—

(*Here describe the dealing; see Note 2.*)

[To be attested.]

Note 1

The expression "matrimonial home" is defined in section 22 of the Matrimonial Homes (Family Protection) (Scotland) Act 1981 as follows:—

> "'matrimonial home' means any house, caravan, houseboat or other structure which has been provided or has been made available by one or both of the spouses as, or has become, a family residence and includes any garden or other ground or building attached to, and usually occupied with, or otherwise required for the amenity or convenience of, the house, caravan, houseboat or other structure."

Note 2
The expression "dealing" is defined in section 6(2) of the Matrimonial Homes
(Family Protection) (Scotland) Act 1981 as follows:—

> "'dealing' includes the grant of a heritable security and the creation
> of a trust but does not include a conveyance under section 80 of the
> Lands Clauses Consolidation (Scotland) Act 1845."

Secure Tenancies (Abandoned Property) (Scotland) Order 1982

(S.I. 1982 No. 981)

[17th June 1982]

In exercise of the powers conferred upon me by section 19 (4) of the Tenants'
Rights, Etc. (Scotland) Act 1980 and of all other powers enabling me in that
behalf, I hereby make the following order:—

Citation, commencement and interpretation
   1.—(1) This Order may be cited as the Secure Tenancies (Abandoned Property)
(Scotland) Order 1982 and shall come into operation on 2nd August 1982.
   (2) In this Order—
"the Act" means the Tenants' Rights, Etc. (Scotland) Act 1980.

Procedure
   2.—(1) Where property is found in a house to which section 19(2) of the Act
applies the landlord shall immediately serve notice on the tenant that the property is
available for delivery into his or his agent's hands at a place specified in the notice
on payment of any sum payable in terms of article 5 (1) of this Order and that if the
property is not collected by the tenant from the specified place on or before the date
specified in the notice (being a date not less than 289 days from the date of service
of the notice and not earlier than the date on which the landlord repossesses the
house) it may be disposed of in accordance with the other provisions of this Order.
   (2) The notice provided for in paragraph (1) of this article shall be served by
posting it to the tenant in a recorded delivery letter addressed to him at his last
known address or by leaving the notice for him at that address.

   3.—(1) Where property in respect of which a notice under article 2 of this
Order has been served on the tenant has not been collected by the date specified
in the notice the property shall, subject to paragraph (2) of this article, be stored
by the landlord for a period of six months from the date on which the landlord
took possession of the dwelling-house and after expiry of the said period the
landlord may sell any item remaining in its custody.
   (2) Paragraph (1) of this article shall not apply to any property the value of
which would not, in the opinion of the landlord, exceed the amount which the
landlord would be entitled to deduct under article 7 of this Order from the
proceeds of any sale of such item.

   4. Where property to which paragraph (1) of the article 3 does not apply and
in respect of which a notice under article 2 has been served on the tenant has not
been collected by the date specified in the notice the landlord may sell or
otherwise dispose of it in the manner which in its opinion is most expedient.

5.—(1) Subject to paragraph (2) of this article, where at any time prior to the sale or disposal of property under this Order the tenant, or any other person who appears to the landlord to have a right of ownership or of possession in the property, arranges for delivery to himself of any item the landlord shall relinquish custody of that item upon receipt of a payment equal to the amount of any expense incurred by the landlord in complying with this Order in relation to that item or such lesser amount (including a nil amount) as the landlord may think fit.

(2) Nothing in this article shall affect the landlord's exercise of its right of hypothec.

6.   Nothing in articles 2 to 5 of this Order shall prevent the exercise by any person or authority of any power under any enactment relating to public health or public safety.

7.   Where a landlord sells property under article 3 of this Order it may deduct from the proceeds of sale the amount of any expense incurred by it in complying with this Order in relation to that property and, if there is any remainder after deduction of such amount, the amount of any arrears of rent.

Register of abandoned property
8.—(1) Landlords shall maintain a register of houses in which property has been found on the exercise of their powers under section 19 of the Act.

(2) A house shall remain on the register until after the expiry of a period of five years from the date on which the landlord took possession of the house.

(3) The landlord shall make the register available for inspection by members of the public at all reasonable times.

Protected Tenancies and Part VII Contracts (Rateable Value Limits) (Scotland) Order 1985

(S.I. 1985 No. 314)

[1st March 1985]

In exercise of the powers conferred on me by sections 1(2) and 64(2) of the Rent (Scotland) Act 1984 and of all other powers enabling me in that behalf, I hereby make the following order:—

Citation and commencement
1. This order may be cited as the Protected Tenancies and Part VII Contracts (Rateable Value Limits) (Scotland) Order 1985 and shall come into operation on 1st April 1985.

Interpretation
2. In this order—
"the Act" means the Rent (Scotland) Act 1984.

Increase in rateable value limits
3. In relation to dwelling-houses comprising or forming part of lands and heritages for which a rateable value is first shown on the valuation roll on or after 1st April 1985, the sum of £600 specified in sections 1(1)(*a*) and 64(1) of the Act shall be increased to £1,600 in each case.

Revocation

4. The Protected Tenancies and Part VII Contracts (Rateable Value Limits) (Scotland) Order 1980 is hereby revoked.

Assured Tenancies (Notices to Quit Prescribed Information) (Scotland) Regulations 1988

(S.I. 1988 No. 2067)

[28th November 1988]

The Secretary of State, in exercise of the powers conferred on him by section 112 of the Rent (Scotland) Act 1984, and of all other powers enabling him in that behalf, hereby makes the following Regulations:

1. These Regulations may be cited as the Assured Tenancies (Notices to Quit Prescribed Information) (Scotland) Regulations 1988 and shall come into force on 2nd January 1989.

2. Where a notice to quit is given by a landlord to terminate an assured tenancy under the Housing (Scotland) Act 1988 that notice shall contain the information set out in the Schedule to these Regulations.

Regulation 2   SCHEDULE

INFORMATION TO BE CONTAINED IN THE NOTICE TO QUIT

1. Even after the notice to quit has run out, before the tenant can lawfully be evicted, the landlord must get an order for possession from the court.

2. If a landlord issues a notice to quit but does not seek to gain possession of the house in question the contractual assured tenancy which has been terminated will be replaced by a statutory assured tenancy. In such circumstances the landlord may propose new terms for the tenancy and may seek an adjustment in rent at annual intervals thereafter.

3. If a tenant does not know what kind of tenancy he has or is otherwise unsure of his rights he can obtain advice from a solicitor. Help with all or part of the cost of legal advice and assistance may be available under the legal aid legislation. A tenant can also seek help from a citizens advice bureau or housing advisory centre.

Assured Tenancies (Exceptions) (Scotland) Regulations 1988

(S.I. 1988 No. 2068)

[28th November 1988]

The Secretary of State, in exercise of the powers conferred on him by section 53(3) of the Housing (Scotland) Act 1988 and paragraph 7 of Schedule 4 to that

Act, and of all other powers enabling him in that behalf, hereby makes the following Regulations:

1. These Regulations may be cited as the Assured Tenancies (Exceptions) (Scotland) Regulations 1988 and shall come into force on 2nd January 1989.

2. For the purposes of paragraph 7 of Schedule 4 to the Housing (Scotland) Act 1988 (tenancies granted to a person who is pursuing or intends to pursue a course of study which cannot be assured tenancies), there are specified the following educational institutions and bodies of persons or classes thereof:—

(*a*) any university, university college and any constituent college, school or hall of a university;

(*b*) any central institution within the meaning of section 135(1) of the Education (Scotland) Act 1980;

¹(*c*) any designated institution within the meaning of section 44(2) of the Further and Higher Education (Scotland) Act 1992;

(*d*) any institution for the provision of further education within the meaning of that section which is administered by an education authority;

²(*dd*) any college of further eduction which is managed by a board of management in terms of Part I of the Further and Higher Education (Scotland) Act 1992;

(*e*) any association approved by the Secretary of State under regulation 8 of the Further Education (Scotland) Regulations 1959; and

(*f*) The Royal College of Surgeons of Edinburgh.

NOTES
¹Substituted by S.I. 1993 No. 995 (effective 5th May 1993).
²Inserted by S.I. 1993 No. 995 (effective 5th May 1993).

Assured Tenancies (Tenancies at a Low Rent) (Scotland) Order 1988

(S.I. 1988 No. 2069)

[28th November 1988]

The Secretary of State, in exercise of the powers conferred on him by section 53(3) of the Housing (Scotland) Act 1988 and paragraph 2 of Schedule 4 to that Act, and of all other powers enabling him in that behalf, hereby makes the following Order:

1. This Order may be cited as the Assured Tenancies (Tenancies at a Low Rent) (Scotland) Order 1988 and shall come into force on 2nd January 1989.

2. For the purposes of paragraph 2 of Schedule 4 to the Housing (Scotland) Act 1988 (tenancies at a low rent), there is specified—

(*a*) in the case of a tenancy where the rent is payable weekly, a rent of £6 per week; and

(*b*) in the case of a tenancy where the rent is payable for any other period, a rent calculated for that period at the rate of £6 per week.

Assured Tenancies (Rent Book) (Scotland) Regulations 1988

(S.I. 1988 No. 2085)

[28th November 1988]

The Secretary of State, in exercise of the powers conferred on him by sections 30(5), 53(3) and 55(1) of the Housing (Scotland) Act 1988, and of all other powers enabling him in that behalf, hereby makes the following Regulations:

1. These Regulations may be cited as the Assured Tenancies (Rent Book) (Scotland) Regulations 1988 and shall come into force on 2nd January 1989.

2. For the purposes of section 30(5) of the Housing (Scotland) Act 1988 (matters relating to which it is the duty of a landlord to provide under an assured tenancy where the rent is payable weekly), every rent book shall contain a notice to the tenant which shall be in the form and relate to such matters as are set out in the Schedule to these Regulations.

Regulation 2   [1]SCHEDULE

Form of notice to be inserted in every rent book used in the case of an assured tenancy where the rent is payable weekly

_____[1]

NOTE
[1]As amended by S.I. 1993 No. 649 (effective 1st April 1993).

_____

INFORMATION FOR TENANT

NOTE 1   Rents for assured and short assured tenancies are freely negotiable between landlord and tenant. In certain circumstances you may, however, have a right to apply to a rent assessment committee for a determination of a market rent.

NOTE 2   Landlords must keep the amounts for rent, furniture and services up to date.

1. Address of the house. ....
....
....

2. Name, address and telephone number of landlord (and agent if any)
....
....
....

Rent to be recovered

3.—(1) If a market rent has been agreed between landlord and tenant (including a case where a market rent for a statutory assured tenancy has been determined by a rent assessment committee but has been varied by agreement between tenant and landlord)—

> (a) the rent payable under the tenancy is £   per week; the date from which the rent applies is   ;
> (b) if furniture or services are provided the amount which is apportioned to them under the tenancy is—
>> Furniture £..........Services £..........

(2) If a market rent has been determined by a Rent Assessment Committee—

> (a) the rent payable under the tenancy as determined by the rent assessment committee is £   per week; the date from which the rent applies is   ;
> (b) if furniture or services are provided the amount to be apportioned to them under the tenancy agreement as determined by the rent assessment committee is—
>> Furniture £..........Services £..........
>
> The date from which these payments apply is

(3) In circumstances in which the landlord is responsible for payment of the council tax the figure for rent payable contained in sub-paragraphs (1)(a) and (2)(b) above includes the tenant's contribution to the council tax.

Type of assured tenancy

4. There are different types of assured tenancy and your rights as tenant in relation to such matters as rent adjustments and security of tenure will depend on the type you have. Your tenancy will be one of three kinds—

> *An assured tenancy*: this is an assured tenancy which is contractual because a tenancy agreement or contract of tenancy is still in force; or
>
> A *statutory assured tenancy*: that is a tenancy which arises after the termination of a contractual assured tenancy but where the tenant continues to retain possession of the house without a new contractual tenancy agreement being created; or
>
> A *short assured tenancy*: that is a special type of assured tenancy in existence for a set period under which the landlord has served on the tenant a notice under section 32 of the Housing (Scotland) Act 1988 informing him that the tenancy is a short assured tenancy. Like a normal assured tenancy a short assured tenancy can either be contractual or statutory. A short assured tenancy gives special rights to a landlord in relation to repossession of the house and special rights to a tenant in relation to applications to a rent assessment committee for a rent determination.

Rent adjustment

5. Rent for most assured and short assured tenancies will be freely negotiated between landlord and tenant. In many cases both parties will also agree on a formal mechanism to allow adjustment to be made on a periodic basis, for example, to allow an annual increase by a certain agreed figure. Such agreements should be clearly set out in the written document which a landlord is obliged to supply to a tenant under an assured or short assured tenancy. Rent adjustment can in certain circumstances be sought other than through a mechanism built into a tenancy agreement. You should note that—

> (a) if yours is a contractual assured tenancy, not later than 12 months after its termination either you or your landlord may, by serving a notice

AT1 on the other, propose new terms for the statutory assured tenancy which arises, and, if appropriate, an adjustment to the rent to take account of the new terms. Both landlord and tenant have a right to refer such new proposals to a rent assessment committee for a determination on the proposed terms and any proposed rent adjustment, but most do so within 3 months of the notice AT1 being served;

(b) if yours is a statutory assured tenancy, your landlord may serve a notice AT2 proposing a new rent at any time (but no more often than once a year). He must give you appropriate notice. If your tenancy is for 6 months or more, he must give 6 months notice. If your tenancy is for less than 6 months, he must give you one month's notice or the same length of time as the duration of the tenancy, whichever is longer. If a notice is served on you there is a right to apply to a rent assessment committee for a determination of a market rent although you must do so before the day on which the new rent proposed by the landlord would take effect;

(c) if yours is a short assured tenancy, paragraphs (a) and (b) will also apply as appropriate. However, if you are a tenant under a short assured tenancy and you believe your rent is excessive you may at any time apply to a rent assessment committee for a rent determination. the Committee will make a determination unless it has previously already done so for the tenancy or unless it has difficulty establishing a market rent for the tenancy because there are insufficient similar tenancies in the locality for comparison purposes;

(d) if yours is a statutory or contractual assured tenancy, your landlord may serve a notice, AT9, proposing a new rent to take account of the council tax during the period commencing on 1st April 1993 and ending on 31st March 1994. If a notice is served on you there is a right to apply to a rent assessment committee for a determination of a market rent although you must do so before the day on which the new rent proposed by the landlord would take effect.

Determination by a rent assessment committee (RAC)

6.—(1) Once a rent determination has been made by the RAC no further increase in rent (other than in the circumstances specified in paragraph 5(d) above) may be made within 12 months unless the landlord and tenant agree otherwise.

(2) Except in the case of a determination made for a short assured tenancy, it is open to a landlord and tenant to agree to vary the terms of the determination made by the RAC if they so wish.

Security of tenure

7.—(1) The landlord can recover possession of a house under an assured tenancy only by obtaining an order for possession from the sheriff. This means that if he serves a notice to quit on you, you do not need to leave by the date stated on the notice. Before you can be evicted the landlord must first get an order for possession from the sheriff. In certain circumstances the sheriff must order possession, for example, if a short assured tenancy has reached its expiry date, or if the landlord requires the premises for his own home, or if a full 3 months rent is in arrears. In other circumstances the sheriff may only grant possession if he considers it reasonable to do so, for example, if the tenant is alleged to have broken or not performed an obligation of the tenancy, or has been guilty of conduct in or in the vicinity of the house which is a nuisance or annoyance.

(2) It is a criminal offence for the landlord or for anyone else to try to make you leave your home by using force, by harassing you or your family, by withdrawing services or by interfering with your home or your possessions. If anyone does this you should contact the police immediately.

Housing benefit
8. If you consider that you cannot afford the rent which is charged you should apply to your local authority for housing benefit. You may obtain further information on housing benefit and on other matters concerning your assured tenancy from your local authority or citizens advice bureau.

Assured Tenancies (Forms) (Scotland) Regulations 1988

(S.I. 1988 No. 2109)

[1st December 1988]

The Secretary of State, in exercise of the powers conferred on him by sections 17(2) and (3), 19(3), 24(1) and (3), 32(2) and (4), 34(1), 48(2), 53(3) and 55(1) of the Housing (Scotland) Act 1988, and of all other powers enabling him in that behalf, hereby makes the following Regulations:

1. These regulations may be cited as the Assured Tenancies (Forms) (Scotland) Regulations 1988 and shall come into force on 2nd January 1989.

2. In these Regulations, "the Act" means the Housing (Scotland) Act 1988.

3. The forms set out in the Schedule to these Regulations shall be the forms to be used for the purposes of the Act in the cases to which those forms are applicable.

Regulation 3   SCHEDULE
List of Forms

Form No. Purpose		References to the Act in forms
AT1(L)	Notice by landlord proposing terms of a statutory assured tenancy different from the terms of the former tenancy	Section 17(2)
AT1(T)	Notice by tenant proposing terms of a statutory assured tenancy different from the terms of the former tenancy	Section 17(2)
AT2	Notice of an increase of rent under an assured tenancy	Section 24(1)
AT3(L)	Application by a landlord to a rent assessment committee for a determination of the terms of a statutory assured tenancy	Section 17(3)
AT3(T)	Application by a tenant to a rent assessment committee for determination of the terms of a statutory assured tenancy	Section 17(3)

AT4	Application by a tenant to a rent assessment committee for determination of a rent for a statutory assured tenancy or short assured tenancy	Sections 24(3) and 34(1)
AT5	Notice by landlord that tenancy is a short assured tenancy	Section 32
AT6	Notice by landlord of intention to raise proceedings for possession of a house let on an assured tenancy	Section 19 as amended by paragraph 85 of Schedule 17 to the Housing Act 1988
AT7	Notice by landlord that the continued or new tenancy is not to be a short assured tenancy	Section 32(4)
AT8	Notice by rent assessment committee served on the landlord or the tenant requiring such information as the committee may reasonably require for the purposes of their functions	Section 48(2)
[1]AT9	Notice of a proposed increase of rent to take account of the council tax	Section 25A as inserted by the Local Government Finance (Housing) (Consequential Amendments) (Scotland) Order 1993 (S.I. 1993 No. 658)

NOTE

[1]Added by S.I. 1993 No. 648 (effective 1st April 1993).

FORM AT1(L): FOR USE ONLY BY A LANDLORD

ASSURED TENANCIES   **AT1(L)**

HOUSING (SCOTLAND) ACT 1988

NOTICE UNDER SECTION 17(2) PROPOSING TERMS OF A STATUTORY ASSURED TENANCY DIFFERENT FROM THE TERMS OF THE FORMER TENANCY

IMPORTANT: INFORMATION FOR TENANT(S)

This notice proposes a change in the terms of your tenancy (and possibly an adjustment to the rent to reflect the change) for the house at the address in part 2. The new terms (and rent, if appropriate) will take effect from the date specified unless you and your landlord negotiate different terms or you refer this notice to a Rent Assessment Committee within three months of the date of service of this notice using a special form AT3(T). The Rent Assessment Committee will determine whether the proposed terms are reasonable and can specify adjustments to the terms and to the rent. You should give your response to the proposed changes by returning part 7 of this notice to your landlord.

Please read this notice carefully before responding.

Part 1.   This notice is served on...(tenant's name) as tenant by...(landlord's name) as landlord under section 17(2) of the Housing (Scotland) Act 1988.

NOTE 1 TO TENANT.
YOUR LANDLORD MAY PROPOSE A CHANGE OF TENANCY TERMS BY THIS MEANS ONLY IF THE TENANCY IS A STATUTORY ASSURED TENANCY. IF YOU ARE IN DOUBT ABOUT WHAT KIND OF TENANCY YOU HAVE YOU SHOULD CONSULT A SOLICITOR OR AN ORGANISATION WHICH GIVES ADVICE ON HOUSING MATTERS.

Part 2.   Address of house to which this notice relates:—

....
....
....
....

(Please be as specific as possible. For example, if the tenancy is of a flat give the location in stair, eg 1F1)

Part 3.   Name, address and telephone number of landlord, and of agent (if any):—

.... landlord(s)   .... agent
....
....
....

NOTE 2 TO TENANT.
THIS NOTICE PROPOSES CHANGES TO THE TERMS OF THE TENANCY FOR THE HOUSE TO WHICH THE NOTICE RELATES. YOUR LANDLORD MUST GIVE YOU AT LEAST THREE MONTHS NOTICE OF THE CHANGES. THEY WILL TAKE EFFECT FROM THE DATE SPECIFIED IF YOU DO NOT ACT WITHIN THREE MONTHS OF THE DATE OF SERVICE OF THE NOTICE. READ THE NOTICE CAREFULLY. IF YOU ARE IN DOUBT ABOUT WHAT ACTION YOU SHOULD TAKE, GET ADVICE IMMEDIATELY FROM A SOLICITOR OR AN ORGANISATION WHICH GIVES ADVICE ON HOUSING MATTERS.

Part 4. I your landlord(s)/I your landlord's agent* give you notice of proposed changes in the terms of your tenancy for the house at the address in part 2. The proposed changes are shown in paragraph (c) of part 6 of this notice and are to come into effect on.................................(date).

Signed ....
Landlord/Landlord's agent

Date ....

NOTE 3 TO TENANT.
YOUR LANDLORD MAY ALSO PROPOSE THAT YOUR RENT IS TO BE ADJUSTED TO TAKE ACCOUNT OF THE PROPOSED NEW TENANCY TERMS. IF SO THE LANDLORD MUST ALSO COMPLETE PART 5 OF THE NOTICE.

***delete as appropriate**

Part 5. I your landlord(s)/I your landlord's agent* give you notice of an adjustment of rent shown in paragraph (d) of part 6 of this notice to take account of the tenancy terms. I am proposing that the adjustment is to come into effect on ....(date).

Signed ....
Landlord/Landlord's agent

Date ....

***delete as appropriate**

NOTE 4 TO TENANT.
IF YOU DO NOT WISH TO ACCEPT THE TERMS PROPOSED OR WISH TO REFER THE PROPOSALS TO A RENT ASSESSMENT COMMITTEE THEN A MEETING WITH YOUR LANDLORD TO DISCUSS THE PROPOSALS MIGHT BE HELPFUL. YOU SHOULD, HOWEVER, KEEP IN MIND THE THREE MONTH TIME-LIMIT FOR REFERRING THE PROPOSALS TO A RENT ASSESSMENT COMMITTEE.

Part 6.

a. Date(s) on which the assured tenancy ....
agreement or contract of tenancy ....
began. ....

b. Date when the notice to quit termi- ....
nating the assured tenancy expired or, ...
if your tenant succeeded to a tenancy, ...
the date on which he succeeded. ....

c. The proposed changes to the terms of ....
the tenancy are: ....
(**Note to the Landlord** ....
The exact nature of the changes ....

should be specified. Attach a copy of   ....
the written document setting out the   ....
terms of the tenancy agreement. Con-   ....
tinue on additional sheets of paper if   ....
necessary.)   ....
                                         ....
                                         ....

d.   Existing rent for the house   £.......(per/week*/month*/year*)
     Proposed adjustment plus/minus   £.......(per/week*/month*/year*)
     Proposed new rent   £.......(per/week*/month*/year*)

*delete as appropriate

NOTE 5 TO TENANT.
TO REFER YOUR LANDLORD'S PROPOSALS TO A RENT ASSESSMENT COMMITTEE YOU MUST USE FORM AT3(T) (OBTAINABLE FROM THE CLERK TO THE RENT ASSESSMENT COMMITTEE, THE RENT REGISTRATION SERVICE, CITIZENS ADVICE BUREAU OR HOUSING ADVISORY CENTRE). THE APPLICATION SHOULD BE SENT TO THE CLERK TO THE LOCAL RENT ASSESSMENT COMMITTEE (SEE TELEPHONE BOOK FOR ADDRESS). THE RENT ASSESSMENT COMMITTEE IS AN INDEPENDENT BODY WHICH CHARGES NO FEE.

NOTE 6 TO TENANT.
DETACH PART 7 AND RETURN IT TO THE SENDER OF THE NOTICE AS SOON AS POSSIBLE. HOWEVER IF YOU DECIDE TO DISCUSS THE PROPOSALS(S) WITH YOUR LANDLORD <u>DO NOT</u> COMPLETE PART 7 NOW, BUT REMEMBER THERE IS A THREE MONTH TIME-LIMIT FOR REFERRING THE PROPOSALS TO A RENT ASSESSMENT COMMITTEE.

NOTE 7 TO TENANT.
THIS IS AN IMPORTANT DOCUMENT AND YOU SHOULD KEEP IT IN A SAFE PLACE.

Part 7.   (This part of the notice is for the use of the tenant.)

To ....(name)
(landlord*/landlord's agent*)

I acknowledge receipt of notice AT1(L) dated...................19..........(date of notice) and give you notice that:— (*delete as appropriate)

* I accept the proposed terms of the statutory assured tenancy [and the proposed adjustment to the rent*.]
* I do not accept the proposed terms of the statutory assured tenancy and/or the proposed adjustment to the rent, and intend to refer this notice to a Rent Assessment Committee.

Signed ....
(Tenant/Tenant's Agent)

Date ....
(If tenancy is a joint tenancy all
tenants or their agents should sign)

FORM AT1(T): FOR USE ONLY BY A TENANT

ASSURED TENANCIES **AT1(T)**

HOUSING (SCOTLAND) ACT 1988

NOTICE UNDER SECTION 17(2) PROPOSING TERMS OF A STATUTORY ASSURED TENANCY DIFFERENT FROM THE TERMS OF THE FORMER TENANCY

IMPORTANT: INFORMATION FOR LANDLORD(S)

This notice proposes a change in the terms of your tenancy (and possibly an adjustment to the rent to reflect the change) for the house at the address in part 2. The new terms (and rent, if appropriate) will take effect from the date specified unless you and the tenant negotiate different terms or you refer this notice to a Rent Assessment Committee using a special form AT3(L)(within three months of the date of service of this notice. The Rent Assessment Committee will determine whether the proposed terms are reasonable and can specify adjustments to the terms and the rent. You should give your response to the proposed changes by returning part 6 of this notice to your tenant.

Please read this notice carefully before responding.

Part 1. This notice is served on...(landlord's name)
as landlord by..(tenant's name) as tenant
under section 17(2) of the Housing (Scotland) Act 1988.

NOTE 1 TO LANDLORD.
YOUR TENANT MAY PROPOSE A CHANGE OF TENANCY TERMS BY THIS MEANS ONLY IF THE TENANCY IS A STATUTORY ASSURED TENANCY. IF YOU ARE IN DOUBT ABOUT WHAT KIND OF TENANCY YOU HAVE YOU SHOULD CONSULT A SOLICITOR OR AN ORGANISATION WHICH GIVES ADVICE ON HOUSING MATTERS.

Part 2. Address of house to which this notice relates:—
....
....
....
....
(Please be as specific as possible. For example, if the tenancy is of a flat give the location in stair, eg 1F1)

> **NOTE 2 TO LANDLORD.**
> **THIS NOTICE PROPOSES CHANGES TO THE TERMS OF THE TENANCY FOR THE HOUSE TO WHICH THE NOTICE RELATES. YOUR TENANT MUST GIVE YOU AT LEAST THREE MONTHS NOTICE OF THE CHANGES. THEY WILL TAKE EFFECT FROM THE DATE SPECIFIED IF YOU DO NOT ACT WITHIN THREE MONTHS OF THE DATE OF SERVICE OF THE NOTICE. READ THE NOTICE CAREFULLY. IF YOU ARE IN DOUBT ABOUT WHAT ACTION YOU SHOULD TAKE, GET ADVICE IMMEDIATELY FROM A SOLICITOR OR AN ORGANISATION WHICH GIVES ADVICE ON HOUSING MATTERS.**

Part 3.   I your tenant(s)/I your tenant's agent* give notice of proposed changes in the terms of the tenancy for the house at the address in part 2. The proposed changes are shown in paragraph (c) of part 5 of this notice and are to come into effect on...(date).

Signed ....
(In a joint tenancy all tenants should sign)

Date   ....

> **NOTE 3 TO LANDLORD.**
> **IF YOUR TENANT PROPOSES THAT YOUR RENT IS TO BE ADJUSTED TO TAKE ACCOUNT OF THE PROPOSED NEW TENANCY TERMS, PART 4 MUST ALSO BE COMPLETED.**

Part 4.   I your tenant(s)/I your tenant's agent* give notice of an adjustment of rent as shown in paragraph (d) of part 5 of this notice to take account of the proposed terms.
The adjustment is to come into effect on................................(date).

Signed ....
(In a joint tenancy all tenants should sign)

Date   ....

*delete as appropriate

> **NOTE 4 TO LANDLORD.**
> **IF YOU DO NOT WISH TO ACCEPT THE TERMS PROPOSED OR WISH TO REFER THE PROPOSALS TO A RENT ASSESSMENT COMMITTEE THEN A MEETING WITH THE TENANT TO DISCUSS THE PROPOSALS MIGHT BE HELPFUL. YOU SHOULD, HOWEVER, KEEP IN MIND THE THREE MONTH TIME-LIMIT FOR REFERRING THE PROPOSALS TO A RENT ASSESSMENT COMMITTEE.**

Part 5.

a. Date(s) on which your assured tenancy ....
   agreement or contract of tenancy ....
   began.

b. Date when the notice to quit termin- ....
   nating the assured tenancy expired or, ...
   if you succeeded to the tenancy, the ....
   date on which you succeeded. ....

c. The proposec changes to the terms of ....
   the tenancy are: ....
   (**Note to the Tenant.** ....
   The exact nature of the changes ....
   should be specified. Attach a copy of ....
   the written document setting out the ....
   terms of the tenancy agreement. Con- ....
   tinue on additional sheets of paper if ....
   necessary). ....
   ....
   ....

d. Existing rent for the house   £.......(per/week*/month*/year*)
   Proposed adjustment plus/minus   £.......(per/week*/month*/year*)
   Proposed new rent   £.......(per/week*/month*/year*)

*delete as appropriate

NOTE 5 TO LANDLORD.
TO REFER YOUR TENANT'S PROPOSALS TO A RENT ASSESSMENT COMMITTEE YOU MUST USE FORM AT3(L) (OBTAINABLE FROM THE CLERK OF THE RENT ASSESSMENT COMMITTEE, THE RENT REGISTRATION SERVICE, CITIZENS ADVICE BUREAU OR HOUSING ADVISORY CENTRE). THE APPLICATION SHOULD BE SENT TO THE CLERK OF THE LOCAL RENT ASSESSMENT COMMITTEE (SEE TELEPHONE BOOK FOR ADDRESS). THE RENT ASSESSMENT COMMITTEE IS AN INDEPENDENT BODY WHICH CHARGES NO FEE.

NOTE 6 TO LANDLORD.
DETACH PART 6 AND RETURN IT TO THE SENDER OF THE NOTICE AS SOON AS POSSIBLE. HOWEVER, IF YOU DECIDE TO DISCUSS THE PROPOSAL(S) WITH YOUR TENANT <u>DO NOT</u> COMPLETE PART 6 NOW, BUT REMEMBER THAT THERE IS A THREE MONTH TIME-LIMIT FOR REFERRING THE PROPOSALS TO THE RENT ASSESSMENT COMMITTEE.

NOTE 7 TO LANDLORD.
THIS IS AN IMPORTANT DOCUMENT AND YOU SHOULD KEEP IT IN A SAFE PLACE.

Part 6. (This part of the notice is for the use of the landlord)

To...(name)
tenant*/tenant's agent*

I acknowledge receipt of notice AT1(T) dated.....................19.........(date of notice)
and give you notice that:—
(*delete as appropriate)

* I accept the proposed terms of the statutory assured tenancy [and the proposed adjustment to the rent.]*

* I do not accept the proposed terms of the statutory assured tenancy and/or the proposed adjustment to the rent, and intend to refer this notice to a Rent Assessment Committee.

Signed ....
(landlord/landlord's agent)

Date ....

*delete as appropriate

¹**FORM AT2: FOR USE ONLY BY A LANDLORD**

———

NOTE
¹As amended by S.I. 1993 No. 648 (effective 1st April 1993).

———

ASSURED TENANCIES **AT2**

HOUSING (SCOTLAND) ACT 1988

**NOTICE UNDER SECTION 24(1) OF AN INCREASE OF
RENT UNDER AN ASSURED TENANCY**

IMPORTANT: INFORMATION FOR TENANT(S)

This notice informs you as tenant(s) that your landlord(s) wish(es) to increase the rent for your assured tenancy. The new rent will take effect unless you reach an agreement with your landlord that the rent should be a different amount or unless you refer this notice to a Rent Assessment Committee for a rent determination using a special form AT4. If you do apply to the Committee you must do so **before the date on which the new rent is due to take effect**. You should give your landlord your response to the proposed new rent by returning to him Part 3 of this notice.

Please read this notice carefully before responding.

Part 1. To. ....
(name of tenant(s))

of ....

....

....

(address of tenant(s))

NOTE 1 TO TENANT.
YOUR LANDLORD MUST GIVE YOU AT LEAST THE FOLLOWING AMOUNT OF NOTICE OF A RENT INCREASE. IF THE ASSURED TENANCY IS FOR 6 MONTHS OR MORE, 6 MONTHS NOTICE MUST BE GIVEN. IF THE TENANCY IS FOR LESS THAN 6 MONTHS, THE NOTICE GIVEN MUST BE THE SAME LENGTH AS THE ORIGINAL TENANCY BUT CANNOT BE LESS THAN ONE MONTH.

Part 2. This give you notice that ....

(name of landlord)

of. ....

....

....

(address of landlord)

proposes to charge a new rent of £..............

[per year]* [per month]* [per week]*

for your tenancy of the house at the address in Part 1.

The new rent is to take effect from................(date)

Signed .... (Landlord(s)/Landlord's Agent)

Date ....

Address of Agent (if appropriate)

....

....

IMPORTANT: FOR THE ATTENTION OF TENANT(S) NOTES 2 TO 4
2. A LANDLORD MAY PROPOSE A NEW RENT BY THIS MEANS ONLY IF THE TENANCY IS A STATUTORY ASSURED TENANCY. IF YOU ARE IN DOUBT ABOUT WHAT KIND OF TENANCY YOU HAVE YOU SHOULD CONSULT A SOLICITOR OR AN ORGANISATION WHICH GIVES ADVICE ON HOUSING MATTERS.

3. THE PROPOSED NEW RENT WILL TAKE EFFECT ON THE DATE SPECIFIED UNLESS YOU REACH SOME OTHER AGREEMENT WITH YOUR LANDLORD OR UNLESS YOU REFER THE NOTICE TO A RENT ASSESSMENT COMMITTEE FOR A RENT DETERMINATION BEFORE THE DATE ON WHICH THE NEW RENT TAKES EFFECT.

4. IF YOU DECIDE TO REFER THIS NOTICE TO THE RENT ASSESSMENT COMMITTEE YOU MUST DO SO USING FORM AT4 (OBTAINABLE FROM THE CLERK TO THE RENT ASSESSMENT COMMITTEE, THE RENT REGISTRATION SERVICE, CITIZENS ADVICE BUREAU OR HOUSING ADVISORY CENTRE). THE APPLICATION SHOULD BE MADE TO THE LOCAL RENT ASSESSMENT COMMITTEE (SEE TELEPHONE BOOK FOR ADDRESS). THE RENT ASSESSMENT COMMITTEE IS AN INDEPENDENT BODY WHICH CHARGES NO FEE.

*delete as appropriate

IMPORTANT: FOR THE ATTENTION OF TENANT(S) NOTES 5 TO 7
5. YOUR LANDLORD CANNOT INCREASE YOUR RENT BY THIS METHOD MORE OFTEN THAN ONCE EVERY 12 MONTHS (EXCEPT DURING THE PERIOD COMMENCING ON 1ST APRIL 1993 AND ENDING ON 31ST MARCH 1994 WHEN HE CAN INCREASE THE RENT TO TAKE ACCOUNT OF THE COUNCIL TAX—A SEPARATE FORM, FORM AT9, HAS TO BE USED FOR THIS PURPOSE).

6. DETACH PART 3 AND RETURN IT TO YOUR LANDLORD AS SOON AS POSSIBLE. HOWEVER IF YOU WISH TO DISCUSS THE PROPOSED NEW RENT WITH YOUR LANDLORD DO NOT COMPLETE PART 3 NOW. BUT REMEMBER IF YOU DECIDE TO REFER THE NEW RENT TO THE RENT ASSESSMENT COMMITTEE YOU MUST DO SO BEFORE THE DATE ON WHICH THE NEW RENT IS DUE TO TAKE EFFECT.

7. THIS IS AN IMPORTANT DOCUMENT AND IT SHOULD BE KEPT IN A SAFE PLACE.

Part 3. (This part is for the use of the tenant.)
To ....
(landlord*/landlord's agent)
*I/We acknowledge receipt of the notice AT2 dated ....19........ and give you notice that

*I/We accept the new rent to apply from
......................................19........
*I/We do not accept the new rent to apply from
......................................19........ and
propose to refer the matter to a Rent Assessment Committee for a rent determination.
Signed ....(Tenant/Tenant's agent)
(If the tenancy is a joint tenancy all tenants or their agents should sign)
Date ....

Address of tenant's agent(s) (if appropriate)

....

....

*delete as appropriate

FORM AT3(L): FOR USE ONLY BY A LANDLORD

ASSURED TENANCIES   **AT3(L)**

HOUSING (SCOTLAND) ACT 1988

Application by a landlord to a Rent Assessment Committee for a determination of the terms of a statutory assured tenancy and, if appropriate, rent for that tenancy under Section 17(3) of the Housing (Scotland) Act 1988.

IMPORTANT: INFORMATION FOR LANDLORDS

This form should be used by a landlord who wishes to refer to a Rent Assessment Committee a Notice AT1(T) served on him by his tenant to propose a change in the terms of a tenancy agreement for the house at the address in part 1. You should read this application form carefully. Complete the form as fully as you can. Insert "NOT KNOWN" where the information is not available. Where boxes are shown tick only one. It would be helpful if you would type your answers or use BLOCK LETTERS in BLACK INK and send 2 copies of the form if possible, to the Clerk to the Rent Assessment Committee.

The form must be with the Clerk to the Committee within 3 months of the date on which your tenant served you Notice AT1(T).

Part 1.   Address of House being let.

....

....

Part 2.   Name, address and telephone number of landlord.

....

....

Name, address and telephone number of landlord's agent (if any).

....

....

Part 3.   Name and telephone number of tenant(s).

....

....

Name, address and telephone number of tenant's agent (if any).

....

....

Part 4.   Details of House

Say what kind of house it is, such as a detached or terraced house or flat or part of a house. (If a flat give location in stair eg 1F1.)

....

Give number and type of rooms (eg bedroom, living room).

....

....

Is there any accommodation or facilities shared with another tenant? If yes, give details.   ☐ No ☐ Yes

....

....

Is there any accommodation or facilities shared between tenant and landlord? If yes, give details.   ☐ No ☐ Yes

....

....

Does the tenancy include a garage, garden, yard or any other separate building or land? If yes, give details.   ☐ No ☐ Yes

....

....

Part 5.   Services

Are services provided under the tenancy (such as cleaning, heating or hot water supply)? If yes, give details   ☐ No ☐ Yes

....

....

What charge is made for these services at present?

....

Part 6.   Furniture

Is furniture provided under the tenancy? If yes, please attach a list of the furniture provided. If you do not have one prepare one and attach it to this form.   ☐ No ☐ Yes

....

....

....

Part 7.   Improvements

During the present or any former tenancy has the tenant or any previous tenant carried out any improvement or replaced fixtures, fittings or furniture for which he is (or he was) **not** responsible under the terms of the tenancy? If yes, give details

including the costs (actual or estimated) and the ☐ No ☐ Yes
approximate date on which the work was carried out

....
....
....
....
....

Part 8. Disrepair

Is there any disrepair or other defect to the house
or to any fixtures, fittings or furniture due to a ☐ No ☐ Yes
failure to comply with the terms of the present
or any former tenancy? If yes, give details.

....
....
....
....
....

Part 9. I apply for the proposed terms of the statutory assured tenancy [and
the proposed adjustment to the rent]* to be determined by a Rent
Assessment Committee.

Signed. ....
      [landlord(s)]   [landlord's agent]*
In the case of joint landlords all landlords should sign.
                  ....(date)

*delete as appropriate

Part 10. In submitting your application you should attach copies of certain
documents which will be required by the Rent Assessment Committee
to help it make a determination. You should attach the following:—

a. A copy of the existing tenancy agreement or
    written document setting out the terms of the tenancy.   ☐

b. A copy of Notice AT1(T) served on you by your
    tenant (including any attachments to that form).   ☐

c. If you provide furniture, a list of the furniture.   ☐

d. If the tenancy is a short assured tenancy a copy
    of Notice AT5 which you served on the tenant.   ☐

Any documents which you send with this application will be returned to you as
soon as possible.

Tick each box to indicate that you have attached the relevant form.

Please send this application form to the Clerk to the Rent Assessment Committee
for your area (see telephone book for the address).

FORM AT3(T): FOR USE ONLY BY A TENANT

ASSURED TENANCIES   **AT3(T)**

HOUSING (SCOTLAND) ACT 1988

Application by a tenant to a Rent Assessment Committee for a determination of the terms of a statutory assured tenancy and, if appropriate, rent for that tenancy under Section 17(3) of the Housing (Scotland) Act 1988.

IMPORTANT: INFORMATION FOR TENANT(S)

This form should be used by a tenant who wishes to refer to a Rent Assessment Committee a notice AT1(L) served on him by his landlord to propose a change in the terms of a tenancy agreement for the house at the address in part 1. You should read this application form carefully. Complete the form as fully as you can. Insert "NOT KNOWN" where the information is not available. Where boxes are shown tick only one. It would be helpful if you would type your answers or use BLOCK LETTERS in BLACK INK and send 2 copies of the form if possible, to the Clerk to the Rent Assessment Committee.

The form must be with the Clerk to the Committee within 3 months of the date on which your landlord served on you Notice AT1(L).

Part 1.   Address of House being let.
....
....

Part 2.   Name, address and telephone number of landlord.
....
....

Name, address and telephone number of landlord's agent (if any).
....
....

Part 3.   Name and telephone number of tenant(s).
....
....

Name, address and telephone number of tenant's agent (if any).
....
....

Part 4. Details of House

Say what kind of house it is, such as a detached or terraced house or flat or part of a house. (If a flat give location in stair eg 1F1.)
....

Give number of rooms (eg bedroom, living room).
....
....

Is there any accommodation or facilities shared
with another tenant? If yes, give details. ☐ No ☐ Yes

....

....

Is there any accommodation or facilities shared ☐ No ☐ Yes
between tenant and landlord? If yes, give
details.

....

....

Does the tenancy include a garage, garden, yard or
any other separate building or land? If yes, give ☐ No ☐ Yes
details.

....

....

Part 5. Services

Are services provided under the tenancy (such as
cleaning, heating or hot water supply)? ☐ No ☐ Yes
If yes, give details.

....

....

What charge is made for these services at present?

....

Part 6. Furniture

Is furniture provided under the tenancy? If yes,
please attach a list of the furniture provided. ☐ No ☐ Yes
If you do not have one prepare one and attach
it to this form.

....

....

....

Part 7. Improvements

During the present or any former tenancy have you
or has any previous tenant carried out any
improvement or replaced fixtures, fittings or
furniture for which you are (or he was) **not** responsible
under the terms of the tenancy? If yes, give details
including the costs (actual or estimated) and the ☐ No ☐ Yes
approximately date on which the work was
carried out.

....

....

....

....

....

Part 8.   Disrepair

Is there any disrepair or other defect to the house or
to any fixtures, fittings or furniture due to a failure
to comply with the terms of the present or any   ☐ No   ☐ Yes
former tenancy? If yes, give details.

....
....
....
....
....

Part 9.   I apply for the proposed terms of the statutory assured tenancy [and
the proposed adjustment to the rent]* to be determined by a rent
assessment committee.
Signed ....
     [tenant(s)]   [tenant's agent]*
In the case of joint tenants all tenants should sign.
                                        ....(date)

*delete as appropriate

Part 10.   In submitting your application you should attach copies of certain
documents which will be required by the Rent Assessment Committee
to help it make a determination. You should attach the following:—

a.   A copy of your existing tenancy agreement or
     written document setting out the terms of the tenancy.   ☐

b.   A copy of Notice AT1(L) served on you by your
     landlord (including any attachments to that form).   ☐

c.   If your landlord provides furniture, a list of the furniture.   ☐

d.   If your tenancy is a short assured tenancy a copy
     of Notice AT5 served on you by the landlord.   ☐

Any documents which you send with this application will be returned to you as
soon as possible.

Tick each box to indicate that you have attached the relevant form. If you do not
have a copy of any of these forms, consult your solicitor, local Citizens Advice
Bureau or Housing Advisory Centre.

Please send this application form to the Clerk to the Rent Assessment Committee
for your area (see telephone book for the address).

[1]   **FORM AT4: FOR USE ONLY BY A TENANT**

———

NOTE
    [1]As amended by S.I. 1993 No. 648 (effective 1st April 1993).

———

ASSURED TENANCIES **AT4**

HOUSING (SCOTLAND) ACT 1988

Application by a tenant to a rent assessment committee for a determination of rent under sections 24(3), 25A and 34(1) of the Housing (Scotland) Act 1988

IMPORTANT: INFORMATION FOR TENANT(S)

This form should be used if you as tenant are seeking a determination of rent from the Rent Assessment Committee for your assured or short assured tenancy. This might be as a result of a Notice AT2 having been served on you by your landlord (a Notice AT2 proposes an increase in rent for an assured tenancy), or, if you are a tenant of a short assured tenancy, because you would like the Committee to look at the rent you are being charged. Please note that tenants of short assured tenancies have different rights to apply to Rent Assessment Committees from other assured tenants. You are therefore advised to read this application form carefully. Complete the form as fully as you can. Insert "NOT KNOWN" where the information is not available. Whether boxes are shown tick only one. It would be helpful if you would type your answers or use BLOCK LETTERS in BLACK INK and send 2 copies of the form, if possible, to the Clerk of the Rent Assessment Committee.

Part 1. Address of House being let.

....

....

Part 2. Name, address and telephone number of landlord.

....

....

Name, address and telephone number of landlord's agent (if any).

....

....

Part 3. Name and telephone number of tenant(s).

....

....

Name, address and telephone number of tenant's agent (if any).

....

....

Part 4. **Details of House**

Say what kind of house it is, such as a detached or terraced house or flat or part of a house. (If a flat give location in stair eg 1F1.)

....

Give number and type of rooms (eg bedroom, living room).

....

....

Is there any accommodation or facilities shared with another tenant? If yes, give details. ☐ No ☐ Yes

....

....

Is there any accommodation or facilities shared with the landlord? If yes, give details. ☐ No ☐ Yes

....

....

Does the tenancy include a garage, garden, yard or any other separate building or land? If yes, give details. ☐ No ☐ Yes

....

....

Part 5. Services

Does the landlord provide any services (such as cleaning, heating or hot water supply)? If yes, give details. ☐ No ☐ Yes

....

....

What charge is made for these services at present?

....

Part 6. Furniture

Does the landlord provide any furniture? If yes please attach a list of the furniture provided. If you do not have one, prepare one and attach it to this forM. ☐ No ☐ Yes

....

....

....

Part 7. Improvements

During the present or any former tenancy have you or has any previous tenant carried out any improvement or replaced fixture, fittings or furniture for which you are (or he was) **not** responsible under the terms of the tenancy? If yes, give details including the costs (actual or estimated) and the approximate date on which the work was carried out. ☐ No ☐ Yes

....

....

....

....

....

Part 8. Disrepair

Is there any disrepair or other defect to the house or to any fixtures, fittings or furniture due to failure to comply

with the terms of the present or any former tenancy?   ☐ No   ☐ Yes
If yes, give details.

....
....
....
....
....

Part 9.   What rent are you paying now?

£.............   [per week*]   [per month*]   [per year*]

If you are responding to a rent increase proposed by your landlord please attach a copy of Notice AT2 which gave notice of the proposed new rent.

*delete as appropriate

Part 10.   I apply to the Rent Assessment Committee for a rent determination for the house at the address in part 1 above.

Signed.. (tenant or tenant's agent)
Date...
(In the case of joint tenants all tenants should sign.)

Part 11.   In submitting your application you should attach copies of certain documents which will be required by the Rent Assessment Committee to help it make a determination. You should attach the following:—

a.   A copy of your existing tenancy agreement or
     written document setting out the terms of the tenancy.   ☐

b.   A copy of Notice AT2 if one has been served on you by
     your landlord (including any attachments to that form).   ☐

c.   If your landlord provides furniture, a list of the furniture;
     and   ☐

d.   If your tenancy is a short assured tenancy a copy
     of Notice AT5 served on you by the landlord.   ☐

e.   A copy of notice AT9 if one has been served on you by
     your landlord.   ☐

Any documents which you send with this application will be returned to you as soon as possible.

Tick each box to indicate that you have attached the relevant form.

Please send this application form to the Clerk to the Rent Assessment Committee for your area (see telephone book for the address).

FORM AT5: FOR USE ONLY BY A LANDLORD

ASSURED TENANCIES   **AT5**

HOUSING (SCOTLAND) ACT 1988

NOTICE UNDER SECTION 32 TO BE
SERVED ON A PROSPECTIVE TENANT
OF A SHORT ASSURED TENANCY

IMPORTANT: INFORMATION FOR PROSPECTIVE TENANT(S)

This notice informs you as prospective tenant(s) that the tenancy being offered by the prospective landlord(s) is a short assured tenancy under Section 32 of the Housing (Scotland) Act 1988

Please read this notice carefully.

Part 1. To ....
(name of prospective tenant(s))

**NOTE 1 TO PROSPECTIVE TENANT.
TO BE VALID THIS NOTICE MUST BE SERVED BEFORE
THE CREATION OF A TENANCY AGREEMENT. A SHORT
ASSURED TENANCY WILL NOT EXIST IF A VALID NOTICE
HAS NOT BEEN SERVED.**

Part 2. I your prospective landlord(s)/I your prospective landlord's agent*
....
(name of landlord(s))
of ....
....
....
(address and telephone number of landlord(s))
give notice that the tenancy being offered to you of the
house at ....
....
....
(address of house)

*delete as appropriate

to which this notice relates is to be a short assured tenancy in terms of Section 32 of the Housing (Scotland) Act 1988.

Signed...
(landlord(s) or landlord's agent)

Date..

NOTE 2 TO PROSPECTIVE TENANT.
A SHORT ASSURED TENANCY IS A SPECIAL FORM OF TENANCY. UNLESS IT FOLLOWS IMMEDIATELY AFTER ANOTHER SHORT ASSURED TENANCY OF THE SAME HOUSE, (WITH THE SAME TENANT) IT MUST BE FOR NOT LESS THAN 6 MONTHS.

NOTE 3 TO PROSPECTIVE TENANT.
A LANDLORD OF A SHORT ASSURED TENANCY HAS SPECIAL RIGHTS TO REPOSSESS THE HOUSE. IF THE LANDLORD TERMINATES THE TENANCY BY ISSUING A VALID NOTICE TO QUIT AND GIVES THE TENANT AT LEAST 2 MONTHS NOTICE (OR A LONGER PERIOD IF THE TENANCY AGREEMENT PROVIDES) OF HIS INTENTION TO REPOSSESS THE HOUSE THE COURT <u>MUST</u> GRANT THE LANDLORD AN ORDER ALLOWING HIM TO EVICT THE TENANT IF HE APPLIES FOR ONE AT THE END OF THE TENANCY PERIOD SET OUT IN THE TENANCY AGREEMENT.

Part 3. Address and telephone number of agents if appropriate

of landlord(s) agent   **of Tenant(s) agent**

....
....
....
....

NOTE 4 TO PROSPECTIVE TENANT.
A TENANT OF A SHORT ASSURED TENANCY HAS A SPECIAL RIGHT TO APPLY TO A RENT ASSESSMENT COMMITTEE FOR A RENT DETERMINATION FOR THE TENANCY.

NOTE 5 TO PROSPECTIVE TENANT.
IF YOU AGREE TO TAKE UP THE TENANCY <u>AFTER</u> YOUR LANDLORD HAS SERVED THIS NOTICE ON YOU YOUR TENANCY WILL BE A SHORT ASSURED TENANCY. YOU SHOULD KEEP THIS NOTICE IN A SAFE PLACE ALONG WITH THE WRITTEN DOCUMENT SETTING OUT THE TERMS OF THE TENANCY WHICH YOUR LANDLORD MUST PROVIDE UNDER SECTION 30 OF THE HOUSING (SCOTLAND) ACT 1988 ONCE THE TERMS ARE AGREED.

NOTE 6 TO PROSPECTIVE TENANT.
IF YOU REQUIRE FURTHER GUIDANCE ON ASSURED AND SHORT ASSURED TENANCIES, CONSULT A SOLICITOR OR ANY ORGANISATION WHICH GIVES ADVICE ON HOUSING MATTERS.

SPECIAL NOTES FOR EXISTING TENANTS

1. If you already have a regulated tenancy, other than a short tenancy, should you give it up and take a new tenancy in the same house or another house owned by the same landlord, that tenancy cannot be an assured tenancy or a short assured tenancy. Your tenancy will continue to be a regulated tenancy.

2. If you have a short tenancy under the Tenant's Rights etc. (Scotland) Act 1980 of the Rent (Scotland) Act 1984 your landlord can offer you an assured tenancy or short assured tenancy of the same or another house on the expiry of your existing tenancy.

3. If you are an existing tenant and are uncertain about accepting the proposed short assured tenancy you are strongly advised to consult a solicitor or any organisation which gives advice on housing matters.

FORM AT6: FOR USE ONLY BY A LANDLORD

ASSURED TENANCIES   **AT6**

HOUSING (SCOTLAND) ACT 1988
AS AMENDED BY PARAGRAPH 85 OF SCHEDULE 17
TO THE HOUSING ACT 1988

NOTICE UNDER SECTION 19 OF INTENTION
TO RAISE PROCEEDINGS FOR POSSESSION

IMPORTANT: INFORMATION FOR TENANT(S)

This notice informs you as tenant that your landlord intends to apply to the Sheriff for an Order for possession of the house at the address in Part 1, which is currently occupied by you.

Part 1. To ....
(name of tenant(s))
of ....
....
....
(address of house)

> **NOTE 1 TO TENANT.**
> **IF YOU ARE UNCERTAIN ABOUT WHAT THIS NOTICE MEANS, OR IF YOU ARE IN DOUBT ABOUT ANYTHING IN IT, OR ABOUT ITS VALIDITY OR WHETHER IT IS FILLED IN PROPERLY YOU SHOULD IMMEDIATELY CONSULT A SOLICITOR OR AN ORGANISATION WHICH GIVES ADVICE ON HOUSING MATTERS. YOU MAY ALSO FIND IT HELPFUL TO DISCUSS THIS NOTICE WITH YOUR LANDLORD.**

Part 2. I/we [on behalf of]* your landlord(s)

....
(name(s) of landlord(s))

of ....

....

....
(address and telephone number of landlord(s))

inform you that I/we* intend to raise proceedings for possession of the house at the address in Part 1 above on the following ground/ grounds* being a ground/grounds* for possession as set out in Schedule 5 to the Housing (Scotland) Act 1988.

....

....

....
(give the ground number(s) and fully state ground(s)
as set out in Schedule 5 to the Housing (Scotland) Act 1988:
continue on additional sheets of paper if required)

NOTE 2 TO TENANT.
A FULL LIST OF THE 17 GROUNDS FOR POSSESSION IN SCHEDULE 5 TO THE HOUSING (SCOTLAND) ACT 1988 TOGETHER WITH INFORMATION ON YOUR RIGHTS AS TENANT IS GIVEN IN THE BOOKLET "ASSURED TENANCIES IN SCOTLAND—A GUIDE FOR LANDLORDS AND TENANTS". IT IS AVAILABLE FROM ANY OFFICE OF THE RENT ASSESSMENT COMMITTEE, CITIZENS ADVICE BUREAU, HOUSING ADVISORY CENTRE OR FROM THE RENT REGISTRATION SERVICE.

Part 3. I/we also inform you that I/we are seeking possession under the above ground/grounds* for the following reasons:—

....

....

....

....
(state particulars of how you believe the ground(s) have arisen:
continue on additional sheets of paper if required)

*delete as appropriate

NOTE 3 TO TENANT.
YOUR LANDLORD MUST GIVE YOU PROPER NOTICE BETWEEN SERVING THIS NOTICE AND RAISING COURT PROCEEDINGS. IF <u>ANY</u> OF GROUNDS, 1, 2, 5, 6, 7, 9 AND 17 APPLY, WITH OR WITHOUT OTHER GROUNDS, 2 MONTHS NOTICE MUST BE GIVEN. YOUR LANDLORD MUST ALSO GIVE YOU 2 MONTHS NOTICE IF YOUR TENANCY IS A SHORT ASSURED TENANCY AND YOUR LANDLORD IS SEEKING REPOSSESSION ON THE GROUND THAT THE TENANCY PERIOD HAS EXPIRED. IF <u>ONLY</u> OTHER GROUNDS APPLY, ONLY 2 WEEKS NOTICE NEED BE GIVEN.

Part 4.   Proceedings will not be raised before................(date) (which is the earliest date at which proceedings can be raised under Section 19 of the Housing (Scotland) Act 1988).

Signed... (Landlord(s) or Landlord's agent)

Date ....

*delete as appropriate

NOTE 4 TO TENANT.
IF YOUR LANDLORD DOES NOT RAISE COURT PROCEEDINGS THIS NOTICE AT6 WILL CEASE TO HAVE EFFECT 6 MONTHS AFTER THE EARLIEST DATE ON WHICH COURT PROCEEDINGS COULD HAVE BEEN RAISED (SEE PART 4 OF THE NOTICE).

NOTE 5 TO TENANT.
IF YOU WANT TO CONTEST YOUR LANDLORD'S INTENTION TO REPOSSESS YOUR HOME, YOU ARE STRONGLY ADVISED TO TAKE LEGAL ADVICE WITHOUT DELAY AND BEFORE THE EXPIRY OF THE TIME LIMIT GIVEN BY THE NOTICE. HELP WITH ALL OR PART OF THE COST OF LEGAL ADVICE MAY BE AVAILABLE UNDER THE LEGAL AID LEGISLATION.

NOTE 6 TO TENANT.
REMEMBER BEFORE YOU MUST LEAVE YOUR HOME, YOUR LANDLORD MUST HAVE DONE 3 THINGS:

1. SERVED ON YOU A NOTICE TO QUIT (NOTE CAREFULLY THAT THIS MAY HAVE BEEN SERVED AT AN EARLIER STAGE IN THE TENANCY TO CHANGE THE TENANCY FROM A CONTRACTUAL TO A STATUTORY ASSURED TENANCY); AND

2. SERVED ON YOU AN AT6 (THIS NOTICE); AND

3. OBTAINED A COURT ORDER.

NOTE 7 TO TENANT.
THIS IS AN IMPORTANT DOCUMENT AND YOU SHOULD KEEP IT IN A SAFE PLACE.

FORM AT7: FOR USE ONLY BY A LANDLORD

ASSURED TENANCIES   **AT7**

HOUSING (SCOTLAND) ACT 1988
NOTICE UNDER SECTION 32(4) THAT A NEW OR CONTINUING TENANCY IS NOT TO BE A SHORT ASSURED TENANCY

IMPORTANT: INFORMATION FOR TENANT(S)

This notice informs you as tenant that your landlord is proposing to offer you a new tenancy which is not a short assured tenancy, or to continue your existing tenancy, as an assured tenancy, not as a short assured tenancy. Please read this notice carefully.

Part 1. To ....
(name of tenant(s))

of ....

....

....
(address of tenant(s))

NOTE 1 TO TENANT.
YOU SHOULD NOTE THAT THIS NOTICE SERVED BY YOUR LANDLORD CHANGES YOUR TENANCY FROM A SHORT ASSURED TENANCY TO AN ASSURED TENANCY. PLEASE READ THIS NOTICE CAREFULLY. IF YOU ARE IN DOUBT ABOUT WHAT IT MEANS, YOU MAY WISH TO DISCUSS THE NOTICE WITH YOUR LANDLORD OR CONSULT A SOLICITOR OR AN ORGANISATION WHICH GIVES ADVICE ON HOUSING MATTERS.

Part 2. I/We* [on behalf of]* your landlord(s)

....
(name(s) of landlord(s))

of ....

....

....
(address and telephone number of landlord(s))

Give notice that:—

* [Your tenancy of the house at the address in Part 1 is to continue with its current terms and conditions but that as from.............(date) it will no longer be a short assured tenancy.]

* [Your new tenancy of the house at the address in Part 1 which takes effect from.............(date) will not be a short assured tenancy.]

Notice AT5 which informed you that your original tenancy was a short assured tenancy, and which was served on you on.............(date of service of notice AT5) no longer applies.

Signed.. (Landlord(s) or Landlord's agent)
Date ....
*delete as appropriate

NOTE 2 TO TENANT.
YOUR LANDLORD MUST SERVE THIS NOTICE ON YOU BEFORE THE BEGINNING OF THE NEW TENANCY OR BEFORE THE EXISTING TENANCY'S EXPIRY DATE IF IT IS TO CONTINUE. IF HE DOES NOT, THE NOTICE HAS NO EFFECT.

NOTE 3 TO TENANT.
AS A TENANT OF AN ASSURED TENANCY (RATHER THAN OF A SHORT ASSURED TENANCY) YOUR RIGHTS TO MAKE AN APPLICATION TO A RENT ASSESSMENT COMMITTEE FOR A DETERMINATION OF YOUR RENT WILL CHANGE. A TENANT OF AN ASSURED TENANCY CAN REFER TO THE RENT ASSESSMENT COMMITTEE A RENT INCREASE PROPOSED BY THE LANDLORD ONLY IN CERTAIN CIRCUMSTANCES. FURTHER INFORMATION ABOUT THIS IS AVAILABLE IN "ASSURED TENANCIES IN SCOTLAND— A GUIDE FOR LANDLORDS AND TENANTS".

NOTE 4 TO TENANT.
IN AN ASSURED TENANCY YOUR LANDLORD CANNOT REPOSSESS YOUR HOME SOLELY BECAUSE THE EXPIRY DATE IN THE TENANCY AGREEMENT HAS BEEN REACHED BUT OTHERWISE THE SECURITY OF TENURE OF AN ASSURED TENANT IS THE SAME AS THAT OF A TENANT WITH A SHORT ASSURED TENANCY.

NOTE 5 TO TENANT.
YOU SHOULD RETAIN THIS NOTICE AND KEEP IT IN A SAFE PLACE ALONG WITH THE WRITTEN DOCUMENT PROVIDED BY YOUR LANDLORD SETTING OUT THE TERMS OF YOUR TENANCY.

ASSURED TENANCIES **AT8**

HOUSING (SCOTLAND) ACT 1988

NOTICE UNDER SECTION 48(2) REQUIRING THAT A LANDLORD OR TENANT SUPPLY THE RENT ASSESSMENT COMMITTEE WITH INFORMATION

IMPORTANT:

This Notice is served on you by the Rent Assessment Committee. It requires you to supply the Committee with the information detailed in Part 3 below. This information is needed to allow the Committee to make a determination of rent or terms of the tenancy as provided for by the Housing (Scotland) Act

1988. You should provide the information by the date in Part 4. Failure to provide the information may make you liable to summary conviction and a fine.

Please read this Notice carefully before responding.

Part 1. To .... landlord/tenant*

Part 2. An application has been made to the Rent Assessment Committee for consideration of:—
* the terms of the statutory assured tenancy
* the terms of the statutory assured tenancy and a consequent adjustment in rent to reflect those terms
* an increase in rent for the statutory assured tenancy
* the rent under the short assured tenancy

for the house at:

....

....

....

(address of house let under the tenancy)

*delete as appropriate

Part 3. To help the Committee consider this application further information is needed from you.
The further information required is:—

....

....

....

....

....

....

....

....

....

....

Part 4. You should send this information to the address given in Part 5 of this Notice by....................(date). **NOTE**: The date must be not less than 14 days after the date on which this notice is served. If you do not comply with this Notice without reasonable excuse you will be liable on summary conviction to a fine not exceeding level 3 on the standard scale. If you are not clear exactly what information you are to provide to the Committee, please contract me immediately.

Part 5. Signed...
for the Rent Assessment Committee

....

....

....

....

(address and telephone number of Committee)
Date...................................

FORM AT9: FOR USE ONLY BY A LANDLORD

ASSURED TENANCIES   **AT9**

HOUSING (SCOTLAND) ACT 1988

NOTICE UNDER SECTION 25A OF A PROPOSED INCREASE OF RENT TO TAKE ACCOUNT OF THE COUNCIL TAX

This notice only has effect where a landlord wishes to increase the rent on account of the council tax.

IMPORTANT: INFORMATION FOR TENANT(S)

This notice informs you as tenant(s) that your landlord(s) wish(es) to increase the rent for your assured tenancy to take account of the council tax. The new rent will take effect unless you reach an agreement with your landlord that the rent should be a different amount or unless you refer this notice to a rent assessment committee for a rent determination using form AT4. If you do apply to the committee you must do so before the date on which the new rent is due to take effect. You should give your landlord your response to the proposed new rent by returning to him Part 3 of this notice.

Please read this notice carefully before responding.

Part 1. To ....
                                                             (name of tenant(s))
        of ....
....
....
                                                 (address of tenant(s))

NOTE 1 TO TENANT.
YOUR LANDLORD MUST GIVE YOU AT LEAST ONE MONTH'S NOTICE OF A RENT INCREASE TO TAKE ACCOUNT OF THE COUNCIL TAX.

Part 2. This gives you notice that ....
                                                         (name of landlord)
        of ....
....
....
                                                  (address of landlord)
Proposes to charge a new rent of £.................. to take account of the council tax.

              [per year]*   [per month]*   [per week]*
for your tenancy of the house at the address in part 1.

*delete as appropriate

The new rent including council tax is to take effect from.............. (date)

Signed ....

(landlord(s)*/landlord's agents)

Date ....

Address of agent (if applicable)

....

....

IMPORTANT: FOR THE ATTENTION OF TENANT(S) NOTES 2 TO 4.

2. A LANDLORD MAY PROPOSE A NEW RENT BY THIS MEANS ONLY IF THE TENANCY IS A STATUTORY OR CONTRACTUAL ASSURED TENANCY. IF YOU ARE IN DOUBT ABOUT WHAT KIND OF TENANCY YOU HAVE YOU SHOULD CONSULT A SOLICITOR OR AN ORGANISATION WHICH GIVES ADVICE ON HOUSING MATTERS.

3. THE PROPOSED NEW RENT WILL TAKE EFFECT ON THE DATE SPECIFIED UNLESS YOU REACH SOME OTHER AGREEMENT WITH YOUR LANDLORD OR UNLESS YOU REFER THE NOTICE TO A RENT ASSESSMENT COMMITTEE FOR A RENT DETERMINATION BEFORE THE DATE ON WHICH THE NEW RENT TAKES EFFECT.

4. IF YOU DECIDE TO REFER THIS NOTICE TO THE RENT ASSESSMENT COMMITTEE YOU MUST DO SO USING FORM AT4 (OBTAINABLE FROM THE CLERK TO THE RENT ASSESSMENT COMMITTEE, THE RENT REGISTRATION SERVICE, CITIZENS ADVICE BUREAU OR HOUSING ADVISORY CENTRE). THE APPLICATION SHOULD BE MADE TO THE LOCAL RENT ASSESSMENT COMMITTEE (SEE TELEPHONE BOOK FOR ADDRESS). THE RENT ASSESSMENT COMMITTEE IS AN INDEPENDENT BODY WHICH CHARGES NO FEE.

IMPORTANT: FOR THE ATTENTION OF TENANT(S) NOTES 5 TO 7.

5. YOUR LANDLORD CANNOT INCREASE YOUR RENT BY THIS METHOD MORE THAN ONCE.

6. DETACH PART 3 AND RETURN IT TO YOUR LANDLORD AS SOON AS POSSIBLE. HOWEVER IF YOU WISH TO DISCUSS THE PROPOSED NEW RENT WITH YOUR LANDLORD DO NOT COMPLETE PART 3 NOW. BUT REMEMBER IF YOU DECIDE TO REFER THE NEW RENT TO THE RENT ASSESSMENT COMMITTEE YOU MUST DO SO BEFORE THE DATE ON WHICH THE NEW RENT IS DUE TO TAKE EFFECT.

7. THIS IS AN IMPORTANT DOCUMENT AND IT SHOULD BE KEPT IN A SAFE PLACE.

Part 3. (This part is for the use of the tenant.)

To ....

(landlord*/landlord's agent)

I/We acknowledge receipt of the notice AT9 dated.............19........and give you notice that

*I/We accept the new rent including council tax to apply from

.... 19.......

*I/We do not accept the new rent including council tax to apply from

.... 19.......and

propose to refer the matter to a rent assessment committee for a rent determination.

Signed ....

(tenant*/tenant's agent)

(If the tenancy is a joint tenancy all tenants or their agents should sign)

Date ....

Address of tenant's agent(s) (if appropriate)

....

....

*delete as appropriate

Rent Assessment Committee (Assured Tenancies) (Scotland) Regulations 1989

(S.I. 1989 No. 81)

[18th January 1989]

The Secretary of State, in exercise of the powers conferred on him by section 53(1)(b) of the Rent (Scotland) Act 1984, and of all other powers enabling him in that behalf, and after such consultation with the Council on Tribunals as is required by section 10(1) of the Tribunals and Inquiries Act 1971, hereby makes the following Regulations:

Citation and commencement

1. These Regulations may be cited as the Rent Assessment Committee (Assured Tenancies) (Scotland) Regulations 1989 and shall come into force on 20th February 1989.

Interpretation

2.—(1) In these Regulations, unless the context otherwise requires—

"the 1984 Act" means the Rent (Scotland) Act 1984;

"the 1988 Act" means the Housing (Scotland) Act 1988;

"assured tenancy" and "short assured tenancy" have the meanings assigned to them respectively by sections 12 and 32 of the 1988 Act and "statutory assured tenancy" has the meaning assigned to it by section 16 of the 1988 Act;

"chairman" means the chairman of a committee;

"committee" means a rent assessment committee, to which a reference is made and which is constituted in accordance with the provisions of Schedule 4 to the 1984 Act;

"hearing" means the meeting or meetings of a committee to hear oral representations made in relation to a reference;

"party" means, in the case where a reference is subject to a hearing, any person who is entitled under regulation 5(2) of these Regulations to receive notice of the date, time and place of the hearing and, in the case where a reference is not to be subject to a hearing, any person who is entitled to make representations in writing to the committee;

"reference" means a matter which is referred to a committee by a landlord or a tenant under regulation 3 of these Regulations.

(2) For the purpose of any of these regulations relating to procedure at a hearing, any reference to a party shall be construed as including a reference to a person authorised by that party to be heard on his behalf, whether or not that person is an advocate or a solicitor.

Application

3. These Regulations apply to any of the following references to the committee—

(*a*) a reference by a landlord or by a tenant under section 17(3) of the 1988 Act of a notice which has been served under section 17(2) of that Act (a notice proposing terms of a statutory assured tenancy and, if appropriate, an adjustment of the rent to take account of the proposed terms);

(*b*) a reference by a tenant under section 24(3) of the 1988 Act of a notice which has been served under section 24(1) of that Act (notice proposing an increase in rent under an assured tenancy);

[1](*bb*) a reference by a tenant under section 25A(4)(*a*) of the 1988 Act of a notice which has been served on him under section 25A(2) of that Act (notice proposing a new rent to take account of any sums payable by the tenant to the landlord in respect of council tax);

(*c*) an application by a tenant under section 34(1) of the 1988 Act (application for a determination of the rent which the landlord might reasonably be expected to obtain under a short assured tenancy).

NOTE

[1]Inserted by S.I. 1993 No. 659 (effective 1st April 1993).

Committee response to a reference

4.—(1) When a reference is made to a committee, the committee shall as soon as practicable thereafter serve on the landlord and on the tenant a notice specifying a period of not less than 14 days from the service of the notice during which either representations in writing or a request to make oral representations may be made to the committee by either party.

(2) Where within the period specified in paragraph (1) of this regulation, or such further period as the committee may allow, the landlord or the tenant requests

to make oral representations, the committee shall give him an opportunity of being heard at a hearing in accordance with regulation 5 below.

(3) The committee may make such inquiries, if any, as they think fit and consider any information supplied or representations made to them relevant to the matters to be determined by them, but shall give the parties adequate opportunity for considering such information and representations and may hold a hearing whether or not the parties have requested one.

Hearings

5.—(1) Where a reference is to be subject to a hearing, the committee shall appoint a date, time and place for a hearing.

(2) A committee shall give not less than 10 days' notice in writing to the landlord and the tenant of the date, time and place so appointed for a hearing.

(3) A hearing shall be in public unless for special reasons the committee otherwise decide, but nothing in these Regulations shall prevent a member of the Council on Tribunals or of its Scottish Committee in that capacity from attending any hearing.

(4) At a hearing—

(*a*) a party may be heard either in person or by a person authorised by him in that behalf, whether or not that person is an advocate or a solicitor;

(*b*) the parties shall be heard in such order and, subject to the provision of these Regulations, the procedure shall be such as the committee shall determine; and

(*c*) a party may call witnesses, give evidence on his own behalf and cross-examine any witnesses called by the other party.

(5) The committee at their discretion may on their own motion, or at the request of the parties or one of them, at any time and from time to time postpone or adjourn a hearing; but they shall not do so at the request of one party only unless, having regard to the grounds upon which the time at which such request is made and to the convenience of the parties, they deem it reasonable to do so. The committee shall give to the parties such notice of any postponed or adjourned hearing as they deem to be reasonable in the circumstances.

(6) If a party does not appear at a hearing, the committee, on being satisfied that the requirements of this regulation regarding the giving of notice of a hearing have been duly complied with, may proceed to deal with the reference upon the representations of any party present and upon the documents and information which they may properly consider.

Documents

6.—(1) Where the reference is to be subject to a hearing, the committee shall take all reasonable steps to ensure that there is supplied to each of the parties before the date of the hearing—

(*a*) a copy of, or sufficient extracts from, or particulars of, any document relevant to the reference which has been received from a party (other than a document which is in the possession of such party or of which that party has previously been supplied with a copy); and

(*b*) a copy of any document which embodies results of any enquiries made by or for the committee for the purposes of that reference, or which contains relevant information in relation to rents or other tenancy terms previously determined for other houses and which has been prepared for the committee for the purposes of that reference.

(2) At any hearing where—

(*a*) any document relevant to the reference is not in the possession of a party present at such hearing; and

(*b*) such party has not been supplied with a copy of, or relevant extracts from, or particulars of, such document by the committee in accordance with the provisions of paragraph (1) of this regulation,

then unless—

(i) such party consents to the continuation of the hearing; or

(ii) the committee consider that such party has a sufficient opportunity of dealing with such document without an adjournment of the hearing,

the committee shall not consider such document until after they have adjourned the hearing for a period which they consider will afford such a party a sufficient opportunity of dealing with such document.

(3) Where a reference is not to be subject to a hearing, the committee shall supply to each of the parties a copy of, or sufficient extracts from, or particulars of, any such document as is mentioned in paragraph (1)(*a*) of this regulation (other than a document excepted from that paragraph) and a copy of any such document as is mentioned in paragraph (1)(*b*) of this regulation, and they shall not reach their decision until they are satisfied that each party has been given a sufficient opportunity of commenting upon any document of which a copy or from which extracts or of which particulars has or have been so supplied, and upon the other party's case.

Inspection of house

7.—(1) The committee may on their own motion and shall at the request of one of the parties (subject in either case to any necessary consent being obtained) inspect the house which is the subject of the reference.

(2) An inspection may be made before, during or after the close of the hearing, or at such stage in relation to the consideration of the representations in writing as the committee shall determine.

(3) The committee shall give such notice in writing as they deem sufficient of an inspection to the party or parties and shall allow each party and his representative to attend any such inspection.

(4) Where an inspection is made after the close of a hearing, the committee may, if they consider that it is expedient to do so on account of any matter arising from the inspection, re-open the hearing; and if the hearing is to be re-opened paragraph (2) of regulation 5 of these Regulations shall apply as it applied to the original hearing, save in so far as its requirements may be dispensed with or relaxed with the consent of the parties.

Decisions

8.—(1) The decision of the committee upon a reference shall be recorded in a document signed by the chairman (or, in the event of his absence or incapacity, by another member of the committee) which shall contain no reference to the decision being a majority (if that be the case) or to any opinion of a minority.

(2) Where the committee are requested, on or before the giving or notification of the decision, to state the reasons for the decision, those reasons shall be recorded in the said document.

(3) The chairman (or, in the event of his absence or incapacity, another member of the committee) shall have power, by a certificate under his hand, to correct any clerical or accidental error or omission in the document.

(4) A copy of the document and of any such correction shall be sent by the committee to the party or parties.

Giving of notices, etc.

9. Where any notice or other written matter is required under the provisions of these Regulations to be served, given or supplied by the committee to a party or parties, it shall be sufficient compliance with the Regulations if such notice or matter is served given or supplied—

(*a*) by delivering it to him or to his agent where a party has appointed an agent to act on his behalf;

(*b*) by leaving it at his or his agent's last known address; or

(*c*) by sending it by recorded delivery letter to him or his agent at that address.

Assured Tenancies (Rent Information) (Scotland) Order 1989

(S.I. 1989 No. 685)

[14th April 1989]

The Secretary of State, in exercise of the powers conferred on him by section 49 of the Housing (Scotland) Act 1988 and of all other powers enabling him in that behalf, hereby makes the following Order:

1. This Order may be cited as the Assured Tenancies (Rent Information) (Scotland) Order 1989 and shall come into force on 17th May 1989.

2. The information with respect to rents under assured tenancies to be kept by the rent assessment panel (whether it is kept in documentary form or otherwise) shall be kept in such manner—

(*a*) that the entry in respect of each tenancy shows, or

(*b*) if kept otherwise than in documentary form that each entry when displayed or printed shows.

the information specified in the Schedule to this Order.

3. The rent assessment panel shall keep the specified information available for public inspection without charge during usual office hours at the office of the panel.

4. A person requiring a copy of any specified information certified under the hand of an authorised officer of the rent assessment panel shall be entitled to obtain it on payment of a fee of £1.50 for the specified information relating to each entry.

Article 2 ¹SCHEDULE

Information with respect to rents under assured tenancies to be kept by rent assessment panel:

1. Address and description of subjects of let.

2. Details of any accommodation which is shared including whether it is shared with the landlord or somebody else.

3. Names and addresses of landlord and tenant.

4. Duration of tenancy if short assured tenancy.

5. Rent applying before application is made.

6. Details of any furniture and services provided by the landlord and the amount of the rent which is attributable to the use of furniture or for services.

6A. Any amount of the rent which is attributable to the tenant's liability to make payments to the landlord in respect of the council tax payable by the landlord.

7. Kind of application, for example, whether (*a*) proposing new terms and rent, (*b*) proposing new rent, (*c*) determination of rent for short assured tenancy or (*d*) an increase under section 25A of the Housing (Scotland) Act 1988 to take account of the tenant's liability to make payments to the landlord in respect of the council tax payable by the landlord.

8. Date and details of determination including revised rent and whether or not linked with change in the terms of the tenancy.

9. Reasons for a refusal to make a determination of the kind mentioned in 7(*c*) above.

10. Any other factor taken into consideration by the rent assessment committee in making a determination.

———

NOTE

[1]As amended by S.I. 1993 No. 645.

———

Limits on Rent Increases (Scotland) Order 1989

(S.I. 1989 No. 2469)

[28th December 1989]

The Secretary of State, in exercise of the powers conferred on him by section 33(1) and (2) of the Rent (Scotland) Act 1984, and of all other powers enabling him in that behalf, hereby makes the following order:

Citation and commencement
1. This order may be cited as the Limits on Rent Increases (Scotland) Order 1989 and shall come into force on 5th February 1990.

Interpretation
2. In this order—
"the 1984 Act" means the Rent (Scotland) Act 1984;
"first period" means the period of 12 months beginning with the date of registration;
"noted amount" means the amount of the registered rent noted as fairly attributable to the provision of services under section 49(2)(*b*) of the 1984 Act;
"permitted increase" means the amount by which the rent for any first period or subsequent period may be increased calculated in accordance with article 5(2) or (3) of this order as the case may be;

"previous rent limit" means, as the case may require and subject to article 3 of this order, either—
- (a) where the increase is the first to be made since the date of registration of the rent, the amount payable by way of rent on that date; or
- (b) in all other cases, the amount payable by way of rent on the most recent anniversary of that date;

"registered" in relation to rent means registered under Part V of the 1984 Act and "registration" shall be construed accordingly; and

"subsequent period" means the period of 12 months beginning on the date of the first anniversary of the date of registration.

Calculation of previous rent limit

3. Where the previous rent limit included a noted amount as defined in article 2 of this order the previous rent limit shall, for the purposes of article 5 of this order, be reduced by the amount or amounts so payable.

Effect of notice of increase

4.—(1) Where a rent for a dwelling-house under a regulated tenancy is registered on or after the date of commencement of this order and the rent payable under the tenancy for any statutory period (or part thereof) is less than the amount so registered, it shall not be increased by a notice of increase under section 29(2)(b) of the 1984 Act except to the extent permitted by article 5 of this order, and any such notice which purports to increase it further shall have effect to increase it to the extent so permitted but no further.

(2) Paragraph (1) of this article shall not affect any increase in respect of a noted amount within the meaning of article 2 of this order.

Permitted increase

5.—(1) Subject to paragraph (4) of this article, the rent may be increased in any first period or subsequent period to the aggregate of the following:—
- (a) the amount of the previous rent limit, calculated in accordance with article 3 of this order; and
- (b) the noted amount (if any) as defined in article 2 of this order; and
- (c) the permitted increase, calculated in accordance with paragraph (2) or (3) of this article, as the case may be.

(2) The permitted increase in respect of the first period shall be the greatest of the following amounts:—
- (a) £104; or
- (b) one-quarter of the previous rent limit, ascertained in accordance with article 3 of this order; or
- (c) one-half of the difference between the previous rent limit ascertained in accordance with article 3 of this order and the registered rent.

(3) The permitted increase in respect of the subsequent period shall be such amount as is required to increase the previous rent limit calculated in accordance with article 3 of this order to the registered rent.

(4) Nothing in this article—
- (a) shall permit the rent to be increased above the amount of the registered rent;
- (b) shall prevent or limit an increase in any sums in a rent which are variable by virtue of section 49(6) of the 1984 Act.

Restriction on rent increases in cases of further registration

6.—(1) Where, on or after the commencement of this order—

(*a*) a registration is superseded by another registration,

(*b*) the new registration permits the rent to be increased above the amount payable under the former registration,

(*c*) the new registration takes effect within 12 months of an increase in rent recoverable in respect of the former registration, and

(*d*) the increase mentioned in sub-paragraph (*c*) above is less than the increase (in consequence of the new registration) permitted by virtue of article 5(4)(*a*) of this order,

the total additional rental income in the period of 12 months (beginning with an anniversary of the date of the former registration) in which the new registration occurs shall not, by virtue of a permitted increase taking effect within 12 months of an increase which falls within sub-paragraph (*d*) of this paragraph, be increased above the permitted increase which, but for article 5(4)(*a*) of this order, would have been recoverable in respect of that period.

(2) Where the circumstances specified in paragraph (1)(*a*) to (*c*) above apply and the date of registration of the former registration occurred before the commencement of this order, the total additional rental income in the period of 12 months in which the new registration occurs shall not exceed the increase, calculated in accordance with article 5(2) or (3) of this order, which would, but for this paragraph, be permitted.

Successive tenancies

7. Where—

(*a*) a rent for a dwelling-house which is subject to a regulated tenancy is registered; and

(*b*) at a time when the rent payable under the tenancy is less than the registered rent the tenant, or any person who might succeed him as statutory tenant, becomes the tenant under a new regulated tenancy of the dwelling-house,

the rent limit for any contractual period of the new regulated tenancy beginning before the registered rent becomes payable shall be the amount to which, if the first mentioned tenancy had continued, the rent payable thereunder could have increased in accordance with the provisions of this order for a statutory period beginning at the same time.

New tenancies

8. This order shall not apply to the rent under any regulated tenancy of a dwelling-house which was granted after the date of registration of the rent if the person to whom it was granted was neither the tenant under any previous regulated tenancy of that dwelling-house nor any person who might have succeeded such a tenant as a statutory tenant of the dwelling-house.

Transitional

9. Where a rent has been registered before the date this order comes into force but the full amount of the registered rent has not become payable by that date, the provisions of this order shall apply to the next permitted increase which would have become due under the Increase of Rent Restriction (Scotland) Order 1980 as if it were a permitted increase due at the beginning of a first period under this order.

10. Where a rent is registered before this order comes into force in the circumstances specified in section 50(2) of the 1984 Act the date of registration shall be deemed to be the date of the first day after expiry of the period of three years mentioned in section 46(3) of the 1984 Act.

11. Where a rent has been registered by the rent officer before the commencement of this order and a rent determined by a rent assessment committee is registered after the commencement of this order in substitution for that rent, the provisions of section 33 of the 1984 Act shall have effect as if only the rent determined by the rent assessment committee had been registered: but the date of registration shall be deemed for the purposes of that section (but not for the purposes of section 29(3) of the 1984 Act) to be the date on which the rent determined by the rent officer was registered.

Supplemental
   12. In ascertaining for the purpose of this order whether there is any difference between amounts or what that difference is, such adjustments shall be made as may be necessary to take account of periods of different lengths: and for that purpose a month shall be treated as one-twelfth and a week as one-fifty-second of a year.

Revocation
   13. The Increase of Rent Restriction (Scotland) Order 1980 is hereby revoked.

Rent Regulation (Forms and Information etc.) (Scotland) Regulations 1991

(S.I. 1991 No. 1521)

[17th June 1991]

The Secretary of State, in exercise of the powers conferred on him by sections 41(1), 53(1), 53(1) as applied by section 56(2), 80(1) and 112 of the Rent (Scotland) Act 1984, and of all other powers enabling him in that behalf, hereby makes the following Regulations:

Citation and commencement
   1. These Regulations may be cited as the Rent Regulation (Forms and Information etc.) (Scotland) Regulations 1991 and shall come into force on 5th August 1991.

Interpretation
   2. In these Regulations—
   (*a*) "the Act" means the Rent (Scotland) Act 1984; and
   (*b*) a reference to a numbered Schedule is a reference to the Schedule to these Regulations bearing that number.

Register of rents
   3. The particulars prescribed in Schedule 1 shall be the particulars with regard to the tenancy which the register of rents is required to contain in pursuance of section 45(2)(*a*) or of that section as applied by section 56(2) of the Act.

Notices to quit
   4. Where a notice to quit is given by a landlord on or after the coming into force of these Regulations to determine—

(*a*) a protected tenancy; or

(*b*) a Part VII contract,

the notice shall contain, in such form as may be, the information set out in Schedule 2.

Form and content of rent books

5.—(1) Every rent book or similar document provided by a landlord for use in respect of a dwellinghouse, which is let on or subject to a regulated tenancy, shall contain a notice to the tenant in the form set out in Schedule 3, or in a form substantially to the same effect, of all the matters referred to in the said form.

(2) Every rent book or similar document, required by section 79(1) of the Act (rent books under Part VII contracts) shall be in the form set out in Schedule 4, or in a form substantially to the same effect, and shall contain the information referred to in the said form.

Forms

6. The forms set out in Schedule 5, or forms substantially to the same effect, shall be the forms to be used for the purposes of the Act in the cases to which those forms are applicable.

Fee for certified copy

7. For the purposes of section 45(4) of the Act (register of rents) the fee to be paid for a certified copy of an entry in the register of rents shall be £1.50.

Revocations and transitional provision

8. The Regulations specified in Schedule 6 are hereby revoked except insofar as the forms, notices and information so prescribed are required to be used in connection with proceedings after the date on which these Regulations come into force and consequent upon action taken before that date.

Regulation 3   SCHEDULE 1

<small>Particulars with Regard to the Tenancy Which the Register of Rents is Required to Contain</small>

1. The name and address of both the landlord and the tenant.

2. The name and address of the landlord's agent (if any).

3. Whether Part VI of the Rent (Scotland) Act 1984 (rent limit for dwellinghouses let by housing associations and the Housing Corporation) applies to the tenancy.

4. Whether furniture is provided by the landlord.

5. The services provided by the landlord.

6. The respective liability of the landlord and the tenant for the maintenance and repair of the dwellinghouse.

[1]**6A.** Whether any amount is payable by the tenant in respect of council tax.

NOTE

[1]Inserted by S.I. 1993 No. 647 (effective 1st April 1993).

---

7. Any other terms of the tenancy taken into consideration in determining a fair rent for the dwellinghouse.

Regulation   SCHEDULE 2

INFORMATION TO BE CONTAINED IN A NOTICE TO QUIT

1. Even after the notice to quit has run out, before the tenant can lawfully be evicted, the landlord must get an order for possession from the court.

2. A tenant who does not know if he or she has any right to remain in possession after a notice to quit runs out or is otherwise unsure of his or her rights should obtain advice without delay and before the notice to quit expires. Advice can be obtained from a solicitor, a Citizens' Advice Bureau, a Housing Aid Centre, a Rent Officer or the office of the Rent Assessment Committee. Some solicitors give a free first interview and help with all or part of the cost of legal advice may be available.

Regulation 5(1)   [1]SCHEDULE 3

FORM OF NOTICE TO BE INSERTED IN EVERY RENT BOOK OR SIMILAR DOCUMENT USED IN RESPECT OF A DWELLING LET ON OR SUBJECT TO A REGULATED TENANCY

———

NOTE

[1]As amended by S.I. 1993 No. 647 (effective 1st April 1993).

———

INFORMATION FOR TENANT

NOTE: YOUR TENANCY IS A REGULATED TENANCY. THIS AFFECTS THE RENT WHICH MAY BE LAWFULLY RECOVERED FOR THE DWELLING AND IMPOSES RESTRICTIONS ON THE LANDLORD'S RIGHT TO RECOVER POSSESSION OF IT. THE LANDLORD MUST KEEP THE ENTRIES UP TO DATE.

1. Address of the dwelling ....
....

2. Name, address and telephone number of the landlord and his agent (if any) ....
....

3. RENT LAWFULLY RECOVERABLE

    (*a*) If no rent is registered—
        (i)   the rent payable as from [date] under the tenancy is £   per

(ii)   if furniture or services are provided the amount (if any) which is apportioned to them under the tenancy agreement is—
Furniture £............. Services £..............

(iii)   where the landlord is responsible for payment of the council tax and a payment in respect of the council tax is included in the rent, the amount which is apportioned to it under the tenancy agreement is £   per   .*

(b) If a fair rent has been registered—

(i)   the registered rent is £   per   including £   for furniture and services and council tax of £   per   .* (The word "variable" should be added after the amount of the registered rent if the entry in the register permits the landlord to vary the rent to take account of changes in the cost of providing services or maintaining or repairing the dwelling in accordance with the terms shown in the register, without having to have a new rent registered.)

*(ii)   The landlord may increase the rent up to the registered rent only by the following annual amounts prescribed by order made under section 33 of the Rent (Scotland) Act 1984

From (date)   by (amount of the increase) £   per   to   £   per
From (date)   by (amount of the increase) £   per   to   £   per

*Delete if inapplicable.

4. ALTERATIONS IN RENT WHERE NO RENT REGISTERED

(a) Where no rent has been registered then, unless you enter into a rent agreement (see paragraph (c) below) the rent can only be increased for one or more of a limited number of reasons, for example increases in the cost of services provided.

(b) You or your landlord or both of you acting together may apply at any time to the rent officer to have a fair rent registered.

(c) As an alternative to having a fair rent registered you and your landlord may agree to increase the rent under the existing tenancy or to enter into a new tenancy agreement for the same house at an increased rent. The agreement must be in writing and contain a conspicuous statement at the top that (1) your security of tenure will not be affected if you refuse to agree; (2) the agreement will not deprive you or the landlord of the right to apply at any time to the rent officer for registration of a fair rent; and (3) if a rent is registered any increase in rent will be subject to a maximum annual limit.

5. ALTERATIONS IN RENT WHERE A FAIR RENT REGISTERED

(a) The landlord may not charge more than the registered rent, or, if the increase of rent is subject to a maximum annual limit (see paragraph 3(b)(ii) above), more than is permitted under the relevant provisions. In certain cases the registered rent may vary to take account of changes in the cost of providing services or of maintaining or repairing the dwelling, but only if there is a note on the register to this effect.

(b) The registered rent normally lasts for three years and cannot be changed without applying to the rent officer.

The only circumstances where a rent officer will accept an application for re-registration within three years are:—

(i) Where the application is made by you and the landlord acting together; or

(ii) Where there has been a change in the circumstances which were taken into account when the rent was registered; or

(iii) Where the application is made by the landlord alone within three months of the expiry of the three year period (but the new registration cannot take effect until the expiry of the three year period);

(iv) Where an increase is sought in the period commencing on 1st April 1993 and ending on 31st March 1994 in respect of the council tax.

At the expiry of that three year period, if you and the landlord have entered into a rent agreement, you may both apply to the Rent Officer for the cancellation of the registration, but the Rent Officer will only cancel it if he is satisfied that the agreed rent does not exceed a fair rent.

(c) Further information on rents of registered tenancies is set out in a Scottish Office Environment Department booklet available free of charge from Rent Officers, Housing Aid Centre, Citizens' Advice Bureaux and local Council Offices.

6. SUB-LETTING

(a) If you sub-let the dwelling and you are not permitted to do this under your tenancy agreement, your landlord may apply to the sheriff for an order for possession to get the dwelling back (see paragraph 7).

(b) If you sub-let any part of the dwelling on a regulated tenancy—

(i) you must give the landlord, within 14 days, a statement in writing of the sub-letting, giving particulars of occupancy, including the rent charged. The penalty for failing to do this without reasonable excuse, or for giving false particulars, is a fine not exceeding level 1 on the standard scale of fines set out in section 298G of the Criminal Procedure (Scotland) Act 1975. When you have once given the landlord the particulars, you need not do so again if the only change is a change of sub-tenant; and

(ii) if you overcharge your sub-tenant, the landlord may apply to the sheriff for an order for possession.

7. SECURITY OF TENURE

(a) The landlord can recover possession of a dwelling-house subject to a regulated tenancy only by obtaining an order for possession from the sheriff. This means that if he serves a notice to quit on you, you do not have to leave by the date stated in the notice. If you feel you cannot move out at that time, before you can be evicted the landlord must first get an order for possession from the sheriff. The sheriff, except in certain cases, will only grant an order for possession if he thinks it reasonable to do so and either there is suitable accommodation available for you to go to or one of a limited number of conditions is satisfied (for example you have failed to pay the rent lawfully due, or you or your family have been a nuisance or annoyance to neighbours).

(*b*) A tenancy cannot be terminated until a valid notice is served. To be valid, a notice to quit must be in proper form and in writing and give the appropriate period of notice which must always be at least four weeks before the date on which it is to take effect. In the case of a short tenancy as defined in section 9 of the Rent (Scotland) Act 1984, the landlord must also serve a notice on the tenant of his intention to apply for an order for possession.

(*c*) It is a criminal offence for the landlord or for anyone else to try to make you leave by using force, by threatening you or your family, by withdrawing services, or by interfering with your home or your possessions. If anyone does this, you should contact the police immediately.

8. HOUSING BENEFIT

If you have difficulty in paying your rent you should apply to your District or Islands Council for Housing benefit. You may obtain further information about Housing Benefit from your local Council Offices, or Citizens' Advice Bureau.

Regulation 5(2)   ¹SCHEDULE 4

The form of, and the information to be contained in, every rent book or similar document required by section 79(1) of the Rent (Scotland) Act 1984 to be provided for use in respect of a dwelling-house under a contract to which Part VII of the Act applies.

_____

NOTE
¹As amended by S.I. 1993 No. 647 (effective 1st April 1993).

_____

INFORMATION FOR TENANTS

NOTE: YOU OCCUPY THIS DWELLING-HOUSE UNDER A
CONTRACT TO WHICH PART VII OF THE RENT (SCOTLAND) ACT
1984 APPLIES. THIS AFFECTS THE RENT WHICH YOUR LANDLORD
MAY LAWFULLY RECOVER AND CONFERS A DEGREE OF
SECURITY OF TENURE. YOUR LANDLORD MUST KEEP THE
ENTRIES UP TO DATE.

1. Address of the dwelling-house and description of the premises to which the contract relates ....
....

2. Name, address and telephone number of the landlord and of his agent (if any) ....
....

3. RENT LAWFULLY RECOVERABLE

(*a*) If no rent is registered—

    (i) The rent payable as from [date] under the contract is £   per week.

    (ii) If furniture or services are provided the amount (if any) which is apportioned to them under the contract is—
Furniture £....... Services £.........

    (iii) where the landlord is responsible for payment of the council tax and a payment in respect of the council tax is included in the rent, the amount which is apportioned to it under the tenancy agreement is £   per   .*

(*b*) If a reasonable rent has been registered following determination by the rent assessment committee

    (i) *A rent of £....... per week for the dwelling-house comprised in the contract was approved by the rent assessment committee on.........

    (ii) *The rent for the dwelling-house comprised in the contract was * reduced/increased* by the rent assessment committee to £........ on ....

*Delete if inapplicable.

4. ALTERATIONS IN RENT

(*a*) Either you or the landlord may refer the contract to the rent assessment committee to fix a reasonable rent. On such a reference, the rent assessment committee may approve the rent payable under the contract or may reduce or increase the rent to such sum as they consider reasonable or may, if they think fit in all the circumstances dismiss the reference. Any approval, reduction or increase may be limited to the rent payable in respect of a particular period.

(*b*) The rent determined by the rent assessment committee is registered and it then becomes a criminal offence for any person to require or receive, on account of rent for that dwelling under any contract, more than the registered rent. Any overpayment of rent may be recovered by you.

(*c*) Once a rent has been registered, then for three years after the rent was last considered by the rent assessment committee no new application for the registration of a different rent can be made, except by you and the landlord acting together, or where there has been a change in the circumstances taken into account when the rent was last considered— for example a change in the terms of the tenancy or in the furniture supplied, or in the condition of the dwelling-house or where an increase is sought during the period commencing on 1st April 1993 and ending on 31st March 1994 in respect of the council tax.

(*d*) If you agree to a change in rent or any other terms of the contract without reference to the rent assessment committee you will no longer have a Part VII contract.

5. SECURITY OF TENURE

(*a*) The landlord can recover possession of a dwelling-house subject to a Part VII contract only by obtaining an order for possession from the sheriff. This means that if he serves a notice to quit on you, you do not have to leave by the date stated in the notice. If you feel you cannot leave at that time, before you can be evicted the landlord must first get an order for possession from the sheriff.

(*b*) A tenancy cannot be terminated until a valid notice is served. To be valid a notice to quit must be in proper form and in writing and give at least four weeks' notice.

(*c*) When the notice to quit takes effect the landlord is entitled, if you do not leave voluntarily, to obtain an order for possession of the dwelling from the sheriff. The landlord cannot evict you from the dwelling without such an order from the sheriff and it is a criminal offence for him or for anyone to try to make you leave by using force, by threatening you or your family, by withdrawing services or by interfering with your home or your possessions. If anyone does this, you should contact the police immediately.

6. HOUSING BENEFIT

If you have difficulty in paying your rent, you should apply to your District or Islands Council for Housing Benefit. You may obtain further information about Housing Benefit from your local Council Offices or Citizens' Advice Bureau.

Regulation 6   SCHEDULE 5

[1]List of Forms

NOTE

[1]As amended by S.I. 1993 No. 647 (effective 1st April 1993).

Form No	Purpose	Relevant provisions of the Act
1	Notice of increase of rent under a regulated tenancy where a rent has been registered under section 49 of the Act	Sections 29(2), 32 and 33
2	Application for the registration of rent, unsupported by a certificate of fair rent where the dwellinghouse is or is to be let under a regulated tenancy or where the interest of the landlord belongs to a housing association	Sections 46 and 56
3	Application for a certificate of fair rent where the dwellinghouse is or is to be let under a regulated tenancy or where the interest of the landlord belongs to a housing association	Sections 47 and 56 and Schedule 6

4	Application for the registration of a rent, supported by a certificate of fair rent, where the dwellinghouse is or is to be let under a regulated tenancy or where the interest of the landlord belongs to a housing association	Sections 47 and 56
5	¹Application by joint applicants or by a landlord alone for the cancellation of a registration of rent	Sections 51 and 52
6	Notice requiring further information to be given to a rent assessment committee	Section 56 and paragraph 8 of Schedule 5
7	Application for an increase of rent in respect of the council tax	Sections 49A

¹Form No. 1

———

NOTE
¹As amended by S.I. 1993 No. 647 (effective 1st April 1993).

———

Rent (Scotland) Act 1984
NOTICE OF INCREASE OF RENT UNDER A REGULATED TENANCY
WHERE A RENT HAS BEEN REGISTERED UNDER SECTION 49 OF
THE RENT (SCOTLAND) ACT 1984 (NOTE 1)

Date..............

To ....

1. A rent of £.............. per .... was registered on..............(*Note 2*) as the fair rent for the dwelling-house situated at.........................of which you are the tenant.

[**2.** In the register it is noted that the fair rent includes an amount in respect of the provision of services provided by the landlord — "the noted amount" — and that the noted amount recorded by the Rent Officer is £..............]

Delete words in square brackets if they do not apply.

3. Accordingly, I hereby give you notice that your rent will be increased from your present rent of £.............. per .... to a new rent of £.............. per .... and the date from which the new rent is to take effect is.............. (*Note 3*).

Your new rent is made up of the following elements—

(*a*) the amount of the previous rent limit (*Note 4*) £.............. per annum
ADD
(*b*) permitted increase (*Note 5*) £.............. per annum
PLUS
(*c*) the noted amount (if any) £.............. per annum
Total of the above, being the rent lawfully recoverable
from you as tenant of the dwellinghouse £.............. per annum
Deduct the amount of the rent which at present is
lawfully payable by you as tenant of the dwellinghouse £.............. per annum
The amount of the increase is £.............. per annum

....
(Signature of landlord or agent)

....
(Address of landlord or agent)

NOTES

(*To be incorporated in the notice*)

1. This notice of increase is required if:
(*a*) The tenancy is a regulated tenancy as defined in the Rent (Scotland) Act 1984 ("the Act"); *and*
(*b*) the tenancy is a statutory tenancy, or will become one as a result of the operation of this notice (see section 32(3) of the Act); *and*
(*c*) a rent has been registered for the house which is higher than the rent payable at present.
The maximum amount by which a rent may be increased may be limited by the phasing arrangements set out in the Limits on Rent Increases (Scotland) Order 1989 (S.I. 1989/2469). These limits cannot be evaded by a landlord granting to the tenant a new tenancy of the house. The limits are described in note 5.

2. Insert the date upon which the rent determined by the rent officer or by the rent assessment committee was registered for the dwellinghouse. The rent register may be inspected at the office of the rent officer.

2A. Where a landlord is responsible for payment of the council tax and the tenant is required to include in his rent a payment in respect of the council tax, such a payment will be included as part of any registered rent.

3. The date from which the new rent takes effect must not be earlier than:
(*a*) the date of registration in paragraph 1 of the notice; *and*
(*b*) four weeks before the date of service of the notice; *and*
(*c*) where an application for a fair rent (other than a joint application or following a change of circumstances) is made within the last three months of the period of three years commencing when the registration of a fair rent took effect, the first day after the expiry of that period of three years; *and*
(*d*) if the tenancy is contractual, the date on which the tenancy could be terminated by a notice to quit served by the landlord at the same time as this notice.

3A. Where a landlord is responsible for payment of the council tax and he seeks increase in respect of the council tax paragraph 3(*c*) to (*d*) above does not apply but an application can not be made after 31st March 1994.

4. The previous rent limit is the amount, excluding the "noted amount" (if any) which was payable for the last rental period beginning—

(*a*) before the date of registration; or

(*b*) as the case may require, before each subsequent anniversary of that date.

5. The permitted increase is set by the Limits on Rent Increases (Scotland) Order 1989. This provides that for the first annual stage (which is the period of 12 months beginning with the date of registration) the rent can be increased by the greatest of:

£104 a year; *or*

one quarter of the previous rent limit; *or*

one half of the total increase required to take the rent payable to the registered rent: Provided that the rent payable can never be increased above the registered rent. For the second stage (which starts on the first anniversary of the date of registration) the rent payable can be increased to the registered rent.

[1]FORM NO. 2

NOTE

[1]As amended by S.I. 1993 No. 647 (effective 1st April 1993).

RENT (SCOTLAND) ACT 1984

APPLICATION FOR REGISTRATION OF A RENT

Use this form when applying for the registration of a rent (UNSUPPORTED BY A CERTIFICATE OF FAIR RENT) where the dwellinghouse is at present let on a regulated tenancy or on a secure tenancy from a registered housing association

All sections MUST be completed. Insert 'NOT KNOWN' where the information requested is not available. Where boxes are shown, please tick. Please send the form to the Rent Registration Office for the area in which the dwellinghouse is situated

1. Address of dwellinghouse

2. a. Name, address and telephone number of landlord: And of agent (if any);
   b. If landlord is a registered housing association   Please tick ☐

3. Name and telephone number of tenant: And of agent (if any) (include address):

RENT

4. Please state the rent which you want
registered as a fair rent
£......per week/month/quarter/year
Include the amount of rent to be charged
for any services or furniture provided
by the landlord

4A. Who is liable for the council tax   The landlord ☐   The tenant ☐
      on the property?

PREVIOUS REGISTRATION

5. Has a rent already been registered for   YES ☐   NO ☐
the dwellinghouse?
If YES
    a.   please state: the registration number   ....
         the effective date of registration   ....

(These details are shown on the Notification of Registration sent to the landlord
and tenant at the time of the last registration).

    b.   Have there been any substantial   YES ☐   NO ☐
         changes (including any   If Yes, please give details
         improvements or alterations) in
         the condition of the dwellinghouse
         since the previous registration?

    c.   If this application is being made
         within two years and nine months
         of the date of the previous registration,
         and it is not a joint application, please
         state why you are applying again:

DETAILS OF DWELLINGHOUSE

6. a.   State what kind of dwellinghouse it is,
        such as a detached or terraced house,
        a flat, or room(s). (If a flat, give
        location in block eg 1 up Right; If
        room(s) give location or room
        number).

   b.   Give number and types of rooms
        (such as kitchen, livingroom):

   c.   Is any accommodation/facility   YES ☐   NO ☐
        (such as bathroom or kitchen)   If Yes, please give details
        shared with others?

d. Does the tenancy include a garage,   YES ☐   NO ☐
    garden, yard or any other separate   If Yes, please give details
    building or land?

SERVICES

7. a. Does the landlord provide any   YES ☐   NO ☐
        services such as cleaning, heating
        or hot water supply?   If Yes, please give details or attach a
                                          separate list if necessary

    b. If YES, what do you think is a fair   £......... per week/month/quarter/year
        charge for services, to be included
        in the rent?

FURNITURE

8. a. Does the landlord provide any   YES ☐   NO ☐
        furniture?
                                          If Yes, please attach a copy of the
                                          inventory of furniture or, if you do
                                          not have a copy, please make up your
                                          own list and attach it.

    b. If YES, what do you think is a fair   £......... per week/month/quarter/year
        charge for furniture, to be included
        in the rent?

BUSINESS USE

9. a. Is any part of the dwellinghouse   YES ☐   NO ☐
        used for conducting any type of   If Yes, please give details:
        business such as a shop, office,
        surgery etc.?

    b. If YES, please state what you   £......... per week/month/quarter/year
        consider to be a fair rent for the
        parts of the dwellinghouse used
        for business purposes:

DETAILS OF TENANCY

10. a. Do you have a copy of the tenancy   YES ☐   NO ☐
        agreement?   (The Rent Officer may wish to
                                            see it later)

    b. When did the tenancy begin?   ....

    c. What is the present rent?   £.........

d. How often is rent payable?

Weekly ☐ Monthly ☐

Quarterly ☐ Yearly ☐

e. Under the terms of the tenancy, what repairs are the landlord's responsibility?

f. Under the terms of the tenancy, what repairs are the tenant's responsibility?

g. Is the tenancy a short tenancy? YES ☐ NO ☐

IMPROVEMENTS AND DISREPAIR

11. a. Has the tenant improved or replaced anything (including furniture if it is provided) which he is not required to do under the tenancy agreement? YES ☐ NO ☐ If Yes, please give details

b. Has the tenant caused any disrepair or other defect to the dwellinghouse (or furniture if it is provided) because he has not complied with the tenancy agreement? YES ☐ NO ☐ If Yes, please give details

I/WE APPLY FOR REGISTRATION OF A RENT

(Signature of Landlord/Agent)   (Signature of Tenant/Agent)

Date ....   Date...

Where there are joint landlords or joint tenants they should each sign unless one acts as an agent for the rest. In such a case he should state that he is acting as agent. In the case of a landlord and tenant applying together, both must sign.

[1]Form No 3

NOTE
[1]As amended by S.I. 1993 No. 647 (effective 1st April 1993).

RENT (SCOTLAND) ACT 1984

APPLICATION FOR CERTIFICATE OF FAIR RENT

Use this form if you are the owner of the landlord intending:

All sections MUST be completed. Insert"NOT KNOWN" where the information requested is not available.

a. to provide a dwellinghouse by erection or conversion of premises; or

Where boxes are shown, please tick.

b. to make improvements in a dwellinghouse; or

Please send the form to the Rent Registration Office for the area in which the dwellinghouse is situated.

c. to let a dwellinghouse which is not already let

and the tenancy will be a regulated tenancy or a secure tenancy by a registered housing association.

1. Address of dwellinghouse	
2. a. Name, address and telephone number of landlord:	And of agent (if any)
b. If landlord is a registered housing association	Please tick ☐
3. a. Is the dwellinghouse vacant?	YES ☐ NO ☐
b. If YES, who should the rent officer contact about access for inspection?	
4. Name and telephone number of tenant (if any):	And of agent (if any) (include address):
(include address if tenant is currently residing elsewhere)	

RENT

5. Please state the rent which you want shown on the certificate of fair rent
£...... per week/month/ quarter/year
Include the amount of rent to be charged for any services or furniture which you provide

5A.	Who is liable for the council tax on the property? The landlord ☐ The tenant ☐

GROUNDS OF APPLICATION (cross out whichever does not apply)

6. a. Erection/conversion
   b. Improvements to dwellinghouse
   c. Proposal to let dwellinghouse

Give a brief description (including the estimated cost) of any proposed works or improvements and attach a copy of any relevant plans and specifications.

PREVIOUS REGISTRATION

7. a. Has a rent already been registered for the dwellinghouse? YES ☐   NO ☐

   b. If YES, please state: the registration number

   ....

   the effective date of registration

   ....

   (These details are shown on the notification of registration sent to the landlord and tenant at the time of the last registration).

DETAILS OF HOUSE

8. a. State what kind of dwellinghouse it is, such as a detached or terraced house or a flat, or room(s). If a flat, give location in block, eg 1 up Right; if room(s) give location or room number.

   b. Give number and type of rooms (such as kitchen, living room):

   c. Does the tenancy include a garage, garden, yard or any other separate building or land? YES ☐   NO ☐

DETAILS OF TENANCY

9A. If the dwellinghouse is ALREADY LET

   a. What is the present rent? £............

   b. How often is rent payable?

   Weekly ☐   Monthly ☐

   Quarterly ☐   Yearly ☐

c. Under the terms of the tenancy
    what repairs are the landlord's
    responsibility?

d. Under the terms of the tenancy
    what repairs are the tenant's
    responsibility?

e. Has the tenant improved or
    replaced anything (including
    furniture if it is provided) which
    he is not required to do under
    the tenancy agreement?

f. Has the tenant caused any   YES ☐   NO ☐
    disrepair or other defect to the   If Yes, please give details
    dwellinghouse (or furniture if it
    is provided) because he has not
    complied with the tenancy
    agreement?

9B.   If the dwellinghouse is NOT
ALREADY LET and it is proposed to
grant a tenancy, please state:

a. The proposed duration of the
    tenancy   ....

b. How often is rent payable?   Weekly ☐   Monthly ☐

                                      Quarterly ☐   Yearly ☐

SERVICES

10. a. Will the landlord provide any   YES ☐   NO ☐
        services? e.g. cleaning, heating,
        hot water supply etc.?   If Yes, please give details or attach a
                                              separate list if necessary

    b. If YES, what do you think is a   £..........per week/month/quarter/year
        fair charge for services, to be
        included in the rent?

FURNITURE

11. a. Will the landlord provide any   YES ☐   NO ☐
        furniture?   If Yes, please give details or provide
                                              a copy of the inventory

    b. If YES, what do you think is a fair
        charge for furniture, to be included
        in the rent?   £..........per week/month/quarter/year

BUSINESS USE

12. a. Is any part of the dwellinghouse to be used for conducting any type of business such as a shop, office, surgery etc.?

    YES ☐   NO ☐
    If Yes, please give details

   b. If YES, please state what you think would be a fair rent for the part of the dwellinghouse used for business purposes:

    £..........per week/month/quarter/year

I/WE APPLY FOR A CERTIFICATE OF FAIR RENT FOR THE PREMISES NAMED IN QUESTION 1 ABOVE

Signed..   (Landlord/Agent) Date.............

If there are joint landlords each should sign unless one acts as an agent for the rest. In such a case he should state that he is acting as agent.

FORM NO. 4

RENT (SCOTLAND) ACT 1984

APPLICATION FOR REGISTRATION OF A RENT

Use this form when applying for the registration of a rent where SUPPORTED BY A CERTIFICATE OF FAIR RENT and the tenancy is a regulated tenancy or a secure tenancy granted by a registered housing association

All sections MUST be completed. Insert 'NOT KNOWN' where the information requested is not available. Where boxes are shown please tick the correct one. Please send the form to the Rent Registration Service Officer for the area in which the dwellinghouse is situated

---

1. Address of dwellinghouse

---

2. Name, address and telephone number of landlord: And of agent (if any):

---

3. Details of certificate of fair rent: i. Number........
   ii. When dated...........

---

4. a. If the dwellinghouse was not subject to a tenancy when the certificate of fair rent was issued, has a regulated tenancy or a secure tenancy from a registered housing association now been granted?

    YES ☐   NO ☐

   b. If YES, please state:

   i.   Name of tenant

   ii.   Date tenancy commenced

   iii. Duration of tenancy and rental
       period

   iv. Whether the terms of the tenancy
       are as shown in the certificate of
       fair rent.

---

5. Where proposed works are specified in   YES ☐   NO ☐
the certificate of fair rent have these   If NO, please give details:
works been carried out in accordance
with the plans and specifications sent
with the application for the certificate
of fair rent?

---

6. If no alterations were mentioned in   YES ☐   NO ☐
the certificate of fair rent, is the
condition of the dwellinghouse still
the same?

---

7. If the certificate of fair rent states an   YES ☐   NO ☐
amount for services and/or furniture,
are these services and/or furniture
being provided?

I/WE APPLY FOR THE REGISTRATION OF A RENT IN ACCORDANCE
WITH THE CERTIFICATE OF FAIR RENT

Signed...   (Landlord/Agent) Date............

If there are joint landlords each should sign unless one acts as an agent for the
rest. In such a case he should state that he is acting as agent.

FORM NO. 5

RENT (SCOTLAND) ACT 1984

APPLICATION FOR THE CANCELLATION OF A REGISTRATION OF RENT

IMPORTANT: AN APPLICATION TO CANCEL THE REGISTRATION OF
             A RENT CANNOT BE ENTERTAINED UNTIL 3 YEARS
             AFTER THE DATE ON WHICH THE REGISTERED RENT
             TOOK EFFECT OR WAS CONFIRMED BY THE RENT
             OFFICER

Use Part A if you are applying under section 51 of the Act which enables a
landlord and tenant who have entered into a rent agreement to apply jointly to
the rent officer for the registration of a rent to be cancelled. Before the rent

officer will agree to such a cancellation he must be satisfied that the rent payable under the agreement does not exceed a fair rent.

Use Part B if you are applying under section 52 of the Act which enables a registration of rent to be cancelled if a landlord applies because the dwellinghouse is no longer let on a regulated tenancy.

PART A

To the Rent Officer   Date..............

We jointly apply, under section 51 of the Rent (Scotland) Act 1984, for the cancellation of the registration of rent for the dwellinghouse situated at ....

We have entered into a rent agreement a copy of which is enclosed. NOTE: YOU *MUST* SEND A COPY OF YOUR RENT AGREEMENT WITH THIS APPLICATION

Date last registration took effect

Name, address, and telephone number   ....
of the landlord

Name, address and telephone number   ....
of the landlord's agent (if any)

Name and address of tenant   ....

Name, address and telephone number   ....
of the tenant's agent (if any)

Has there been any change in the   YES☐   NO☐
condition of the dwellinghouse since
the date of last registration?

If YES, is the change due to
  (i) any disrepair or other defect   YES☐   NO☐
      attributable to a failure by the
      tenant (including a former tenant)
      to comply with the forms of the
      tenancy, or
  (ii) any improvement (including the
      replacement of any fixture or
      fitting) carried out by the tenant
      (including a former tenant) other than
      under the terms of the tenancy   Signed ....
                                               Landlord/agent

                                               ....
                                               Tenant/agent

PART B

To the Rent Officer   Date.............

I apply under section 52 of the Rent (Scotland) Act 1984 for the cancellation of the registration of rent for the dwellinghouse situated at.....................

The dwellinghouse is not currently let on a regulated tenancy.

Date last registration took effect   ....
Name, address and telephone number of   ....
the landlord

Name, address and telephone number   ....
of the landlord's agent (if any)

Date on which the dwellinghouse ceased   ....
to be let on a regulated tenancy

Signed ....
Landlord/agent

FORM No. 6

RENT (SCOTLAND) ACT 1984

NOTICE REQUIRING A LANDLORD OR TENANT TO SUPPLY THE RENT ASSESSMENT COMMITTEE WITH INFORMATION

IMPORTANT: This Notice is served on you by the Rent Assessment Committee. It requires you to supply the Committee with the information detailed in Part 3 below. This information is needed to allow the Committee to make a determination of rent as provided for by the Rent (Scotland) Act 1984. You should provide the information by the date in Part 4. Failure to provide the information may make you liable to summary conviction and a fine.

Please read this Notice carefully before responding

Part 1. To.. landlord/tenant*

Part 2. The Rent Officer has referred to the Rent Assessment Committee the application for the registration of rent for the house at:
....
....
(address of house let under the tenancy)

*delete as appropriate

Part 3. To help the Committee consider this application further information is needed from you. The further information required is:—

....
....
....
....
....
....
....
....
....
....
....
....

Part 4. You should send this information to the address given in Part 5 of this Notice by.........(date). **NOTE**: The date must be not less than 14 days after the date on which this notice is served. If you do not comply with this Notice without reasonable excuse you will be liable on summary conviction to a fine not exceeding level 3 on the standard scale. If you are not clear exactly what information you are to provide to the Committee, please contact me immediately.

Part 5. Signed....................
for the Rent assessment Committee

....
....
....
....

(address and telephone number of Committee)

Date............

———

NOTE

[1]Added by S.I. 1993 No. 647 (effective 1st April 1993).

———

RENT (SCOTLAND) ACT 1984: SECTION 49A

APPLICATION FOR AN INCREASE OF RENT IN RESPECT OF COUNCIL TAX

USE THIS FORM WHEN THE LANDLORD IS RESPONSIBLE FOR PAYMENT OF COUNCIL TAX AND YOU WISH TO APPLY TO THE RENT OFFICER FOR A REGISTRATION OF RENT WHICH INCLUDES A CONTRIBUTION TOWARDS THE COUNCIL TAX

All sections MUST be completed. Insert "NOT KNOWN" where the information requested is not available. Where boxes are shown please tick the correct one.
Please sent the form to the Rent Registration Service Office for the area in which the dwellinghouse is situated.

Who is liable for council tax? Landlord ☐ Tenant ☐

If Landlord then complete this form.

To the rent officer

---

1. Address of dwellinghouse

---

2. a. Name, address and telephone
       number of landlord and of agent
       (if any)
   b. Is landlord a registered housing   YES ☐   NO ☐
       association?

---

3. Name and telephone number of tenant
   and of agent (if any) (and agent's address)

---

4. Details of dwellinghouse. State what
   type of dwellinghouse it is, for example,
   a house, flat or room(s). If it is a flat or
   room(s), say what floor or floors it is on.
   Give number and type of rooms.

---

5. Does the tenancy include any other   YES ☐   NO ☐
   property? Such as garage, or other
   separate building or land? If "Yes",
   give details.

---

6. Does the tenant share any
   accommodation
   a. with the landlord?   YES ☐   NO ☐
   If "Yes", give details.
   b. with another tenant?   YES ☐   NO ☐
   If "Yes", give details.

---

7. Has the rent officer previously   YES ☐   NO ☐
   registered a fair rent for the
   dwellinghouse?
   If Yes, when did it come into effect?

---

8. What is the rent now?   £   per (e.g. week, month,
                                                 quarter etc.)

---

9. What is the amount of council tax   £   per annum
   payable for the property?
   Please give details of banding.

---

10.   What rent do you want the rent   £   per (e.g. week, month,
      officer to register as a fair rent?   quarter etc.)

11.   I/We apply for a registration
       of a rent.

       Signed   Signed

       Say whether you are the landlord or   Say whether you are the tenant or
       the landlord's agent   the tenant's agent

       Date   Date

       If signed by agent, name and address of
       agent

If the application is being made jointly by landlord and tenant, both should sign. If this is a joint application, the rent officer may register the rent asked for at question 11 without further consultation. If he does so, there is no right of objection to a rent assessment committee. In an application by joint tenants or joint landlords, they should each sign, unless one signs as agent for the rest with their agreement. In such a case he should state that he is acting as agent.

NOTE
The registration will not have any effect on the existing rent registration period or the time of the next review.

Regulation 8   SCHEDULE 6

REVOCATIONS

[Revocations of enactments reproduced in the *Parliament House Book* have been given effect.]

Secure Tenants (Right to Repair) (Scotland) Regulations 1994

(S.I. 1994 No. 1046)

[6th April 1994]

The Secretary of State for Scotland, in exercise of the powers conferred on him by sections 60 and 338 of the Housing (Scotland) Act 1987 and of all other powers enabling him in that behalf, hereby makes the following Regulations:

Citation and commencement
   1. These Regulations may be cited as the Secure Tenants (Right to Repair) (Scotland) Regulations 1994 and shall come into force on 1st October 1994.

Interpretation
   2.—(1) In these Regulations—
   "landlord" means a person prescribed in regulation 4;
   "maximum time" means the time prescribed in regulation 9 and the Schedule;

"qualifying repair" means a repair prescribed as such in regulation 5 and the Schedule;

"working day" means a day which is not a public holiday, a Saturday or a Sunday.

(2) In these Regulations any reference to a numbered regulation or to the Schedule is a reference respectively to a regulation bearing that number in or to the Schedule to these Regulations.

Entitlement

3.—(1) A secure tenant of a landlord shall be entitled to have a qualifying repair carried out to the house of which he is such a tenant, subject to and in accordance with these Regulations.

(2) In respect of any single qualifying repair the landlord shall pay for the work so carried out up to a maximum of £250.

Landlord

4. A landlord is—

(*a*) an islands or district council, or a joint board or joint committee of an islands or district council or the common good of an islands or district council, or any trust under the control of an islands or district council; or

(*b*) a regional council, or a joint board or joint committee of two or more regional councils, or any trust under the control of a regional council; or

(*c*) a development corporation (including an urban development corporation); or

(*d*) Scottish Homes.

Qualifying repair

5. A qualifying repair is a repair of a house which is a repair of a defect specified in column 1 of the Schedule and is the responsibility of the landlord.

List of contractors

6. A landlord shall maintain a list of contractors prepared to carry out qualifying repairs including the usual contractor.

Procedure

7. Where a secure tenant applies to his landlord for a qualifying repair to be carried out to the house of which he is the secure tenant—

(*a*) if the landlord considers it necessary to inspect the house to ascertain whether the repair is a qualifying repair, the landlord shall forthwith inspect the house;

(*b*) in any case the landlord shall let the tenant know whether the subject of the tenant's application is a qualifying repair and where it is—

    (i) the maximum time within which the qualifying repair is to be completed;

    (ii) the last day of the maximum time;

    (iii) the effect of these Regulations;

    (iv) the arrangements for access; and

    (v) the name, address and telephone number of at least one other listed contractor where available, and

(*c*) if the subject of the tenant's application is a qualifying repair, the landlord shall issue a works order to the usual contractor and let him know—

(i) that a qualifying repair is involved;
(ii) the maximum time within which the qualifying repair is to be completed;
(iii) the last day of the maximum time; and
(iv) the arrangements for access.

Failure to provide access
8. Where the secure tenant has failed to provide access to the house of which he is a tenant for the purpose of enabling the qualifying repair to be inspected under regulation 7(*a*) or carried out, although he has been given a reasonable opportunity to do so, the procedure under regulation 7 shall be cancelled and the provisions of regulations 9 to 12 shall cease to apply.

Maximum time
9.—(1) The maximum time within which a qualifying repair is to be completed is the number of working days specified in column 2 of the Schedule opposite the defect specified in column 1 of the Schedule.
(2) The maximum time shall start on the first working day after—
(*a*) the date of receipt of notification of the qualifying repair by the landlord; or
(*b*) where the landlord inspects the house under regulation 7(*a*), the date of inspection.

Instructing another listed contractor
10.—(1) Subject to paragraph (4) where the usual contractor has not started the qualifying repair by the last day of the maximum time the secure tenant may instruct another listed contractor to carry out the qualifying repair.
(2) As soon as the other listed contractor receives the instruction from the secure tenant, he shall inform the landlord that he has been so instructed and shall be entitled on request to obtain a copy of the works order from the landlord.
(3) The landlord on being informed under paragraph (2) shall let the other listed contractor know the number of working days in the maximum time.
(4) Paragraph (1) does not apply if compliance with that paragraph would infringe the term of a guarantee for work done or materials supplied of which the landlord has the benefit.

Compensation
11.—(1) Where the usual contractor has failed to carry out the qualifying repair by the last day of the maximum time the landlord shall pay to the secure tenant a sum of compensation calculated in accordance with paragraph (2) below.
(2) The amount of compensation referred to in paragraph (1) above shall be the sum of—
(*a*) £10 and
(*b*) £2 for every working day, if any, in the period—
(i) commencing on the day after the last day of what would have been the maximum time if the maximum time had applied to the other listed contractor and had started on the day after the day of his receipt of his instruction; and
(ii) ending with the day on which the qualifying repair is completed subject to a maximum amount of compensation of £50.

Suspension of maximum time

12.—(1) The running of the maximum time shall be suspended for so long as there are circumstances of an exceptional nature, beyond the control of the landlord or the contractor who is to carry out the qualifying repair, which prevent the repair being carried out.

(2) The landlord shall let the secure tenant known of the suspension of the running of the maximum time.

Providing information about these Regulations

13. A landlord shall let its secure tenants know in writing once every year of the provisions of these Regulations and of the list of contractors prepared to carry out qualifying repairs.

Regulations 2, 5 and 9   SCHEDULE

DEFECTS, REPAIRS OF WHICH ARE QUALIFYING REPAIRS AND MAXIMUM TIME FOR COMPLETION

1 *(Defect)*	2 *(Maximum time in working days from date after date of notification of qualifying repair or inspection)*
Blocked flue to open fire or boiler.	1
Blocked or leaking foul drains, soil stacks, or toilet pans where there is no other toilet in the house.	1
Blocked sink, bath or basin.	1

Electric power—
    loss of electric power;
    partial loss of electric power.
	
	1
	3

Insecure external window, door or lock.	1
Leaks or flooding from water or heating pipes, tanks, cisterns.	1
Loss or partial loss of gas supply.	1
Loss or partial loss of space or water heating where no alternative heating is available.	1
Toilet not flushing where there is no other toilet in the house.	1
Unsafe power or lighting socket, or electrical fitting.	1

Water supply—
    loss of water supply;   1
    partial loss of water supply.   3

Loose or detached bannister or hand rail.   3

Unsafe timber flooring or stair treads.   3

Mechanical extractor fan in internal kitchen or
bathroom not working.   7

INDEX

succession—*cont.*
secure tenancies, 5–102–104, 9–15—9–31
declinature, 9–21
definitions
family, 9–23—9–27
living together as husband and wife, 9–28
occupation, 9–30, 9–31
only or principal home, 9–29, 9–31
residing with, 9–30
effect of moving to other secure tenancies, 9–22
qualified persons, 9–17—9–20
supported accommodation, 1–13
exclusive occupation, 2–60
occupancy agreements, 2–53

tacit relocation, 1–22—1–23, 5–02
contracting out, 1–23
defects, 1–23
notice to quit by one joint tenant, 1–28
short assured tenancies, 2–48, 5–59
short tenancies, 5–92
tempest, repairing obligations, 3–51
temporary accommodation
and secure tenancies, 2–67—2–70, 5–123
right to buy, 7–09, 7–15
tenancies of shops, 2–07, 2–15, 2–35
tenantability, *see* **habitability**
tenants
definition, secure tenancies, 1–30
obligations, *see* **tenants' obligations**
tenants' obligations, 1–43—1–48
breaches, remedies, 1–49—1–55
misrepresentations, 1–48
rent, payment, 1–45
subjects
access for repairs, 1–47
duty of care, 1–44
possession, 1–43
restriction on use, 1–46
tenants' rights
breach of repairing obligations, 3–84—3–98
actings of third parties, 3–108
choice of remedies, 3–84
damages, 3–88—3–89
defects obvious at beginning of leases, 3–105
effect of landlords' assurances, 3–103—3–104

implement, 3–86—3–87
natural disasters, 3–106
quantification of damages, 3–85
reasonable time to effect repairs, 3–85
renunciation of leases, 3–90
restrictions, 3–99—3–108
statutory scheme for small repairs, *see* **small repairs statutory scheme**
tenants' negligence, 3–107
voluntary acceptance of risk, 3–100–102
withholding rent, 3–91
choice of new landlords, 7–53—7–60
third-party actings
damages, 3–108
possession, 1–55
repair obligations, 3–22
tied houses, *see* **service occupancies**
tolerable standard, enforceability by tenants, 3–81—3–82
trespassers, 6–04

unlawful eviction, 6–05
common law, 6–04
damages, 6–10—6–14
amount, 6–13—6–14
reinstatement, 6–11
defences, 6–12
historical background, 6–01—6–02
remedies, 1–54—1–55
'unlawfully deprive', meaning, 6–04
uses
illegal/immoral, eviction
assured tenancies, 5–38
Part VII tenancies, 5–131
protected tenancies, 5–78
secure tenancies, 5–111
restriction, 1–43, 1–46

vandalism, landlords' obligations, 1–55, 3–16, 3–17, 3–108
ventilation, treatment of dampness, 3–35, 3–75
vermin infestation, repairing obligations, 3–39
volenti non fit injuria, 3–100, 3–103

water supply, repairing obligations, 3–38, 3–50
wind and water tight, 3–29
written leases, landlords' obligations, 1–38—1–39, 3–16